*Organi*

D1584312

The globalized nature of modern organizations presents new and intimidating challenges for effective relationship building. Organizations and their employees are increasingly being asked to manage unfamiliar relationships with unfamiliar parties. These relationships not only involve working across different national cultures, but also dealing with different organizational cultures, different professional cultures and even different internal constituencies. Managing such differences demands trust. This book brings together research findings on organizational trust building across cultures. Established trust scholars from around the world consider the development and maintenance of trust between, for example, management consultants and their clients, senior international managers from different nationalities, different internal organizational groupings during times of change, international joint ventures, and service suppliers and the local communities they serve. These studies, set in a wide variety of national settings, are an important resource for academics, students and practitioners who wish to know more about the nature of cross-cultural trust building in organizations.

MARK N. K. SAUNDERS is Professor in Business Research Methods in the School of Management, University of Surrey.

DENISE SKINNER is Associate Dean (Applied Research) and Professor of Human Resource Management in the Faculty of Business, Environment and Society, Coventry University.

GRAHAM DIETZ is Lecturer in Human Resource Management at Durham Business School, Durham University.

NICOLE GILLESPIE is Senior Lecturer in Management at UQ Business School, The University of Queensland.

ROY J. LEWICKI is Irving Abramowitz Memorial Professor of Business Ethics and Professor of Management and Human Resources at the Max M. Fisher College of Business, The Ohio State University.

# Cambridge Companions to Management

*Cambridge Companions to Management* is an essential new resource for academics, graduate students and reflective business practitioners seeking cutting-edge perspectives on managing people in organizations. Each *Companion* integrates the latest academic thinking with contemporary business practice, dealing with real-world issues facing organizations and individuals in the workplace, and demonstrating how and why practice has changed over time. World-class editors and contributors write with unrivalled depth on managing people and organizations in today's global business environment, making the series a truly international resource.

# Organizational Trust

## A Cultural Perspective

Edited by

**MARK N. K. SAUNDERS**
*University of Surrey*

**DENISE SKINNER**
*Coventry University*

**GRAHAM DIETZ**
*Durham University*

**NICOLE GILLESPIE**
*University of Queensland*

AND

**ROY J. LEWICKI**
*Ohio State University*

CAMBRIDGE
UNIVERSITY PRESS

CAMBRIDGE UNIVERSITY PRESS
Cambridge, New York, Melbourne, Madrid, Cape Town, Singapore,
São Paulo, Delhi, Dubai, Tokyo

Cambridge University Press
The Edinburgh Building, Cambridge CB2 8RU, UK

Published in the United States of America by Cambridge University Press, New York

www.cambridge.org
Information on this title: www.cambridge.org/9780521737791

© Cambridge University Press 2010

First published 2010

Printed in the United Kingdom at the University Press, Cambridge

*A catalogue record for this publication is available from the British Library*

*Library of Congress Cataloguing in Publication data*
Organizational trust : a cultural perspective / edited by Mark N. K. Saunders ... [et al.].
   p.   cm. – (Cambridge companions to management)
ISBN 978-0-521-49291-1 (hardback)
1. Business ethics. 2. Trust. 3. Organization – Psychological aspects. I. Saunders,
Mark, 1959– II. Title. III. Series.
HF5387.O74   2010
302.3'5–dc22

                                                                        2010000324

ISBN 978-0-521-49291-1 Hardback
ISBN 978-0-521-73779-1 Paperback

# Contents

# Figures

# Tables

# Editors

*Mark N. K. Saunders* is Professor in Business Research Methods at the University of Surrey, School of Management. He was formerly Assistant Dean (Director of Research and Doctoral Programmes) and Professor of Business Research Methods at Oxford Brookes University Business School. He is a visiting professor at Newcastle Business School, Northumbria University. His research interests include human resource aspects of the management of change including trust and downsizing, and research methods. He has published in management journals including *Personnel Review*, *European Journal of Work and Organisational Psychology*, *Service Industries Journal*, *Employee Relations*, *Accounting Forum* and *International Journal of Public Sector Management*. He is a member of the editorial boards of *Personnel Review*, *Journal of Services Research* and the *Electronic Journal of Business Research*. He is lead author of *Research Methods for Business Students* (2009, 5th edition), which has also been translated into Chinese, Dutch and Russian, and has co-authored a range of other books including *Strategic Human Resource Management* (2007) and *Dealing with Statistics: What you Need to Know* (2008).

*Denise Skinner* is Associate Dean (Applied Research) and Professor of Human Resource Management (HRM) in the Faculty of Business, Environment and Society at Coventry University. Her current research interests in the fields of HR and change management include diversity, evaluation, trust in the context of the employment relationship, relationship repair and the end-user experience of HRM and change processes. Her publications include refereed articles in the *British Journal of Management*, *International Journal of HRM*, *Management Learning*, *Personnel Review*, *Human Resource Management Journal*, *Women in Management Review*, *Evaluation* and *International Journal of Public Sector Management*. She was co-editor of *Experiencing Human Resource Management: The Inside Story* (1998).

*Graham Dietz* is Lecturer in HRM at Durham Business School. His research interests include the development, maintenance and repair of trust inside organizations; the impact of HRM practices on employees' trust and organizational performance, and the development of trust in joint consultative committees. He has published articles on trust in several management journals including *Academy of Management Review*, *International Journal of Human Resource Management*, *Human Resource Management Journal*, *Personnel Review*, *International Small Business Journal*, and *Employee Relations*. He is an editorial board member for the *Journal of Management Studies*.

*Nicole Gillespie* is Senior Lecturer in Management at the University of Queensland. Prior to this she held faculty and research positions at Warwick Business School, Melbourne Business School and Swinburne University of Technology. Her research interests include trust in organizational contexts, particularly building and repairing trust, trust measurement and developing trust across cultures. She is also actively involved in research on leadership and team processes, stress and well-being at work, and processes of organizational change. Nicole's research appears in leading management journals including *Academy of Management Review*, *Journal of Management*, *Work and Stress*, and the *International Journal of Human Resource Management*, as well as in books and book chapters.

*Roy J. Lewicki* is the Irving Abramowitz Memorial Professor of Business Ethics and Professor of Management and Human Resources at the Max M. Fisher College of Business, The Ohio State University. He maintains research and teaching interests in the fields of trust and trust repair, negotiation and dispute resolution, managerial leadership and ethical decision making. He is an author or editor of thirty-three books, including *Negotiation* (2010), *Negotiation: Readings, Exercises and Cases* (2007), *Essentials of Negotiation* (2007), *Making Sense of Intractable Environmental Conflicts: Frames and Cases* (2003, winner of the 2004 Best Book Award from the International Association of Conflict Management), multiple volumes of *Research on Negotiation in Organizations*, and numerous book chapters and research articles. He served as inaugural editor of *Academy of Management Learning and Education*. He is a past president (2000) of the International Association of Conflict Management. He was selected as a fellow of the Academy of Management in 2003, and received its Distinguished Educator Award in 2005.

# Contributors

*Stephanos Avakian* is Senior Lecturer in Organisational Behaviour and Human Resource Management at Brighton University, Business School. His research interests focus on the study of the management consulting industry and its trends, the interpersonal dynamics of the consultant–client relationship, and the study of the social factors responsible for the legitimation of consulting knowledge.

*Reinhard Bachmann* is Professor of Strategy at the University of Surrey. He has published widely in journals such as *Organization Studies, British Journal of Sociology, Cambridge Journal of Economics* etc. Together with Christel Lane he edited *Trust Within and Between Organizations* (1998/ 2000), and with Akbar Zaheer he edited the *Handbook of Trust Research* (2006/2008) and the *Landmark Papers on Trust* (2008). Currently, he serves on the editorial boards of *Organization Studies* and *Organization*. His work emphasizes the role of social mechanisms (trust, power, etc.) and societal influences (institutional arrangements, cultural traditions) on the structure and quality of organizational relationships and business strategies.

*Georgia T. Chao* is Associate Professor of Management at the Eli Broad Graduate School of Business at Michigan State University. She has a BS in psychology from the University of Maryland and MS and PhD in industrial/ organizational psychology from the Pennsylvania State University. Her primary research interests lie in the areas of cultural influences on organizational behaviour, organizational socialization, mentoring and career development. She is currently examining cultural influences on trust relationships, team processes in emergency medical teams, the emergence and measurement of team knowledge, and work adjustment issues for the current generation of young adults. She has been an invited speaker in over a dozen countries around the world. She is a fellow of the American Psychological Association (APA) and the Society for Industrial and Organizational Psychology (SIOP) and currently serves on four editorial boards. Dr. Chao was elected and served on the APA Council and on executive committees in the Academy of Management and SIOP.

*Timothy Clark* is Professor of Organisational Behaviour at Durham Business School, Durham University. Over the past fifteen years he has conducted a series of research projects into different aspects of consultancy work and more recently focused on the role of management gurus. These have resulted in a series of publications, including *Critical Consulting: New Perspectives on the Management Advice Industry* (2002, with R. Fincham), *Management Speak: Why We Listen to What the Management Gurus Tell Us* (2005, with D. Greatbatch) and *Management Consultancy: Boundaries and Knowledge in Action* (2009, with A. Sturdy, K. Handley and R. Fincham).

*Mark R. Dibben* is an Associate Professor in the Department of Management at Monash University, Australia. His research focuses on 'applied process thought' to study the nature of (managerial) life experience. Within this, a central theme is the role of trust in personal and organizational growth. He has published on this topic in philosophy, medicine, information systems and sociology – as well as various management sub-disciplines including entrepreneurship, marketing and philosophy of management. He serves on the editorial boards of *Philosophy of Management, Cosmos and History* and *Process Studies*, and is the Executive Director of the International Process Network (IPN), the international body charged by its member organizations with enabling process philosophical research across the globe (www.processnetwork.org).

*Ina Ehnert* is Lecturer at the University of Bremen and currently represents the field of sustainable management there. Her research interests are in the fields of sustainable human resource management, theory development in HRM, trust across cultures, multiparadigm enquiry, expatriate training and preparation and evaluation of cross-cultural training. She has single- and co-authored several book chapters, books and international conference papers in mono- and cross-cultural collaboration.

*Elaine Farndale* is Assistant Professor in the Department of Human Resource Studies at Tilburg University in the Netherlands, and is a member of the Change Management Consortium at Cass Business School, City University, UK. Elaine completed her PhD at Cranfield School of Management (UK) in 2004. Her research in the fields of international HRM, the HR department and change management has been published in both academic and practitioner journals and books, and presented at numerous international conferences.

*Donald Ferrin* is Associate Professor of Organizational Behavior and Human Resources at Singapore Management University. Donald earned his PhD in

2000 from the University of Minnesota. His research focuses on interpersonal trust and negotiation in the organizational context. Specific topics include the development of trust, repair of trust, organizational trust networks, trust spirals and the role of trust in negotiation.

*Veronica Hope-Hailey* is Professor of Strategic Human Resource Management at the Cass Business School at City University, London. Her particular research and teaching interests centre on issues of change at both a strategic and organizational level, and also at the level of individual managerial practice and personal development. Veronica is also the Director of the Change Management Consortium which conducts collaborative research with ten major private sector and public sector organizations including GlaxoSmithKline, Ernst & Young, GKN, Her Majesty's Revenue and Customs. She consults within the private, public and voluntary sectors on an international basis and is the author of two books: *Strategic Human Resource Management* and *Exploring Strategic Change*.

*Jane Kassis Henderson* is Associate Professor of English and International Business Communication at ESCP Europe Paris campus. She holds a PhD from the University of St Andrews, Scotland, UK. She has taught in higher education in France in universities and management schools and has delivered seminars and lectures on different aspects of intercultural communication in various professional organizations. In addition to her research on trust in international management teams, one of her current research interests is the use of English as a working language in international business and academic contexts. She also conducts research on teaching multicultural audiences and learning in multicultural student groups in business schools and universities in Europe.

*Clare Kelliher* is Senior Lecturer in Strategic Human Resource Management at Cranfield School of Management, Cranfield University. She is a member of the Change Management Consortium Research team at Cass Business School, City University. Clare holds a PhD in Organizational Behaviour from London Business School, an MA in Industrial Relations from the University of Warwick and a first degree in management from the University of Surrey. Her research interests centre around the organization of work and the management of the employment relationship in the context of organizational change. She has a long-standing interest in flexible working and currently directs a major project concerned with examining the impact of flexible working on performance, in conjunction with the charity Working Families and sponsored by seven companies. Clare is the author of many published papers and book chapters and regularly presents at national and international conferences. She has considerable experience running management programmes and advising organizations both in the UK and overseas. Prior to joining Cranfield she was at the University of Surrey where she held appointments in the postgraduate Surrey European Management School and in the School of Management Studies for the Service Sector.

*Roderick M. Kramer* is the William R. Kimball Professor of Organizational Behavior at Stanford University's Business School. Kramer received his PhD in social psychology from the University of California, Los Angeles. He has authored more than one hundred scholarly articles and essays. His work has appeared in leading academic journals, such as the *Journal of Personality and Social Psychology*, *Administrative Science Quarterly* and the *Academy of Management Journal*, as well as popular journals such as the *Harvard Business Review*. He is also the author or co-author of a number of scholarly books, including *Negotiation in Social Contexts, The Psychology of the Social Self, Trust in Organizations, Power and Influence in Organizations, The Psychology of Leadership, Trust and Distrust Within Organizations* and most recently *Organizational Trust*. Kramer has been a visiting scholar at various academic institutions and think tanks, including the London Business School, Northwestern University, Oxford University, Harvard University and the Hoover Institution.

*Fergus Lyon* is Professor of Enterprise and Organisations in the Centre for Enterprise and Economic Development Research, Middlesex University, UK. His research interests include trust and cooperation in networks and clusters; enterprise behaviour, market institutions and social inclusion in less developed countries and the UK, entrepreneurship and business support. Recent work also involves trust in business science relationships and he has established a five-year ESRC-funded research programme on the Third Sector and Social Enterprises in the UK. This will involve research on trust in relationships between public, private and third sector organizations.

*Isabelle Mari* is a PhD candidate in business administration at Jönköping International Business School, Sweden. She has a full-time position at EDHEC Business School as coordinator of the Management and Strategy Department (graduate and undergraduate programmes). She has worked in business education for fourteen years and has taught on undergraduate and graduate programmes. In 2005, she spent a one-year leave as a visiting researcher at the Australian Graduate School of Management (AGSM), Sydney, Australia. Her research revolves around the role of trust in family-firm strategy. Her dissertation addresses the trust relationships between the corporate governance actors in determining strategy in family firms. She aims to provide a better understanding of the specific nature of trust that characterizes these relationships in family firms.

*Guido Möllering* is Senior Research Associate at the Max Planck Institute for the Study of Societies in Cologne, Germany. He holds a PhD in Management Studies from the University of Cambridge, UK. His research is generally in the area of inter-organizational relationships and the constitution of markets with specific interests in trust and institutional entrepreneurship. He has published numerous articles and book chapters on trust, some of them in leading journals such as *Organization Science* and *Sociology*. He is the author of the book *Trust: Reason, Routine, Reflexivity*, published in 2006.

*Gina Porter* is Senior Research Fellow in the Department of Anthropology, Durham University, UK. She has a long-standing interest in trader relations in West Africa (notably Ghana and Nigeria), where she has undertaken research for over thirty years. Her research on trust has been conducted in trade and other contexts, including North–South NGO relations, and NGO–state relations. Currently she is leading a research study of child mobility in Ghana, Malawi and South Africa.

*Joanne Roberts* is Senior Lecturer in Management at Newcastle University Business School and a member of the Centre for Knowledge, Innovation, Technology and Enterprise, both at Newcastle University, UK. Her research interests include knowledge-intensive services, new information and communication technologies and knowledge transfer, inter- and intra-organizational knowledge transfer and the internationalization of business services. Her current research is focused on two areas: the role of business services in the transfer of knowledge, and critiques of knowledge in contemporary economy and organization. She is a member of the Dynamics of Institutions and Markets in Europe (DIME) Network of Excellence and co-founder and co-editor of the journal *Critical Perspectives on International Business*. Her most recent book, co-edited with Ash Amin, is *Community, Economic Creativity, and Organization* (2008).

*Jacob M. Rose* is Associate Professor of Accounting at the University of New Hampshire. Prior to joining the University of New Hampshire, he was Professor of Accountancy and PhD programme director at the School of Accountancy, Southern Illinois University. He teaches courses in accounting information systems and behavioural research methods. His research emphasizes behavioural experimentation in the areas of accounting judgment and decision making, the effects of information systems on accounting and audit practitioners, corporate governance and the role of trust in audit practice. He serves on the editorial boards of the *Journal of Information Systems*, the *International Journal of Accounting Information Systems* and *Issues in Accounting Education*.

*Ulrike Schwegler* is Director and co-founder of the Institute for Applied Trust Research in Stuttgart, Germany. Her business and research interests cover both 'for-profit' and 'not-for-profit' organizations in Southeast Asia, the Middle East, North Africa and Europe. Her business activities link trust to strategic management processes such as leadership, global team working and international business partnering. For seven years, Ulrike has been working for various NGOs in Indonesia. As for her academic activities, Ulrike is currently a research associate at the Ruhr-University Bochum, as well as a visiting lecturer at the University of Applied Science at Konstanz. She frequently teaches courses on organizational psychology, intercultural communication, intercultural training and cultural diversity in Indonesia. She has published books on trust-building processes in intercultural cooperation and on intercultural competence training for Germans working in Arabic countries. She holds a PhD from the University of Chemnitz.

*L. Ripley Smith* is Professor of International Communication at Bethel University in St. Paul, Minnesota, USA. He lectures and writes in the areas of intercultural social networks, refugee resettlement and cross-cultural partnership development. His recent research has explored *liminality, communitas* and identity reconstruction among KaRen and Somali refugee populations. A Fellow in the International Academy of Intercultural Research, Dr. Smith's published work has appeared in *The International Journal of Intercultural Relations*, the *International and Intercultural Communication Annual*, the *International Journal of the Sociology of Language* and the *International Journal of Communication*. He currently serves as the Chairman of the Board for World Relief, MN. He holds a PhD from the University of Minnesota.

*Florian Stache* is a doctoral candidate in the Free University of Berlin's doctoral programme on Organizational Paths. Previously, he worked as a management consultant in Russia and Ukraine. He holds a degree in Business Administration (*Diplom-Kaufmann*) from the Free University of Berlin, Germany. His master's thesis on Cooperation with Eastern European Firms has been published in German by Verlag Dr. Müller. His main current research interest is the transformation of Russian health care systems.

*Hwee Hoon Tan* is Associate Professor of Organizational Behavior and Human Resources at the Lee Kong Chian School of Business, Singapore Management University. She earned her PhD from the Krannert School, Purdue University. Her research interests include emotions in the workplace and interpersonal trust. Her work has been published in journals such as *Academy of Management Journal*, *Journal of Applied Psychology*, *Journal of Organizational Behavior* and *Leadership Quarterly*.

*S. Arzu Wasti* is Associate Professor of Management and Organization Studies at the Faculty of Management, Sabanci University, Turkey. She received her PhD in Industrial Relations and Human Resource Management from University of Illinois at Urbana-Champaign. Her cross-cultural research on organizational commitment, sexual harassment, organizational trust and organizational culture has appeared in such journals as *Journal of Applied Psychology*, *Journal of Management*, *Journal of Personality and Social Psychology*, *Journal of International Business Studies* and *Leadership Quarterly*. She is a recipient of several research awards, including the International Academy of Intercultural Relations' *Best Dissertation Award*, the Academy of Management's *Lyman Porter and Carolyn Dexter Best Paper Awards* and the Turkish Academy of Sciences *Encouragement Award*.

*Alex Wright* is Lecturer in Strategy at the Open University Business School, UK. His research interests focus on strategy-as-practice, which views strategizing as a sociolinguistic construction constituted by strategists. He is interested in practice-based methodologies in general and how they may be used to study actors organizing activities. He has been a 'Visiting Scientist' at the University of Bremen.

*Hèla Yousfi* is Associate Professor of Management and Organization at the University of Paris-Dauphine. She received her PhD in Management Studies from University Paris X Nanterre, France. She teaches graduate courses on cross-cultural management, strategic management and organization theory. She specializes in the field of sociology of organizations. She has more than seven years of experience in consultancy and research on the role of culture in economic development. She has undertaken extensive studies of management practices in North Africa and the Middle East, including Lebanon, Jordan, Tunisia, Egypt, Algeria and Morocco. She is also an experienced trainer in intercultural management. Her work has centred on issues such as democratization, good governance, public–private partnerships and socioeconomic transformations in North Africa and Middle East regions.

# Foreword

Trust is widely studied yet remains elusive. Everyone agrees that it is important, that social life could not exist without it, and that it is valuable, since the cost of building structures and controls that substitute for trust in and between organizations is enormous. More elusive still is how trust is established and sustained across cultures by those doing organizational work. Trust requires sending signals of trustworthiness, and differences in the meaning and interpretation of signals is the very essence of different cultures. As this volume's editors, Mark Saunders, Denise Skinner, Graham Dietz, Nicole Gillespie and Roy Lewicki note, people from different cultures often bring mutually alien values and beliefs, uninterpretable behaviours, and incompatible assumptions to their organizational work, all of which can undermine the trust necessary to successful interactions and fruitful collaboration. These scholars address such fundamental questions as how do people from different cultures understand and develop trust in one another? How do they go about building, maintaining and repairing trust in their own culture, and with those in other cultures? Which practices work best to build and sustain successful cross-cultural trust in particular settings? This book reports the current state of our knowledge about cross-cultural trust building, and helps to further our deeper understanding of cross-cultural trust building in and across organizations.

This book brings together leading-edge conceptual thinking and empirical research on the nature, meaning and development of trust across multiple cultural boundaries. It is genuinely international, pulling together the leading trust scholars from around the world. Here readers will find strong empirical comparisons of how trust is created and maintained in organizations operating in the same industry but in different countries, comprehensive reviews of how trust is created and maintained in various organizational contexts in different national cultures, innovative theoretical lenses for interpreting cross-cultural differences in trust development, and conceptual, risk-taking papers that provoke and challenge our understandings of trust. The volume aims to unify the extant research on trust across different cultures, and to stimulate new research directions.

We feel that this book makes a fundamental contribution to the literature. The editors are to be congratulated for putting together a coherent, innovative and scholarly volume of distinguished international scholars. We hope that this book will stimulate debate on these increasingly critical questions for all of us working in and with organizations over the next decades.

## Series Editors

Cary Cooper,
Lancaster University Management School

Jone L. Pearce,
University of California, Irvine

# Editors' acknowledgements

Our thanks go first and foremost to the UK's Economic and Social Research Council (ESRC) for providing support through grant RES 451–25–4135 for the seminar series 'Building, maintaining and repairing trust across cultures: theory and practise' in which this book has its origins.

We are also grateful for the personal and professional contributions made by our colleagues and friends who provided us with valuable comments on the book manuscript and assisted in the genesis of this book. In particular our thanks go to Jane Errington, for her administrative support throughout the seminar series and during the preparation of the manuscript, and to Paula Parish our Commissioning Editor at Cambridge University Press.

# PART I

# The conceptual challenge of researching trust across different 'cultural spheres'

# 1 | *Unravelling the complexities of trust and culture*

GRAHAM DIETZ, NICOLE GILLESPIE AND
GEORGIA T. CHAO

## Introduction

Badri is an Iranian businesswoman representing her firm in first-round negotiations with a new alliance partner from Munich, Germany.[1] When she
enters the room, her counterpart from the German firm, Johann, reaches
out his hand for her to shake as a first gesture of goodwill. Badri hesitates,
but takes Johann's hand briefly, shakes it once, smiling the whole time. Then
she sits down. Johann is impressed by her apparent openness; for him, this
bodes well for the talks ahead. Behind him, a few colleagues wince at his
indiscretion, but are relieved when it appears he has got away with it. Behind
her, Badri's male colleagues from Iran are shocked. Some are disgusted. For
women to touch unfamiliar men is neither customary nor appropriate in their
culture. But Badri has studied and worked in the States for several years and,
though she finds such incidents uncomfortable, she has learned to 'switch'
between styles of working when required. Plus, for her, the priorities of her
employer mean that nurturing a solid, trusting relationship with their
German partner is of paramount importance.

Sean and Nils are elected employee representatives sitting on the European
Works Council of the Anglo–Dutch steel firm, Corus, for whom they both
work.[2] Nils is Dutch and works in his native Holland; Sean is Irish but works
in a smelting works in England. They are both union members (though in
different unions), both Corus employees, and both engineers. But when Corus
attempted to divest a profitable Dutch aluminium business to prop up flag-
ging UK plants (including the one where Sean works), Nils and the Dutch reps
invoked Dutch law to prevent the sale. This tactic infuriated Sean and his
UK constituents, and it soured relations between the two national workforces. However, when Corus tried to force through further job cuts, Sean

---

[1] Scenario adapted from Molinsky (2007: 625).
[2] Scenario adapted from Timming (2008).

approached Nils to coordinate a joint protest on behalf of all Corus workers, regardless of nationality or function. Their 'new' shared fate sealed both parties' commitment to the campaign, and trust was repaired. (Now, both men work for an Indian company, after TATA Group bought Corus.)

In July 2008, the *Financial Times* reported a real case from the Airbus manufacturing plant in Toulouse (Hollinger and Wiesmann, 2008), where production problems with their giant A380 aircraft were attributed to major cross-cultural differences between the local French workforce and a group of 200 German technicians transferred in to repair errors made in the company's Hamburg factory (in Germany). Some within the Toulouse plant claimed that German working patterns (including a marked preference for written instructions) were anathema to the French, and vice versa (the Germans were startled to see French men greet each other with a kiss in the morning). Yet others noted that the handsomely compensated 'transferees' were not Airbus employees but contract workers, and this was the real source of the 'them and us' frustration.

These vignettes highlight both the complexity and the ordinariness of cross-cultural trust building in today's globalized world of business. Organizations and their employees are increasingly enmeshed in complex interdependencies across national, organizational and professional borders, meaning that people from different 'cultures' are being asked to manage unfamiliar relationships with unfamiliar parties.

Such contexts demand trust. Trust's vital role in securing sustainable relations among disparate parties, especially in ambiguous situations characterized by uncertainty (such as between parties from different 'cultures'), is now well established. Trust has been shown to have a beneficial impact on a range of individual, group and organizational performance outcomes (see Dirks and Ferrin, 2001 for a review). Interpersonal trust is associated with cooperation (Golembiewski and McConkie, 1975), the quality of group communication and problem solving (Butler *et al.*, 1999; Zand, 1972), knowledge transfer (Levin and Cross, 2004), employees' extra effort (Korsgaard *et al.*, 2002; Mayer and Gavin, 2005), team performance (Dirks, 2000), even sales (Salamon and Robinson, 2008) and organizational revenue and profit (Davis *et al.*, 2000; Simons, 2002). At the inter-organizational level, Madhok (1995) notes trust's 'cost reduction and value enhancing properties' in the form of more efficient and effective cooperation and information sharing between firms, and the expansion of the range of potential partners (see also Gulati, 1995: 107; Zaheer *et al.*, 1998). Indeed, trust is held to be a major contributor to organizational competitiveness because it cannot be easily imitated or replicated (Barney and Hansen, 1994).

Many scholars argue further that the degree of trust in a particular society profoundly influences that nation's economic wellbeing and global competitiveness (Fukuyama, 1995; Inglehart, 1999; Zak and Knack, 2001). Additionally, trust and reciprocity form the basis of all human systems of morality (Nowak and Sigmund, 2000, cited in Buchan *et al.*, 2002: 168). Putnam (2000) sees both as the very foundation of society and civilization, and reciprocated trusting relationships are key to human happiness (Haidt, 2006; Layard, 2005).

Yet developing and maintaining trust between different 'cultures' is a formidable challenge. People from different cultures often bring to relationship-building efforts 'alien' values and beliefs, 'peculiar' behaviours and even incompatible assumptions, which can prevent successful interactions and fruitful collaboration (e.g. Arino *et al.*, 2001; Branzei *et al.*, 2007; Farris *et al.*, 1973; Thompson, 1996). It is little wonder that cross-cultural interaction often involves misunderstandings, embarrassment, feelings of low self-efficacy, even psychological distress (Molinsky, 2007).

Our goal with this book is to bring together leading-edge conceptual thinking and empirical research on the nature, meaning and development of trust across multiple cultural boundaries, in order to facilitate a cumulative body of knowledge on this richly complex process. It has its origins in an exciting seminar series funded by the UK's Economic and Social Research Council (ESRC) between 2005 and 2007, which involved more than fifty scholars from around the world. The aim and scope of the book, echoing Noorderhaven (1999), is to unify the extant research on trust across different 'cultures', and to stimulate new research directions. Despite substantial research on what constitutes trust and trustworthiness, we know surprisingly little about how people from different cultures understand this complex and enigmatic construct, and how they go about building, maintaining and repairing trust in their own culture, and across cultural divides. This book seeks to address this gap in our understanding, and serves as a staging post in mapping the terrain of cross-cultural trust building, finessing our understanding of what is required to foster trust between people from different 'cultures'.

## Cross-cultural engagement: multiple 'cultural spheres' and the 'cultural mosaic'

The challenge of establishing and maintaining trust in cross-cultural relations is most apparent across national borders. It is a truism of globalization that the worldwide transfer of capital, labour and investment, coupled with the network-oriented nature of organizations and their markets, and the fluid employment and social environments within which many now operate, entail elaborate interdependencies within and between workforces in different countries (Caldwell and Clapham, 2003; Child, 2001; Gulati, 1995).[3] Yet, although the 'globalized' nature of work is rendering national cultural boundaries somewhat 'fuzzy' (Doney *et al.*, 1998), the influence of national cultural traits and norms on people's perceptions, beliefs, values and behaviours endures (Pothukuchi *et al.*, 2002), and remains particularly problematic for trust building (Dyer and Chu, 2000; Johnson and Cullen, 2002).

Importantly, however, we do not see cross-cultural engagement as being limited to *national* boundaries. Mergers, strategic alliances, joint ventures and outsourcing arrangements bring people together from different *organizational* cultures (Child, 2001; Luo, 2002; Madhok, 1995; Maguire and Phillips, 2008; Ring and van de Ven, 1994; Zaheer *et al.*, 1998). *Multiprofessional* arrangements include the relationships between management consultants and auditors, and their clients. Meanwhile, new patterns of working are emerging *within* organizations that require employees to negotiate and manage an ever more complex network of relationships (Kasper-Fuehrer and Ashkanasy, 2001; Rubery *et al.*, 2002): the shift to flatter, more flexible internal structures (e.g. cross-functional teams; 'virtual' teams; joint working parties; one-off projects), combined with the influence of 'lateral' and 'portfolio' career moves, bring people together from very different *professional* or *functional* cultures (e.g. HR, Finance, Marketing, R&D, lawyers) and different *sub-organizational cultures*.

Schneider and Barsoux (2003: 51–79) view these multiple cultural groupings as interacting 'cultural spheres'. Each sphere may shape a person's thinking or conduct independently or simultaneously with another sphere. Chao and Moon (2005) use the metaphor of a 'mosaic' of multiple cultural identities to convey the same idea. Many different 'tiles' create the overall mosaic picture of the cultural identities of a person or organization (they include nationality, ethnicity, sector/industry, organization, profession and subcultures), yet each tile remains a distinct part of the whole. Figure 1.1 illustrates both ideas.

---

[3] It is worth reflecting, however, that this has in fact been happening for centuries (Wright, 2000). The trade routes along the Silk Road from China to Venice, for example, saw people traverse entire continents thousands of years ago. It is, therefore, misleading to imagine that cross-cultural collaboration and trust building is a new phenomenon.

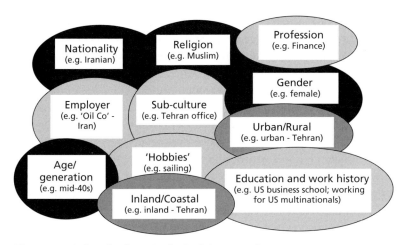

**Figure 1.1** Cultural spheres in the Badri case study

Figure 1.1 illustrates these ideas from the perspective of Badri, from the opening vignette: she is Iranian by birth and a Muslim, but is also socialized in the West and its ways of conducting business, loyal and committed to her firm, and focused on finance by profession. So, to what extent was her thinking and behaviour influenced by her nationality, religion, industry, corporate culture or professional culture – or by some combination of these?

In short, it is increasingly difficult to discern what is distinctively 'local' about individuals' conduct when many people have been subject to a myriad of multicultural influences, and also when – as we shall see – certain spheres or tiles dominate in certain circumstances, may recede in influence in others, and idiosyncratic new cultural forms may emerge from parties' interactions. The existence of, and interaction among, these multiple 'cultural spheres' or 'tiles' renders cross-cultural engagement, and the effective establishment and maintenance of trust amongst unfamiliar parties, even more delicate (Molinsky, 2007). This book takes a 'cultural mosaic' perspective to unravel the complexity of the processes involved.

## The research agenda

We can split the research challenge into two essential questions and types of studies:

1. *The etic vs. emic debate*: is there a universally applicable model of trust and trust development [*etic*], or do people from varying cultures understand and enact trust differently [*emic*]?

Much of the research on trust has adopted an *etic* perspective (Zaheer and Zaheer, 2006), assuming trust concepts, models and measures developed in Western countries are adequate for the study of trust in other (national) cultural contexts. This approach has been criticized by Noorderhaven (1999) who argues, 'it is much more productive to explore and compare the meaning of trust and its antecedents and consequences as perceived in various cultures'. Zaheer and Zaheer (2006: 22) call for a 'fresh approach' that starts from the premise that the level, nature and meaning of trust may vary across different national contexts. They conclude that an integrated emic/etic approach is a promising avenue for future research. This book takes that approach explicitly. The majority of chapters offer an 'emic' or an integrated 'emic'/'etic' view on trust across cultural contexts, and extend beyond the *national* cultural sphere to other cultural spheres, such as across professional and organizational cultures.

2. *Intercultural* studies: how can Party A from Culture #1 develop a trust relationship with Party B from Culture #2?

This question focuses our attention on interaction among individuals, groups or organizations from different cultural spheres. Relevant questions here include: What factors or conditions facilitate the development of trust and/or the reduction of distrust? Does this differ depending on the cultural sphere under examination? What role does cultural learning and adaptation play in the trust-development process? Can common cultural identities be used to overcome barriers to trust resulting from divergent cultural identities? Is the influence of culture on trust building and repair overplayed? Additionally, are there situations in which cultural differences are insurmountable, and attempts to overcome them are ill-advised?

## This volume

To address these questions meaningfully, and advance our research agenda, requires a *cross-disciplinary* approach. We have selected a highly diverse set of contributors in this volume (itself an example of multiple interacting cultural spheres). The selected authors represent several different countries themselves, and they come from a wide range of academic disciplines, including accounting, anthropology, management, strategic HRM, psychology, sociology and linguistics.

We have also consciously adopted a *multi-level* approach (see Klein and Kozlowski, 2000), recognizing – as Keyton and Smith (2008) have done in relation to the *Handbook of Trust Research* (Bachmann and Zaheer, 2006), and Tung (2008: 43) has done in relation to culture – that the nature of both constructs ought not to be limited to single-level analysis. Indeed, a core theoretical proposition of this book is that trust is fundamentally interpersonal, but is shaped by latent and overt influences at multiple levels, and that some of the strongest influences are cultural in origin. Moreover, as we have already seen, cultural influences may materialize at the level of the individual (e.g. ethnicity, gender), team or group, the organization, interorganizationally, as well as societal levels. These variables also interact across the levels. Our contributions reflect this: they present trust-building and repair processes across very different 'cultural spheres', including between international joint venture partners, senior international managers from different nationalities, service suppliers (such as consultants, auditors, utilities firms) and the clients they serve, different internal organizational groupings during times of change, and within family firms.

Each chapter is rooted in a specific empirical study or conceptual project. The source data for the empirical chapters come from different national settings, including Britain, China, France, Germany, Ghana, Lebanon, Nigeria, Turkey and the United States. A further diversity characteristic of the contributions is the variety of research methods used, including surveys, interviews and ethnographies. Indeed, a distinctive feature of this book is that the majority of the empirical studies make use of rich qualitative methods, unlike much of the existing literature.

In the remainder of this introductory chapter, we clarify the conceptualization of trust adopted in the book. We then unravel our second core concept, culture, and discuss further the notion of multiple interacting cultural spheres, or tiles. Third, we critically review current perspectives on the influence of culture on trust, including dominant approaches to building trust across cultural barriers. In so doing, we summarize the limits and prominent gaps in this literature. The final section provides the reader with a preview of the chapter contributions.

## Trust: an overview

### Conceptualizing trust

Given the prominence of trust for individual and organized behaviour, it is not surprising that trust has been studied from a number of disciplines, including psychology, sociology, economics, political science and moral philosophy. These disciplines differ in how they approach and conceptualize trust (for a review, see Rousseau *et al.*, 1998), in part because they focus on different phenomena at different levels of engagement and interaction. In line with Rousseau and colleagues' (1998) overview of trust research and theory, we conceptualize trust as a 'meso' concept which integrates micro-level psychological processes (intrapersonal, interpersonal) and group dynamics with macro-level organizational, societal and institutional forms. The contributions in this book examine trust from various disciplines, and at various levels.

*Trust definition.* In their cross-disciplinary review, Rousseau *et al.* (1998: 395) noted convergence around the following definition of trust:

a psychological state comprising the intention to accept vulnerability based upon positive expectations of the intentions or behavior of another.

This definition highlights two fundamental components of trust evident in earlier conceptualizations: the *willingness to be vulnerable* in a situation of *risk* (see Mayer *et al.*, 1995; Zand, 1972) and *confident positive expectations* (see Baier, 1986; Cook and Wall, 1980; Lewicki *et al.*, 1998; Mayer *et al.*, 1995). Although other definitions of trust exist (e.g. Möllering, 2006), we adopt this as the chosen definition, as our intention in this book is to move beyond long-standing but moribund debates on what trust is, to enable a focused examination of the interplay between trust and culture.

In line with Mayer *et al.*'s (1995) influential integrative model, as well as recent reviews (see Dietz and den Hartog, 2006; McEvily *et al.*, 2003) and meta-analyses (Colquitt *et al.*, 2007), we distinguish trust from trustworthiness beliefs, propensity to trust and trusting behaviour.

*Trustworthiness beliefs.* Trustworthiness beliefs are the subjective set of confident beliefs that the trustor has about the other party and their relationship with that party. These beliefs inform the decision to trust. Mayer *et al.* (1995) identify three prominent dimensions of trustworthiness: *ability* (the group of skills, competencies and characteristics that enable a party to have influence within some specific domain); *benevolence* (perception of a positive orientation of the trustee toward the trustor, including expressions of genuine concern and care); and *integrity* (perception that the trustee adheres consistently to a set of principles acceptable to the trustor, such as honesty and fairness).

*Propensity to trust.* As well as the trustor's perceptions of the other party's trustworthiness, their propensity to trust will also influence their decision to trust (Colquitt *et al.*, 2007), particularly unfamiliar actors. Propensity to trust (also known as 'generalized trust') is a person's predisposition towards trusting other people in general (Rotter, 1967). It is understood to be a facet of personality influenced by early developmental experiences, and by cultural background (see Hofstede, 1991), and remains relatively stable throughout adulthood (Rotter, 1967).

*Trusting behaviour.* While trust involves a willingness to render oneself vulnerable, and implies the *intention* to act in a trusting manner, risk only occurs in the behavioural manifestation of trust: the act of making oneself vulnerable to the other party (Mayer *et al.*, 1995). Gillespie (2003) identifies two dominant categories of trusting behaviour in work contexts: *reliance* (relying on another party's skills, knowledge, judgments or actions, including delegating and giving autonomy), and *disclosure* (sharing work-related or personal information of a sensitive nature with another party). While trusting behaviour is the likely outcome of trust, this is by no means guaranteed as other contextual factors beyond the immediate trustee–trustor relationship can influence trust behaviour (e.g. control systems, perception of risk in the situation, power relations, social network implications – see Dietz and den Hartog, 2006; Mayer *et al.*, 1995).

The empirical contributions in this volume draw on these four causally related trust constructs (trust, trustworthiness beliefs, propensity to trust, trusting behaviour) to inform our understanding of the influence of culture on trust. We now go on to consider how trust is formed and develops over time.

## Trust development and forms of trust

Several models of trust development have been proposed (for a review, see Lewicki *et al.*, 2006). All highlight that trust is based on a body of evidence about the other party's motives and character, from which a belief, prediction or faith judgment about that party's likely *future* conduct is derived. That is, the trustor generates an initial judgment about the other party's trustworthiness (i.e. their ability, benevolence and integrity) on the basis of available evidence. They then recalibrate that judgment in light of subsequent evidence, and/or the outcomes of their trusting behaviour towards the party (Mayer *et al.*, 1995). As Zand (1972) describes, if one party expects the other to be trustworthy, then they disclose information, relax controls and accept influence and interdependence. Should the other party vindicate that trust, the relationship may deepen and develop further through reinforcing cycles of reciprocated trust. In contrast, when reciprocation is not forthcoming, trust often erodes and distrust may result. As relationships mature through experience in different contexts and around different interdependencies, parties accumulate deeper and more extensive knowledge about each other's strengths and weaknesses. Thus trust development is an ongoing, dynamic process influenced by reciprocation (Blau, 1964) and the outcome of trusting behaviour (Zand, 1972).

Central to the trust process, therefore, is the quality of evidence gathered, and the quality of the interpretation of that evidence. We can distinguish between direct and presumptive bases of trust. *Direct evidence* comes from interaction and first-hand knowledge of that party (e.g. their past performance, conduct and character). In contrast, *presumptive* bases facilitate placing trust in individuals without prior *direct* knowledge, and relying on other sources of evidence (see Dietz and den Hartog, 2006). Presumptive bases of trust include: 1) information about that party's membership of a *social or organizational category* (e.g. a certain 'culture' such as nationality, profession, or an affiliation) or *social network* (see Meyerson *et al.*, 1996); 2) *information from third parties* (e.g. gossip or testimonials from boundary spanners and auditors; see Burt and Knez, 1996; Ferrin *et al.*, 2006); 3) *role expectations*: the expectation that others will behave in accordance with the obligations, responsibilities and system of expertise attached to their role (e.g. the 'Hippocratic Oath' signed by doctors, see Barber, 1983); and 4) *institutions and regulations* (i.e. explicit and implicit rules, norms, routines and exchange practices which define what is and isn't acceptable behaviour, such as legislation and codes of conduct; see Sitkin and Roth, 1993; Zucker, 1986). Kramer (1996), Johnson and Cullen (2002) and Lewicki *et al.* (2006) all provide more detailed reviews of these bases of trust.

Parties weigh up the evidence from these multiple sources in the aggregate, to make their judgment on whether to trust or not, acting as 'intuitive auditors' of others' trustworthiness (Kramer, 1996). Thus, trust is, at once, calculative (in the sense of weighing up evidence) *and* predictive (in the sense of anticipating likely future behaviour). Moreover, it can be based on *relational* bonds as much as, or even in tandem with, *institutional* supports. Over time, information from within the relationship typically becomes a more salient and valid basis of trust than presumptive and external sources of evidence. With repeated cycles of successful exchange and fulfilment of expectations, trust strengthens and parties expand the resources and level of reliance on, and disclosure to, each other. At the narrowest level, parties may only trust each other on the strength of a cost–benefit analysis (i.e. calculative trust), but at the broader end of a continuum of intensity, parties can identify fully with each other's interests and desires, and operate with such a high level of mutual understanding that they can act for each other (i.e. identification-based trust; see Lewicki and Bunker, 1996). But the dreaded prospect of betrayal is ever-present, even if it is not subjectively felt. Trust falls between hope and certainty.

Two further strands of the trust literature are particularly salient for this volume. The first is the relationship between trust and forms of control. There are two opposing perspectives on this relationship: trust and control are complements or substitutes (for reviews see Costa and Bijlsma-Frankema, 2007; Poppo and Zenger, 2002). In the former, trust and control may coexist: one may trust another because of the existence of controls, or may happily accede to controls because of one's trust in another. In the substitution thesis, the presence of controls obviates the need for trust as the controls render the level of risk minimal, or one cannot be said to trust another if one imposes controls as well (Schoorman *et al.*, 2007). Both the theorizing and empirical data to date lend support to the complementarity argument (Costa and Bijlsma-Frankema, 2007). Different cultures may have preferred types of control (e.g. formal institutionalized rules versus more informal normative or relational pressures) to promote trust, or to cope with having to trust (see Griffith *et al.*, 2000; Thompson, 1996). Understanding the relationship between culture, trust and control would be valuable.

Related to the trust/control debate, a commonly held assumption is that trust and distrust sit at contrasting ends of the same continuum. On the basis of this assumption, distrust and related mechanisms of suspicion, control and monitoring are viewed as indicators of low trust or the absence of trust – the substitution thesis above. Contrary to this view, Sitkin and Roth (1993) and Lewicki *et al.* (1998) conceptualize trust and distrust as separate and potentially *coexisting* constructs with distinct determinants and effects, empirical work by Saunders and Thornhill (2004) providing support. Sitkin and Roth (1993) propose that trust violations occur when expectations about task reliability are not met, whereas distrust occurs in response to value incongruence. Lewicki and colleagues (1998) argue that *ambivalence* (the simultaneous existence of trust and distrust) is more common in most professional relationships than either a broad trusting or distrusting stance toward another. The accumulation of evidence over time results in an understanding of the limits of trust and potentially the areas of distrust within the relationship. Lewicki and colleagues (1998) propose a two-by-two matrix of working relationships with high and low levels of trust on one axis (characterized by hope, faith, confidence, assurance and initiative) and distrust on the other (characterized by fear, scepticism, cynicism, watchfulness and vigilance).

Having examined definitions of trust, the process of trust development, and some relevant debates within the literature, we now move on to consider our other complicated concept: culture.

## Culture: an overview

Within the social sciences, more than 50 years have passed since Kroeber and Kluckhohn's (1952) review famously identified more than 160 definitions of culture. Today, the definition of culture still remains fragmented and diverse. This section examines some contemporary definitions of culture to provide a workable definition for use in this book.

Much of the ongoing confusion lies in the level at which culture is defined, or the degree to which cultural manifestations are visible to an observer (Schein, 1997). Schein describes three levels of culture. First, *artifacts* are the observable manifestations of culture – an observer can see, smell, taste, hear and/or touch them. In an organizational context, these include the physical buildings and furnishings, organizational charts, company logos, forms of dress, styles of interaction, language and communication, etc. (Schneider and Barsoux, 2003: 24–30). Although observable, it is often difficult for an outsider to correctly decipher the true meaning of these cultural artifacts. For example, cows roam freely in Indian cities, but the significance of this may be unclear to a Westerner. (Small children roam freely in restaurants in Italy; this too may be unsettling for outsiders!)

Second, *values* express a group's beliefs about how things should be (Doney *et al.*, 1998). Rokeach defined values as 'enduring beliefs that a specific mode of conduct or end-state of existence is personally or socially preferable to an opposite or converse mode of conduct, or end-state of existence' (1973: 5). Values (pre-)judge our behaviour and that of others. Understanding these values and their derivatives (i.e. the artifacts) helps an observer form a stable and meaningful description of another culture (Schneider and Barsoux, 2003: 30–4). For example, the concept of 'saving face' may help explain why an Asian subordinate would refrain from criticizing a superior's decision, even if the decision were flawed. However, Schein (1997) cautions that what a culture espouses and what it actually does may be *very* different. Examples of organizations espousing ethical values while engaging in illegal activities are testament to the incongruence between professed cultural values and actual behaviour.

The third and deepest level of culture is *basic assumptions*. These are the unconscious beliefs that define certain actions as normal, correct or good (Schneider and Barsoux, 2003: 34–46). For Schein (1997), these assumptions are the ultimate source of cultural values and behaviour. Together with values, they are learned from an early age, and reinforced throughout a person's socialization into a culture such that they are taken for granted and rarely questioned. Examples include one's relationship with time (e.g. having a future, past or present orientation; short-term or long-term orientation), one's relationship with the environment (e.g. to submit to Nature's will, or strive to overcome external constraints) and, most crucially perhaps, one's relationships with other people and society (e.g. an individualist versus collectivist orientation; deference to authority). Behaviour not based on our own basic assumptions may be inconceivable or hard to accept.

Gibson *et al.* (2009: 47–8) have put forward a definition of culture that encapsulates these different levels of culture. For its malleability and accordance with much of the extant literature, we adopt this definition as a general framework for the book:

the configuration of basic assumptions about humans and their relationship to each other and to the world around them, shared by an identifiable group of people. Culture is *manifested* in individuals' values and beliefs, in expected norms for social behavior, and in artifacts such as social institutions and physical items.

In her classic work on culture, Smircich (1983) discusses five ontological and epistemological conceptualizations of culture. All five are highly pertinent to the research informing this book, and so it is instructive to reflect on each for their insights into cross-cultural trust building (though they overlap, to some extent).

In the first conceptualization, culture is the independent variable, an input into an organization or person that occurs through membership of external groups (e.g. nationality and affiliations, such as to professional communities). This is very much the standard conceptualization in the literature on trust across cultures (Doney *et al.*, 1998; Johnson and Cullen, 2002): culture is a variable that exists beyond the immediate group boundaries that exerts influence on what happens within the group.

Culture can also be an internal variable that 'expresses the values or social ideals and the beliefs that organization members come to share... conveys a sense of identity [i.e. generating in-group and out-group memberships]... facilitates the generation of commitment to something larger than the self... enhances social system stability... [and] serves as a sense-making device that can guide and shape behaviour' (Smircich, 1983: 344–6). This conceptualization, of culture impacting on trust from within, implies a need to explore how groups create their own distinctive culture, rather than be influenced by external cultural variables. Perrone *et al.*'s work (2003) on 'boundary spanners' in international alliances is an example (also Caldwell and Clapham, 2003).

The cognitive perspective presents culture as a 'system of shared cognitions or a system of knowledge and beliefs'. Organizations or groups are 'networks of subjective meanings or shared frames of references that organization members share to varying degrees and which, to an external observer, appear to function in a rule-like or grammar-like manner' (Smircich, 1983: 348–9). Thus, culture provides 'a template for cognitive processes' used for processing information about one's experiences and about other people in particular (Erez and Earley, 1993). Culture influences the content of 'schemas' [i.e. cognitive filters used by people to understand their experiences], the structure of those schemas [i.e. the priority given to different information] and the propensity to process information using those schemas (Gibson *et al.*, 2009: 50). When an individual interacts with someone from another culture, they are required to comprehend the 'rules or scripts that guide action' (Smircich, 1983: 350), and potentially to modify their behaviours accordingly. The key question arising from this approach is: what are the cognitive processes for uncovering, interpreting and accommodating different cultures' rules for trusting others, and how does one demonstrate one's own trustworthiness in an alien culture?

The 'symbolic' perspective differs from the cognitive view, in that culture is less about rules than about 'system[s] of shared symbols and meaning [producing] themes that orient or stimulate social activity' (Smircich, 1983: 350). Symbolic processes shape members' activities more so than do cognitive evaluations of a set of 'rules', she argues: coordinated activity in any given culture requires a 'common interpretation' of the situation (Smircich, 1983: 351). The challenge here for researchers in cross-cultural trust is to understand how these 'consensually determined meanings' are generated and agreed upon.

Finally, the 'structuralist' and 'psycho-dynamic' approaches are concerned with how culture is 'the expression of [members'] *unconscious* psychological processes', including desires and convictions, and how these are manifested in behaviour. They imply a need to identify these unconscious desires, and see how these are expressed in a culture.

We now explore how culture shapes thinking and behaviour in general terms, before considering the special case of trust.

## The influence of culture on thinking and behaviour

Smircich (1983: 341) argues that culture expresses the values, social ideals and beliefs that group members come to share; it conveys a sense of identity and facilitates commitment to the group (generating in-groups and out-groups); it enhances social system stability, and it serves as a sense-making device that guides and shapes behaviour (Smircich, 1983: 344–6). Schein (1997: 22) similarly describes culture as defining for us 'what we pay attention to, what things mean, how to react emotionally to what is going on, and what actions to take in various kinds of situations', to reduce the anxiety of dealing with unpredictable and uncertain environments. Culture 'provides insight into how to be a person in the world, what makes for a good life, how to interact with others, and which aspects of situations require more attention and processing capacity' (Gibson *et al.*, 2009: 48); culture is the source of 'scripts for social interaction [that] implicitly guide everyday behaviour' (49).

In short, culture determines in part, how we think and what we do (Tinsley, 1998), including what we understand as foundational to trust and what we consider trustworthy conduct from ourselves and from others (Zaheer and Zaheer, 2006). That said, culture's effect on individual and group *behaviour* is far from straightforward; its impact comes 'through its influence on more proximal outcomes' such as values and beliefs (Gibson *et al.*, 2009: 52). Moreover, culture's effect is 'highly indirect and likely moderated by a variety of other variables' (46); Gibson and colleagues identify moderator variables operating at the *individual* level (propensities, preferences and capabilities); *group* features (such as homogeneity and history) and dynamics (internal strength of the culture's identity, its cohesion and stage of development), and *situational* factors (including the degree of uncertainty, complexity, munificence and volatility). As noted by numerous authors, aspects of culture are likely to work in concert, rather than singly (Berry *et al.*, 2002; Chao and Moon, 2005; Kirkman and Shapiro, 1997). It is therefore important to understand the multiplicity of cultural identities.

## The multiplicity of cultural identities

Recent conceptualizations of culture rightly emphasize that it is 'a multi-level, multi-layer construct' (Leung *et al.*, 2005; Tung, 2008: 43). Following Schneider and Barsoux's (2003) notion of interacting cultural spheres and Chao and Moon's (2005) metatheory of culture, we argue that individuals and organizations have multiple cultural memberships that arise from different social identities. Social identity theory describes how an individual's self-concept can be derived from his or her group memberships (Tajfel, 1981). Social identity is based on a *cognitive* component, an awareness of a group membership; and an *evaluative* component, the value of a group membership. In this way, we categorize people into different groups, we identify with the groups to which we belong, and we compare our groups' standings with other groups. Although most of the research on social identity theory involve only two groups, an in-group and an out-group, Tajfel (1981) acknowledged that multiple group identities contribute to an individual's social identity. Groups that are valued and hold emotional significance are typically most salient for an individual's social identity. Significant groups, associated with cultural identities, help guide the individual's self-image and relationships with others.

Chao and Moon's (2005) 'cultural mosaic' model categorizes multiple cultural identities into three groups. *Demographic* tiles include physical, innate attributes such as age, gender, race, ethnicity and nationality.[4] *Geographic* tiles include natural or human-made aspects of a locale, such as tropical/temperate, urban/rural, coastal/inland: thus, a person's cultural identity may be shaped by the place where they live. Finally, *associative* tiles include those groups that individuals choose to be involved with, such as family, religion and political affiliations. In organizational contexts, industry, employing organization and professional/functional groups are particularly salient associative tiles. Each 'tile' or 'sphere' represents a culture or subculture, with its own artifacts and behaviours, beliefs and values, and underlying assumptions that may influence that person's thinking and conduct. How then can we analyse the impact of idiosyncratic mosaic-like combinations of multiple cultural identities on human behaviour?

Chao and Moon's metatheory depicts how cultural 'tiles' may complement each other, coexist or clash, depending on the strength and salience of each cultural identity in a given situation (see also the interaction effects among cultures proposed by Schneider and Barsoux, 2003: 51–77). While this may appear to render culturally derived behaviour chaotic and unpredictable, Chao and Moon draw upon complexity theory to argue that three types of discernible 'localized' structures can emerge (i.e. significant 'patches' of regular pattern in the mosaic). These are:

(a) Some tiles may dominate others,
(b) Some tiles may self-organize into a consolidated identity, and
(c) Other tiles may maintain independent influences (Chao and Moon, 2005: 1131–5).

These 'localized structures' can help parties identify reliable behaviour patterns in other groups or cultures. For example, one may have a 'unified identity' (e.g. being Italian), or a 'dominant cultural identity' (e.g. mainly

---

[4] Interestingly, although nationality is most often viewed as a demographic tile – something we are born into – we recognize that people can adopt new nationalities (e.g. immigrants seeking US citizenship; being brought up in a country other than where one was born; affiliating oneself with one's parent's nationality, such as some ethnic Pakistanis born and bred in the UK). In these cases, nationality is *associative*. However, since the vast majority of people grow up in the country of their birth, for most encounters, nationality can be considered a demographic tile.

Italian, but with some American traits) – both are consistent with structure (a) above. Or, one may have a 'merged' or 'hybrid' identity (e.g. an Italian-American, which, in some respects, is its own culture) – structure (b) above. Such localized structures render parties from alien cultures more predictable, and hence potentially more trustworthy. However, when a party's cultural 'tiles' remain independent, this is likely to produce unpredictable and potentially disorienting patterns of behaviour, as with a 'compartmentalized' identity (e.g. Italian at home; American at work). Badri's decision to shake Johann's hand in our introductory vignette is an example: she drew on her Western-trained business culture and/or organizational identity, rather than her Iranian/Muslim culture, which would predict that she refuse the handshake.

We acknowledge two further complexities that must be tackled in cross-cultural trust research. First, cultural identities are dynamic: parties adopt new group memberships, terminate some old group memberships, and other identities evolve and mature, or fade in significance over time. Moreover, they can be modified and even newly created by others (Hatch, 1993). Second, people may not be consciously aware of their cultural identities (Schein, 1997); nor are people always aware of the myriad cultural identities of those they interact with.

In summary, multiple cultural spheres or tiles profoundly shape people's thinking and behaviour in organizational contexts. Our research challenge is to understand how culture influences trust, and how trust develops between individuals and groups separated by cultural boundaries. This is no easy task. We now turn our attention to some of the theoretical frameworks and empirical studies that might advance our understanding.

## The interaction of trust and culture: putting the pieces together

When two parties from within a given culture interact, the processes of signalling and interpreting trust 'cues' *should* be relatively straightforward. As previously argued, individuals with shared cultural memberships are likely – courtesy of their shared norms, values and socialization experiences – to hold a common understanding and set of expectations about what is required to establish and maintain a trusting relationship. Because the 'trust cues' are familiar to both parties – that is, 'because the direction the target takes to earn trust is the same route the trustor follows to establish whether the target is trustworthy' (Doney *et al.*, 1998: 616) – trust tends to grow quickly (Branzei *et al.*, 2007: 62; Griffith *et al.*, 2000: 306).

However, this 'familiarity' (see McKnight *et al.*, 1998) is not available when engaging with a party from another culture. When party A from 'culture #1' meets party B from 'culture #2', the relationship parameters are a mix of potentially shared objectives and mutual gain, but dissimilar backgrounds. 'A' and 'B' may hope to collaborate, but may be fearful of separate interests and being exploited. It is this mix of agendas and unfamiliarity that challenges trust from the outset (Banai and Reisel, 1999; Sullivan *et al.*, 1981). The 'assumptions of symmetry' between parties in understanding, and enacting, trust processes 'may need revising' (Zaheer and Zaheer, 2006: 22). How can 'A' and 'B' go about realizing a fruitful exchange?

Whether unconsciously or deliberately, A and B will give off cues about their trustworthiness, and about the prospects of a trusting relationship forming between them. The degree of trust in a relationship pivots around the signals interpreted from these cues (Bacharach and Gambetta, 2001: 135, cited in Branzei *et al.*, 2007). B's own cultural background will, to an a-priori unknown degree, determine her conduct and what she thinks will engender A's trust. Her 'trust cues' are, to some extent, a manifestation of her own culture(s). But culture also affects A's processing of B's behaviour, by shaping how the information received from the cues is used to make the judgment about B's trustworthiness, and the consequent decision to trust. Finally, cultural filters ('schemas') affect how A and B will weight and prioritize different cues and symbols (Gibson *et al.*, 2009). 'People deal with complex environments by comparing new events to categories already stored in memory' (Shapiro *et al.*, 2008: 75). As Branzei and colleagues found (2007: 78), 'cultural norms and values that are conducive to efficient trust production in one setting may be impotent, misleading and even damaging in another'. What A from culture #1 may *understand* by the concepts of 'ability', 'benevolence' and 'integrity', and might consider *reliable* indicators of each, may not resonate with people from B's culture. In this respect, culture inhibits efforts to understand a foreign party.

A few examples can illustrate this influence of culture on trust. Trompenaars (2003) devised a scenario in which his research subject is in a car being driven by a friend, who knocks down a pedestrian at illegal speed. The friend appeals to the research subject to lie on his behalf to the authorities about how fast he was going, in order to escape punishment. Trompenaars famously showed that people in cultures with 'universalistic' values and people in cultures with 'particularistic' values have incompatible logics. The former (privileging honesty and compliance with the law regardless of the situation) might say of the latter, 'you cannot trust these people, they would lie to protect their friends'; the latter (recognizing few or no absolute principles, and that one's actions should reflect circumstances) might say of the former, 'you cannot trust these people, they wouldn't even lie to protect their friends'.

The recommendation of a family friend is highly influential in Chinese *guanxi* for facilitating business ties, but such an endorsement – while interesting – seldom suffices in Anglo-American business culture. In American business relations, a formal contract tends to precede trust by underwriting it; in China, strong trust seems to be a pre-condition of signing any contract. For both cultures, how they act is 'normal' and even expected; to encounter different assumptions and conduct is likely, therefore, to be unnerving.

In an altogether different 'cultural' scenario, Elsbach and Kramer (2003) found that people pitching ideas to Hollywood producers who did not act in an offbeat, quirky manner were felt to be lacking in creativity – even though, contrary to *presumed orthodoxies* in the film industry, creative people are often methodical thinkers. In other words, 'Hollywood culture' anticipates quirkiness as a cue for creativity (i.e. ability); failing to conform to this expectation is likely to be viewed with scepticism.

In short, culture *influences* the formation of trust cues in relationships, and serves as a *filter* for cues encountered from another culture. Both the delivery and interpretation of cues is far from clear-cut, as we have seen, and this can 'hinder the production of initial trust in cross-cultural encounters' (Branzei *et al.*, 2007: 79). Plenty can get lost in translation. Indeed, this has been found in cross-cultural trust research, where findings are mixed and contradictory, even counterintuitive (for reviews see Ferrin and Gillespie, this volume; Arino *et al.*, 2001; Johnson and Cullen, 2002). When incomprehension and confusion do result, culture can serve as a *refuge*, reaffirming one's own identity while disparaging that of the other party (Brewer and Yuki, 2007; Gibson *et al.*, 2009: 49). Molinsky (2007) cites Weldon *et al.* thus: 'if the interaction is anxiety producing, then the trained subject may fall back upon old responses with a new tenacity'. This can hamper trust further.

This leads to the general question: which cues, and which cultural tiles, are rated highly during trust building, and which are rejected or are too difficult to comprehend and process? Additionally, are certain cues or tiles privileged during first impressions, and do others become more decisive later? We might speculate that nationality, ethnicity and gender may dominate the earliest phase of a relationship, or perhaps associative tiles (e.g. shared professional community or employer) 'trump' demographics. Gibson *et al.* (2009: 57) suggest that members of a 'subculture' – smaller, more distinctive, closer to the person – are likely to have more aligned values than members of the same nation: thus, a shared organization may trump nationality, a shared

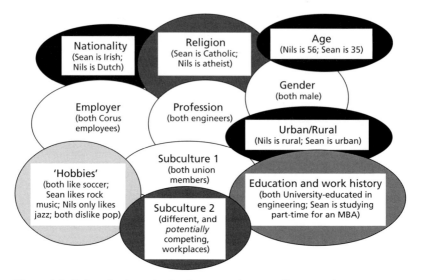

**Figure 1.2** Cultural spheres in the Corus works council case study

workplace may trump organization, etc. Indeed, in their study of international joint ventures involving Indian firms and partners from countries such as the United States, Japan and the Netherlands, Pothukuchi *et al.* (2002) found that *organizational* culture explained the variance in the impact of 'partner dissimilarity' on international joint venture performance better than *national* cultural differences (see also Gerhart (2009) for a recent review of the modest impact of national culture on organizational culture). Meyerson *et al.* (1996) found that cues from *professional* identities established trust quickly on Hollywood film sets, regardless of *demographic* or *organizational* identities. These effects remain to be investigated.

We can now illustrate these dynamics by returning to the opening vignette featuring Sean and Nils as employee representatives on Corus's European Works Council. Figure 1.2 depicts their congruent and antagonistic cultural spheres/tiles: the lighter shading reflects commonality; dark shading indicates no common culture. They do not share nationality, or urban/rural living, or ethnicity, but they have a similar educational background and hobbies profile, and they share gender, profession, employer and the trade union subculture. In the vignette, neither employer nor profession nor union membership could overcome the primacy of national/workplace interests and values – at least, not *initially*. But later their shared 'union' identity and employee cultures, broadly defined, did lead them to trust each other, when workplace differences faded in the face of perceived employer hostility.

To sum up, it is clear from the insights presented in this chapter that we need models and frameworks of cross-cultural trust that accommodate both individual agency as well as [cultural] embeddedness (Möllering, 2006): trust is a matter of choice for individuals, but constrained by external influences, including multiple cultures. Cross-cultural trust is an idiosyncratic accomplishment, but one that, through theorizing and empirical study, we can aspire to predict. The next section offers a number of ways forward.

## Frameworks and toolkits for understanding and building trust across cultures

'A' has two basic options when dealing with 'B' from another culture: one is to interpret B's conduct through the prism(s) of her own multifarious cultural schemas, potentially giving rise to misunderstandings. The alternative is to try to *accommodate* B's cultural background when interpreting their behaviour, and adapting appropriately. In other words, trustors and trustees may have to 'switch' from one system of trust production – derived from their own culture – to another (see Molinsky, 2007). In this section, we review several frameworks that explore these processes, and we locate them within each of Smircich's perspectives. In the concluding section, we propose a synthesized model of trust development across cultural boundaries, drawing on each of these frameworks.

The first model, from Doney and colleagues (1998), examines how the norms, values and assumptions apparent in *national* cultures, based on Hofstede's dimensions, impact on the way individuals attend to, prioritize and process trust-relevant information. Hence, their framework takes Smircich's first concept of culture, that is, as the independent variable. They propose, for example, that trustors from individualist cultures place greater weight on the target's capability to fulfil promises than do those from collectivist cultures. In contrast, trustors from collectivist cultures place greater weight than individualists on the target's predictability, motivations and 'proof sources' transferred from other trusted parties/groups (this has been confirmed in a study involving Canadian and Japanese nationals: Branzei *et al.*, 2007).

Johnson and Cullen (2002) also make a number of propositions about how national cultural differences, as an independent variable, influence the salience of certain bases of trust. But they make explicit use of symbolic interactionism to depict cross-cultural trust building as fundamentally a process of generating *symbols* and the attachment of *meaning* to them.

Parties in intercultural exchanges must 'mutually develop and agree on what behaviour, activity or gesture in the relationship serves as a trust signal' (Johnson and Cullen, 2002: 358). It is a process of 'formative mutual realignment' (344). The following factors facilitate intercultural trust: investing time and effort in overcoming cultural barriers, including fostering cultural sensitivity, extensive information exchange and two-way communications, flexibly adjusting to differences, and social controls in the form of repeated interactions and the development of a shared joint venture culture (i.e. a newly created, shared cultural 'tile'). Yet their overall conclusion, from a selected review of empirical studies on alliances, is that 'when trusting involves a specific referent, [national] cultural differences do not seem to play a significant role'. In other words, reinterpreting this from a Chao and Moon standpoint, a specific referent comes with many specific cultural identities, any of which may overshadow nationality effects in a trust-building context. (Recall that 'organization' superseded 'nationality' in Pothukuchi *et al.*, 2002.)

Zaheer and Zaheer (2006) discuss the 'asymmetries of trust' in encounters between people from 'high' and 'low' [pre-dispositional/generalized] trust cultures (i.e. low–low; high–high; low–high), exclusively in international scenarios. Their framework therefore depicts culture not as an external, national variable, but an internal variable, one that determines parties' response to another. They put forward five propositions on anticipated recourse to regulatory institutions and/or investments in trust building based on these asymmetries.

The 'cross-cultural code-switching' process proposed by Molinsky (2007) has clear implications for trust building. He defines code-switching as 'the act of purposefully modifying one's behaviour, in a specific interaction in a foreign setting, to accommodate different cultural norms for appropriate behaviour' (Molinsky, 2007: 623). Rather than either seeking to persuade the other party to change or withdrawing personally from the relationship, code-switching 'forces an individual to consciously override [her/his] dominant, ingrained cultural response... [and] entails deviating from accustomed behaviour in one's native culture in order to engage in behaviour appropriate to a foreign culture' (Molinsky, 2007). In this respect, it reflects Smircich's cognitive, rule-based perspective on culture. The extent of the psychological toll that the switch exerts is shaped by three contextual variables (the complexity of the norms involved, the discrepancy between the required norms for the situation and the person's own norms, and the degree of psychological safety (see Edmondson, 1999) in the situation) and by two personal variables (the person's cultural knowledge and capabilities, and their own personal values). The presence of these factors may help to account for parties' progress in trust-building efforts across cultures.[5]

Shapiro *et al.*'s model (2008) of the emergence of 'cultural sensitivity' conceptualizes it as 'some composite of knowledge of cultural facts [about the other culture] and the cognitive, motivational and behaviour skills needed to adapt' (2008: 72). Their research involved interviews with twelve American managers dealing with alliance parties in the Pacific Rim. They found four distinct phases toward 'cultural sensitivity', beginning when the newcomer is a 'romantic sojourner' with passionate interest and affection for the other culture, albeit at a superficial level. (S)he becomes a 'foreign worker' as greater awareness and understanding of the full complexity of the host culture is attained, and (s)he accumulates a set of 'tactical' and 'borrowed' frames of meaning (i.e. picking up rules of thumb and superficially congenial patterns of behaviour in dealings with people from the host culture). However, the shock of coping with this stage can lead to disappointment and frustration. As relations develop over time, the person creates frames of meaning with the locals, and comes to share them in common: the 'foreign worker' now becomes a 'skilled worker', adept at forging strong bonds of trust with locals while at the same time reconciled to the status of an outsider (see also Gibson *et al.*, 2009: 54). Finally, few people become true 'partners', with 'nuanced situated knowledge' and 'transcultural understanding', though the authors insist that it is possible. Thus, in Smircich's terms (1983), Shapiro *et al.* take a primarily cognitive approach to understanding culture, but also address the (co-)creation of symbols and meanings. Throughout this progress toward full cultural sensitivity, different forms of trust are said to emerge or, rather, appear more salient: indicators of ability are most crucial in the earlier stages, and signs of genuine benevolence only come much later. While this

---

[5] Three studies provide interesting evidence to reinforce Molinsky's view that code-switching, even modifying one's underlying assumptions, is achievable under certain conditions. Kuhlmann (2005) observed a modification response among German and Mexican collaborators, who acted as if trying to 'contradict the assumed heterostereotype of the typical German or the typical Mexican'. The German business partners 'attached great importance to close, friendly relationships', whereas their Mexican partners sought to 'demonstrate competence, reliability and honesty' (Kuhlmann, 2005: 46). Sullivan *et al.*'s (1981) study involving forty-eight American and seventy two Japanese managers found that, while both cultures viewed trust in similar ways – as based on 'the deliberate development of a close personal relationship' (Sullivan *et al.*, 1981: 813) – the Japanese *modified their cultural preferences* for managing relationships, depending upon whether an American or fellow Japanese was in charge of the project. Finally, Rao and Hashimoto (1996) found that Japanese managers needing to influence their Canadian subordinates used 'reason' much more than they might have felt necessary to do at home.

study compartmentalizes trust into different 'types' based only on the content of the beliefs, much like Doney *et al.* (1998) and Johnson and Cullen (2002), and the sample size is small, the insights are compelling, and may apply to trust development in other cross-cultural settings. Schneider and Barsoux (2003) similarly urge managers to adopt as 'reflexive activities' the observation of a given party's artifacts and behaviours, asking questions to elicit others' core values and beliefs and interpreting accurately others' underlying assumptions (see also Earley and Peterson, 2004; Peterson, 2004).

Chao and Moon's (2005) metatheory of culture offers several further insights for identifying which cues from which cultural tiles best serve trust building. Our *dominant* cultural tiles shape our initial attitudes, behaviours and dealings with others: we may be either wholly typical of our dominant culture and act in a culturally uniform manner, or particular tiles may be more influential. For example, someone may think and act as an archetypal German, or overwhelmingly in investment banker mode, or like every other 'IBMer'. They may also interpret everyone else's conduct through this prism (see Maguire and Phillips, 2008, for a case study). In such a case, that party's behaviour and response to others' behaviour will be more 'predictable'.

But other tiles may maintain independent influences on behaviour, depending on circumstances. An American academic may act in a typically forthright 'American' manner when demanding decent customer service in a London restaurant, but may be equivocal and even-handed in discussions with unfamiliar fellow academics around the table. This may render that person's behaviours unpredictable in cultural terms (which 'tiles' are to be dominant, in any given situation?) Hence, there are independent *and* additive effects from cues from different tiles.

Adapting Chao and Moon's model for our purposes, an individual's initial search for cues and signals might be taken from visible 'surface-level' tiles, because they are the most apparent. *Demographic* tiles related to ethnicity, gender and age – whichever might be most salient to the trustor – might be the most obvious sources of cues for initial trust. Alternatively, clear signals of professional identity (e.g. a doctor's medical apparel – an *associative* tile) or role (see Meyerson *et al.*, 1996) may provide stronger cues.

Interactions between trustor and trustee can uncover additional cultural identities that can serve as cues for trust. Prolonged interactions between the trustor and trustee (i.e. relational trust) can move the relationship beyond surface cues to deeper aspects. Over time, differences in demographics may be overcome by appeal to *associative* tiles in particular (e.g. organizational, professional, extra-curricular, such as hobbies or interests). Professional cultures often serve this purpose during collaborative endeavours between 'rival' organizations, such as joint ventures or projects (see Smith and Schwegler, this volume). For example, the French and German Airbus engineers at the troubled Toulouse plant in our opening vignette could bond over their common employment status or profession (i.e. *associative* tiles), despite their demographic differences. Equally, ingrained cultural values may prevent the possibility of parties creating their own unique cultural identity to share (see Hope-Hailey *et al.*, this volume). Leaders have a role in articulating common purpose and fostering a shared identity; their power and influence may overcome cultural differences, or compel their resolution.

In sum, trust may emerge from: 1) recognition and promotion of shared cultural identities (i.e. coming from the same culture); 2) an alignment of tiles and identities (i.e. having compatible yet different tiles); 3) one party's acceptance of, and possibly adaptation toward, the other's dominant culture (i.e. a relationship based on one party's superior power); or 4) from the 'self-organizing' creation of a new, *shared* cultural identity created by the parties for themselves (as with a merger such as GlaxoSmithKline, for example, and *not* with Daimler-Chrysler). But if the other party's tiles are mystifying, even alienating, we may interpret them as indicative of their lack of trustworthiness, given that 'culture' implies a *values* dimension wherein shared values facilitate trust, while antagonistic values damage trust. Trust may, accordingly, falter. This is Chao and Moon's attractor/repellor thesis. Mary Jo Hatch's (1993) work explains how an organizational culture might be modified, including how to align disparate groups' value-sets.

These propositions all point to people engaging across cultures needing to understand how their own, and other parties', cultural influences might manifest themselves, and how they are interpreted. It also highlights the influence of networks that facilitate linkages among people from a shared culture or from different cultures (e.g. 'you can be confident about X, he's a friend of mine'/ 'I can vouch for her' (she's from 'our' culture, or a 'friendly' one)). In particular, 'boundary spanners' (Perrone *et al.*, 2003) and third parties play a crucial role. The latter predict trust '*indirectly* by shaping behaviour within [interpersonal] dyads and *directly* by conveying trust judgments' about the other parties (Ferrin *et al.*, 2006: 879). Yet group diversity levels may lead to the creation of cliques, with attendant consequences for trust development within the cliques (likely to be good), and across the cliques (likely to be bad).

Lastly, Mesquita's (2007) model for third-party interventions for developing inter-firm trust contrasts two basic approaches: attempting to eliminate distrust from every relationship dimension to build trust in its place, versus reconstructing what he calls 'aggregate trust: the net balance of trust and distrust across the several domains of a relationship' (Mesquita, 2007: 75). Interestingly for our purposes, he advocates the latter.

## Concluding understanding of trust building across cultures

In the concluding section, we draw upon the insights gathered herein to present a tentative four-stage process of trust building across cultures, based upon Lewicki and Bunker's (1996) original staged model of trust development. We have annotated it with references to particular insights from the literature reviewed previously:

1. **Context:** Prior to the first encounter, parties arrive with their own cultural preconceptions [Doney *et al.*; Johnson and Cullen; Shapiro *et al.*; Zaheer and Zaheer], which vary in degree of complexity [Molinsky] and compatibility [Chao and Moon; Zaheer and Zaheer], shaping the likelihood of trust from the outset. Parties also come with a set level of cross-cultural awareness and capabilities, and motivation to adapt [Chao and Moon; Molinsky; Shapiro *et al.*]. At sufficient levels these attributes have the potential to offset any 'cultural gap'.

2. **Opening stance:** Parties will arrive either with good reasons to trust each other (i.e. the presence of signals indicating shared cultural tiles/spheres), or to distrust the other (such as between people from nations or ethnic groups with antagonistic histories, or companies facing a hostile merger or acquisition). More likely, perhaps, there will be a willingness to suspend judgment [Mesquita; Shapiro *et al.*]. This opening stance will, to some extent, be culturally determined, both by immediate assessments of the other's values and by each culture's receptiveness to unfamiliar and possibly uncomfortable scenarios. Active distrust leaves parties prone to confirmation bias and self-fulfilling prophecies; a willingness to trust or a suspension of judgment is more conducive to successful engagement.

3. **Early encounters:** In early encounters, parties initiate communication, gather trust-relevant information, seek and interpret cues, test assumptions, and potentially try to modify the expectations of the other party, and their own [Chao and Moon; Johnson and Cullen; Molinsky; Shapiro *et al.*]. Each party will have a level of determination to overcome frustrations and misunderstandings [Molinsky].

Then, depending on how the parties' trust-building efforts fare. . .

4a. **The 'breakthrough':** In positive relationships, parties gather sufficient insights into the other party to recognize or create commonalities and/ or reconcile differences [Johnson and Cullen; Mesquita; Molinsky;

Shapiro *et al.*]. Parties may proactively modify their own behaviour to realize this [Molinsky]. Accommodation or acceptance of the other party results, *despite* cultural differences (the influence of which diminishes) or due to the sharing of a new common cultural identity. This leads to *trust*.

4b. **The 'breakdown'**: Parties fail to reach insights into the other party's culture, or they reach insights that are culturally intolerable or discomforting. They are incapable of reconciling their differences. Suspicion of the other party remains, *due to* cultural differences [Doney *et al.*; Zaheer and Zaheer]. This results in *distrust*.

The outcome paths are different, depending on the success of the trust-building process:

5. **Consequences**: A trusting relationship should mature as insights into the other develop further [Shapiro *et al.*; Lewicki and Bunker]. Mutual understanding, and even affection, may be possible and cultural influences on parties' interpretation of the other should recede in significance. By contrast, a distrusting relationship will either fail to progress beyond the breakdown and be terminated or, if the relationship must continue, suspicion will be its governing principle until understanding can be reached (and this may never come). A second distrust scenario is a violation of trust expectations suffered by one party sometime in the future, caused by a cultural misunderstanding. This may require a trust repair effort, if the violator wishes for the relationship to endure. In this respect, trust processes have a built-in feedback loop, and a breakthrough can still be realized. In later encounters, parties' capacity to code-switch, or to retain tolerance of cultural differences, will endure as an influence.

Figure 1.3 represents this staged process in diagrammatic form. In each chapter, we can see how the parties from different cultural spheres, and with different cultural tiles, negotiate their progress through these stages.

Before we preview the book chapters, we note three reasons for caution in considering the influence of culture on trust. First, researchers may overestimate the impact of culture. Perhaps individuals' behaviour is independent of culture, and simply idiosyncratic, in which case any *cultural* assumptions derived from behaviour may be inaccurate and potentially misleading, even offensive (e.g. treating all Arabs the same). Likewise for assumptions about behaviour derived from cultural stereotyping (e.g. making absurd generalizations about multi-ethnic and multicultural communities). Though interactions are culturally embedded, individual agency remains (Möllering, 2006). Plenty of evidence from cross-cultural research on trust suggests that this note of caution is warranted.

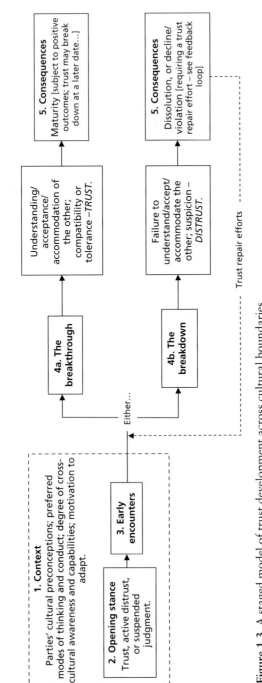

**1. Context**
Parties' cultural preconceptions; preferred modes of thinking and conduct; degree of cross-cultural awareness and capabilities; motivation to adapt.

**2. Opening stance**
Trust, active distrust, or suspended judgment.

**3. Early encounters**

Either...

**4a. The breakthrough**

Understanding/acceptance/accommodation of the other; compatibility or tolerance –*TRUST.*

**5. Consequences**
Maturity [subject to positive outcomes; trust may break down at a later date....]

**4b. The breakdown**

Failure to understand/accept/accommodate the other; suspicion – *DISTRUST.*

**5. Consequences**
Dissolution, or decline/violation [requiring a trust repair effort – see feedback loop]

Trust repair efforts

**Figure 1.3** A staged model of trust development across cultural boundaries

Second, behaviour may be driven not so much by culture but by *institutions* (Zucker, 1986). Child and Möllering's (2003) study of Hong Kong managers' trust in their mainland Chinese workers found that institutional bases (e.g. a reliable legal system, consistent conduct from local Chinese officials) had a stronger predictive effect on trust than the Hong Kong managers' personal attempts to foster trust (such as with efforts to build rapport, recruiting locals to key positions and the transfer of operating standards). However, the authors note that the absence of reliable institutions makes these personal efforts at 'active trust development' more important. Timming's study of international squabbles on a European Works Council (2008) provides another compelling example of the influence of different institutions on cross-cultural trust – in this case, employment-rights legislation. Of course, a complicating argument is that institutions may be considered a manifestation of a culture.

A final objection to the presumed powerful impact of culture comes from the difficulty of identifying which of the multiple 'cultural tiles' is dominant during any given interaction, and then disentangling this effect from effects caused by individual dispositions and preferences, group dynamics as well as institutional sources of trust. In short, isolating the unique influence of 'culture' on trust is extremely complicated! In this volume, to gain insight into the complex relationships between culture and trust, we adopt a multi-disciplinary, multi-method and multi-level approach: that is, we combat the complexity of the research agenda with a diversity of perspectives, research methodologies and settings.

## The book: an overview

The book is structured in four parts: the first part sets the scene conceptually, defining trust and culture, reviewing what we know so far and introducing the contributions. The second and third parts are focused, respectively, on inter-organizational and intra-organizational studies. The broad themes and issues are illustrated by a striking variety of cross-cultural scenarios. The final part draws out patterns of insight and suggests practical advice and future research agendas.

### *Preview summary of contributions*

In Chapter 2, Ferrin and Gillespie ask the question: does interpersonal trust and its development, functions and meaning differ between people from different *national–societal* cultures? Their review of over fifty empirical studies reveals evidence of cross-cultural differences (particularly on generalized trust), but also evidence of trust universals. They conclude that trust operates as a 'variform universal' (the general principle of trust holds across cultures, however, specific manifestations exist in different cultures) and a 'variform functional universal' (a relationship between trust and another variable is typically found, but the magnitude and/or direction of the relationship differs across cultures). They propose two routes for future cross-cultural trust research.

Bachmann argues in Chapter 3 that inter-organizational trust is an inherently context-bound concept. Drawing on data from supplier relations in the UK and Germany, he shows that the nature and quality of inter-organizational trust varies greatly over different cultural and institutional environments. He further argues that appropriate research methodology for examining trust in a comparative perspective needs to draw on a mixed method approach involving different techniques to collect and analyse data, and he describes in detail the repertory grids method.

Wright and Ehnert produce a compelling counter-argument to the positivistic assumptions and methodologies that presently dominate the trust literature. In Chapter 4, they argue instead that trust, and culture, are best understood as 'social constructions', and that context (temporal and physical) and people's own stories should be privileged accordingly. They reflect upon the implications for this alternative perspective on both practice and research agendas.

The second part focuses primarily on inter-organizational trust situations. Beginning with Chapter 5, Avakian, Clark and Roberts explore the multiplicity of intercultural dynamics on display in interactions between management consultants and representatives from their client organizations. Their study explains how the former try to persuade the latter of the legitimacy of their knowledge and prescriptions, and how the latter interpret these efforts. Trust is essential to this process. Based on an empirical study of a selection of consultants and clients, their perspective is drawn explicitly from Chao and Moon's cultural mosaic metatheory, and the processes outlined in this chapter. The authors use these lenses to understand these dynamics and uncover evidence of code-switching and value-alignment tactics.

Dibben and Rose's chapter (6) looks into similar dynamics, but their focus is on auditors' and accountants' servicing of their clients. They too use a 'cultural mosaic' perspective to examine how individual auditors attempt to reconcile the competing values and interests implied by the different cultures of which they are a member (e.g. their employer; their profession; their own values). Results from their own research point to a number of disconcerting patterns of cultural inertia in the auditing profession, with potentially grave implications for the credibility of the profession.

In Chapter 7, Kramer examines barriers to trust within the context of cross-cultural negotiations. He discusses both the psychological and social barriers to trust in this context, including categorization processes, cognitive biases, inter-group dynamics, third-party influences and constituent accountability. He then focuses attention on both behavioural and institutional approaches to overcoming these barriers, illustrating their use through several high-profile cases. He concludes with the practical implications of the review, and directions for future research on trust in cross-cultural negotiations.

Möllering and Stache (Chapter 8) draw on a qualitative analysis of field interviews and personal observations of German–Ukrainian business relationships, to investigate the potential actors have to creatively respond to institutional contexts, cultural differences and the challenge of trust development. They conclude that the trust dilemma in international business relationships can be overcome through reflexivity and creativity, and provide many practical examples of what this means.

In Chapter 9, Yousfi explores how national cultural differences between partners involved in a contractual relationship may interfere with the development of trust. This is illustrated through an ethnographic case study of a partnership between a French private company (Promostate) and a public Lebanese company (SONAT). Yousfi argues that due to differences in national cultural backgrounds, the French and Lebanese parties had different conceptions of what 'good cooperation' means and differing expectations of trustworthy behaviour, which hindered trust development. These challenges were exacerbated by differing organizational cultures and power asymmetries.

Lyon and Porter examine cooperation in the Nigerian and Ghanaian food sectors in Chapter 10. This is a context characterized by a highly fragmented system of micro-entrepreneurs from diverse ethnic groups, who both compete and cooperate with each other. The ethnographic research reveals how the traders draw on both personalized social relations and semi-formal institutional forms (such as professional codes of conduct and associations) to operate across cultural boundaries.

The third part looks into scenarios *within* organizations. Bridging the 'gap' between predominantly inter-organizational studies and intra-organizational studies, Smith and Schwegler's chapter (11) takes us into the world of international NGOs (non-governmental organizations) such as medical charities operating in developing countries. NGOs cannot realistically solve all of the problems they face, and so their choice of partner NGOs in the field is a critical strategic decision which, of course, must involve trust building across a multitude of cultural boundaries. Drawing on a study involving interviews inside sixteen American and German NGOs, the authors show how parties' different cultural spheres impact on this decision-making process, noting which spheres seem to dominate the process within each organization.

In Chapter 12, Wasti and Tan argue that US models of dyadic trust building at work have been applied to foreign contexts without a careful understanding of the culture-specific workways in such contexts (i.e. the pattern of workplace beliefs, mental models and practices about what is true, good and efficient within the domain of work). Drawing on sixty interviews from two countries (Turkey and China), the authors argue that both personal and professional life domains are important for understanding supervisor–subordinate trust in collectivist cultures.

Hope-Hailey, Farndale and Kelliher's chapter (13) reports findings from a long-standing UK study into change-management processes. Drawing on quantitative and qualitative data from nine large organizations, and using insights from the 'cultural mosaic' model in their analysis, the authors examine how different cultures (geographic; demographic; associative) seem to affect levels of employees' trust in their employer, and their line manager. Of particular interest for practical recommendations is the mediating role available to effective line managers.

In Chapter 14, Kassis Henderson notes that, in most multinationals, senior executives can expect to work in multicultural and multi*lingual* project teams. In her chapter, she presents findings from her own research, and other studies, into how language features in cross-cultural team situations. She finds that the international business language of English can serve as a unifying force, but also a barrier, to trust building. Intriguingly, the dominance of English can bring people from different non-English-speaking national cultures together, as an extended 'out-group' of their own.

Finally, Mari explores trust building in the context of family firms. She argues that three interacting subcultures (family, business and ownership) influence CEO and owner behaviour in family firms, and because of distinct values and norms of behaviour, the interactions of these subcultures often result in conflict and distrust. Through an exploratory case study, Mari examines and illustrates how family firm CEOs can enhance their legitimacy and thus build, maintain and repair trust.

The conclusion summarizes the key findings presented within each section of the book, identifying the emerging patterns and themes across the conceptual contributions and empirical studies. These are considered in relation to our two initial questions, firstly: is there a universally applicable model of trust and trust development [*etic*], or do people from varying cultures understand and enact trust differently [*emic*]? And, secondly: how can Party A from Culture #1 develop a trust relationship with Party B from Culture #2? We then highlight the implications of these patterns and themes for practitioners, and point to directions for future research.

## References

Arino, A., de la Torre, J. and Ring, P. S. 2001. 'Relational quality: managing trust in corporate alliances'. *California Management Review*, 44(1), 109–31.

Bachmann, R. and Zaheer, A. 2006. *A Handbook of Trust Research*. Cheltenham: Edward Elgar.

Baier, A. 1986. 'Trust and antitrust'. *Ethics*, 96, 231–60.

Banai, M. and Reisel, W. D. 1999. 'Would you trust your foreign manager? An empirical investigation'. *International Journal of Human Resource Management*, 10(3), 477–87.

Barber, B. 1983. *The Logic and Limits of Trust*. New Brunswick, NJ: Rutgers University Press.

Barney, J. B. and Hansen, M. H. 1994. 'Trustworthiness as a source of competitive advantage'. *Strategic Management Journal*, 15, 175–90.

Berry, J. W., Poortinga, Y. Y., Segall, M. H. and Dasen, P. R. 2002. *Cross-cultural Psychology: Research and Applications*, 2nd edn. New York: Cambridge University Press.

Blau, P. 1964. *Exchange and Power in Social Life*. New York: Wiley.

Branzei, O., Vertinsky, I. and Camp II, R. D. 2007. 'Culture-contingent signs of trust in emergent relationships'. *Organizational Behavior and Human Decision Processes*, 104, 61–82.

Brewer, M. B. and Yuki, M. 2007. 'Culture and social identity'. In S. Kitayama and D. Cohen (eds.) *Handbook of Cultural Psychology*. New York: Guilford, 307–22.

Buchan, N. R., Croson, R. T. A. and Dawes, R. M. 2002. 'Swift neighbours and persistent strangers: a cross-cultural investigation of trust and reciprocity in social exchange'. *American Journal of Sociology*, 108(1), 168–206.

Burt, R. S. and Knez, M. 1996. 'Trust and third party gossip'. In R. M. Kramer and T. R. Tyler (eds.) *Trust in Organizations: Frontiers of Theory and Research*. Thousand Oaks, CA: Sage, 68–89.

Butler, J. K. Jr., Cantrell, R. S. and Flick, R. J. 1999. 'Transformational leadership behaviors, upward trust, and satisfaction in self-managed work teams'. *Organization Development Journal*, 17(1), 13–28.

Caldwell, C. and Clapham, S. E. 2003. 'Organizational trustworthiness: an international perspective'. *Journal of Business Ethics*, 47(4), 349–64.

Chao, G. T. and Moon, H. 2005. 'The cultural mosaic: a metatheory for understanding the complexity of culture'. *Journal of Applied Psychology*, 90(6), 1128–40.

Child, J. 2001. 'Trust – the fundamental bond in global collaboration'. *Organizational Dynamics*, 29(4), 274–88.

Child, J. and Möllering, G. 2003. 'Contextual confidence and active trust development in the Chinese business environment'. *Organization Science*, 14(1), 69–80.

Colquitt, J., Scott, B. and LePine, J. 2007. 'Trust, trustworthiness, and trust propensity: a meta-analytic test of their unique relationships with risk taking and job performance'. *Journal of Applied Psychology*, 92, 909–27.

Cook, J. and Wall, T. D. 1980. 'New work attitude measures of trust, organizational commitment and personal need non-fulfilment'. *Journal of Occupational Psychology*, 53, 39–52.

Costa, A. C. and Bijlsma-Frankema, K. 2007. 'Trust and control inter-relations: new perspectives on the trust-control nexus: towards integrated perspectives'. *Group and Organization Management*, 32(4), 392–406.

Davis, J. H., Schoorman, F. D., Mayer, R. C. and Tan, H. H. 2000. 'The trusted general manager and business unit performance: empirical evidence of a competitive advantage'. *Strategic Management Journal*, 21(5), 563–76.

Dietz, G. and den Hartog, D. 2006. 'Measuring trust inside organizations'. *Personnel Review*, 35, 557–88.

Dirks, K. T. 2000. 'Trust in leadership and team performance: evidence from NCAA basketball'. *Journal of Applied Psychology*, 85, 1004–12.

Dirks, K. T. and Ferrin, D. 2001. 'The role of trust in organizational setting'. *Organizational Science*, 12, 450–67.

Doney, P. M., Cannon, J. P. and Mullen, M. R. 1998. 'Understanding the influence of national culture on the development of trust'. *Academy of Management Review*, 23(3), 601–20.

Dyer, J. H. and Chu, W. 2000. 'The determinants of trust in supplier-automaker relationships in the U.S., Japan and Korea'. *Journal of International Business Studies*, 31(2), 259–85.

Earley, C. P. and Peterson, R. S. 2004. 'The elusive cultural chameleon: cultural intelligence as a new approach to intercultural training for the global manager'. *Academy of Management Learning and Education*, 3(1), 100–15.

Edmondson, A. 1999. 'Psychological safety and learning behavior in work teams'. *Administrative Science Quarterly*, 44, 350–83.

Elsbach, K. D. and Kramer, R. M. 2003. 'Assessing creativity in Hollywood pitch meetings: evidence for a dual-process model of creativity judgements'. *Academy of Management Journal*, 46(3), 283–301.

Erez, M. and Earley, C. P. 1993. *Culture, Self-identity and Work*. Oxford University Press.

Farris, G. F., Senner, E. E. and Butterfield, D. A. 1973. 'Trust, culture and organizational behaviour'. *Industrial Relations*, 12(2), 144–57.

Ferrin, D. L., Dirks, K. T. and Shah, P. P. 2006. 'Direct and indirect effects of third-party relationships on interpersonal trust'. *Journal of Applied Psychology*, 91(4), 870–83.

Fukuyama, F. 1995. *Trust: the Social Virtues and the Creation of Prosperity*. London: Hamish Hamilton.

Gerhart, B. 2009. 'How much does national culture constrain organizational culture?' *Management and Organization Review*, 5(2), 241–60.

Gibson, C. B., Maznevski, M. and Kirkman, B. L. 2009. 'When does culture matter?' In R. S. Bhagat and R. M. Steers (eds.) *Handbook of Culture, Organizations, and Work*. Cambridge University Press.

Gillespie, N. 2003. 'Measuring trust in working relationships: the behavioral trust inventory'. Paper presented at the Academy of Management Conference, Seattle, WA, August.

Golembiewski, R. T. and McConkie, M. 1975. 'The centrality of interpersonal trust in group processes'. In C. L. Cooper (ed.) *Theories of Group Processes*. New York: Wiley.

Griffith, D. A., Hu, M. Y. and Ryans, J. K. 2000. 'Process standardization across intra- and inter-cultural relationships'. *Journal of International Business Studies*, 31(2), 303–24.

Gulati, R. 1995. 'Does familiarity breed trust? The implications of repeated ties for contractual choice in alliances'. *Academy of Management Journal*, 38(1), 85–112.

Haidt, J. 2006. *The Happiness Hypothesis: Putting Ancient Wisdom to the Test of Modern Science*. London: Arrow Books.

Hatch, M. J. 1993. 'The dynamics of organizational culture'. *Academy of Management Review*, 18(4), 657–93.

Hofstede, G. 1991. *Culture and Organizations: Software of the Mind*. London: McGraw Hill.

Hollinger, P. and Wiesmann, G. 2008. 'Airbus is hampered by cultural differences'. *Financial Times*, 15 July 2008.

Inglehart, R. 1999. 'Trust, well-being and democracy'. In M. E. Warren (ed.) *Democracy and Trust*. Cambridge University Press, 88–120.

Johnson, J. L. and Cullen, J. B. 2002. 'The bases and dynamics of trust in cross-cultural exchange relationships'. In M. J. Gannon and K. L. Newman (eds.) *The Blackwell Handbook of Cross-Cultural Management*. Oxford: Blackwell, 335–60.

Kasper-Fuehrer, E. C. and Ashkanasy, N. M. 2001. 'Communicating trustworthiness and building trust in interorganizational virtual organizations'. *Journal of Management*, 27, 235–54.

Keyton, J. and Smith, F. L. 2008. 'Nascent and complex: what is the focus of trust research?' *Academy of Management Review*, 33(1), 274–6.

Kirkman, B. L. and Shapiro, D. L. 1997. 'The impact of cultural values on employee resistance to teams: toward a model of globalized self-managing work team effectiveness'. *Academy of Management Review*, 22, 730–57.

Klein, K. J. and Kozlowski, S. W. J. (eds.) 2000. *Multilevel Theory, Research, and Methods in Organizations: Foundations, Extensions and New Directions*. San Francisco: Jossey-Bass.

Korsgaard, M. A., Brodt, S. E. and Whitener, E. M. 2002. 'Trust in the face of conflict: the role of managerial trustworthy behavior and organizational context'. *Journal of Applied Psychology*, 87(2), 312–19.

Kramer, R. M. 1996. 'Divergent realities and convergent disappointments in the hierarchic relation: trust and the intuitive auditor at work'. In R. M. Kramer and T. R. Tyler (eds.) *Trust in Organizations: Frontiers of Theory and Research*. Thousand Oaks, CA: Sage, 216–45.

Kroeber, A. and Kluckhohn, C. 1952. *Culture: A Critical Review of Concepts and Definitions*. Papers of the Peabody Museum of Archaeology and Ethnology, 47(1), Cambridge, MA: Harvard University.

Kuhlmann, T. M. 2005. 'Formation of trust in German–Mexican business relations'. In K. M. Bijlsma-Frankema and R. Klein Woolthuis (eds.) *Trust Under Pressure: Empirical Investigations of Trust and Trust Building in Uncertain Circumstances*. Cheltenham: Edward Elgar, 37–54.

Layard, R. 2005. *Happiness: Lessons from a New Science*. London: Penguin.

Leung, K., Bhagat, R. S., Buchan, N. R., Erez, M. and Gibson, C. B. 2005. 'Culture and international business: recent advances and their implications for future research'. *Journal of International Business Studies*, 36(4), 357–78.

Levin, D. Z. and Cross, R. 2004. 'The strength of weak ties you can trust: the mediating role of trust in effective knowledge transfer'. *Management Science*, 50(11), 1477–90.

Lewicki, R. and Bunker, B. B. 1996. 'Developing and maintaining trust in work relationships'. In R. M. Kramer and T. R. Tyler (eds.) *Trust in Organizations: Frontiers of Theory and Research*. Thousand Oaks, CA: Sage 114–39.

Lewicki, R., McAllister, D. J. and Bies, R. J. 1998. 'Trust and distrust: new relationships and realities'. *Academy of Management Review*, 23(3), 438–58.

Lewicki, R., Tomlinson, E. C. and Gillespie, N. 2006. 'Models of interpersonal trust development: theoretical approaches, empirical evidence, and future directions'. *Journal of Management*, 32(6), 991–1022.

Luo, Y. 2002. 'Building trust in cross-cultural collaborations: toward a contingency perspective'. *Journal of Management*, 28(5), 669–94.

Madhok, A. 1995. 'Revisiting multi-national firms' tolerance for joint ventures: a trust-based approach'. *Journal of International Business Studies*, 26(1), 117–37.

Maguire, S. and Phillips, N. 2008. '"Citibankers" at Citicorp: a study of the loss of institutional trust after a merger'. *Journal of Management Studies*, 45(2), 372–401.

Mayer, R. C. and Gavin, M. B. 2005. 'Trust in management and performance: who minds the shop while the employees watch the boss?' *Academy of Management Journal*, 48(5), 874–88.

Mayer, R. C., Davis, J. H. and Schoorman, F. D. 1995. 'An integrative model of organizational trust'. *Academy of Management Review*, 20, 709–34.

McEvily, B., Perrone, V. and Zaheer, A. 2003. 'Trust as an organizing principle'. *Organization Science*, 14(1), 91–103.

McKnight, D. H., Cummings, L. L. and Chervany, N. L. 1998. 'Initial trust formation in new organizational relationships'. *Academy of Management Review*, 23, 473–90.

Meyerson, D., Weick, K. E. and Kramer, R. M. 1996. 'Swift trust in temporary groups'. In R. M. Kramer and T. R. Tyler (eds.) *Trust in Organizations: Frontiers of Theory and Research*. Thousand Oaks, CA: Sage, 166–95.

Mesquita, L. F. 2007. 'Starting over when the bickering never ends: rebuilding aggregate trust among clustered firms through trust facilitators'. *Academy of Management Review*, 32(1), 72–91.

Molinsky, A. 2007. 'Cross-cultural code-switching: the psychological challenges of adapting behavior in foreign cultural interactions'. *Academy of Management Review*, 32(2), 622–40.

Möllering, G. 2006. *Trust: Reason, Routine and Reflexivity*. Oxford: Elsevier.

Noorderhaven, N. G. 1999. 'National culture and the development of trust: the need for more data and less theory'. *Academy of Management Review*, 24(1), 9–10.

Perrone, V., Zaheer, A. and McEvily, B. 2003. 'Free to be trusted? Organizational constraints on trust at the boundary'. *Organization Science*, 14(4), 422–39.

Peterson, B. 2004. *Cultural Intelligence: a Guide to Working with People from Other Cultures*. Yarmouth, ME: Intercultural Press.

Poppo, L. and Zenger, T. 2002. 'Do formal contracts and relational governance function as substitutes or complements?' *Strategic Management Journal*, 23(8), 707–25.

Pothukuchi, V., Damanpour, F., Choi, J., Chen, C. C. and Park, S. H. 2002. 'National and organizational culture differences and international joint venture performance'. *Journal of International Business Studies*, 33(2), 243–65.

Putnam, R. D. 2000. *Bowling Alone: the Collapse and Revival of American Community*. New York: Simon and Schuster.

Rao, A. and Hashimoto, K. 1996. 'Intercultural influence: a study of Japanese expatriate managers in Canada'. *Journal of International Business Studies*, 27(3), 443–66.

Ring, P. S. and van de Ven, A. H. 1994. 'Developmental processes of cooperative inter-organizational relationships'. *Academy of Management Review*, 19(1), 90–118.

Rokeach, J. 1973. *The Nature of Human Values*. New York: Free Press.

Rotter, J. B. 1967. 'A new scale for measurement of interpersonal trust'. *Journal of Personality*, 35(4), 651–65.

Rousseau, D. M., Sitkin, S. B., Burt, R. S. and Camerer, C. 1998. 'Not so different after all: a cross-discipline view of trust'. *Academy of Management Review*, 23(3), 393–404.

Rubery, J., Earnshaw, J., Marchington, M., Cooke, F. L. and Vincent, S. 2002. 'Changing organizational forms and the employment relationship'. *Journal of Management Studies*, 39(5), 645–72.

Salamon, S. D. and Robinson, S. L. 2008. 'Trust that binds: the impact of collective felt trust on organizational performance'. *Journal of Applied Psychology*, 93(3), 593–601.

Saunders, M. N. K. and Thornhill, A. 2004. 'Trust and mistrust in organisations: An exploration using an organisational justice framework.' *European Journal of Work and Organisational Psychology*, 13(4), 492–515.

Schein, E. H. 1997. *Organizational Culture and Leadership*, 2nd edn. San Francisco, CA: Jossey-Bass.

Schneider, S. C. and Barsoux, J.-L. 2003. *Managing Across Cultures*. London: FT/Prentice-Hall.

Schoorman, D., Mayer, R. C. and Davis, J. 2007. 'An integrative model of organizational trust: past, present, and future'. *Academy of Management Review*, 32, 344–54.

Shapiro, J. M., Ozanne, J. K. and Saatcioglu, B. 2008. 'An interpretive examination of the development of cultural sensitivity in international business'. *Journal of International Business Studies*, 39, 71–87.

Simons, T. 2002. 'The high cost of lost trust'. *Harvard Business Review*, 80(9), 18–19.

Sitkin, S. B. and Roth, N. L. 1993. 'Explaining the limited effectiveness of legalistic 'remedies' for trust/distrust'. *Organization Science*, 4, 367–92.

Smircich, L. 1983. 'Concepts of culture and organizational analysis'. *Administrative Science Quarterly*, 28(3), 339–58.

Sullivan, J., Peterson, R. B., Kameda, N. and Shimada, J. 1981. 'The relationship between conflict resolution approaches and trust – a cross-cultural study'. *Academy of Management Journal*, 24(4), 803–15.

Tajfel, H. 1981. *Human Groups and Social Categories: Studies in Social Psychology*. Cambridge University Press.

Thompson, A. G. 1996. 'Compliance with agreements in cross-cultural transactions: some analytical issues'. *Journal of International Business Studies*, 27(2), 375–90.

Timming, A. R. 2008. 'Trust in cross-national labour relations: a case study of an Anglo-Dutch European Works Council'. *European Sociological Review*, 25(4), 1–12.

Tinsley, C. 1998. 'Models of conflict resolution in Japanese, German and American cultures'. *Journal of Applied Psychology*, 83(2), 316–23.

Trompenaars, F. 2003. *Did the Pedestrian Die? Insights from the Greatest Culture Guru*. London: Capstone.

Tung, R. L. 2008. 'The cross-cultural research imperative: the need to balance cross-national and intra-national diversity'. *Journal of International Business Studies*, 39, 41–6.

Wright, R. 2000. *Nonzero: History, Evolution and Cooperation*. London: Abacus Books.

Zaheer, S. and Zaheer, A. 2006. 'Trust across borders'. *Journal of International Business Studies*, 37, 21–9.

Zaheer, A., McEvily, B. and Perrone, V. 1998. 'Does trust matter? Exploring the effects of inter-organizational and interpersonal trust on performance'. *Organization Science*, 9(2), 141–59.

Zak, P. J. and Knack, S. 2001. 'Trust and growth'. *The Economic Journal*, 111, 295–321.

Zand, D. E. 1972. 'Trust and managerial problem solving'. *Administrative Science Quarterly*, 17, 229–39.

Zucker, L. G. 1986. 'Production of trust: institutional sources of economic structure, 1840–1920'. In B. M. Staw and L. L. Cummings (eds.) *Research in Organizational behavior*. Greenwich, CT: JAI Press, 8, 53–111.

# 2 | Trust differences across national–societal cultures: much to do, or much ado about nothing?

DONALD L. FERRIN AND NICOLE GILLESPIE

## Summary

Does trust and its development, functions and meaning, differ between people from different national–societal cultures? There is considerable anecdotal evidence and some theoretical argumentation to suggest it does, but are these supported by empirical research? This chapter reviews the available empirical evidence on the effects of national–societal culture on interpersonal trust. It focuses largely on quantitative empirical evidence to consider the extent to which, and the ways in which, interpersonal trust differs across national–societal cultures. In every category of our review we found evidence of cross-cultural differences, particularly on generalized trust, and also evidence of trust universals across cultures. In evaluating these findings, we conclude that trust may operate as a variform universal and variform functional universal. We conclude with two proposed routes for future research, and implications for practice.

## Introduction

To an ever-increasing extent, 'work' involves close interaction and cooperation with people who come from a national–societal cultural background different from one's own. This emerging reality of work can be attributed to

Initial findings of this review were presented at the Economic and Social Research Series Seminar on Building, Maintaining and Repairing Trust Across Cultures, Durham University, UK, 26 June 2006 and the Fourth European Institute for Advanced Studies in Management (EIASM) Workshop on Trust Within and Between Organisations, Vrije Universiteit (Free University) Amsterdam, Netherlands, 25 October 2007. We would like to express our gratitude to the organizers – Katinka Bijlsma-Frankema, Graham Dietz, Mark Saunders, Sim Sitkin and Denise Skinner – for their support and encouragement of this research. We also thank Guido Möllering and Roxanne Zolin who, as editors of the First International Network on Trust quarterly newsletters, provided a rich bibliography of trust articles, many of which we may not have found otherwise. We also thank Mabel Reo Cimei and Radhika Kanuga for research assistance.

a number of factors. First, with the unrelenting advance of globalization, more and more organizations are taking a global approach to operations, including the operation of overseas international joint ventures and alliances, working with offshore suppliers and customers, and conducting global searches for talent. Second, the advance of communication technologies such as e-mail and videoconferencing has fostered a movement toward global virtual teams involving individuals from a variety of different cultural backgrounds. Third, whereas the world economy during most of the twentieth century was dominated by North America, Europe, Japan and Southeast Asia (with most of the developing world serving as a source of inexpensive materials and labour), the last decade has seen countries such as India, China, Brazil, and Russia become major global players in the world economy. Fourth, because talent is increasingly mobile, even companies whose operations are entirely domestic will often still have a culturally diverse workforce. Consequently, managers are increasingly called upon to gain and manage the trust of individuals whose cultural backgrounds are 'foreign' and unfamiliar.

Meanwhile, in the organizational sciences there is no longer any serious debate about whether trust matters. At the societal level, trust stimulates economic growth because individuals need to expend fewer resources to protect themselves from being exploited in economic transactions (Slemrod and Katuščásk, 2005; Zak and Fakhar, 2006); consequently, high-trust societies provide stronger incentives to innovate and to accumulate physical and human capital (Knack and Keefer, 1997). At the organizational and corporate level, empirical evidence indicates that the level of internal trust in large publicly-listed companies (as measured by the Fortune Great Place to Work Trust Index) results in increased market valuation and financial performance (Filbeck and Preece, 2003). Finally, at the individual and interpersonal level, a large body of research has documented the impact of trust on outcomes including job performance, satisfaction, commitment, turnover intentions, citizenship behaviours and commitment to leader decisions (see Colquitt *et al.*, 2007; Dirks and Ferrin, 2002 for meta-analytic reviews).

Thus, it is critical and timely to consider whether and how national–societal culture influences interpersonal trust. We are not the first scholars to consider this issue. Doney *et al.* (1998) proposed a conceptual framework in which Hofstede's (1980) four cultural dimensions (individualism versus collectivism, masculinity versus femininity, high versus low power distance and high versus low uncertainty avoidance) are theorized to influence the way trustors develop trust in a target (specifically, whether trust is based on calculative, prediction, intentionality, capability or transference processes).

They concluded that there is a greater chance of trust forming when a trustor and trustee share the same norms and values because, in such cases, trustee actions to earn trust are likely to be consistent with trustor assumptions about the types of actions that indicate whether trust is warranted. As an example, they theorized that in individualistic and masculine cultures, trust is more likely to form through calculative- (i.e. based on the costs versus rewards of a target acting in an untrustworthy manner) and capability-based (i. e. assessment of the target's ability) processes, whereas in collectivist and feminine cultures, trust is more dependent on prediction (based on confidence that the targets' behaviour can be predicted), intentionality (assessment of the target's motives) and transference (based on third-party or proof sources from which trust is transferred to a target). Similarly, Chen *et al.* (1998) posited that because cognition-based trust is based on knowledgeable role performance whereas affect-based trust is based on emotional bonds between partners (McAllister, 1995), cognition-based trust will be a stronger determinant of cooperation in individualist cultures than in collectivist cultures, whereas affect-based trust will be a stronger determinant of cooperation in collectivist than individualist cultures.

Johnson and Cullen (2002) provided a more general framework that describes how elements of national culture become manifested as trust-related behaviours and perceptions in cross-cultural relationships. Specifically, national culture influences the bases of trust that are relevant within a culture (e.g. calculus-based trust, experience, reputation, level of dispositional trust). These bases of trust are then manifested in individuals' trust-related behaviours (negotiation behaviours, leadership behaviours, etc.), which in turn function as a signal of trustworthiness in a cross-cultural relationship. Because the framework recognizes that the trustor and trustee may be from different cultures, it allows that the two parties may operate with different bases of trust, and therefore may interpret signals of trustworthiness differently. The model is not specific to any culture, but instead can potentially incorporate the norms and trust bases of any culture.

These frameworks provide a useful analysis of the effects of well-established dimensions of national–societal culture on interpersonal trust. Yet, we also have some reservations about accepting these conclusions wholesale. First, rather than being induced from the empirical reality of trust in a variety of cultural contexts, the propositions were deduced primarily from logic and argumentation. Therefore, there may be many important elements of trust across cultures that have been unwittingly omitted from the models. As Noorderhaven (1999: 9) noted, 'It is much more productive to explore and compare the meaning of trust and its consequences and antecedents as perceived in various cultures than to try to come up with a general model of how particular dimensions of cultures influence particular dimensions of trust.'

Second, the objectives of these conceptual frameworks were to identify and understand differences in trust across cultures. Such an approach ignores the possibilities that trust could be universal, and that trust as a universal could be desirable. For example, in their review, Aguinis and Henle (2003) noted that a number of organizational behaviour phenomena, such as work motivators (e.g. achievement, pay, growth, interesting work), the pressure to conform to group norms and the transformational/transactional leadership paradigm, can be considered universal across cultures. And, as noted by Tjosvold *et al.* (2001), in an increasingly global world, 'Theories … that cannot be applied in more than one culture are increasingly irrelevant'.

Considering that research on interpersonal trust has burgeoned over the last two decades, it is possible that answers to the questions of whether and how national–societal culture influences trust already exist in the trust literature. To date, there has been no attempt to systematically review and analyse this literature to draw out conclusions regarding the potential effects of culture on interpersonal trust. Accordingly, in this chapter we will comprehensively review and analyse the empirical quantitative and qualitative research dealing with the potential effects of national culture on interpersonal trust. Our intention is to keep speculation to a minimum and focus rather on analysing and interpreting the empirical results to date as a collective whole.

## Chapter overview

In the following sections, we first discuss the concepts of trust and culture. We then describe the method used for identifying and including studies in the review. The review is then presented in five sections, each considering the evidence for and against the following propositions:

(1) mean *levels of trust* vary across cultures;
(2) the *determinants of trust* differ across cultures;
(3) the *consequences of trust* differ across cultures;
(4) the *role of trust* (mediation, moderation) differs across cultures; and
(5) the *meaning of trust* differs across cultures.

We conclude the chapter with a summary of the empirical findings, the limitations of the review and a discussion of the implications of our findings for future research and practice.

## Defining trust

Rousseau *et al.* (1998: 395) provided an integrative definition of trust as 'a psychological state comprising the intention to accept vulnerability based on positive expectations of the intentions or behaviour of another'. In their integrative model of organizational trust, Mayer *et al.* (1995) posited that trust is based on *perceived ability* (the group of skills, competencies, and characteristics that enable a party to have influence within some specific domain), *perceived benevolence* (perception of a positive orientation of the trustee toward the trustor) and *perceived integrity* (perception that the trustee consistently adheres to a set of principles acceptable to the trustor such as honesty and fairness). Trust is also influenced by the trustor's *propensity to trust* (i.e. a predisposition towards trusting other people in general), as well as the outcomes of previously trusting the party. Propensity to trust – or generalized trust as we will refer to it in this chapter – is typically understood to be a personality trait (e.g. Mayer *et al.*, 1995; Rotter, 1971), however it is also understood to be influenced by the level of trust in society, which is shaped by societal culture (Fukuyama, 1995). Finally, Mayer *et al.* (1995) posited that trust predicts risk taking in the relationship. Thus, the trust domain reflects a family of constructs – namely (using the Mayer *et al.* terminology) trust, perceived ability, perceived benevolence, perceived integrity, propensity to trust and risk taking in the relationship – that are connected together in a causal model.

Unfortunately, there is a great deal of inconsistency and disagreement in the trust literature about which of these constructs should be called 'trust' and which should not (Ferrin *et al.*, 2008). We therefore anticipate that, in conducting our review, we will find articles on 'trust' that study a range of related constructs. Rather than recharacterizing each study according to some imposed definition of trust, we will accept each author's definition of trust at face value. This will result in heterogeneity in the trust studies reviewed, but that heterogeneity simply reflects the heterogeneity that exists in the trust literature itself.

## Defining national–societal culture

Consistent with most cross-cultural organizational behaviour research, we are interested in the cultural values and beliefs held by individuals that differ systematically across nations and societies. National culture can be defined as 'shared beliefs, attitudes, norms, roles, and values found among speakers of a particular language who live during the same historical period in a specified geographic region' (Triandis, 1995: 6). Organizational scholars typically focus on specific dimensions of culture, such as individualism–collectivism, power distance, uncertainty avoidance, masculinity–femininity and Confucian Dynamism (e.g. Hofstede, 1980; Hofstede and Bond, 1988) to understand how national–societal culture affects work-related beliefs, perceptions, behaviours, and other phenomena of interest.

Cross-cultural research on trust has typically taken one of two forms: Either it examines the effects of key cultural values such as individualism–collectivism and power distance (Hofstede, 1980), or it simply compares trust across two or more cultures or countries. Of Hofstede's cultural dimensions, trust has most frequently been related to individualism versus collectivism. 'Individualism stands for a society in which the ties between individuals are loose: Everyone is expected to look after him/herself and her/his immediate family only. Collectivism stands for a society in which people from birth onwards are integrated into strong, cohesive in-groups, which throughout people's lifetime continue to protect them in exchange for unquestioning loyalty' (Hofstede, 2001: 225).

In our review, we will include studies that provide insight into the effect of cultural differences that are directly measured (e.g. the correlation of power distance and trust) or inferred (e.g. correlations between trust and its consequences for participants from different countries). The inclusion of the latter category of studies requires a simplifying assumption that people from different nations have significantly different cultural values. As noted by Triandis (1994), country boundaries are only approximately equivalent to cultural boundaries. For example, the question of whether Canadians are culturally distinct from Americans will typically stimulate a vigorous debate. However, in the large majority of country comparisons there would be no serious debate. To be conservative, we will exclude from our review any studies that include individuals from nations where the cultural differences are sincerely debatable.

Finally, in our review we will separately consider two types of cultural studies: *intra-cultural* comparisons (i.e. studies that examine how individuals with different cultural values or national–societal backgrounds might vary in the nature, level, determinants, or effects of trust they experience or report) and *intercultural* studies (i.e. studies that examine the nature, level, determinants or effects of trust in samples of individuals engaged in intercultural interactions).

## Method

### Identification of studies

Our objective is to identify and evaluate a large, representative sample of published empirical studies that can provide insight into the questions of whether and how national–societal culture influences the meaning, level, determinants and/or functions of trust. We conducted extensive electronic searches for the keywords 'trust' and 'culture' on a range of databases including PsychINFO, EBSCO, ABI/Inform, and Business Source Premier. In addition, we examined for relevance all articles announced in the First International Network on Trust (FINT) Newsletters to date (17 editions published since 1999), chapters in books on trust, and articles in our own personal trust libraries.

To be included in the review, the study had to: 1) include data on a construct called 'trust' or 'trustworthiness' that met the definition as specified in this chapter, 2) examine generalized trust or interpersonal trust (i.e. trust in individuals, not a specific group, an organization, or management),[1] 3) include data on a construct that reflected national–societal cultural values, or used country as a proxy, and 4) have undergone a process of peer review.

Where country of origin was used as a proxy for cultural values, only research examining multiple national–societal cultures *within the same study* was included. The problem in comparing multicultural country findings *across* studies is that differences between nations could be due to any number of uncontrolled factors such as organizational culture, structure, age, industry, demographics, history, leadership, internal competitive environment, education levels, etc. That said, we did include one single-country study (Tan and Chee, 2005) because it explicitly considered whether Western conceptualizations of trust and its development transfer to the country (Singapore) under examination. Throughout the review, all findings reported as significant met or exceeded the commonly accepted probability level of $p < .05$, unless otherwise indicated.

## Results of empirical review

In total, fifty-six relevant studies were identified; these studies are marked with an asterisk in the reference list. The review is divided into studies examining: 1) the level of trust, 2) the determinants of trust, 3) the consequences of trust, 4) the role of trust, and 5) the meaning of trust. For each of these five sub-sections, we first review evidence suggesting that cultural differences in trust exist, followed by evidence suggesting that trust universals hold across cultures. Studies with results relevant to multiple sections are

---

[1] On this basis, studies such as Child and Möllering (2003) and Branzei *et al.* (2007) that assess trust in specific work groups (e.g. local staff) or an organization (e.g. joint-venture partner organization) are excluded from this review.

discussed in each of those sections, noting that the study has been previously reported.

## The level of trust

### Evidence for national-societal cultural differences in trust levels

This section reviews empirical studies assessing cross-national differences in the level of trust toward others. Most of these studies examine generalized trust (i.e. impersonal trust between strangers and acquaintances), as opposed to personalized trust in specific others.

The most comprehensive study of this kind is based on the World Values Survey, hereafter WVS (1990 and 1995–1997 waves) (Delhey and Newton, 2005). Participants from sixty countries responded to the question: 'Generally speaking, would you say that most people can be trusted, or that you can't be too careful in dealing with people?' Trust is measured as the percentage of respondents in each country who replied 'most people can be trusted', as opposed to 'can't be too careful' (binary choice). National average scores ranged from a high of 65 per cent (Norway) to 3 per cent (Brazil). High-trust countries (>50 per cent) were primarily Western European, plus Japan, China, India, South Korea, USA, Canada, and Australia, whereas low- or no-trust countries tended to be Eastern European, South American and African. Knack and Keefer (1997) also examined trust using the WVS in a sample of twenty-nine market economies (measured either in 1981 or 1990–91). They reported very similar findings to Delhey and Newton (2005), with trust levels ranging from 61 per cent in Norway to 7 per cent in Brazil.

The *Living Conditions, Lifestyle and Health* survey of post-Soviet countries (Sapsford and Abbott, 2006) examined generalized trust across representative samples from Armenia, Belarus, Georgia, Kazakhstan, Kyrgyzstan, Moldova, Russia, and Ukraine. They found large variance across countries in responses to the question 'A majority of the people can be trusted', ranging from Kyrgyzstan (70 per cent agree) to Russia (55 per cent) to Moldova (29 per cent). In explaining the results, they refer to local cultural norms, local political and social conditions, rate of political and economic change, and economic recovery.

In a comparative study of the political cultures of Denmark and Korea, Kim *et al.* (2002) conducted a survey using a stratified national sample of 1,236 Danish and 1,000 Koreans. This study differs from the ones reported above in that it examined generalized trust towards specific groups. They found little difference between Danish and Korean participants' trust toward close in-group members (family, friends and neighbours) or strangers (university alumni, fellow countrymen, and foreigners), however Koreans were less likely than Danes to trust their work colleagues and superiors. Similarly, Danish participants believed other people were generally trustworthy, while Koreans did not.

Holm and Danielson (2005) compared trust in Tanzania (N = 220) and Sweden (N = 130). A unique aspect of this study is that it examined trust across countries using both survey data and trust-game behaviour.[2] While they found almost identical results across the two countries for trust-game behaviour (A-players sent 51 and 53 per cent of initial endowments in Sweden and Tanzania, respectively, and B-players returned 35 and 37 per cent, respectively), they found significant differences in generalized trust levels, with 74 per cent of Swedes reporting that they trust others, compared to only 41 per cent of Tanzanians. The authors explain the difference between survey response and trust-game behaviour partly in terms of the different referents: the trust survey referred to trusting the 'average citizen', whereas trust behaviour was directed to 'a fellow undergraduate student'. Hence, the results suggest different levels of generalized trust across the countries, but similar levels of trust behaviour toward fellow students. (Interestingly, the trust measures predicted trust-game behaviour in the Swedish group but not the Tanzanian group.)

Although in the large cross-country studies based on the WVS, Japan and the USA are both classified as high-trust countries, there is repeated strong evidence suggesting that the level of generalized trust is higher in American society than in Japanese society. Using the same item for generalized trust as the WVS, Yamagishi and Yamagishi (1994) found that Americans are higher in generalized trust than Japanese. This result was robust across four samples (male/female student population; male/female general population). A critique of Yamagishi and Yamagishi's (1994) study is that it did not use a representative sample. However, a similar cross-national difference in generalized trust was found in a more systematic study which used representative national samples (Hayashi *et al.*, 1982, cited in Yamagishi *et al.*, 1998). In response to the question 'Do you think you can put your trust in most people, or do you

---

[2] In the trust game, participants are given money and must decide how much to keep and how much to entrust to another participant who may or may not return the money. For example, a Player may be given $6. Player A can choose to keep any portion of it, which then becomes his/her personal profit for that round. If Player A gives $3 to Player B, the amount is tripled and given to Player B, who then decides how much to keep and how much to send back to Player A. The amount Player A gives to Player B is considered an indicator of A's trust in B. The amount Player B gives back to Player A is considered either an indicator of B's trustworthiness or of reciprocity. The game creates tension between self interest and the mutual benefit of exchange.

think it's always best to be on your guard?', 47 per cent of the American sample (N = 1,571) responded 'People can be trusted', in contrast to 26 per cent of the Japanese sample (N = 2,032).

This difference in generalized trust between the USA versus Japan can be explained through Yamagishi's 'emancipation' theory of trust which proposes that strong family and group ties, typically observed in collectivist cultures such as Japan, prevent trust from developing beyond the group boundaries (Yamagishi and Yamagishi, 1994; for similar arguments see also Fukuyama, 1995). This results in less generalized trust between members than in societies where social and interpersonal ties are weaker (Yamagishi *et al.*, 1998). To put it differently, in comparison to Americans, Japanese feel a greater sense of security within established and stable relationships but are more distrustful of people outside of such relationships.

In a repeated trial variation of the trust game, Yamagishi (1988) found further evidence that trust differs in Japan compared to the USA. The results revealed that under conditions that did not provide the opportunity for mutual monitoring and sanctioning, the Japanese were less cooperative and trusting with strangers (44 per cent contributed) than Americans (56 per cent contributed). However, under conditions that did enable mutual monitoring and sanctioning, the Japanese were as cooperative and trusting (75 per cent contributed) as Americans (75 per cent contributed). Yamagishi interpreted the results as suggesting that the Japanese cooperate in achieving group goals, not because of internalized 'collectivist' values around cooperation and trust, but rather because of the strong institutionalized informal monitoring and sanctioning in Japanese society.

Other studies have compared trust between Americans and a range of other countries. Drawing largely on Yamagishi's work, Huff and Kelley (2003) examined the level of trust in individualistic (United States) versus collectivist cultures (China, Malaysia, Hong Kong, Japan, Korea, Malaysia and Taiwan). Using a survey design (N = 1,282 mid-level bank managers), they found that generalized trust was higher among individualist bank managers (US) compared to collectivist bank managers, and propensity to distrust was lower for individualist versus collectivist bank managers. In a longitudinal questionnaire study of two US-based housing cooperatives with culturally diverse memberships (N = 183 respondents matched across time), Van Dyne *et al.* (2000) found that generalized trust was higher for American versus non-American co-op members (r = –0.38), and the correlation of collectivism to generalized trust was not significant (r = 0.14). In contrast, in two samples of English (N = 74) and American (N = 86) employees within a single multinational company, Earley (1986) found that trust in supervisor was positively correlated with collectivism (r = .19 and r = .44) and negatively correlated with power distance (r = −.32 and r = −.42). In a sample of six companies, two from the USA and four from Hungary, Pearce *et al.* (2000) found that country was a weak but significant predictor of trust in co-workers (B = −.13).

Buchan *et al.* (2002) used a one-shot experimental trust game with student participants from four countries: China (N = 128), Japan (N = 140), Korea (N = 140), and the USA (N = 140). Their findings revealed that Americans and Chinese were more trusting than Japanese and Koreans. In a similar but separate study, Buchan *et al.* (2006) used the same trust game with students from the same four countries (China N = 50; Korea N = 50; Japan N = 44; USA N = 44) and found that Chinese participants were slightly more trusting than American participants (adopting a $p<0.10$ criterion). Contrary to their earlier study, there were no significant differences in trust between Japanese and US samples.

Using data from the WVS (1990 wave, Inglehart *et al.*, 1998), Buchan and Croson (2004) examined differences between China and the USA in their trust toward specific groups. They report that the level of trust toward one's own family is comparative and high for both China and the USA, however once the target moves from family to non-family groups, the levels of trust differ markedly between countries, with levels of trust in the USA toward strangers remaining relatively high – around 50 per cent, while those in China dropped to 10 per cent.

Johnson and Cullen (2002) examined country-level correlations of selected cultural dimensions with the trust measures from the WVS (1994 wave, Inglehart *et al.*, 1998). The number of countries in the sample ranged from nine to forty-one across the cultural dimensions. They report that generalized trust was significantly higher in countries with high uncertainty avoidance, high power distance, high context language and in collectivist countries. However, this generalization warrants caution and further investigation given that five of the six 'high-trust' countries identified by the WVS (i.e. Norway, Sweden, Denmark, the Netherlands, and Canada; 1990 and 1996 waves) have the opposite pattern of cultural dimensions (i.e. individualistic with low uncertainty avoidance, low power distance and low context language). The exception is China. Johnson and Cullen further report that when trusting involved a specific referent (e.g. family, or people from one's own country) as opposed to a general predisposition, cultural differences played a weaker role.

*Intercultural studies*

More recently, studies have examined trust differences in intercultural studies, as opposed to cross-national studies. Takahashi *et al.* (2008) studied trust in three collectivist, high power distance East Asian countries. Using a modified trust game, university students from Japan (N = 236), China (N = 240), and Taiwan (N = 212) interacted in real time over the Internet with participants from their own society (in-group) and another society (out-group). Participants earned real money by playing six rounds of one-shot trust games with three in-group members and three out-group members. Across three experiments involving two interacting societies each, Japanese were found to be less trusting and trustworthy exchange partners compared to cultural Chinese. The authors interpret the finding as suggesting that Japanese collectivism is based more on long-term assurance networks, whereas Chinese collectivism provides a more expansive, guanxi-based approach to building new social networks.

Kuwabara *et al.* (2007) used a web-based 'virtual lab' to study trust and trustworthiness between Japanese and Americans in real-time interaction. Participants played a variation of the trust game in two different experimental conditions: a 'flags-on' condition in which everyone's nationality was publicly identified during the session, and a 'flags-off' condition in which participants did not know who was Japanese or American. The Japanese players were more likely than Americans to trust and were more trustworthy (i.e. more likely to return money entrusted to them), but only to the extent that they were in durable relationships. Outside of these relationships, they were no more trusting or trustworthy than their American counterparts. This difference is interpreted by the authors to be due to the exchange relationships built by the Japanese players. Americans chose to 'play the field' and transact with multiple players (i.e. develop trust to explore opportunities), while Japanese were more likely to commit to exchanging with fewer people (build on existing relationships), which reduced untrustworthy behaviour within these relationships.

Sullivan *et al.* (1981) studied Japanese (N = 48) and American (N = 72) managers' responses to a scenario regarding resolution of a dispute in a Japanese–American joint venture. American managers reported greater future trust in the joint venture president than did Japanese managers, regardless of the manner of dispute resolution or the nationality of the joint venture president. In a qualitative and quantitative study (N = 92) of employees and managers in German–Czech companies, Bürger *et al.* (2006) found that German participants considered their Czech colleagues to be less trustworthy than their German colleagues, even though

Czech participants perceived their German colleagues to be as trustworthy as their Czech colleagues. This coincided with statements by Czech interviewees that the Germans did not trust them. In a study of eighty-four managers involved in US–Mexican strategic alliances, Rodríguez and Wilson (2002) found that Mexican managers perceived higher levels of trust in the alliance relationship than their US counterparts. And in a qualitative and quantitative study of thirty German and thirty Mexican boundary-spanners for German–Mexican cooperative small and medium enterprises (SMEs), Kühlmann (2005) reported that while managers of both nationalities tended to base their trust judgments on similar characteristics (e.g. competence, openness, discretion, and comprehensibility), Mexicans indicated considerably higher levels of trust in their German counterparts than vice versa.

In a study of cruise line managers (N = 367 representing 49 countries), Testa (2002) examined the impact of leader–subordinate cultural congruency (i.e. same or different national culture) on subordinate perceptions and trust in their leader. The results indicate that subordinates in congruent dyads reported higher levels of trust and satisfaction with their leader and evaluated their leaders significantly higher on consideration behaviours, than those in the incongruent group. The authors interpret the findings as suggesting that national culture systematically impacts how subordinates evaluate and feel about their leaders.

### Evidence for similar levels of trust across national-societal cultures

In our review, we found four studies comparing levels of trust that reported no differences between countries. Using an experimental trust game with students in China (N = 50) and the USA (N = 44), Buchan and Croson (2004) found no difference in the level of trust (amount given) or trustworthiness (amount returned) across the two countries. In Sullivan *et al.*'s (1981, previously reported) study of Japanese and American managers' responses to a scenario of a dispute in a Japanese–American joint venture, the main effect for nationality of the joint venture president on future trust toward the president was non-significant. In a US-based study of 175 manager-peer dyads, McAllister (1995) found that ethnic similarity (e.g. White–White; Hispanic–Hispanic) was not significantly associated with trust in one's peer. And in a study of seventy-five diverse teams (comprising 4–6 masters students located in different countries), Jarvenpaa and Leidner (1999) found no significant difference in trust levels between participants from individualistic versus collectivist countries. Jarvenpaa and Leidner considered this last study a 'weak test' of the influence of culture on trust levels: 'The insignificance of culture in predicting perceived levels of trust . . . may be related to the fact that the respondents were of similar ages, functional backgrounds, and educational levels. Additionally, electronically facilitated communication may make cultural differences less salient: the lack of nonverbal cues eliminates evidence of cultural differences, such as different ways of dressing, gesticulating, and greeting' (p. 811).

## Conclusion

Taken together, the results of these studies provide robust support for the view that there are national–societal differences in the average level of generalized trust. These differences have been found repeatedly across a variety of countries, using different methodologies (e.g. surveys, experimental trust games) and different measures of generalized trust. However, it is important to note the marked inconsistency among the findings, even for the same 'culture' (e.g. in some studies US participants have higher levels of trust than Japanese or Chinese participants, in others there is no significant difference). And in some studies, not all countries examined differ significantly in the level of trust.

## *The determinants of trust*

**Evidence for national-societal cultural differences in the determinants of trust**
In this section, we review evidence supporting the idea that the determinants of trust are affected by culture. We first review the evidence that the determinants of trust differ across cultures (cross-national studies). Then we examine the evidence that the formation of trust differs in intercultural relationships. It should be noted that we include studies reporting correlates of trust, for which the direction of causality is not directly tested.

### *Macro-level institutional, economic, biological, social, and/or environmental factors*
Drawing on experimental evidence suggesting that neuroactive hormones (particularly oxytocin) are associated with trusting behaviour (see Kosfeld *et al.*, 2005), Zak and Fakhar (2006) hypothesized that people living in environments associated with higher levels of oxytocin and/or oestrogen will have higher levels of generalized trust. Using thirty-one measures associated with neuroactive hormone levels for forty-one countries, they found that biological, social and environmental proxies explained 70 per cent of the variance in generalized trust (as measured by the WVS). Sample proxies included: 1) biological factors (frequency of having sex, fertility rate, proportion of females in population, rate of breastfeeding); 2) social factors (telephone usage, population density, home ownership, percentage rural

population, proportional representation of the six major religions); and 3) environmental factors (ambient temperature, distance from equator, presence of synthetic hormones from pesticides (such as DDT), pharmaceuticals (such as oestrogen), household products, and water pollution).

Knack and Keefer's study (1997, previously reported), using WVS data in a sample of twenty-nine market economies, found that trust was stronger in nations that have higher and more equal incomes, with institutions that restrain predatory actions of chief executives and arbitrary actions of government, and with better-educated and ethnically homogeneous populations. Also drawing largely on the WVS data, Zak and Knack (2001) examined the correlates of trust in forty-one countries and came to many of the same conclusions, reporting that trust is stronger in nations with higher and more equal incomes, higher levels of education, greater land equality, and stronger formal institutions (as indicated by property rights, low corruption, contract enforceability, and investor rights). A noteworthy difference was the finding that ethnic homogeneity had a significant, non-linear relationship with trust, with mid-range levels of homogeneity most significantly and negatively predicting trust. The authors explain that the salience of group differences is maximized when there is a limited number of sizable groups (such as in Fiji and Trinidad) rather than a proliferation of small groups (e.g. Tanzania), in which case no one group poses a threat to dominate all others. They also report that the percentages of the population that are Catholic and Muslim each significantly and negatively predicts trust.

Delhey and Newton (2005, previously reported) found similar results in their study of sixty countries using WVS data. Trust levels correlate with ethnic homogeneity, good government (e.g. democracy, law and order, low corruption, public expenditure on health and education), national wealth (gross domestic product per capita), income equality and Protestant traditions. The authors concluded that generalized social trust is tightly integrated into a syndrome of ethnic/cultural, social, economic, and political characteristics. While this conclusion seems justified based on the data, the fact that the six 'high-trust' countries comprise three Nordic countries (Norway, Sweden, Denmark) plus the Netherlands, Canada, and also China (whose religious traditions, national wealth and governance are quite distinct from the five others), highlights the need for a better understanding of factors leading to trust in non-Western regions of the world. Finally, in a crossed-lagged panel study based on the 1980 and 1990 WVS data sets, Paxton (2002) found that democracy positively predicted generalized trust, and industrialization negatively predicted generalized trust, across the forty-two countries in the sample.

## Cultural norms and values

In a Hong Kong sample of university employees, Lee *et al.* (2000) found that power distance moderated the effect of procedural justice on trust in supervisor ($\Delta R^2 = 0.01$). The result is explained by the tendency for low-power-distance people to defer less to authorities, which in turn inclines them to react negatively to injustice.

Several studies suggest that the tendency to trust in-group members is influenced by culture. Three of these were studies conducted by Buchan and her colleagues. In the first, Buchan *et al.* (2002, previously reported) used an experimental trust game with student participants from four countries (China, Japan, Korea, and the USA). They reported that participants with an individualistic cultural orientation (US) increased their levels of trust in unknown others (amount of money invested) when an arbitrary category boundary was introduced that provided exchange participants with a common social group identity (i.e. the participant became a member of the 'in-group'). In contrast, the category identity made no difference on participants with a collectivist orientation.

In Buchan *et al.*'s study (2006, previously reported) using different participants from the same four countries, group membership was manipulated by randomly assigning participants to one of several colour-coded groups of about twelve participants. The participants spent ten minutes in either personal or impersonal communication before engaging in the 'investment game' (similar to the trust game), with either an in-group or out-group member. They found that in the USA, individuals send and return more to their in-group than to their out-group, however in China the effect of social distance is reversed participants send and return more to their out-group than to their in-group. Using questionnaires to assess cultural orientation of participants (individualistic versus collectivist), they further showed that individually oriented participants exhibited an in-group bias in amounts sent and proportions returned while collectively oriented participants sent relatively equal amounts, regardless of social distance to the partner. The authors interpret the results as suggesting that the manner in which groups are formed may moderate the extent to which an in-group bias is demonstrated in various cultures. In line with previous work, the results demonstrate a strong in-group bias among even experimentally constructed temporary groups in the United States, but a limit to this influence when it comes to collectively oriented participants. They surmise that the influence of social distance in prompting in-group biases in collectivist cultures is only evident among naturally occurring groups in society.

A third study by Buchan and Croson (2004, previously reported) used the same experimental trust game with students in China and the USA. They examined how reported trust and trustworthiness change as the social distance to one's partner increases. The social distance of the seven targets ranged from a member of their family (parent, sibling, cousin), a member of their social network (student you know well, student from another university, stranger from your home town) or an absolute stranger from another country. With these naturally occurring groups, they found that trust declined as the social distance of the target increased, with no significant difference between the countries. They also found that expectations about the trustworthiness of others declined as social distance increased, however this was more pronounced for US than Chinese students. The authors explained that this finding differs from their earlier work because it examines naturally occurring groups rather than minimal groups.

Yuki *et al.* (2005) provided a related set of findings based on two experiments comparing the influence of in-group bias on trust in the USA (N = 215 and 146) and Japan (N = 199 and 122). Across both studies, they found Americans tended to trust strangers based on whether or not they were members of a categorical in-group, whereas having an acquaintance in the out-group had no effect on levels of trust. The Japanese also showed an in-group bias, however in contrast to the Americans, the presence of potential cross-group relationships had a strong effect on out-group trust for Japanese.

In their survey study (N = 1,282) based on the WVS, Huff and Kelley (2003, previously reported) found that Asian bank managers (China, Hong Kong, Japan, Korean, Taiwanese) had a stronger in-group bias (viewing family and people of the same ethnicity as more trustworthy than outsiders and people of different ethnicity) than did American bank managers. They concluded that the stronger in-group bias in collectivist cultures leads to the lower generalized trust in these societies. This finding conflicts with the finding of both Buchan and Croson (2004) and Yuki *et al.* (2005) that both Americans and Chinese/Japanese show a similar in-group bias in trust. The difference in results may reflect the different methods used to assess in-group bias. Huff and Kelley (2003) use a comparative question (e.g. 'I can trust people from my own ethnic group more than people from other ethnic groups'). In comparison, Buchan and Croson (2004) and Yuki *et al.* (2005) use separate trust ratings for the various in-group and out-group targets (e.g. how much would you send/return to your: parent, sibling, cousin, fellow student, stranger, etc?). Additionally, Buchan and Croson (2004) and Yuki *et al.* (2005) both recognized that other factors may be at play beyond simple category-based effects. Buchan and Croson (2004) noted the possibility that trust may be based on assurance, for example mutual monitoring or social sanctions that could be available even for socially distant trustees. Yuki *et al.* (2005) similarly recognized that trust in Japan is more relationship-based and dependent on the structure of interrelationships within groups, especially the likelihood of sharing direct or indirect possible links, whereas for Western cultures such as the USA, trust is based more heavily on depersonalized categorical distinctions between in-groups and out-groups.

### Indicators of trustworthiness

Cook *et al.* (2005) conducted laboratory experiments to examine the cross-cultural effects of risk taking on trust building. Based on a variation of the Prisoner's Dilemma game, they found that in the absence of opportunities to engage in risk to signal willingness to trust, Americans (N = 106) were less cooperative than their Japanese (N = 192) counterparts. However, given the opportunity to signal willingness to trust a partner, the Americans were not only more willing than the Japanese to take risks (offering 8.92 versus 7.35 'coins') in order to create trusting relations, they also became more cooperative and built stronger trust relations. The authors concluded that risk taking is a critical element of trust building for Americans, but less so for the Japanese. This result can be explained by the difference in uncertainty avoidance across the two countries, with America rating very low and Japan very high. The results also support the general claim that Americans are relatively more inclined toward risk taking and trust building.

In a critical incident-based, interview study of interpersonal trust (supervisor, peer, subordinate) in Turkey and China, Tan *et al.* (2007) reported that while Turks (N = 30) and Chinese (N = 30) saw ability, benevolence and integrity as antecedents of trust, some specific manifestations were different from those reported in Western samples. For example, integrity can be manifested as 'correcting mistakes' in Chinese culture, and benevolence can include material support (e.g. a business owner may provide financial support for an employee's marriage and son's birth expenses). Importantly, the authors concluded that four factors emerged as new, emic antecedents: identification (Turkey), delegation (China), and humility and closeness (China and Turkey).[3]

In an exploratory, interview-based study of seventeen Chinese Singaporeans, Tan and Chee (2005) reported, that interviewees cite affective

---

[3] Wasti and Tan elaborate further on this study in Chapter 12.

determinants of trust (personal relationship, openness, mutual help, frequency of contact, mutual understanding) much more frequently than cognitive determinants of trust (professionalism, competence, performance, dependability/reliability). They further observed that while ability, benevolence, and integrity indeed emerged as antecedents of trust, there are also antecedents unique to the Confucian setting such as filial piety, diligence, perseverance, thriftiness, respect for authority, shared value of collective effort, harmonious relationship in office, humility and magnanimous behaviour. They concluded that affective antecedents take priority over cognitive antecedents for the development of trust in Chinese working relationships.

In Holm and Danielson's (2005) comparative study of trust (previously reported), the authors found that Tanzanians (N = 220) and Swedes (N = 130) differed in the underlying mechanism driving trust game behaviour. Most importantly, there was a positive reciprocity mechanism for the Swedes (i.e. the more they received the more they sent back), but there was no evidence of reciprocity amongst the Tanzanian subjects. The authors concluded that care should be exercised when generalizing results from trust studies conducted in rich post-modern countries to developing countries.

Using a longitudinal ethnographic approach, Tillmar (2006) examined trust in Tanzania and Sweden. More specifically, she compared the preconditions for trust formation in small businesses across the two countries. Despite the very different levels of institutional trust in these countries (high distrust of police and judiciary in Tanzania versus very high trust in Sweden), the author identified several common factors that influenced trust development in both contexts. However, the specific manifestations of these factors differed markedly across cultures. In both countries, informal institutions, particularly 'tribalism' and gender-based stereotypes, influenced trust. In both cases, people from other parts of the country were less trusted in terms of their benevolence, and locals were less trusted in terms of their competence ('tribalism'). However, gender-based stereotypes manifested in very different ways. In Tanzania, female business owners were trusted for their commitment and benevolence more than men (women cannot leave town due to child-raising responsibilities), but less for their competence. Tanzanian cultural norms inhibiting men and women discussing business and socializing as colleagues adversely affected trust development. In Sweden, female business owners were less trusted than males to be committed to their business (seen as a 'hobby' for women). In both contexts, creating arenas where business owners could meet regularly and interact facilitated trust, although together with business training, this had a greater impact in Tanzania. Fear and jealousy inhibited trust in both contexts, however in Sweden this was influenced by 'Jante' Law (norm of equality), whereas in Tanzania beliefs about witchcraft played an important role. The author reported that the greater need for cooperation in Tanzania, coupled with the inadequate formal institutional environment, evoked initiatives and entrepreneurial approaches to trust creation not apparent in Sweden. These included drawing on the sanctioning mechanisms embedded in traditional institutions (tribal community) and using existing 'hostages' (e.g. limited mobility due to child-raising responsibilities and ownership of fixed assets).

### Intercultural studies

In their study of US–Mexican strategic alliances, Rodríguez and Wilson (2002, previously reported) found that for US managers, trust is built mainly on economic and strategic cooperation, whereas for Mexican managers, trust is driven predominantly by social and affective dimensions.

Two studies suggest that cultural distance is associated with lower trust. In a study of twelve cross-functional, geographically distributed student work teams (USA, Switzerland, the Netherlands, Germany, Slovenia, Japan), dyads whose members had a different country of origin (N = 108 dyads) reported lower perceived trustworthiness, perceived follow-through, and trust compared to dyads whose members originated from the same country (Zolin *et al.*, 2004). As this result was stronger after month three than month one, the authors interpreted the finding as indicative of cultural misunderstandings arising through the conduct of the project, rather than initial cultural prejudice. In a study of international strategic alliances in China (N = 255), Luo (2002) reported that interpersonal trust between local and expatriate managers was significantly negatively correlated (r = −0.14) with perceived cultural distance.

Similarly, Takahashi *et al.* (2008, previously reported) used a modified trust game with participants from Japan, China, and Taiwan. Across three experiments involving two interacting societies each, the Japanese showed less in-group favouritism in both trust and trustworthiness (or conditional fairness) at the national level compared to Chinese and Taiwanese. The authors interpreted this finding as evidence that culture-specific learning may influence ethnocentrism at the national level. More specifically, Japanese collective guilt over WWII, combined with widespread schooling that nationalism in the form of in-group favouritism or out-group derogation is unacceptable, overrides the generalized tendency towards in-group favouritism in minimal groups.

*Intercultural adaptation*

The above studies suggest that cultural differences influence the determinants of trust. That being the case, the effects of these cultural differences may be mitigated, and trust may therefore be enhanced, to the extent that one party successfully adapts to the other's foreign culture. In his study of relationships between boundary-role persons in Mexican–German cooperative SMEs, Kühlmann (2005, previously reported) found that Mexican managers attempted to gain the trust of their German counterparts by demonstrating honesty, competence and reliability, whereas German managers attempted to gain the trust of their Mexican counterparts by systematic nurturing of personal relationships including phone calls, letters, visits, dinner invitations, sightseeing trips, and presents. Evidently, both sets of managers attempted to demonstrate adaptation to the foreign culture – 'code-switching' in Molinsky's (2007) term (see also Chapter 1) – and also dispel stereotypes about their own culture, in building trust.

Are such efforts to adapt to the foreign culture effective? Pornpitakpan has conducted a series of scenario-based studies investigating the effect of cultural adaptation by American business people on their trustworthiness as perceived by Asians (including Thais, Japanese, Malaysians, and Chinese). In the first laboratory study (N = 145), Pornpitakpan (1998) found that Thais and Japanese trusted an American who adapted highly to their culture (language, manners, greetings, dress) more than one who did not adapt. These results were replicated in later studies with Americans adapting to Chinese in the People's Republic of China (N = 140, Pornpitakpan, 2002), Malaysians (N = 140, Pornpitakpan, 2004), and Indonesian Chinese (N = 140, Pornpitakpan, 2005). The author concluded that 'the results support the commonly advocated strategy of "When in Rome, do as the Romans do". Cultural adaptation, if done properly, reduces cultural distance and increases perceived trustworthiness' (Pornpitakpan, 2005: 83).

Sullivan *et al.* (1981, previously reported) studied Japanese and American managers' responses to a scenario regarding resolution of a dispute in a Japanese–American joint venture. They found that when an American was president, Japanese participants saw future trust developing better if contracts required binding arbitration rather than conferral. No such preference was found when the president was Japanese, or for American participants.

Research by Thomas and Ravlin (1995) echoes the above findings and also provides insight into the mechanisms through which cultural adaptation may impact trust. US-based employees (N = 223) of Japanese subsidiaries were assigned to view a videotaped scenario in which a Japanese manager was seen adapting versus not adapting to US cultural norms. Cultural adaptation (as compared to non-adaptation) by the Japanese manager caused participants to report higher levels of perceived similarity with the manager, which in turn had a positive impact on their intentions to trust the manager. However, cultural adaptation also caused participants to view the manager's behaviour as less internally motivated, which then resulted in lower intentions to trust. Thus, the results suggest that cultural adaptation will be effective if it emphasizes similarity to the target and also is perceived as being internally motivated. This study also highlights the potential for using similarity-attraction and attribution theory to understand cultural attribution.

Conversely, emphasizing cultural differences may exacerbate trust problems between groups. Newell *et al.* (2007) conducted an in-depth ethnographic study of IT work teams whose members were located in geographically distributed sites (USA, Ireland, and India). The results confirm the problematic nature of trust building among globally distributed teams, with an 'Us versus Them' attitude and distrust prevailing between the sites, which inhibited knowledge sharing. The traditional approaches used by the organization to address the challenges of global collaboration were found to be ineffective, and cultural sensitivity training actually inhibited trust building as it led onshore workers (US) to attribute the behaviour of offshore workers to negative cultural stereotypes rather than situational factors. The negative impact of nationality on trust was increased by the organization, putting the distributed sites into a competitive frame. This study highlights how cultural differences can negatively impact trust development, particularly when used to attribute blame to internal, 'unchangeable' causes.

## Evidence for culturally universal determinants of trust
### Cross-national studies
Buchan and Croson's study (2004, previously reported) using the trust game with students in China and the USA found that trust declined as social distance of the target increased, with no significant difference between the countries. Similarly, in two experiments (questionnaire study and online money allocation game) exploring impersonal trust towards strangers, Yuki *et al.* (2005, previously reported) found that Japanese and Americans both favoured in-group members (same university, same city of residence or same home nation) over out-group members ($\eta^2 = 0.06$ and $0.03$, respectively). The results support the view that categorical distinctions and cross-group relationships influence trust for both Americans and Japanese. In an experimental trust game study with seventy-nine Japanese and eighty-three Australian participants, Kiyonari *et al.* (2007) also found no cultural differences in in-group trust.

Buchan *et al.*'s (2006, previously reported) investment game study found that, across all four countries (China, Korea, Japan, the USA), personal non-game related communication powerfully increased trusting behaviour, and did so more than impersonal communication.

In laboratory studies examining trust repair, Ferrin *et al.* (2007) found that for Americans (Study 1) and Singaporeans (Study 2), reticence was consistently inferior to apology and denial as a response to integrity- and competence-based violations. Furthermore, the expected interaction of apology/denial × violation type (integrity/competence) was supported in both samples. In a study of strategic alliances in Korea (N = 143), Park *et al.* (2002) report that entry mode (wholly-owned subsidiaries versus international joint ventures) predicted managers' interpersonal trust in peers, but nationality (American versus Korean manager) did not.

While Tan and Chee (2005) reported unique determinants of trust in Confucian settings (see earlier discussion) in their exploratory interview study of seventeen Singaporeans, they also found that the factors of ability, benevolence, and integrity identified in Western trust research (Mayer *et al.*, 1995) generalize to the Singaporean context. Similarly, while Tan *et al.* (2007) found some emic trust antecedents, their interview study also revealed that Turks (N = 30) and Chinese (N = 30) saw ability, benevolence and integrity as antecedents of trust (albeit if some specific manifestations were different from those reported in Western samples).

## Intercultural studies

In contrast to many of the previous studies reporting an in-group bias for trust, in an experimental trust game involving half American (N = 44) and half Japanese (N = 38) participants, Mashima *et al.* (2004) found no effect of nationality information (knowing the nationality of other participants) or the nationality of the subject on trusting behaviour. Nor did they find any tendency to favour in-groups in the choice of trustees.

In forty-five six-person MBA teams spanning ten countries on four continents, team members trusted geographically separated fellow group members less when that group member was a member of a culturally homogeneous (versus heterogeneous) co-located subgroup (Polzer *et al.*, 2006). As this finding held irrespective of the participant's or fellow group member's country of origin, it suggests a universal principle. Furthermore, national similarity (coded 1/0) was an insignificant predictor of trust (MRQAP $\beta = 0.09$). In a European-run US white-collar work setting (N = 68, comprising ten Western Europeans and fifty-eight Americans), Ferrin *et al.* (2006) found that national background similarity did not predict interpersonal trust in co-worker (MRQAP beta = 0.00).

Finally, Kühlmann (2005, previously reported) reported that Mexican and German boundary-role spanners both cited information sharing, respectful interactions, and partner support as important determinants of trust in their cooperative SME relationships.

## Conclusion

Collectively, the studies reviewed in this section examine a broad range of trust determinants, including: biological, economic, institutional, social, and environmental factors; a range of culturally oriented values and preferences; aspects of trustworthiness; strategies for repairing trust; and in intercultural studies, in-group bias and indicators of cultural similarity and social distance. Taken together, these findings suggest that:

1) some determinants of trust are culturally specific including: a) country-level macro factors such as national wealth, income equality, education, democracy and 'good' government, strong formal institutions and ethnic homogeneity[4] (although as noted above, these factors may more accurately predict trust levels in Western than Eastern countries), and b) cultural differences around power distance, risk taking and reciprocity;
2) some determinants may be universal including personal and impersonal communication, and strategies for repairing interpersonal trust (e. g. apology and denial);
3) there are mixed results regarding the impact of cultural distance and national background similarity, however, there is evidence that managers do show adaptation behaviours, and adaptation to the local culture increases perceived trustworthiness;
4) it is unclear whether the influence of in-group bias and boundaries on trust is culturally specific or holds equally across national–societal cultures; and
5) the trustworthiness characteristics of ability, benevolence, and integrity appear to be universal determinants of trust, yet there are also additional, emic aspects of trustworthiness, at least in some countries.

All of these conclusions should be considered preliminary because there is very little replication of the findings, the selection of countries and cultures for

---

[4] We note that some of these macro-level factors are structural (institutional) and hence not strictly cultural in nature. However, as Bachmann (this volume) argues, culture and institutions are highly intertwined, with cultural traditions embedded in institutional arrangements.

study is relatively haphazard, and the studies employ different dependent variables (e.g. generalized versus interpersonal trust).

## The consequences of trust

### Evidence for national-societal cultural differences in the consequences of trust

In this section, we review studies that have explored the different consequences that trust may have across different cultures. In their study of forty-one countries based on the WVS data, Zak and Knack (2001, previously reported) found that generalized trust predicted national investment (as a percentage of GDP) and growth (annual growth per capita). Slemrod and Katuščásk (2005) also used WVS data (1990) across eighteen countries (from Europe, Asia, North and South America) and found that general trust positively predicted, and being trustworthy negatively predicted, household income. However, the financial payoff to being individually trustworthy increases with the average level of trust in a country: in high-trust cultures, being individually trustworthy had a positive payoff in terms of household income, whereas in low-trust cultures being individually trustworthy had a negative payoff. The authors explain this result: as dishonest behaviour is likely to be disclosed to future trading partners, being untrustworthy then has a higher cost in terms of foregone future transactions in high-trust than in low-trust countries.

In a survey study of democratic values using 821 university students from Australia, Japan, South Korea, and the USA, Matsuda *et al.* (2001) report that generalized trust predicts democratic values and commitment to human rights, respectively, for Japanese and South Korean students, but not for Australian or American students. They interpret the finding as suggesting that democratic choices are influenced by generalized trust for Koreans and Japanese, whereas honouring individualism and tolerance were more important for Australians and Americans.

In a study using the GLOBE data for fifty-nine societies ($N = 13,537$), Resick *et al.* (2006) found that country cluster (countries grouped according to similarity of cultural values and practices) predicted endorsement of 'character/integrity' (being trustworthy, sincere, just and honest) as a characteristic that contributes to outstanding leadership ($\eta^2 = 0.31$). The mean endorsement varied from 5.65 for societies included in the Middle Eastern cluster (Low) to 6.40 for societies included in the Nordic European cluster (High) on a scale of 1 to 7. All other clusters (Anglo, Confucian Asian, Eastern European, Germanic European, Latin American, Latin European, South East Asian, and Sub-Saharan African) were ranked in between (Medium). While the high mean scores indicate that character/integrity is universally viewed as facilitating a person being an effective leader, societies in the Nordic European cluster endorsed character/integrity to a significantly greater degree than societies in the Middle Eastern cluster.

### Evidence for culturally universal consequences of trust

Several studies have identified consequences of trust that appear to be universal. Returning to Resick *et al.*'s (2006) study, despite the fact that cultures differed in their degree of endorsement of 'character/integrity' as a characteristic that contributes to outstanding leadership (discussed previously), all country clusters endorsed it strongly. The authors conclude that character/integrity operates as a variform universal: a principle that is viewed similarly around the world, although cultural subtleties lead to differences in the enactment of that principle across cultures (Hanges *et al.*, 2000).

In two studies using buyer–seller tasks (N = 197; N = 157), Yamagishi *et al.* (1998) found generalized trust predicted commitment formation equally for Japanese and American subjects. Those low in generalized trust towards others in both societies were more likely to form commitment relationships with trustworthy persons despite the opportunity costs involved. In a study of international strategic alliances in China, Luo (2002, previously reported) found that cultural distance between the international partners did not moderate the positive relationship between trust and firm performance (return on investment, sales per asset). That is, trust was equally predictive of firm performance in culturally diverse and culturally homogeneous alliances.

Finally, Kühlmann (2005, previously reported) provided qualitative evidence that trust produces universal and also culturally specific outcomes in intercultural business relationships. Whereas both Mexican and German managers in German–Mexican cooperative SMEs noted that trust resulted in greater open discussion, problem solving and realization of the cooperative's goals, German managers tended to view trust as important for time saving, while Mexicans viewed trust as important for stabilizing cooperation for the longer term.

### Conclusion

Based on the limited studies conducted to date, there is preliminary support for both culturally specific consequences of trust (e.g. household income, democratic values, and commitment to human rights) and universal consequences (e.g. positive perceptions of one's supervisor, commitment formation) in comparative and also intercultural studies. Effective leadership is a consequence of trust that fits both categories. We are also surprised at how little research has been conducted in this area relative to research on cultural differences in determinants of trust.

## The role of trust

Relatively few studies have examined the role of trust across national cultures.

### Evidence for national-societal cultural differences in the role of trust

Casimir *et al.* (2006) found that trust mediated the relationship between transformational leadership and subordinate citizenship behaviours in Australian subjects, but not in Chinese subjects. They argued that in collectivist cultures heavily influenced by Confucian values supportive of power distance, individuals may be more accepting of autocratic leadership practices, but acceptance does not necessarily translate into trust in the leader. Further, they proposed that in low power distance cultures, transformational leadership behaviours directly engender feelings of trustworthiness.

### Evidence for cultural universals in the role of trust

In a laboratory comparison of the effects of transformational leadership on follower performance (idea generation) for individualists (Caucasian-American students, N = 194) versus collectivists (Asian-American students, N = 153), Jung and Avolio (1998) found several differences (e.g. Caucasian-Americans performed better under transactional leaders whereas Asian-Americans performed better under transformational leaders). However, the effects were mediated by trust in the leader for both groups. An interesting aspect of this study is the use of intra-national comparisons across two American subcultures. In a study of trust, feedback, and performance, Earley (1986) found that although English and Americans differed in their response to feedback (praise and criticism influenced American's performance, whereas only praise but not criticism influenced English performance), trust in supervisor mediated all feedback effects in both countries across two studies (a field experiment and a field survey).

### Conclusion

Based on these few studies, there is preliminary evidence that trust may universally mediate certain relationships across varying cultural contexts, whilst the mediating role of trust in other relationships may be culturally specific.

## The meaning of trust

In this section, we review evidence suggesting that the conceptual meaning of trust either varies across the different cultures of the world, or is universally understood. Three of the five studies provide evidence supporting both of these perspectives, and for this reason are reviewed first.

**Evidence for culturally universal and culturally specific meanings of trust**
Nishishiba and Ritchie (2000) used a card-sorting task (thirty trust-related words) to explore the structure of Japanese (N = 115) versus American (N = 121) business people's concept of trustworthiness. They found qualitative evidence of both similarities and differences in their understanding of trustworthiness. While four trust facets (characterized as responsible behaviour, professional competence, relational quality and communication) were nearly the same across cultures, the Japanese had a unique fifth facet termed organizational commitment (how the trustee relates to the organization) which involves a positive attitude, trying to do a better job, being committed and loyal. While the Japanese emphasized organizational commitment in judging the trustworthiness of others, the Americans placed a greater emphasis on personal integrity. In addition, two higher-order clusters emerged in both cultures: personal qualities and organizational qualities. However, there were also differences in two higher-order clusters, with the Japanese differentiating between accountability and effectiveness, versus the Americans differentiating between flexibility and integrity. The authors interpreted the differences as evidence of an interdependent (emphasizing individuals' relation to the group and organization) versus an independent (emphasizing individual behaviours and attributes that hold regardless of the group or organization to which one belongs) view of trustworthiness in an organizational setting, consistent with the cultural differences of collectivism versus individualism. Similarly, in their exploratory, interview-based study of seventeen Chinese Singaporeans, Tan and Chee (2005, previously reported) conclude that there are emic differences in the meaning of trust in Confucian settings.

In a critical incident, qualitative study of German–Czech work relations, Bürger *et al.* (2006, previously reported) examined German and Czech participants' implicit theories of trustworthiness. The results showed that abstract categories of perceived trustworthiness (namely, reliability, openness, commitment/helpfulness, and loyalty) are similar for Germans and Czechs, but the behavioural actions underlying these categories are somewhat different. For example, apologies and/or excuses for unreliability were generally accepted by Czech participants, and their impact on the perceived trustworthiness of the person were not as strong as for Germans and depended on the existing personal relationship of the actors. Similarly, while openness and honesty were very important for Germans, they were perceived as positive but not necessarily a prerequisite to trust for Czechs. The researchers also found that, for Czech participants, work and personal domains were equally important for trustworthiness, whereas for Germans the work-related domain was much more emphasized. The authors note that these findings are consistent with differences in German–Czech cultural standards.

Wasti *et al.* (2007) conducted an invariance test of the trust scales developed by Mayer and Davis (1999) across three samples of employees: US (N = 334 restaurant employees), Turkish (N = 434 automotive employees), and Singaporean (N = 207 employees from four organizations). Establishment of metric invariance indicates that individuals from different cultures respond to items in the same way. Perceived integrity was found to be invariant across all three samples (i.e. metrically the same). Perceived ability and perceived benevolence were found to be partially invariant and appeared to be interpreted differently by respondents from collectivist–high power distance versus individualist–low power distance cultures. In regards to ability, the authors suggested that items tapping into task performance are unlikely to make universal sense across cultural groups. In regards to benevolence, differences may reflect cultural variations in the relevance and acceptability of supervisor involvement in the personal domain (e.g. in paternalistic cultures, supervisors may act as mediators in subordinates' family disputes and provide financial assistance for the education of subordinates' children). The metric invariance of the trust scale (willingness to be vulnerable) could not be tested due to poor psychometric properties and inadequate fit across all samples.

### Evidence for cultural universals in the meaning of trust

Ding and Ng (2007) translated McAllister's cognitive and affective based trust scale into Chinese, and found support for its reliability and two-dimensional factor structure in a study of architects (N = 211) in Mainland China. The authors also found the scale predicted the intention to share knowledge in the project, providing some support for the validity of the scale in a Chinese context. However, one of the ten items (item 3 affective trust factor) did not translate well in the Chinese context and was excluded from the analysis. Finally, in her ethnographic comparative study of trust formation in Swedish and Tanzanian cooperatives, Tillmar (2006, previously reported) found three aspects of trust(worthiness) were relevant across settings: commitment, benevolence ('goodness') and competence ('capability').

## Conclusion

These few studies provide preliminary evidence suggesting that at least some dimensions of trust and trustworthiness hold across a range of cultures, perhaps universally. However, collectively the studies also clearly suggest that some aspects of trust and trustworthiness are unique to certain cultures.

## Discussion

We began this endeavour with the hope that, by reviewing the empirical literature on the impact of culture on interpersonal trust, we could answer the question, 'Are the raw levels of interpersonal trust, its determinants and consequences, its role as mediator and moderator, and its underlying meaning, primarily culture-specific or primarily universal across cultures?' In other words, is there 'much to do' in terms of the research needed to understand the effects of culture on trust, or is there 'much ado about nothing' among trust scholars who have been ardently trying to uncover culture-specific aspects of trust when in fact trust is primarily universal? We are pleased to report that there is a relatively large body of empirical work documenting the impact of culture on interpersonal trust. We are disappointed to report that the answer this body of work provides is equivocal: in almost every category we reviewed, there is evidence that interpersonal trust is culture specific, and also that it is culturally universal.

Consequently, in this discussion we have set three major objectives. First, we present preliminary conclusions that can be drawn despite the overall equivocal nature of our findings; we will also enumerate the limitations of our review and highlight some alternative perspectives for understanding culture-related trust problems. Second, and perhaps most importantly, we highlight alternative paths for future research; we hope that in doing so we encourage scholars interested in the impact of culture on trust to break from the status quo. Third, we present a set of relatively simple guidelines that indicate how the insights from our review can be put into practice despite their equivocal nature.

### Preliminary conclusions

As highlighted by the review, the findings are thinly spread across numerous studies, draw on many disparate theoretical perspectives, examine a very large list of potential correlates of trust, have been extracted from a haphazardly selected list of countries and cultures, and have limited replication. This makes it difficult to deduce definitive, bold conclusions. However, we can draw out a number of tentative preliminary conclusions:

- There is robust support for the view that there are meaningful differences across countries in the average level of generalized trust. This finding has been found repeatedly in multiple studies, across multiple countries and using a variety of methodologies.
- There is considerable support for the view that there are both culturally specific and universally applicable determinants and consequences of trust. Several country-level, macro factors (such as national wealth, income equality, education, 'good' government, strong formal institutions, and ethnic homogeneity) have been consistency associated with average levels of generalized trust across nations. In addition, there is mixed support for the role of cultural distance and societal background similarity as determinants of trust, and it is unclear from the studies conducted to date whether the influence of in-group bias on trust is culturally specific or holds equally across national–societal cultures.
- Based on the handful of studies examining the mediating role of trust across cultural contexts, there is preliminary evidence suggesting that trust universally mediates certain relationships (e.g. between leadership/ leader feedback and subordinate performance), while its mediating role in other relationships (e.g. between leadership and subordinate citizenship behaviour) appears to be culturally specific.
- There is evidence to suggest that the trustworthiness characteristics of ability, benevolence, and integrity are universally applicable, yet there are also culturally specific manifestations and interpretations of these characteristics in at least some countries. Furthermore, there are additional, emic aspects of trustworthiness (e.g. thriftiness, respect for authority, organizational commitment) that are important in certain countries.

With the exception of the findings related to trust levels, all other conclusions should be considered preliminary due to the limited replication and limited number of countries or cultural dimensions examined. Our findings should also be considered in light of their limitations, which are enumerated in the next section.

Overall, the results suggest trust operates as a variform universal (Dickson *et al.*, 2001; Lonner, 1980). As a variform universal, the general principle of trust holds across cultures, although some of its specific manifestations differ across cultures. Unlike a universal principle, a variform universal means the dimensions of trust and its enactment can differ across cultures (e.g. what one needs to do to be perceived as benevolent may vary across countries). The findings of the review also suggest that in relation to most variables, trust operates as a variform functional universal (see Bass, 1997): a relationship between trust and another variable is typically found, however, the magnitude (and in some cases the direction) of the relationship differs across countries and cultures. We also see a few examples in our review where trust appears to operate as a functional universal (Lonner, 1980), where the within-group relationship between trust and another variable is the same across cultures. For example, Buchan *et al.* (2006) reported that personal communication positively predicts trust, and does so more than impersonal communication, with no significant differences in the relationships across four countries.

## Limitations of our review

It is important to consider some limitations of our review. First, although we attempted a comprehensive search to identify studies for inclusion, it is possible that we did not locate all relevant studies. Additionally, we did not include unpublished studies (e.g. dissertations, unpublished working papers). It is possible that unpublished studies might reveal a different pattern of results as compared to published studies.

Second, the conclusions of our review are only as strong as the articles reviewed. Many of the studies we reviewed did not measure cultural variables directly, but instead used country as a proxy for cultural differences. Obviously, any single nation reflects a constellation of cultural values, and every individual within a nation is actually 'multicultural' because he or she is a member of numerous cultural groups (profession, gender, community, religion, school, socioeconomic status) (Aguinis and Henle, 2003) that combine into a mosaic of 'cultural tiles' that differentiates each individual from others (Chao and Moon, 2005; see Chapter 1). Thus, the use of country as a proxy for culture is a simplifying assumption with obvious limitations. Additionally, for pragmatic reasons, most of the studies included in our review examined only a handful of countries, used convenience samples that were not necessarily representative of the national–societal culture, and in most cases did not control for differences in job context, organizational culture, education levels, language, etc. across countries that might enable a stronger isolation of the effects of culture. Finally, few of the quantitative studies that reported trust similarities and differences across cultures tested for measurement equivalence across those cultures.

A number of the studies did in fact measure one or more cultural differences rather than using country as a proxy. However, as Gibson *et al.* (2008) note, 'while specific elements of culture can be separated, analysed, and compared with elements of other cultures in useful ways, the interaction of combined elements has effects different from those expected by a simple summation of the effects of the individual elements'. Similarly, Kirkman and Shapiro (1997: 747) noted that 'Since people's beliefs and attitudes are likely to be influenced by more than one cultural value, cultural values considered in concert (rather than singly) are more likely to form a more dynamic and complex explanation for employee behaviour.' Chao and Moon (2005) extend this line of thinking by noting that the particular elements of culture ('cultural tiles') that are predictive of an individual's behaviour are extremely dynamic, changing moment by moment as individuals shift from one social context to another. This suggests that, in addition to testing the effects that individual cultural dimensions have on trust, an accurate understanding requires examining how the various cultural dimensions interact together to influence trust at different times and in different situations.

Third, as noted previously, rather than imposing a single definition of trust, we took trust articles at 'face value' and accepted the authors' definitions of trust. Therefore, the papers included in our review reflect the same variety of trust definitions that exists in the present-day trust literature. This would be a major concern if the definitions of trust were empirically independent and operated in distinct nomological networks. Fortunately, a recent meta-analysis indicates that most of these alternative trust definitions are moderately to highly correlated with each other, operate within a common nomological network and in fact are functionally equivalent to a large degree (Colquitt *et al.*, 2007). Nevertheless, it will be important in future research to distinguish better between these alternative definitions of trust.

Fourth, it is likely that the literature overstates the true effects of culture on trust due to structural factors within academia that encourage the design, conduct, and publication of research on cross-cultural differences, and discourage the design, conduct and publication of research on cross-cultural universals. First, drawing on 'the folly of rewarding A while hoping for B' (Kerr, 1995), although as a research community we may want knowledge that is unbiased, we reward evidence of cultural differences in organizational phenomena, limitations to existing theories, and complex interactions and contingencies, and we punish evidence of generalizability (e.g. by summarily refusing to publish virtually any replication studies). This problem is exacerbated by the file-drawer effect (Rosenthal, 1979), which recognizes that studies with non-significant results are less likely to be published than studies with significant results. The file-drawer effect occurs because authors who report non-significant findings are less likely to submit those findings for publication in journals (Reysen, 2006), and even if they do submit them, journals are less likely to publish those findings, in comparison to significant effects. In combination, the folly of rewarding A implies that authors are more likely to undertake research on cultural differences than cultural similarities, and the file-drawer effect suggests that for those studies that are undertaken, the ones that empirically demonstrate cultural differences in trust are more likely to be published than the ones that fail to demonstrate cultural differences.

## Implications of the empirical findings

Everyday life is in fact replete with cross-cultural trust problems. Some sample trust-related problems are documented in cringe-inducing detail in the trust literature. Botti (1995) provided a detailed description of how Japanese and Italians held very different expectations and assumptions about promotion, recruitment, conflict, gift-giving, and job security, which in turn led to violated behavioural expectations and, in various ways, violations of trust. Wu and Laws (2003) provided a detailed analysis of how, within a single day, an e-mail interaction among Argentine and Russian software programmers spiral into extreme mistrust and relationship rupture due to different cultural interpretations of basic elements of communication such as cc's on an e-mail message.

Do the findings from our review bring clear answers to help prevent and manage such situations? To a certain extent, perhaps yes. For example, the review suggests that managers operating in foreign contexts who adapt to local norms will be perceived as more trustworthy by locals than managers who do not adapt. However, we should not necessarily assume that understanding and addressing these problems requires a theory of cultural differences in the nature, determinants, or functions of trust. Cultural miscommunications can be understood via communication theory (recognizing, for instance, that differences in languages, dialects, idioms, etc. across cultures may cause miscommunications that in turn could affect trust; (see Kassis Henderson, this volume), violations of cultural norms can be understood via norm theory (recognizing, for instance, that norms differ across cultures, yet a violation of any norm tends to be interpreted as a violation of trust expectations, which could negatively impact trust) and difficulties of building trust across cultures can be understood with self-categorization theory (recognizing, for instance, that people tend to overemphasize and negatively evaluate group differences in order to preserve their own group-based esteem, which could have a negative impact on trust across the cultural divide). In each of these three instances, existing theories (communication, norm and self categorization) provide apt insights into the nature of the problem, and existing trust theory can readily explain how and why these problems of miscommunications (e.g. Elsbach, 2004), norm violations (e.g. Lewicki and Bunker, 1996), and group differences (e.g. Brewer, 1981), are likely to influence trust. Perhaps additional theory on cultural differences in the nature and correlates of trust might add yet more understanding, but it is obvious that a great deal of understanding can be achieved with existing theories, and these should not be overlooked.

What our review does offer, in addition to its detailed documentation of the empirical evidence regarding the impact of culture on trust, is an opportunity for trust scholars to consider the state of the literature at this point: what we know and don't know, the research methods used to develop our empirical knowledge to date, the samples studied so far, the level of consistency and replication in our findings the availability of suitable theoretical frameworks for making sense of the findings, and the extent to which the findings can be or have been transmitted to practice. This knowledge is critical if we are to make an informed decision about the optimal route(s) for future research.

## Directions for future research

How should our limited research resources be best employed in the future to advance our understanding of the effects of culture on interpersonal trust? Based on our review and evaluation, we foresee two very distinct routes for future research.

### Route 1: Extending our understanding of the effects of culture on trust

This first route involves a starting assumption that culture does impact trust. Therefore, studies should be undertaken to develop a systematic understanding of when culture will affect trust and when it will not, and/or a culturally grounded understanding of the effects of culture on trust. For example, Gibson *et al.* (2008) identified a number of factors that are posited to moderate the effect of culture on individual outcomes at the individual level (e.g. personality characteristics including social adaptability, and conformity, and exposure to and identification with other cultures), group level (e.g. group homogeneity, cohesion, identification, and level of collectivism), and societal level (e.g. economic uncertainty, political volatility and strength of technical environment). They concluded that 'Culture always matters, but there are certain circumstances in which culture matters more, and others in which culture matters less' (p. 31). The opportunity in this approach is that it may result in a more nuanced and predictive understanding of the operation of trust in different cultures, and an explanation for why some determinants, consequences, and moderators function universally, whereas others appear to be culturally contingent. However, a risk in this line of research is that it may result in an even larger number of particularistic findings that lack an organizing framework through which they can be understood.

The literature would also benefit from more emic, qualitative and/or quantitative studies to induce an understanding of the nature and operation of trust in different cultures around the world. For example, in countries where Confucian, Hindu, or Islamic values are deeply rooted (these three religions/philosophies representing the majority of the earth's population), trust is likely to have unique and fascinating manifestations. The opportunity in this approach is that it is likely to result in a richer understanding of the nature and operation of trust across cultures, and it may also produce knowledge that is practically useful to individuals managing across cultures. Yet, this approach also represents a large investment of research resources – an investment that from a pragmatic standpoint may not be warranted given the rapid globalization of business practices and the apparent ability of many of today's managers to operate with reasonable effectiveness across cultural boundaries despite having a limited understanding of emic manifestations of trust.

### Route 2: Attempting to understand trust as a variform universal phenomenon

The second route is to undertake research whose starting assumption is that trust operates as a variform universal (Lonner, 1980) and variform functional universal (Bass, 1997). The aim then is to validate in what ways trust has universal properties, determinants, and functions across cultures, as well as identify the limits to a universal approach to trust.

Is there a potential to develop theories and measures of trust that are *robust* across cultures? There are at least two reasons for optimism. First, as noted above, Aguinis and Henle (2003) have concluded that many organizational phenomena are in fact universal. Their conclusion offers some hope that trust may also, at least to some degree, be a universal. Second, there is substantial evidence that trust has already been effectively studied as a universal. As noted above, our review uncovered many studies of trust across multiple cultures that essentially reported insignificant culture- or nationality-related differences in trust. In addition, we found, but have excluded from our review, literally dozens of single-country non-Western studies that successfully used Western-based trust measures and/or stimulus materials, and proposed hypotheses and reported findings that could easily be expected to apply in the Western context. We have also excluded a handful of studies that used Western-based approaches to study trust and its correlates in culturally heterogeneous contexts such as global virtual teams. Altogether, these three sets of studies suggest that trust can often be studied as a universal in non-US contexts and multicultural contexts.

Route 2 offers several potential advantages. First, it is economical: it starts, at least in part, with research and measures that have already been validated, and in most cases already validated in multiple cultures. Second, this approach reflects the trends of the world toward globalization not only of business transactions, but also business practices and values. Third, if trust can be understood at least in part as a universal, then it can be used to bridge other cultural problems such as cultural miscommunications and violations of cultural norms.

Our recommendation to study trust as a variform universal and variform functional universal echoes the call from Wasti *et al.* (2007) to form 'a multi-national team of trust and leadership scholars to develop scales in which items reflect not a single culture but are more applicable both in meaning and choice of expression to many cultures'. Finally, we join Wasti *et al.* in recommending that researchers carefully examine the reliability and convergent and discriminant validity of trust measures within each culture and evaluate measurement equivalence across cultures, so that we can more effectively assess the universality of trust and its operationalizations. Research from this approach also needs to actively test for and examine the limits of a universal approach so that we can better understand the ways trust may be culturally bound.

### Route 3: Continuation of the status quo

A third approach, which we discourage, is to continue the status quo. Our concern is that if research continues without redirection towards a systematic understanding of when culture matters, the emic nature of trust, and/or trust as a universal, any update of this literature performed say a decade from now will certainly include a much larger number of studies, but risks arriving at essentially the same conclusion – that although there are reliable differences across countries in their levels of generalized trust, some determinants, consequences, functions and meanings of trust appear to be culturally contingent, whilst others appear universal.

## Implications for practice

What is it that managers operating across national cultures would like? We believe they would appreciate a simple answer to the question 'What should I do?' What answer, then, can we give them? On the basis of our review, our answer for practising managers is as follows:

1.  Do *not* ignore trust. It is crucial for organizational success and individual wellbeing.

2. Ignore cultural differences at your peril. Understanding cultural norms, values, assumptions, and beliefs, and how they are manifested in workplace behaviours and attitudes, is critical for organizational success and individual wellbeing. Plus, culture is one of the most fascinating and enriching elements of managing in the multicultural context.
3. Recognize that there are cultural variations in the enactment of trust. Appreciate that what it takes to be perceived as trustworthy in one country may differ (however subtly) in another country. When in a foreign culture, adapting one's behaviour to be in line with important local cultural norms typically helps engender trust.
4. Please check back with us trust scholars regularly. With time, we may develop some more robust, consistent, and actionable insights into the effects of culture on trust.

## Concluding comments

In reviewing the empirical literature, we did our utmost to conduct an unbiased analysis, ardently seeking evidence that supports and does not support the proposition that culture influences trust. Having presented these findings, we then used our best judgment to develop conclusions about the actual and potential implications of this research for theory and practice. Given the fundamental importance of trust in organizational life, and the many ways – both obvious and subtle – in which cultural differences have become interwoven into everyday work life, we cannot imagine a more fascinating and important area of research. If this chapter helps to stimulate and direct such research, it will have been more than worth the effort.

## References

Note: References marked with an asterisk indicate studies included in the empirical review.

Aguinis, H. and Henle, C. A. 2003. 'The search for universals in cross-cultural organizational behavior'. In J. Greenberg (ed.) *Organizational Behavior: the State of the Science*, 2nd edn. Mahwah, NJ: Lawrence Erlbaum Associates, 373–411.

Bass, B. M. 1997. 'Does the transactional-transformational leadership paradigm transcend organizational and national boundaries?' *American Psychologist*, 52, 130–9.

Botti, H. F. 1995. 'Misunderstandings: a Japanese transplant in Italy strives for lean production'. *Organization*, 2, 55–86.

Branzei, O., Vertinsky, I. and Camp II, R. D. 2007. 'Culture-contingent signs of trust in emergent relationships'. *Organizational Behavior and Human Decision Processes*, 104, 61–82.

Brewer, M. B. 1981. 'Ethnocentrism and its role in interpersonal trust'. In M. B. Brewer and B. E. Collins (eds.) *Scientific Inquiry and the Social Sciences*. San Francisco: Jossey-Bass, 345–60.

*Buchan, N. R. and Croson, R. T. A. 2004. 'The boundaries of trust: own and others' actions in the US and China'. *Journal of Economic Behavior & Organization*, 55, 485–504.

*Buchan, N. R., Croson, R. T. A. and Dawes, R. M. 2002. 'Swift neighbors and persistent strangers: a cross-cultural investigation of trust and reciprocity in social exchange'. *American Journal of Sociology*, 108, 168–206.

*Buchan, N. R., Johnson, E. J. and Croson, R. T. A. 2006. 'Let's get personal: an international examination of the influence of communication, culture and social distance on other regarding preferences'. *Journal of Economic Behavior & Organization*, 60, 373–98.

*Bürger, J., Luke, M. and Indeláová, H. 2006. 'Interpersonal trust in German–Czech work relations: mutual expectations and suggestions for improvement'. *Journal of Organizational Transformation & Social Change*, 3, 173–99.

*Casimir, G., Waldman, D. A., Bartram, T. and Yang, S. 2006. 'Trust and the relationship between leadership and follower performance: opening the black box in Australia and China'. *Journal of Leadership & Organizational Studies*, 12, 68–84.

Chao, G. T. and Moon, H. 2005. 'The cultural mosaic: a metatheory for understanding the complexity of culture'. *Journal of Applied Psychology*, 90, 1128–40.

Chen, C. C., Chen, X.-P. and Meindl, J. R. 1998. 'How can cooperation be fostered? The cultural effects of individualism-collectivism'. *Academy of Management Review*, 23, 285–304.

Child, J. and Möllering, G. 2003. 'Contextual confidence and active trust development in the Chinese business environment'. *Organization Science*, 14, 69–80.

Colquitt, J. A., Scott, B. A. and LePine, J. A. 2007. 'Trust, trustworthiness, and trust propensity: a meta-analytic test of their unique relationships with risk taking and job performance'. *Journal of Applied Psychology*, 92, 909–27.

*Cook, K. S., Yamagishi, T., Cheshire, C., Cooper, R., Matsuda, M. and Mashima, R. 2005. 'Trust building via risk taking: a cross-societal experiment'. *Social Psychology Quarterly*, 68, 121–42.

*Delhey, J. and Newton, K. 2005. 'Predicting cross-national levels of social trust: global pattern or Nordic exceptionalism?' *European Sociological Review*, 21, 311–27.

Dickson, M. W., Hanges, P. J. and Lord, R. G. 2001. 'Trends, developments and gaps in cross-cultural research on leadership'. *Advances in Global Leadership*, 2, 75–100.

*Ding, Z. and Ng, F. 2007. 'Reliability and validity of the Chinese version of McAllister's trust scale'. *Construction Management & Economics*, 25, 1105–15.

Dirks, K. T. and Ferrin, D. L. 2002. 'Trust in leadership: meta-analytic findings and implications for research and practice'. *Journal of Applied Psychology*, 87, 611–28.

Doney, P. M., Cannon, J. P. and Mullen, M. R. 1998. 'Understanding the influence of national culture on the development of trust'. *Academy of Management Review*, 23, 601–20.

*Earley, P. C. 1986. 'Trust, perceived importance of praise and criticism, and work performance: an examination of feedback in the United States and England'. *Journal of Management*, 12, 457–73.

Elsbach, K. D. 2004. 'Managing images of trustworthiness in organizations'. In R. M. Kramer and K. S. Cook (eds.) *Trust and Distrust in Organizations: Dilemmas and Approaches*. New York: Sage, 275–92.

Ferrin, D. L., Bligh, M. C. and Kohles, J. C. 2008. 'It takes two to tango: an interdependence analysis of the spiraling of perceived trustworthiness and cooperation in interpersonal and intergroup relationships'. *Organizational Behavior and Human Decision Processes*, 107, 161–78.

*Ferrin, D. L., Dirks, K. T. and Shah, P. P. 2006. 'Direct and indirect effects of third-party relationships on interpersonal trust'. *Journal of Applied Psychology*, 91, 870–83.

*Ferrin, D. L., Kim, P. H., Cooper, C. D. and Dirks, K. T. 2007. 'Silence speaks volumes: the effectiveness of reticence in comparison to apology and denial for responding to integrity- and competence-based trust violations'. *Journal of Applied Psychology*, 92, 893–908.

Filbeck, G. and Preece, D. 2003. 'Fortune's best 100 companies to work for in America: do they work for shareholders?' *Journal of Business Finance & Accounting*, 30, 771–97.

Fukuyama, F. 1995. *Trust: the Social Virtues and the Creation of Prosperity*. New York: Free Press.

Gibson, C. B., Maznevski, M. L. and Kirkman, B. L. 2008. 'When does culture matter?' In R. S. Bhagat and R. M Steer (eds.) *Handbook of Culture, Organizations, and Work*. Cambridge University Press, 46–70.

Hanges, P. J., Lord, R. G. and Dickson, M. W. 2000. 'An information-processing perspective on leadership and culture: a case for connectionist architecture'. *Applied Psychology: An International Review*, 49, 133–61.

*Hayashi, C., Suzuki, T., Suzuki, G. and Murakami, M. 1982. *A Study of Japanese National Character* (in Japanese with an English summary) (Vol. IV). Tokyo: Idemitsushoten.

Hofstede, G. 1980. *Culture's Consequences: National Differences in Thinking and Organizing*. Beverley Hills, CA: Sage.

2001. *Culture's Consequences: Comparing Values, Behaviors, Institutions, and Organizations Across Nations*, 2nd edn. Thousand Oaks, CA: Sage.

Hofstede, G. and Bond, M. H. 1988. 'The Confucius connection: from cultural roots to economic growth'. *Organizational Dynamics*, 16, 5–21.

*Holm, H. and Danielson, A. 2005. 'Tropic trust versus Nordic trust: experimental evidence from Tanzania and Sweden'. *Economic Journal*, 115, 505–32.

*Huff, L. and Kelley, L. 2003. 'Levels of organizational trust in individualist versus collectivist societies: a seven-nation study'. *Organization Science*, 14, 81–90.

Inglehart, R., Basáñez, M. and Moreno, A. 1998. *Human Cultures and Beliefs: A Cross-Cultural Sourcebook: Political, Religious, Sexual, and Economic Norms in 43 societies: Findings from the 1990–1993*. World Values Survey. Ann Arbor: The University of Michigan Press.

*Jarvenpaa, S. L. and Leidner, D. E. 1999. 'Communication and trust in global virtual teams'. *Organization Science*, 10, 791–815.

*Johnson, J. L. and Cullen, J. B. 2002. 'Trust in cross-cultural relationships'. In M. J. Gannon and K. Newman (eds.) *The Blackwell Handbook of Cross-Cultural Management*. Oxford, UK: Blackwell, 335–60.

Jung, D. I. and Avolio, B. J. 1998. 'Examination of transformational leadership and group process among Caucasion- and Asian-Americans: are they different?' *Research in International Business and International Relations*, 7, 29–66.

Kerr, S. 1995. 'On the folly of rewarding A, while hoping for B'. *The Academy of Management Executive*, 9, 7–14.

*Kim, U., Helgesen, G. and Ahn, B. M. 2002. 'Democracy, trust, and political efficacy: comparative analysis of Danish and Korean political culture'. *Applied Psychology: An International Review*, 51, 318–53.

Kirkman, B. L. and Shapiro, D. L. 1997. 'The impact of cultural values on employee resistance to teams: toward a model of globalized self-managing work team effectiveness'. *Academy of Management Review*, 22, 730–57.

*Kiyonari, T., Foddy, M. and Yamagishi, T. 2007. 'Effects of direct and indirect exchange on trust of in-group members' [in Japanese]. *Japanese Journal of Psychology*, 77, 519–27.

*Knack, S. and Keefer, P. 1997. 'Does social capital have an economic payoff? A cross-country investigation'. *Quarterly Journal of Economics*, 112, 1251–88.

Kosfeld, M., Heinrichs, M., Zak, P. J., Fischbacher, U. and Fehr, E. 2005. 'Oxytocin increases trust in humans'. *Nature*, 435, 673–76.

*Kühlmann, T. M. 2005. 'Formation of trust in German–Mexican business relations'. In K. M. Bijlsma-Frankema and R. Klein Woolthuis (eds.) *Trust under Pressure: Empirical Investigations of Trust and Trust Building in Uncertain Circumstances*. Cheltenham, UK: Edward Elgar, 35–53.

*Kuwabara, K., Willer, R., Macy, M. W., Mashima, R., Terai, S. and Yamagishi, T. 2007. 'Culture, identity, and structure in social exchange: a web-based trust experiment in the United States and Japan'. *Social Psychology Quarterly*, 70, 461–79.

*Lee, C., Pillutla, M. and Law, K. S. 2000. 'Power-distance, gender and organizational justice'. *Journal of Management*, 26, 685–704.

Lewicki, R. J. and Bunker, B. B. 1996. 'Developing and maintaining trust in work relationships'. In R. M. Kramer and T. R. Tyler (eds.) *Trust in Organizations: Frontiers of Theory and Research*. Thousand Oaks, CA: Sage, 114–39.

Lonner, W. J. 1980. 'The search for psychological universals'. In H. C. Triandis and W. W. Lambert (eds.) *Handbook of Cross-Cultural Psychology*. Boston: Allyn & Bacon, 143–204.

*Luo, Y. 2002. 'Building trust in cross-cultural collaborations: toward a contingency perspective'. *Journal of Management*, 28, 669–94.

*Mashima, R., Yamagishi, T. and Macy, M. 2004. 'Trust and cooperation: a comparison of ingroup preference and trust behavior between American and Japanese students'. *Japanese Journal of Psychology*, 75, 308–15.

*Matsuda, Y., Harsel, S., Furusawa, S., Kim, H.-S. and Quarles, J. 2001. 'Democratic values and mutual perceptions of human rights in four Pacific Rim nations'. *International Journal of Intercultural Relations*, 25, 405–21.

Mayer, R. C. and Davis, J. H. 1999. 'The effect of the performance appraisal system on trust for management: a field quasi-experiment'. *Journal of Applied Psychology*, 84, 123–36.

Mayer, R. C., Davis, J. H. and Schoorman, F. D. 1995. 'An integrative model of organizational trust'. *Academy of Management Review*, 20, 709–34.

*McAllister, D. J. 1995. 'Affect- and cognition-based trust as foundations for interpersonal cooperation in organizations'. *Academy of Management Journal*, 38, 24–59.

Molinsky, A. 2007. 'Cross-cultural code-switching: the psychological challenges of adapting behavior in foreign cultural interactions'. *Academy of Management Review*, 622–40.

*Newell, S., David, G. and Chand, D. 2007. 'An analysis of trust among globally distributed work teams in an organizational setting'. *Knowledge and Process Management*, 14, 158–68.

*Nishishiba, M. and Ritchie, L. D. 2000. 'The concept of trustworthiness: a cross-cultural comparison between Japanese and U.S. business people'. *Journal of Applied Communication Research*, 28, 347–67.

Noorderhaven, N. G. 1999. 'National culture and the development of trust: the need for more data and less theory'. *Academy of Management Review*, 24, 9–10.

*Park, H., Gowan, M. and Hwang, S. D. 2002. 'Impact of national origin and entry mode on trust and organizational commitment'. *Multinational Business Review*, 10, 52–61.

*Paxton, P. 2002. 'Social capital and democracy: an interdependent relationship'. *American Sociological Review*, 67, 254–77.

*Pearce, J. L., Branyiczki, I. and Bigley, G. A. 2000. 'Insufficient bureaucracy: trust and commitment in particularistic organizations'. *Organization Science*, 11, 148–62.

*Polzer, J. T., Crisp, C. B., Jarvenpaa, S. L. and Kim, J. W. 2006. 'Extending the faultline model to geographically dispersed teams: how colocated subgroups can impair group functioning'. *Academy of Management Journal*, 49, 679–92.

*Pornpitakpan, C. 1998. 'The effect of cultural adaptation on perceived trustworthiness'. *Journal of Global Marketing*, 11, 41–64.

    2002. 'The effect of cultural adaptation on perceived trustworthiness: Americans adapting to People's Republic of China Chinese'. *Journal of International Consumer Marketing*, 15, 25–41.

    2004. 'The effect of Americans' adaptation to Malaysians on perceived trustworthiness'. *Journal of International Consumer Marketing*, 16, 7–23.

    2005. 'The effect of cultural adaptation on perceived trustworthiness: Americans adapting to Chinese Indonesians'. *Asia Pacific Journal of Marketing and Logistics*, 17, 70–88.

*Resick, C. J., Hanges, P. J., Dickson, M. W. and Mitchelson, J. K. 2006. 'A cross-cultural examination of the endorsement of ethical leadership'. *Journal of Business Ethics*, 63, 345–59.

Reysen, S. 2006. 'Publication of nonsignificant results: a survey of psychologists' opinions'. *Psychological Reports*, 98, 169–75.

*Rodríguez, C. M. and Wilson, D. T. 2002. 'Relationship bonding and trust as a foundation for commitment in U.S.–Mexican strategic alliances: a structural equation modeling approach'. *Journal of International Marketing*, 10, 53–76.

Rosenthal, R. 1979. 'The "file drawer problem" and tolerance for null results'. *Psychological Bulletin*, 86, 638–41.

Rotter, J. B. 1971. 'Generalized expectancies for interpersonal trust'. *American Psychologist*, 26, 443–52.

Rousseau, D. M., Sitkin, S. B., Burt, R. S. and Camerer, C. 1998. 'Not so different after all: a cross-discipline view of trust'. *Academy of Management Review*, 23, 393–404.

*Sapsford, R. and Abbott, P. 2006. 'Trust, confidence and social environment in post-communist societies'. *Communist and Post-Communist Studies*, 39, 59–71.

*Slemrod, J. and Katuščásk, P. 2005. 'Do trust and trustworthiness pay off?' *Journal of Human Resources*, 40, 621–46.

*Sullivan, J., Peterson, R. B., Kameda, N. and Shimada, J. 1981. 'The relationship between conflict resolution approaches and trust: a cross cultural study'. *Academy of Management Journal*, 24, 803–15.

*Takahashi, C., Yamagishi, T., Liu, J. H., Wang, F., Lin, Y. and Yu, S. 2008. 'The intercultural trust paradigm: studying joint cultural interaction and social exchange in real time over the Internet'. *International Journal of Intercultural Relations*, 32, 215–28.

*Tan, H. H. and Chee, D. 2005. 'Understanding interpersonal trust in a Confucian-influenced society: an exploratory study'. *International Journal of Cross Cultural Management*: 5, 197–212.

*Tan, H. H., Wasti, S. A. and Eser, S. 2007. 'Location, location, location: antecedents of trust across hierarchical and geographical positions'. Paper presented at the European Group for Organisation Studies.

*Testa, M. R. 2002. 'Leadership dyads in the cruise industry: the impact of cultural congruency'. *International Journal of Hospitality Management*, 21, 425–41.

*Thomas, D. C. and Ravlin, E. C. 1995. 'Responses of employees to cultural adaptation by a foreign manager'. *Journal of Applied Psychology*, 80, 133–46.

*Tillmar, M. 2006. 'Swedish tribalism and Tanzanian entrepreneurship: preconditions for trust formation'. *Entrepreneurship and Regional Development*, 18, 91–107.

Tjosvold, D., Hui, C. and Law, K. S. 2001. 'Cooperative conflict in China: cooperative conflict as a bridge between East and West'. *Journal of World Business*, 36, 166–83.

Triandis, H. C. 1994. *Culture and Social Behavior*. New York: McGraw-Hill.
    1995. *Individualism and Collectivism*. Boulder, CO: Westview Press.

*Van Dyne, L., Vandewalle, D., Kostova, T., Latham, M. E. and Cummings, L. L. 2000. 'Collectivism, propensity to trust and self-esteem as predictors of organizational citizenship in a non-work setting'. *Journal of Organizational Behavior*, 21, 3–23.

*Wasti, S. A., Tan, H. H., Brower, H. H. and Önder, Ç. 2007. 'Cross-cultural measurement of supervisor trustworthiness: an assessment of measurement invariance across three cultures'. *The Leadership Quarterly*, 18, 477–89.

Wu, J. and Laws, D. 2003. 'Trust and other-anxiety in negotiations: dynamics across boundaries of self and culture'. *Negotiation Journal*, 19, 329–67.

*Yamagishi, T. 1988. 'The provision of a sanctioning system in the United States and Japan'. *Social Psychology Quarterly*, 51, 265–71.

*Yamagishi, T. and Yamagishi, M. 1994. 'Trust and commitment in the United States and Japan. *Motivation & Emotion*, 18(2), 129–66.

*Yamagishi, T., Cook, K. S. and Watabe, M. 1998. 'Uncertainty, trust, and commitment formation in the United States and Japan'. *American Journal of Sociology*, 104, 165–94.

*Yuki, M., Maddux, W. W., Brewer, M. B. and Takemura, K. 2005. 'Cross-cultural differences in relationship- and group-based trust'. *Personality and Social Psychology Bulletin*, 31, 48–62.

*Zak, P. J. and Fakhar, A. 2006. 'Neuroactive hormones and interpersonal trust: international evidence'. *Economics & Human Biology*, 4, 412–29.

*Zak, P. J. and Knack, S. 2001. 'Trust and growth'. *The Economic Journal*, 111, 295–321.

*Zolin, R., Hinds, P. J., Fruchter, R. and Levitt, R. E. 2004. 'Interpersonal trust in cross-functional, geographically distributed work: a longitudinal study'. *Information and Organization*, 14, 1–26.

# 3 | Towards a context-sensitive approach to researching trust in inter-organizational relationships

REINHARD BACHMANN

## Summary

This chapter argues that trust is an inherently context-bound concept. With reference to the results of the Cambridge Vertical Contracts Project (CVCP) which examined supplier relations in the UK and Germany, it is shown that the nature and quality of inter-organizational trust varies greatly over different cultural and institutional environments. As a consequence, it is suggested that an appropriate research methodology needs to either draw on a mixed method approach involving different techniques to collect and analyse data (as has been done in the CVCP), or – perhaps even more suitably – utilize repertory grids to research a social phenomenon as complex as trust in a comparative perspective. The potential of the repertory-grid method is illustrated with reference to an empirical project on collaborative relationships in two virtual organizations in Switzerland.

## Introduction

Over the past two decades or so, trust has attracted much attention in the management literature. Many scholars have tried to come to grips with this phenomenon and discovered many aspects of it which seem worth thorough investigation. The relationships between trust and contracts, trust and innovation and trust and institutions are among the most developed sub-themes of trust research. Key publications have recently tried to summarize where we stand and to take stock of the major results in this research field (e.g. Bachmann and Zaheer, 2006; Bachmann and Zaheer, 2008; Kramer, 2006). As these publications show, significant progress has been made and some very important insights have been gained into how trust works in business relationships.

Researchers of inter-organizational trust have also developed a variety of often cited classifications of different trust types. Among these is Sako's (1992) well-known differentiation between 'contract trust' (i.e. trust that the other party is willing to adhere to the contractual arrangements), 'competence trust' (i.e. trust that the other party will be able to fulfil its promises) and 'goodwill trust' (i.e. the expectation that the other party is prepared to give and take). Other scholars have suggested stage models of trust development. Lewicki and Bunker's (1996) contribution (calculative trust as an initial step, followed by knowledge-based trust and eventually by identification-based trust) is just one such example which has been widely discussed in the research community and was applied in empirical contexts, for example, by Child (1998). While classifications and abstract models are without doubt generally useful they, however, have one obvious deficit which is often overlooked. They do not work equally well across different contexts and it emerges that 'for any theory of organizational trust, the devil is in the detail, and the details are in the context' (Kramer, 2006: 13). In relation to this observation we must admit that despite all the advances we are still in need of viable conceptualizations of the phenomenon of trust that are less universalistic and more context sensitive. Context may mean industry-specific conditions or refer to the specific circumstances in which a firm may be placed in terms of market position, but in a world of high levels of cross-border trade and international competition, it – not least – means the country-specific environment that determines the quality of business relationships and thereby the competiveness of whole business systems.

The insight that the nature and quality of trust differs across different national and regional contexts is not completely new. As Zaheer and Zaheer (2006) point out, trust scholars have engaged with this issue at least since the mid-1990s (e.g. Doney *et al.*, 1998; Madhok, 1995). But, as they also rightly state, 'a decade later, researchers have still barely begun to explore the related idea that trust may differ systematically across cultures' (Zaheer and Zaheer, 2006: 21). Universal concepts that explicitly or – more often – implicitly claim that they are always and everywhere valid and applicable are questionable and yet they are the norm in most of the current trust literature. Without doubt, universalistic concepts (for another prominent example, see Mayer *et al.*, 1995) can provide some initial orientation but all too soon they reach the limits of their explanatory capacity if actually applied to concrete real-world settings. The latter becomes particularly visible when comparative research on the nature and quality of business relations is conducted.

The argument developed in this chapter is based on the assumption that inter-organizational trust varies greatly over cultural and institutional environments, and that it is time to overcome the predominantly context-ignorant conceptualizations of this phenomenon. In so doing, we will – drawing on a comparative Anglo-German analysis – show in which dimensions and why trust differs across territorial contexts (section 2). Then (section 3), we will examine the methodological implications of a context-sensitive approach to researching trust in inter-organizational settings. In the final section (section 4), we will suggest some consequences and draw our final conclusions.

## How and why does trust differ across territorial contexts?

### Business environments: a comparative analysis of the UK and Germany

The literature on business systems (Hall and Soskice, 2001; Lane, 1995; Whitley, 1999, 2003) shows that – despite the globalization of many business activities – the diversity of cultural and institutional inventories of regions and countries remains considerable. According to this literature, business systems can be distinguished from each other on the basis of dimensions such as long-termism vs. short-termism, individualistic vs. collectivistic decision-making processes etc. With regard to trust, Fukuyama (1995) looked at various systems around the globe and made us aware of significant differences of levels of trust, for example between Asia and other regions of the world. Nonetheless, important questions remain unanswered and contradictory findings have not been sufficiently reconciled in this literature. While, for example, a study by Dyer and Chu (2003) largely confirmed Fukuyama's view and found that trust can in certain circumstances be much more developed in Japan than in the United States, Yamagishi *et al.* (1998) as well as Huff and Kelley (2003) came to the conclusion that a relatively high level of trust exists in business relationships in the United States, and a significantly lower level of trust characterizes Japanese business relationships. Clearly such conflicting findings call for more research and a more differentiated understanding of how and why trust differs across different countries.

Comparing the nature and quality of cooperative relationships across national boundaries, a significant stream of conceptual and empirical literature focuses on the UK and Germany, showing interesting differences in terms of cultural and institutional arrangements. Such Anglo-German comparisons have a long tradition, going back at least to Fox (1974), who primarily looked at industrial relations in both countries and concluded that there is a much higher level of trust in relationships between employers and employees in Germany than in the UK. This as well as other studies (e.g. Geppert, 2005; Geppert *et al.*, 2003; Lane, 1992; Stewart *et al.*, 1994) very deliberately focused not only on substantial differences at the cultural level, but also on the different institutional arrangements in the two countries. It is a body of research which draws on the assumption that culture and institutions are highly intertwined. Studies merely highlighting the differences in culture (e.g. Hofstede, 1991) are shown to be based on questionable premises and do not reach far enough to explain why actors in different countries behave in different ways when confronted with the same economic situation. If it was only cultural tradition that makes all the difference then we would surely have to assume that individual actors' behaviour is driven by a deterministic logic rather than free will and bounded rationality. What makes more sense is to start from the assumption that social actors are knowledgeable and make their decisions in the face of risks and opportunities which are often created on the basis of specific institutional arrangements in a specific business environment (Giddens, 1976). This is not to say that actors are only oriented to politically created explicit conditions of economic exchange and thus completely rational or even calculative in their behaviour. The latter would be as unrealistic as the assumption that social behaviour is completely determined by uncontrollable abstract forces. The premise that socially embedded individuals interact with one another in the face of different environmental conditions and on the basis of 'good reasons' (Bachmann, 2001) seems most appropriate and is the conceptual perspective that was, for example, applied in the Cambridge Vertical Contracts Project (CVCP). This project was carried out in the mid-1990s, and its key findings on the quality of supplier relationships in the UK and Germany seem particularly useful to explain significant country-specific differences with regard to the dominant types of trust, the dominant ways of developing trust, the generally prevalent levels of trust and the ways that trust can be interlinked with other social coordination mechanisms such as, for example, power.

## Social, judicial and technical norms

Consistent with previous conceptual research (e.g. Lane, 1992), the CVCP found ample empirical evidence that the German business system is characterized by a much higher degree of institutional regulation than the UK system (Lane and Bachmann, 1996). Social, judicial and technical norms are strong and business people comply with these in their routines and everyday behaviour. Take, for example, the legal system. German law is based on the tradition of Roman law which was revived in continental Europe under Napoleon Bonaparte's reign. This system of 'civil law' builds on a written legal code which consists of explicit and general rules. For each particular case an applicable rule is to be found and applied. Once this rule ('if... then...') is found the consequences are evident (Merryman, 2007). The code is meant to be comprehensive and leaves little room for exceptions and interpretations. Thus, a uniform body of commercial law provides a very stable basis for business behaviour and aggressive individual claims can easily be rejected by business partners who can always refer to these general rules representing the collective interest of the business community. In contrast, English 'common law' is generally not based on a written code and lawyers need to find single precedent cases to establish the consequences of breaching the law that are consistent with previous legal ruling (Glenn, 2005). Business people are thus less aware of the relevant legal norms and interpret situations in a much more particularistic manner. Clearly, this legal system reflects and reconfirms a high degree of individualism in society as a whole. As in the German case, *mutatis mutandis*, the influence of the legal system on business behaviour illustrates how strongly culture and institutional arrangements are intertwined and how difficult it would be if one wanted to conceptually separate both levels of behavioural control, only to reconstruct a unidirectional causal relationship between both levels of social coordination and structure.

### Industry association

Another example of an important element of the institutional frameworks of the two business systems is the role that industry associations play in representing industry-wide collective interests and setting the standards of acceptable business behaviour (Lane and Bachmann, 1997). Despite the fact that some erosion of the traditional associational system has become apparent in Germany in the last ten years or so, industry associations in this country are all in all still very powerful not-for-profit organizations, often with a membership which is congruent with the large majority of business organizations active in a particular industry. By contrast, industry associations in the UK tend to be smaller, take a high membership fee and sell various consultancy services to their members. A single industry thus often has a number of such associations and none can claim to represent the interests of the industry as a whole. As a consequence, UK firms sometimes need to fall back on their own capabilities when it comes to political lobbying activities, for example where industry-wide safety standards are at stake. This, of course, is not always a viable strategy and often leaves firms without any powerful representation, especially if they are small. In Germany, a large industry association can more easily speak for a whole industry and is thus much more influential than its UK counterparts in setting standards, both with regard to technical questions as well as legal and social norms of business behaviour. As in the case of law, the role of industry associations reflects old traditions. While the medieval guild system with compulsory membership shines through in the highly institutionalized associational system in Germany, individualism and competition rule supreme in the UK's associational system.

### Professional education and other institutional arrangements

The system of education and training is just another example that shows the differences between a business system which is based on strong generalized rules and standards and a system which leaves much to the discretion of individuals and single organizations that follow their own particularistic interests and philosophies. Despite the fact that Germany has sixteen regional governments ('Länder') which are in theory relatively independent in their educational policies, there is considerable uniformity both where school degrees and university education are concerned. A Master's degree from the University of Heidelberg, for example, has about the same value as a degree from Chemnitz or Siegen. In fact, there exist very few differences in the quality of education at German universities and most potential employers know this as well. A higher education degree certificate is thus very easy to evaluate, while personal references, which are so important in the UK labour market, are sometimes also used but not taken too seriously in Germany. The UK system, by contrast, perceives considerable variation in standards in the higher education sector, with some employers placing much greater value upon degrees from particular universities such as Oxford and Cambridge. Again, the same pattern emerges: while the UK system is based on particularistic arrangements and individual skills profiles, the German system works on the basis of generalized powerful institutions which have strong equalizing and stabilizing effects within the business system and society as a whole.

A closer look at more elements of the institutional framework of both business systems, for example, the system of financing practices or the nature and quality of relationships between industry associations and government agencies, trade unions and employer associations, etc. would only add to the overall picture and confirm the basic insight that, on the one hand, the German system reduces risk and supports long-term-oriented collective decision making. The UK system, on the other, is a lot more flexible and allows more risk and opportunity to be accepted and enjoyed by competing individuals or single firms. Such orientations have long traditions. They are engrained in deep-seated layers of cultural knowledge (Doney *et al.*, 1998) and very effectively reproduced through the institutional order that is dominant in the wider socioeconomic system (Lane and Bachmann, 1996).

To be aware of the specific cultural practices and institutional arrangements is a vital precondition of successfully establishing cooperative business relationships within one country. Such country-specific characteristics of business environments are even more important where relationships across national borders are to be built. Undoubtedly, they have a very strong influence on the type of trust that is produced in business relationships, how much of it is generated and what is the specific interrelationship between trust and other social coordination mechanisms. In the following we will examine these issues in more detail.

## Characteristics of business systems and trust building

### Interaction-based trust and institution-based trust

The form of trust that is prevalent in many UK business relationships comes close to our intuitive understanding of trust and is also present in many academic accounts, especially from the Anglo-Saxon context. This concept of trust assumes that two individuals meet frequently face-to-face, develop some familiarity and then find each other's behaviour relatively predictable (James, 2002; Lewicki *et al.*, 1998, etc.). It is a form of trust which is generated in interactions between individuals and has no intrinsic connection with general rules of behaviour embodied in far-reaching institutional arrangements. We may call this form of trust *interaction-based trust*.

As the German case shows, however, rules, standards and institutions can also be highly conducive to building trust in business relationships (Zucker, 1986). In Germany, for example, the legal system can provide very clear and widely accepted juridical standards of contracting. Furthermore, both parties are likely to be members in the same industry association which produces explicit and implicit guidelines of business behaviour, and the workforce of a supplier firm will have gone through a reliable and uniform national system of higher education and professional training. In these circumstances, we may assume that each party's behaviour is not much less predictable than if the two parties had known each other for a longer period of time at face-to-face level. In an environment characterized by a high level of institutional regulation, the buyer firm as well as the supplier firm have strong reasons to believe that the risk of betrayal is relatively low. Of course, in principle it may happen that the supplier does not deliver the promised quality of inputs or that the buyer firm does not pay for the delivered goods within the agreed period. But such behaviour is relatively unlikely because social actors normally tend to orient their behaviour to generally accepted rules which – if necessary – might be enforced by the business community. Thus, with reference to stable and reliable institutional structures of the business system, individual managers as well as the firms they represent can easily develop trust in business partners even if they do not know each other at a personal level. The simple fact that both parties to the relationship inhabit a shared world of clear rules and reliable standards makes their behaviours mutually relatively predictable. In accordance with Zucker (1986), we may call the resulting form of trust *institution-based trust*.

In Germany, institution-based trust is strongly developed and influential in many business relationships. By contrast, in the UK, which has a considerably weaker institutional framework, business people need to develop trust much more at the level of the interpersonal contacts and experiences they make with one another over a longer period of time. Of course, it would be wrong to assume that there is no interaction-based trust in Germany and no institution-based trust in the UK, but empirical research in the context of the CVCP showed that, in each country, the dominant form of trust and trust-building processes were strong and deeply rooted in their very specific environments. Reliable and effective institutions, as present in the German system, reduce the intrinsic risk of trust, so that individual as well as organizational actors can often avoid own individual efforts and costs that would occur if trust was constitutively or even solely produced at the level of face-to-face interaction. However, this does not mean that institution-based trust is a costless resource. It certainly implies collectively shared costs when institutions are built and maintained but, importantly, these costs are not due in situations where individual and organizational actors actually need to fall back on them.

It may well be that compared to interaction-based trust, institution-based trust usually is of a slightly lower quality, but this does not necessarily mean that it is insufficient. For example, in the initial stages of a relationship or when the asset specificity of the products or services exchanged is relatively low, this form of trust seems most adequate and efficient. Generally, we suggest that institutional trust has its highest value in business systems with a high degree of institutional regulation. In countries which, like Germany, have large and relatively mature industries swift trust is often of the essence (Bachmann and Inkpen, 2007). By contrast, we may assume that in a more or less de-industrialized country like the UK, high quality interaction-based trust is more important than high quantities of institution-based trust. Its risky science-based businesses and its sophisticated services sector, including the financial services, make the UK a country where the availability of strong forms of trust that are carefully crafted at the level of interaction are key to building successful business relationships. We may thus conclude that the strong institutional framework of the German business system and the existence of a high quantity of relatively weak institution-based trust fits this country with its strong industrial basis. Similarly, the relatively weak institutional arrangements that are characteristic of the UK business system are consistent with the fact that the services sector and the science-based industries, which often are in need of small portions of strong forms of trust, are more developed in the UK.

Clearly, there are many exceptions but, *cum grano salis*, this insight seems to hold: Much more strongly than the German system, the UK business system encourages interaction-based trust which means that the overall level of trust will be relatively low in terms of quantity and high in terms of quality. This is consistent with the fact that Germany is often described as a risk-averse culture, whereas the UK rates relatively high when risk taking behaviour is measured (e.g. Hofstede, 1991). In Germany, abundantly available trust, namely institution-based trust, is produced at low ad hoc costs for individual actors. The latter is often sufficient to enable quick and reliable decisions in business relationships although it might not always have the quality that would be needed for some very risky transactions. High quality trust, by contrast, may generally be a scarce resource but it seems sufficiently available in key situations in a risk-taking culture such as present in the UK.

## Trust and power

Following from this, we may conclude that in conceptual – but also in empirical and practical – terms the question of whether there are substitutes or amplifiers of trust to make up for the relatively low quantity of trust in the UK and the relatively low quality of trust in the German system seems particularly important. The answer to this question is not overly difficult to find. Since we see trust as a basic social coordination mechanism (Bachmann, 2001), we would indeed be inclined to assume that there should be one or more other coordination mechanisms to help facilitate cooperation in business relationships if trust is not produced in sufficient quantity or quality. Imagine, for example, a situation where an engineering firm operating in the weakly regulated UK business environment wants to buy in some mechanical parts on a buyer's market. This firm may find a suitable small supplier but as the quantity of the exchanged parts might be low and the parts technically trivial, it could appear that the development of interaction-based trust would be disproportionately costly while institution-based forms of trust development are not a realistic option in this environment. Nonetheless, we would argue that some form of coordinating mutual expectations still seems necessary to enter into a market transaction of this kind. Our prediction would be that in this situation the buyer firm will be inclined to use its power to effectively coordinate the exchange relationship. It might, for example, hint to the chance that there could be some future business between both firms if large discounts are granted this time, deliveries are exactly on time, etc. In other words, trust may be substituted, wholly or partially, by power where neither interaction-based trust nor institution-based trust is a possibility to coordinate expectations and interaction in an inter-organizational relationship.

Similarly, imagine a buyer–supplier relationship in the German business context. There might be a certain level of institutional trust, but further need for additional controls to supplement trust in its function as coordination mechanism might seem important, especially when high risks are involved in an envisaged transaction. Power, we would argue, might also be a solution to fill the gap here. Of course, this always builds on the assumption that resources of power are actually available and can be credibly referred to by one of the business partners in a relationship. Where this is the case, power can – like trust – play a significant role in the coordination of business relationships.

Generally, we may say that where the level of trust is relatively low or of insufficient quality, individual and organizational actors are more likely to consider power as a coordination mechanism and actually employ it (as a substitute for trust or as a safeguard in addition to trust). If that was not the case, many profitable transactions would simply not be possible as the coordination of expectations is simply a *conditio sine qua non* for the possibility of successful interaction, particularly in relationships that transcend organizational boundaries.

On closer inspection, the form of power that is dominant in the German business system is very characteristic of an institutionally highly regulated system based on a collectivistic cultural tradition. It thus seems quite different from the form of power that is dominant in UK business relationships. We may call it *institution-based power* (Bachmann, 2001) because it emanates from exactly those strong forms of institutional order that also foster the development of institution-based trust. Though institution-based power may not be neutral in a historical and political dimension (Berger and Luckmann, 1966), it is a depersonalized form of power which represents collective interests and is hardly utilizable for individual interests and situational purposes. Take, for example, the powerful legal rule that deliveries must be paid within thirty days unless there are very special circumstances. This is a form of power which is fundamentally different from the type of power that individuals and single organizations can mobilize when they have resources available that emanate from private ownership of capital or a market-leader position within their industry. The latter is less important as a coordination mechanism in the German business environment and may be called *individual power* or perhaps *interaction-based power*, if the categorical similarities to interaction-based trust are to be highlighted. Both forms of power contribute, to different degrees, to coordinating expectations and interaction in any business system, just as this is the case with trust. But an important question is whether trust and power can substitute or amplify each other, and in this respect institution-based forms of trust and power, as dominant in the German system, are different from the interaction-based forms of trust and power that are dominant in business relationships in institutionally weakly regulated systems, such as the UK.

In the Anglo-Saxon business environment, trust and power predominantly appear as interpersonal trust and individual power, and these forms of trust and power are relatively difficult to reconcile. At least, it is necessary that the two parties to a relationship are clear about which of these coordination mechanisms should ultimately govern the relationship. While institution-based forms of trust and power go hand in hand, and depersonalized forms of power can actually support the development of trust in business relationships, strong forms of individual power are not conducive to building trust. This is an insight which is consistent with the Anglo-Saxon tradition of socio-legal research that suggests that tight contracts do not foster trust (Macaulay, 1963). Power incorporated in idiosyncratic contracts drafted mainly by the more powerful party is more likely to encourage distrust than trust in an environment such as the UK (Sako, 1992). In contrast to this, the CVCP found very clear evidence that in Germany lengthy and detailed contracts drawing on the power of strong legal norms have no detrimental effect on the process of trust building in a relationship. On the contrary, they were found to be very effective safeguards that helped to establish trust between business partners (Arrighetti *et al.*, 1997). Thus we can say that power and trust amplify one another in a highly regulated system like Germany, whereas trust and power tend to be mechanisms that can substitute for each other with regard to their function of coordinating business relationships in weakly regulated socioeconomic environments such as the UK.

## Methodological implications

As we have seen, inter-organizational trust can differ greatly in terms of how it is produced, what specific form it takes, the overall level it reaches in a business system and its interrelationship with other mechanisms such as power. Against this background we may argue that if a phenomenon like trust appears differently in different cultural and institutional contexts, this has serious methodological implications, especially when researching across different (national) business environments. Nonetheless, as already pointed out above, the bulk of the current research on organizational trust generously ignores this insight and believes that a 'one-questionnaire-fits-all' approach is appropriate when doing comparative research, or finds single-country studies sufficient to draw sweeping conclusions on the nature of trust in business relationships generally. Whether this is an appropriate approach is more than questionable when looking at fundamental differences with regard to trust and trust building in countries as geographically and historically close as the UK and Germany. Admittedly, there is also a plausible argument that holds scholars of international business relationships back from all too context-sensitive research designs: if the responsiveness of the research instrument to local circumstances is increased this usually implies the need to change the research instrument across research contexts. In that case the comparability of results might no longer exist and comparisons are difficult to make. However, this can hardly be the final conclusion. It rather points to an intricate methodological dilemma: context-ignorant research has a validity problem, whereas context-sensitive research has to deal with a comparability problem. The question is whether there is a viable strategy to escape both of these problems by way of a methodological approach that is best suited for research on trust in cross-country inter-organizational relationships.

## The mixed-method approach

The CVCP, whose results were discussed above, attempted to avoid this dilemma largely by using an eclectic methodological approach to get a comprehensive picture of the research field and to balance out the disadvantages of different research instruments. For example, the questionnaire that was designed consisted of a mix of closed and open questions. The sample size (62 respondents) was relatively low for a quantitative analysis and very high for a case-based qualitative study. Thus, both quantitative and qualitative analysis techniques could be used: small sample statistics and cluster analysis, on the one hand, and content analysis of verbal responses and written documents, on the other. The research team was multilingual – with native speakers of each of the researched countries (UK, Italy, Germany) – and multidisciplinary, involving three different social sciences (Sociology, Economics and Law). In our view, this seemed the most promising approach for a cross-country comparative study on the forms and functions of cooperation and trust in buyer–supplier relations in two selected industries (mining machinery and kitchen furniture) (Arrighetti *et al.*, 1997; Lane and Bachmann, 1996).

In fact, the results of this project were useful and helped us understand the phenomenon of trust at a time when the academic community was only just becoming aware of the importance of this coordination mechanism in business relationships. The CVCP contributed to set the research agenda for the following years and articles that came out of this project were reprinted in a number of reference books (e.g. Bachmann and Zaheer, 2008; Kotabe and Mol, 2006). One may conclude from this that the philosophy that led the researchers of the CVCP to a mixed-method approach proved to be adequate and quite successful with regard to empirically studying trust in a comparative setting.

## Repertory grids

### The state of the art

In our view, another promising approach to researching the phenomenon of trust in inter-organizational relationships is the so-called repertory grid method. While not yet having received any attention in the comparative trust literature, it has been explored in the context of a study of two Swiss virtual organizations (Clases *et al.*, 2003) and found to be very useful in reconstructing the respondents' subjective theories of trust, i.e. the different denotations and connotations that social actors link to the concept of trust. It is a method that is rooted in Personal Construct Theory (Jankowicz, 2003; Kelly, 1955) and has a relatively long tradition in psychology, but which for many decades was not recognized as a powerful research instrument in organizational and management contexts. Unsurprisingly, it has also been ignored when trust became a key issue in this literature. In our view, however, there is evidence that repertory grid-based techniques allow for very insightful in-depth research on what individuals, groups, organizations or nations mean when they refer to the concept of trust. Repertory grids seem to be ideal to elicit often subtle and sometimes obvious differences in the meaning of trust across (country-specific) contexts. And what is more, this method appears to allow the research instrument to be kept constant while maintaining a high level of local responsiveness. In the following we want to explain what can be achieved with this method in the research on trust in inter-organizational relationships.

As an input from the interviewer, the repertory grid method requires simply a list of 'elements' that may be assumed to be relevant with regard to trust in the cognitive world of the respondents. Such elements may be persons, groups, organizations, abstract concepts, specific types of exchange relationships (for example, to preferred suppliers), etc. In the named study of the two virtual organizations in Switzerland, a list of twenty-two elements was created on the basis of a number of informal talks with experts, i.e. individuals who knew the two virtual organizations and their practical operations well. In this research project, examples of elements were: the firm itself, other firms that participated in its virtual organization, the broker who allocated in-coming orders among members of the virtual organization, the market, trust, conflict, etc. (Clases *et al.*, 2003: 13). These elements were identified as playing important roles in the world of the individual members of the virtual organizations and were used as an input in the subsequent repertory grid-based interview sessions in which the respondents were asked for attributes that they felt described each element best. The elements later became the nodes of graphical representations of the respondents' 'meaning space' (i.e. mental maps) that were reconstructed for each interviewed individual. All of these maps included all – in this study twenty-two – elements, which were kept constant over all interviews, but the location of these elements on the maps was to be determined solely on the basis of the answers that were collected in the individual interview sessions, i.e. the attributes that were used by the respondents to describe the elements in their own specific views.

More specifically, the two stages of the data collection process can be described as follows: in the first part of each repertory grid-based interview session the aim was to generate a list of attributes that the respondent thought were relevant in relation to at least one of the elements. This list of attributes was established in that pairs of elements were randomly selected by the interviewer and the respondent was asked to describe the two elements with adjectives or short phrases with regard to what, in the respondents' view, makes these elements similar or dissimilar vis-à-vis each other. If the selected pair was, for example, 'broker' and 'conflict', or 'own organization' and 'conflict', 'trust' and 'long-standing member of one's own virtual organization' etc., the attributes could have been – just to give an example – 'helpful' (for the broker) and 'not helpful' (for conflict) in the case that the two elements were perceived as dissimilar, or just 'helpful' (or just 'not helpful') if both elements were perceived as similar. In the first case two attributes were generated and added to the interviewer's list of attributes; in the second case only one attribute was generated and noted. This procedure was continued, always randomly picking two elements and asking the respondent for attributes that describe them best. Over time a longer list of attributes was generated and the procedure was ended when the answers seemed not to generate any more new attributes. This was often the case after a list of about thirty attributes was created by the interviewee.

In the second part of each repertory grid-based interview session, all established attributes were tested over all elements whereby the respondent could only say whether the particular attribute was valid or not valid for a specific element. In this way each element accumulated a number of 'valid' and 'not valid' attributes, and thus acquired a unique attributes-based profile. The 'broker' might have been 'helpful' while an attribute like, for example, 'useful to detect mistakes' might not have been actualized for this element by the respondent. However, the latter attribute might, for example, have been actualized for one or more of the other elements. As a result, attribute-based profiles, consisting of lists of attributes, were created and attached to all twenty-two elements.

As already mentioned, the results were visualized in the form of a mental map for each respondent where the similarity of profiles of the elements determined the distances between them, i.e. their location on the map. Two elements appearing in close proximity on this two- or three-dimensional map (depending on the software used to support the visualization) meant that they had similar attributes-based profiles, while a relatively large distance between two elements on the map indicated that the respondent had described the two elements by a relatively different set of attributes.

The relative distance of each element to the trust element on the map was, of course, of particular interest. For example, in this research context it was revealed that many individual respondents put 'conflict' not as distant from 'trust' as one might assume, and 'the typical network partner with whom they had only little experience with' surprisingly close to the 'trust' node. Many interesting conclusions about the respondents' subjective theory of trust, i.e. the meaning that they attached to the concept of trust, could be derived. Clases *et al.* (2003) report in detail the results of this exploratory study of two Swiss virtual organizations.

**The potential for comparative research**

What the project described above did not do – but what simply seems to be the next step in order to fully exploit this method's potential with regard comparative research – is to generate collective rather than individual maps. If a number of such individual mental maps are produced in different firms, different industries or different countries, it seems possible to aggregate data and visualize firm-specific, industry-specific or country-specific collective mental maps. These maps can represent 'collective minds' which are 'ideal types' in Max Weber's sense as no one single individual is likely to fully correspond with the established pattern. From our point of view, it would be particularly interesting to create country-specific collective maps, so that meanings of trust which vary between different cultural and institutional socioeconomic systems can be reconstructed.

In the context of this research it would also be possible to analyse the relative variance of patterns of nodes within firms, specific industries and within countries. For example, if it is difficult to establish typical country-specific patterns because the variance of data is too great, whereas typical industry-specific patterns are easy to reconstruct because individual maps sorted according to this criterion are much more similar, then the conclusion could be drawn that the country variable has relatively little explanatory power and the business environment is more determined by the industry context than by culture and institutions. However, against the background of previous research in the context of the CVCP we would assume that clear country-specific patterns do emerge and that differences in what is meant when business people talk about trust are significant between countries. If a repertory grid-based study over many different contexts came to the same result, this would clearly confirm our suggestion that there are hardly any universal insights to be revealed into the processes of trust creation and that only comparative research can shed light on the differences that need to be understood, especially where international cooperative relationships between organizations are to be established and maintained.

### Advantages over questionnaire-based research

In our view, a repertory grid-based approach has significant advantages over conventional questionnaire-based data collection and probably even over mixed-method approaches in the context of comparative research. While the elements that are relevant with regard to trust are gathered across different cultural contexts and kept constant across country-specific (and other) contexts in the repertory grid-based interviews, the characterization of these elements by attributes are solely in the hands of the respondents. Compared to a questionnaire-based interview, the input by the interviewer is minimal. The construction of a questionnaire to research trust in organizational relationships is typically based on a number of relatively unsubstantiated assumptions with regard to what the main indicators of trust might be. For example, frequency of contact is often seen as an important element in the operationalization of the concept of trust which is assumed to hold everywhere and at any time. In repertory grid-based interviews such strong assumptions are not necessary. If at all, it is the respondent who makes such connections. Thus the frequency of contact may be revealed as an indicator of the level of trust in some contexts, but might appear to be irrelevant in other cultural and institutional contexts. In other words, by way of the repertory grid-based method the indicators of trust are established by the respondents themselves in the interview session, which makes this instrument much more sensitive to different contexts and respondents' own interpretations of the concept of trust. Although very qualitative at the stage of data collection, in terms of data analysis it allows for a quantitative processing of data and representation of results.

The repertory grid method is also open to various combinations with other techniques of empirical research. The development of the list of elements should usually draw on informal interviews. But the results of repertory grid-based research can also be used when constructing a more responsive questionnaire in a more conventional manner. Furthermore, the results of a repertory grid-based investigation can be compared with the results of research drawing on other methodological techniques in the sense of a triangulation. Thus we believe that while repertory grids are certainly not the only method for conducting insightful research on trust, they are a very strong tool to bring about significant advances in this research field and lead to a more context-sensitive understanding of trust in business relationships. It can therefore deliver fundamental new insights into the nature of trust especially in the context of comparative research designs.

## Conclusions

### Implications

As shown above, we are only at the beginning of a full understanding of the phenomenon of trust in business relationships. Key to further advances in trust research is to build more context-sensitivity into our methodological approaches. This, in our view, is due to the very nature of trust as a social mechanism that is deeply engrained in cultural traditions and constitutively embedded in institutional arrangements. Research designs that cut off these contexts leave trust as a trivial concept. What trust really means, what it can achieve and how it can be utilized to the benefit of individuals and organizations can only be understood if this phenomenon is recognized in its intrinsic and irreducible social nature and researched accordingly. For that purpose adequate research methods are very important.

### Directions for future research

Although many conceptual advances have been made in organizational trust research in the past two decades or so, in the future we need to make progress at the methodological front in order to come to grips with the contextual subtleties of trust and trust-building processes. For this purpose it seems inevitable to use more innovative methods that are sensitive to the intrinsic contextual embeddedness of a social coordination mechanism as fundamental as trust. Further advances of our understanding of the role of trust, especially in relationships that transcend organizational, cultural and institutional boundaries, seem to crucially depend on the utilization of sophisticated qualitative and quantitative research methods. The mixed-method approach is certainly a step in the right direction. Repertory grid-based analyses may be even more effective in fully understanding the role of trust in different (country-specific) cultural and institutional contexts.

## Concluding remarks

The question of whether trust is just a relatively short-lived phenomenon in the contemporary business literature, among other things, depends on whether we manage to conduct academically sound and practically helpful research on key coordination mechanisms in business relationships. If it is seen as a soft and normative concept that can be used by managers and scholars to portray themselves as 'responsible', 'ethical', etc. towards their workforce, their suppliers, their students and colleagues, it is not worth making a big fuss about. There is ample evidence, however, that trust will remain of very high interest to practitioners and researchers because it is a key concept in understanding economic and social reality. As such it was almost forgotten in the social sciences. But this has changed fundamentally in the last two decades. Now is the time to refine our theoretical and empirical research on trust to unleash its full potential to explain the socioeconomic world in which we live and to facilitate productive forms of individual and organizational cooperation. Comparative research designs will be a major vehicle for achieving this goal.

## References

Arrighetti, A., Bachmann, R. and Deakin, S. 1997. 'Contract law, social norms and inter-firm cooperation'. *Cambridge Journal of Economics*, 21, 171–95.

Bachmann, R. 2001. 'Trust, power and control in trans-organizational relations'. *Organization Studies*, 22, 337–65.

Bachmann, R. and Inkpen, A. C. 2007. 'Trust and Institutions'. Research Paper 84, Sociological Series. Vienna: Institute of Advanced Studies.

Bachmann, R. and Zaheer, A. (eds.) 2006. *Handbook of Trust Research*. Cheltenham: Edward Elgar.

2008. *Landmark Papers on Trust.* 2 Volumes. Cheltenham: Edward Elgar.

Berger, J. and Luckmann, T. 1966. *The Social Construction of Reality.* Garden City, NY: Doubleday.

Child, J. 1998. 'Trust and international strategic alliances: the case of Sino-foreign joint ventures'. In C. Lane and R. Bachmann (eds.) *Trust Within and Between Organizations. Conceptual Issues and Empirical Applications.* Oxford University Press, 241–72.

Clases, C., Bachmann, R. and Wehner, T. 2003. 'Studying trust in virtual organizations'. *International Studies of Management and Organization,* 33, 7–27.

Doney, P. M., Cannon, J. P. and Mullen, M. R. 1998. 'Understanding the influence of national culture on the development of trust'. *Academy of Management Review,* 23, 601–20.

Dyer, J. H. and Chu, W. J. 2003. 'The role of trustworthiness in reducing transaction costs and improving performance: empirical evidence from the United States, Japan and Korea'. *Organization Science,* 14, 57–68.

Fox, A. 1974. *Beyond Contract: Work, Power and Trust Relations.* London: Faber.

Fukuyama, F. 1995. *Trust: the Social Virtues and the Creation of Prosperity.* New York: Free Press.

Geppert, M. 2005. 'Competence development and learning in British and German subsidiaries of MNCs – why and how national institutions still matter'. *Personnel Review,* 34, 155–77.

Geppert, M., Williams, K. and Matten, D. 2003. 'The social construction of contextual rationalities in MNCs: an Anglo-German comparison of subsidiary choice'. *Journal of Management Studies,* 40, 617–41.

Giddens, A. 1976. *New Rules of Sociological Method.* London: Hutchinson.

Glenn, P. 2005. *On Common Laws.* Oxford University Press.

Hall, P. A. and Soskice, D. (eds.) 2001. *Varieties of Capitalism: the Institutional Foundations of Comparative Advantage.* Oxford University Press.

Hofstede, G. 1991. *Cultures and Organizations: Software of the Mind.* London: McGraw-Hill.

Huff, L. and Kelley, L. 2003. 'Levels of organizational trust in individualist versus collectivist societies: a seven-nation study'. *Organization Science,* 14, 81–90.

James Jr., H. S. 2002. 'The trust paradox: a survey of economic inquiries into the nature of trust and trustworthiness'. *Journal of Economic Behavior and Organization,* 47, 291–307.

Jankowicz, D. 2003. *The easy guide to repertory grids.* Chichester: Wiley.

Kelly, G. A. 1955. *The Psychology of Personal Constructs: A Theory of Personality.* New York: Norton & Co.

Kotabe, M. and Mol, M. (eds.) 2006. *Global Supply Chain Management.* 2 Volumes. Cheltenham: Edward Elgar.

Kramer, R. M. (ed.) 2006. *Organizational Trust.* Oxford University Press.

Lane, C. 1992. 'European business systems: Britain and Germany compared'. In R. Whitley (ed.) *European Business Systems – Firms and Markets in their National Contexts*. London: Sage, 64–97.

1995. *Industry and Society in Europe: Stability and Change in Britain, Germany and France*. Cheltenham: Edward Elgar.

Lane, C. and Bachmann, R. 1996. 'The social constitution of trust: supplier relations in Britain and Germany'. *Organization Studies*, 17, 365–95.

1997. 'Cooperation in inter-firm relations in Britain and Germany: the role of social institutions'. *British Journal of Sociology*, 48, 226–54.

Lewicki, R. and Bunker, B.B. 1996. 'Developing and maintaining trust in work relationships'. In R.M. Kramer and T.R. Tyler, *Trust in Organizations: Frontiers of Theory and Research*. Thousand Oaks, CA: Sage 114–39.

Lewicki, R., McAllister, D.J. and Bies, J.J. 1998. 'Trust and distrust. New relationships and realities'. *Academy of Management Review*, 23, 438–58.

Macaulay, S. 1963. 'Non-contractual relations in business. a preliminary study'. *American Sociological Review*, 45, 55–69.

Madhok, A. 1995. 'Revisiting multinational firms' tolerance for joint ventures: a trust-based approach'. *Journal of International Business Studies*, 26, 117–37.

Mayer, R.C., Davis J.H. and Schoorman, F.D. 1995. 'An integrative model of organizational trust'. *Academy of Management Review*, 20, 709–34.

Merryman, J.H. 2007. *The Civil Law Tradition: an Introduction to the Legal Systems of Europe and Latin America*, 3rd revised edn. Stanford University Press.

Sako, M. 1992. *Prices, Quality and Trust: Inter-firm Relationships in Britain and Japan*. Cambridge University Press.

Stewart, R., Barsoux, J.-L., Kieser, A., Ganter, H.-D. and Walgenbach, P. 1994. *Managing in Britain and Germany*. London: Anglo-German Foundation.

Whitley, R. 1999. *Divergent Capitalisms: The Social Structuring and Change of Business Systems*. Oxford University Press.

2003. 'The institutional structuring of organizational capabilities: the role of authority sharing and organizational careers'. *Organization Studies*, 24, 667–95.

Yamagishi, T., Cook, K.S. and Watabe, M. 1998. 'Uncertainty, trust, and commitment formation in the United States and Japan'. *American Journal of Sociology*, 104, 165–94.

Zaheer, S. and Zaheer, A. 2006. 'Trust across borders'. *Journal of International Business Studies*, 37, 21–9.

Zucker, L. 1986. 'Production of trust: institutional sources of economic structure, 1840–1920'. *Research in Organizational Behavior*, 6, 53–111.

# 4 | Making sense of trust across cultural contexts

ALEX WRIGHT AND INA EHNERT

## Summary

In this chapter we argue that one way of better understanding how people make sense of trust across cultures is by framing it as a social construction. This recognizes the fluidity and unevenness of trust, thereby questioning any notion of trust being fixed or static. Although trust as a social construction has been recognized before, we argue that the fuller consequences of this have not been explored adequately. Within this chapter we aim to address this, conceptualizing trust as constituted within cultural contexts that are themselves ongoing social constructions. We also discuss how actors construct social phenomena and focus on the role of narrative in this process, leading us to conceptualize trust as a narrative process. Subsequently we discuss a possible research agenda to improve our knowledge of trusting across cultures, and propose research questions to help achieve this.

## Introduction

This chapter presents an argument that one way of understanding better how people make sense of trust is by framing it as a social construction. By doing this the fluidity and unevenness of trust is recognized, which questions any notion of trust being fixed or static. This leads us to advocate an understanding of trust in its verb form. Trust as a social construction has been recognized before (e.g. Child and Möllering, 2003; Lewis and Weigert, 1985), but we believe the fuller consequences of this have not been adequately explored. We do this and conceptualize trust as constituted within cultural contexts that are themselves ongoing social constructions. We also discuss

The two authors would like to express their appreciation to the editors who commented on an earlier draft of this chapter. Although they hold differing perspectives to those expressed here, their feedback and suggestions were always constructive and helpful, and we greatly appreciate this.

how actors construct social phenomena and focus on the role of narrative in this process, leading us to conceptualize trust as a narrative process. We then discuss a possible research agenda to improve our knowledge of trust across cultures and propose four research questions to help achieve this.

## A look at trust

Traditionally, quantitative approaches have dominated trust research (Möllering *et al.*, 2004). These have tended to take the form of laboratory experiments, standardized surveys and the use of Likert-scaled measurement instruments aimed at hypothesis testing and modelling. Kramer (1999) notes that the rational-choice perspective is the most influential image of trust in organizational science, but acknowledges that criticisms of this dominance are becoming increasingly difficult to ignore. For example, rational-choice perspectives negate emotion and social influences, and therefore their usefulness and relevance for practitioners is questionable. Trust research is also surprisingly acontextual (Kramer, 1996), which Zaheer and Zaheer (2006) see as limiting its utility for understanding trust across cultures. The predominance of acontextual studies into cross-cultural trust lead Möllering *et al.* (2004: 560) to call for a 'reality check' on research. We agree with the view that context-free trust research oversimplifies and sanitizes trust to the point where its potency for practitioners is doubted. Therefore, our aim in this chapter is to provide a conceptual discussion of trust that will help stimulate research that speaks of the actual lived experiences of actors. We achieve this by discussing trust as a social construction that sees agents influenced by differing temporal orientations and from within contexts that are being continually reconstrued.

## What is trust?

The first issue we would like to address is the notion that trust is best understood as a psychological state or event (Kramer, 1999; Lewis and Weigert, 1985; Möllering, 2006), which is encapsulated in Rousseau *et al.*'s (1998: 395) frequently cited definition of trust as 'a psychological state comprising the intention to accept vulnerability based upon positive expectations of the intentions or behaviour of another'. Such a framing is necessary if we hold the epistemological stance that trust can and should be measured. States can be measured as they are relatively fixed and stable (Dietz and den Hartog, 2006). These approaches have resulted in measures and ratings of trustworthiness (Ferres *et al.*, 2004), and pursuit of the antecedents of trust (e.g. Mayer *et al.*, 1995). Yet, to conceive of trust in purely static terms is clearly problematic. Trust alters, it is a dynamic phenomenon, but how this is resolved presently in the literature is to describe it in an oversimplistic way; trustors are said to move sequentially through different levels of trust (Lewicki and Bunker, 1996). This movement, it is suggested, is achieved once the requirements of the previous level have been satisfied.

Similarly, if trust is not always the same differences have to be explained. To overcome the difficulty of pinning trust down multiple types of trust have been identified. We are informed that there are such categories as competence-based trust, motive-based trust, role-based trust and calculative-based trust (Atkinson, 2004; Kramer, 1999; Williamson, 1993); indeed, Möllering (2001: 404) notes eight different types of trust present in the literature influenced by diverse disciplinary origins.

That trust is contextual and relational is generally agreed upon (e.g. Atkinson, 2004; Kramer, 1999; Mayer *et al.*, 1995), but the way this is then dealt with in research reports is largely to ignore it, to assume it away. Similarly, there is an increasing recognition that trust is fundamentally a social construction (e.g. Child and Möllering, 2003), but the implications of this on trust research have yet to be fully explored. The conceptualization of trust as a socially constituted phenomenon is still to have a significant effect on mainstream trust research.

From a constructionist's perspective, trust is *always* shaped by contexts, histories and other actants (both human and non-human), and it is these other elements that need to be studied if we are to produce meaningful research narratives. Burt and Knez (1996) provide one of the few accounts that acknowledges the possibility that third parties influence how trust is created. However, the main point they seem to make is to say third parties can affect trust intensity but not direction (Burt and Knez, 1996: 74): third-party gossip serves only to reinforce existing relations not to change them. This is a meagre rendering of the influence of third parties. To reduce their potential impact to this simple unidirectional relationship fails to appreciate the complexity of social interaction. Third parties *always* influence how trust is construed and this relationship may be direct or indirect, conscious or unconscious, intended or unintended. What trust researchers need to be interested in is how the trusting parties feel they have been influenced by these multiple third parties; whose voices did they listen to and why, and whose voices did they ignore and why.

A conceptualization of trust as a social construction dismisses any notion that trust is best understood as a state or event. Trust is better seen as part of the ongoing flow of living that should not be artificially halted in order that it can be measured. Actors are never in any particular state of trust, but are in a ceaseless and uneven flow of trusting. As contexts unfold the need for trusting activity fluctuates. Sometimes human trusting is acute and critical, at other times it is quiet and calm. What is important, from a constructionist perspective, is how trust is constituted and how this contributes to the overall meaning-making of actors. Trust is not something that can be turned on and off; like 'sensemaking' (Weick, 1995) it is something we have been doing all our lives and will continue to do as long as we live. Social constructs, like trust, cannot be accurately measured as they are never stable enough to be pinned down in any quantitative way; attempts to do so oversimplify the phenomena, leading to the 'reality check' on trust research Möllering *et al.* (2004) have called for. In practice, actors do not move through different levels of trust in a linear and sequential way; they skip back and forth continually and, mostly, unknowingly, between times when trusting is vitally important to ongoing organizing and times when it is less crucial.

The next section focuses on this and discusses the ontological outlook of social constructionism, which is advanced as one means of crafting knowledge on how cross-cultural trust is enacted.

## Culture and trust

Chao and Moon's (2005) conceptualization of culture as a pattern of cultural identities mirrors earlier work by Kroeber and Kluckhohn (1952) that sees culture as consisting of patterns, explicit and implicit, of and for behaviour. Culture, in this sense, is understood as both a guide to behaviour, and a product of that behaviour (Dietz *et al.*, this volume). The metaphor of a mosaic is used by Chao and Moon (2005) to represent what they claim are the underlying structures of behaviour patterns. Actors from different cultural groups can provide alternative explanations for behaviour, which are influenced by their cultural identity (Triandis, 1989). Culture theorists reason that these cross-cultural differences may lead not only to alternative explanations, but to attributions for behaviour that can lead to misinterpretations, misunderstandings, cause offence or conflict, or are simply wrong. Additionally, difficulties and complications can emerge in cross-cultural situations, through actors being unfamiliar with their interaction partner's cultural norms or value systems (Schwegler, 2006). For these reasons, culture and trust researchers often portray cultural differences as obstacles or barriers to trust building (e.g. Bird and Osland, 2006; Osland and Bird, 2000).

Osland and Bird (2000) question the practical usefulness of explaining national cultures in terms of their propensity towards 'individualistic' versus 'collectivistic', or 'high-context' versus 'low-context' communication tendencies. The application of these cultural dimensions in practice is likely to lead to what the authors term *sophisticated stereotyping*, as the complexities and subtleties of different national contexts and emerging cultural paradoxes are neglected or ignored. They assert that, for those exposed to another culture for anything but the briefest period of time, it seems very difficult to make useful generalizations 'since so many exceptions and qualifications to the stereotypes, on both a cultural and individual level, come to mind' (Osland and Bird, 2000: 65).

While it seems reasonable to assume that if cultural differences and paradoxes are neglected this can detrimentally affect cross-cultural, interpersonal interactions and relationships, the notion of culture can be overemphasized. Privileging a cultural perspective when understanding social phenomena can only ever result in a partial story of human organizing, never the whole story. Culture is but one of several considerations that influence and mediate human organizing, and in dynamic, culturally informed interactions, bi-polar dimensions are too static and contextually inadequate to usefully represent this complex phenomenon. When two or more cultures interact a new hybrid culture is formed that is bound by time and unique to that particular context (Chao and Moon, 2005; Osland and Bird, 2000). This contextual sensitivity is important when at least one of the parties in a multicultural situation adapts to and learns from the other. However, adaptation by one party does not mean the other party remains unaffected by the interaction. Equally, it would be taking the notion of generalization too far to assume that how one person from a particular culture has adapted to a situation will be replicated by others from the same culture. Not all the characteristics associated with a culture will be shared by all members from that culture. Similarly, *how* individuals from a culture adapt to new situations will not be uniformly consistent, but will be influenced by other considerations than just culture, for example, previous experience of similar situations to that being encountered will also have an influence on subsequent behaviour.

Zaheer and Zaheer (2006) highlight that research on trust across cultures can be conducted from either an etic (culture-general) or emic (culture-specific) perspective. The 'etic' position dominates and is based on the assumption that trust is a universal social phenomenon occurring across different cultural settings, and that any observable differences can be usefully measured and compared in the same way across cultures (Zaheer and Zaheer, 2006). From the alternative 'emic' perspective, scholars have highlighted that although trust may be universal, in the sense of being important to human beings all over the world (e.g. Schwegler, 2006), considerable differences have to be taken into account with regard to the levels of trust (Dyer and Chu, 2003; Yamagishi *et al.*, 1998), and the degree, nature and objects of trust (Zaheer and Zaheer, 2006).

What our brief review of culture and trust has shown is that this branch of the trust lexicon mirrors its broader colleague in that the focus has been on identifying different types of trust across national cultures. There have been some criticisms of this approach, and Zaheer and Zaheer's (2006) distinction between etic and emic perspectives offers a useful basis for developing a more culture-specific understanding of how trust is developed in cross-cultural contexts.

## Social constructionism

Although Berger and Luckmann (1966) brought the notion of social construction to the attention of sociologists, it was Astley (1985: 509) who first concluded that administrative science is itself a socially constructed product (see Cunliffe (2008) for an up-to-date discussion of the influence of social constructionism on management research). However, despite this, social constructionism has still tended to operate at the (increasingly wide) margins of organization study, which is still dominated by positivist-inspired studies. Social constructionism appears to be not wholly understood, although the label is attached to more and more research output. A social constructionist perspective of phenomena privileges the view that reality emerges through the shared, meaningful interpretations of actors as they cope with their everyday existence. This reality is largely created through the generative power of discursive acts, which frames social phenomena as a fundamentally linguistic accomplishment. Organization therefore, is seen as being constituted through, and not just represented by, shared discourses. Examples of this approach include Brown's (2004) analysis of how a government inquiry report is socially constituted as authoritative and verisimilitudinous, and Vaara *et al.*'s (2004) work that examines how strategies are discursively constructed.

Social constructionism privileges the role of narrative in the creation of human phenomena. The terms 'story' and 'discourse' are best understood as being constituents of 'narrative'. 'Story' consists of a plot comprising causally related episodes culminating in a solution to a problem. For example, practitioners may tell the story of how colleagues from across different cultures worked together to create a common strategy. 'Discourse' is the system of statements that allow certain ways of talking and rule out others, and can comprise written documents, speech acts, pictures and symbols. Here, discourse refers to the accepted norms of communication established between actors; it denotes the ways people discuss things. For example, there exists an accepted trust discourse between academics that admits certain ways of talking about it and marginalizes others. This situation is not unique to trust research of course; all academic topics have their dominant discourse. 'Narrative' incorporates both story and discourse, but is also a mode of knowing and understanding as well as a mode of communication (Czarniawska, 1997, 2004). Therefore, narrative can be seen as a way of constructing experience through stories, which are always embedded within wider social discourses. What a constructivist perspective reminds us is that narratives do not reflect an external reality, but are authored through humans selectively drawing from elements of experience which are combined into a meaningful, coherent, liveable and adequate whole.

This understanding raises several important issues about how actors construct their worlds. First, social constructionism dismisses the possibility that people use a neutral language in their discourses. This means that *all* social encounters involve individuals who bring with them to their discourses identities, histories, motivations, emotions, hopes, fears and expectations, which influence and shape these discourses in unknowable ways. If actors *always* use a non-neutral language, it follows that power is, equally, *always* present in any encounter involving more than one person, as, from a constructionist perspective, every instance of discourse is a power-infused experience. Power is no longer seen as just something that is monopolized by elites, but as an integral aspect of social life.

Second, social happenings are mediated by actors' pasts, presents and futures, which are constantly created and re-created in everyday experiences. Social encounters occur in temporal flows where pasts are continually reinterpreted, presents are enacted and futures are reframed and reconceptualized. Emirbayer and Mische (1998) suggest that individuals act within temporal orientations, so that during any encounter one actor may act from a past orientation, meaning he/she is more influenced by interpretations of the past; another may be focused on the present; whereas a third may act with a clearer focus on the future and how today's actions may play out in the future. They claim different temporal orientations influence actor behaviour in different ways.

Third, context comes alive in constructionism, such that artificial separations of actors, organizations and environments are eschewed in favour of constituting an understanding of these. Practitioners do not work in a context; they help create contexts with their acts. Organizations do not operate within fixed and static environments; through the interpretations of its actors they construct their environments. Contexts do not exist as some separate, objective entity; they are socially constituted. Latour (2005) argues, in our view convincingly, that actors are continually contextualizing and that it is their ongoing framing and reframing that constitutes organizing.

## Trust as a social construction

To say that trust is a social construction has important consequences. It implies trust is a narrative phenomenon, which is created through social processes of interaction and conversation. Trust is present in the stories we relate; it can be the focus of the story, as in 'how we created trust', or it can be present implicitly in the stories of cross-cultural working that could not progress without the actors trusting one another. Trust is also present in the relationship between storyteller and story-listener. At its simplest, trust must exist such that the storyteller trusts his/her audience to listen to his/her story, and the story-listener trusts the teller to deliver an interesting and engaging story. Within this understanding it is difficult to conceive of any story, or storytelling situation, where trust is not present.

No story is told in isolation; it is always constitutive of, and representative of, the wider meta-discourses of which it is part. These need to be appreciated as they help us understand the role of power in the social construction of trust. In human interaction's humblest form – the meeting of two people – power exists and influences what is said and done. These two people have histories, styles of talking and conventions of behaviour they bring with them to the encounter that help form the power relationships between them. When stories about trust are related, they are power-infused; meaning that the wider meta-discourses mediate what stories are told and what are not, why these stories and not others, and why in this form and not in another. Each of these stories is but one from an infinite number of potential stories that could be told. What an appreciation of discourse does is help remind us that what we are speaking about, listening to or reading, has been selectively drawn from a whole range of possible experiences. When we hear a story about cross-cultural trust we need to ask ourselves the questions: why this story? what makes this an authentic story? what other stories could be told? why aren't other stories being told? This questioning does not de-legitimate what we are hearing, but means we understand that the story is shaped by power-fuelled wider discourses. Additionally, both the story and the discourses do not reflect any objective reality, but are social constructions, created by humans to help them cope and make their worlds meaningful.

Conceiving trust as a social construction conceptualizes it as a narrative phenomenon. It shares this status with sensemaking, where a consensus has emerged that it is a narrative process (e.g. Brown, 2000). Actors make sense of their experiences by selecting cues from their encounters and forming these into workable wholes; both the selecting and the forming are narrative processes as they are done inter-subjectively and interpretively. Narrative phenomena are inter-subjective experiences. Trust, therefore, is an inter-subjective occurrence, in the sense that it is formed through an actor's conscious and unconscious thoughts, emotions and perceptions, self-insight and attitude to the surrounding world (Alvesson, 2003). The actor constitutes these through narrative into a meaningful interpretation of trust, which is socially situated and temporal. To think of trust as a narrative process, inter-subjectively construed through actors interpreting selected cues, emphasizes it as a plurality rather than as a mono-expression. It also highlights that understanding trust as an end product or as an aggregation of antecedents dehumanizes trust, turning it into an object or commodity. As a narrative process trust is socially constitutive, it produces knowledge, social identities and relationships between people through its becoming. Indeed, organizing could not occur without trusting, both of which are largely achieved through narrating.

Studying cross-cultural trust from this perspective, therefore, requires that researchers immerse themselves into the research setting, placing their best intellect into the thick of what is going on, listening to conversations, holding conversations and being aware of the macro-contexts that influence these.

## Pasts, presents and futures

Constructionism challenges the value of ahistorical organization research. Berger and Luckmann (1966) suggested several decades ago that to understand social phenomena something of their histories should be comprehended. Individual and shared histories matter when actors are constructing their trusting relationships. To ignore this suggests that each interaction is created anew, with no previous experiences for individuals to draw from. When actors are constructing trust their conversations and thought processes are shaped by their previous experiences and the reported historical experiences of others. This is not to say that constructionists perceive the past as predetermining the present. The notion of a path-dependence leading to a predictive outcome is rejected in favour of a call for better understanding of how meanings are assigned to historical events and choices. Constructionists view the past as irrevocable, but assert that the meanings and interpretations drawn from it are not. The meanings subjectively assigned to historical events can and do change as a result of reinterpretations made by actors. In cross-cultural contexts the meanings assigned to historical events and happenings play a significant role in how actors establish dominating discourses – the acceptable ways of talking about a topic – that shape interactions and help form effective relationships.

Emirbayer and Mische's (1998) discussion of human agency highlights how temporal orientations matter in social encounters. Actors who are trusting from a past orientation are said to be more influenced in their actions by previous experiences, suggesting they will be guided more by interpretations of the past than any other temporal association. Those with a present orientation act very much in the here-and-now, with a focus on the immediacy of actions. Those who act from a future orientation are guided by what may happen in the future as a result of their present-day agency. What Emirbayer and Mische (1998) identify is that actors involved in cross-cultural trusting may all be influenced in their trusting activity from differing temporal orientations at any one time and that this contributes to the contextual environment shaping behaviour. A more nuanced understanding of complex, cross-cultural trusting requires researchers to consider what the temporal associations agency is shaped by.

Seeing trust as part of the temporal flow of social activity constructs it as an unfolding narrative; we never quite 'trust' in any final sense but are always in a process of 'trusting'. Through its objectification and commodification in the dominant trust discourse, 'trust' the verb has been superseded by 'trust' the noun. From a constructionist stance we would recommend the lead offered by Weick (1995) be followed and we consider trust as a verb, as this helps represent it as a truly dynamic process that has no fixed status. Möllering (2006: 102) comes close to a similar understanding when he talks of 'trust-in-the-making', which suggests a continually evolving, fluid, social phenomenon. However, he also talks of a 'carrier of trust' (2006: 7), which turns trust into an object, a 'thing' that can be carried, a noun. Verbs are not stable enough to be carried, they are too fluid; but nouns can be. This confusion and inconsistency can be addressed by replacing the word 'trust' with the terms 'trusting' or 'trust-in-the-making', which better represent it as a process that is an emerging, ongoing, social accomplishment. Conceiving cross-cultural trusting in this way encourages researchers to consider the differing temporal perspectives shaping agent behaviour. It is likely that actors themselves will be unaware of these influences and part of the skill of the researcher is to help research subjects develop a deeper understanding of their own practice through more in-depth reflections on their cross-cultural organizing.

## Trusting and contextualizing

The call for more contextual trust research (e.g. Kramer, 1999) arises from a recognition that acontextual trust research holds little relevance for practitioners. However, the consequences of contextualist research that conceptualizes trusting as a social construction need deeper consideration if the fuller benefits of such an approach are to be realized. If we accept that trusting is created through acts of social construction, we must question the idea that this occurs within contexts that are themselves fixed and static. A constructionist perspective of social worlds holds that *all* social phenomena are socially constituted; it would be wrong to single out elements and say that they are social constructs and that others are not. For social constructionists, trusting is socially constituted within unfolding contexts that are also socially constituted. Latour (2005) suggests that *all* human activity is contextualizing, so trusting cannot be removed from the contexts within which it is occurring; and that by trusting actors are also contextualizing, as by trusting they are influencing and changing their contexts. Context-free trust research, therefore, removes it from what makes it a lived experience.

Contexts contain physical artifacts, of course, but the presence of these alone do not a context make. It is the meaning actors assign to these that is important for context; and meaning is socially constituted and subject to change. Johann's handshake with Badri, in the Introduction to this volume, is a small physical act that is open to multiple interpretations that shape future interactions between those present in various ways. Similarly, a document's presentation may be intended to communicate authority and legitimacy in a certain culture, but in another may be seen as an attempt to exert control and as obfuscatory. These are tangible examples of the constituents of contextualizing whose meanings are assigned by people who draw from their own experiences, histories, perspectives and feelings to imbue them with their subjective significance. This significance is always unevenly assigned and its influences on behaviour are contingent upon situated understandings. This makes context-rich study difficult, but rewarding, as researchers have to make choices about what aspects of context they include in their accounts. The best guidance for this is to be led by the research subjects and hear from them what they feel have been the key contextualizing factors that have influenced them, while at the same time bearing in mind similar questions to those presented earlier, such as: what is missing from their stories? why are these aspects mentioned and not others? and, what other possible contextual aspects could be influencing actors without them being aware of it?

Non-physical contextual aspects reside in the people who are acting out the encounter. They bring with them their emotions and thoughts to the interaction, and these shape how the experience is accomplished. Understanding how these influence trusting in any quantifiable way is simply not knowable, but what is possible is that insight is gained into how trusting and contextualizing evolve together. This is achieved through researchers being sensitive to the aspects of context that are hidden from view and which may also affect the actor in ways he/she is unaware of. Actors arrive at trusting experiences with assumptions they have built up from their previous experiences, from the stories related to them by others and from what they receive from the media; these are integrated and sense is made that allows human agency to take place. From a pragmatic perspective, actors in an encounter must do something, even if that something is nothing, and to do this there must be an interpretation made which assigns that act meaning – contextualizing has taken place. Cross-cultural trusting takes place within contexts that are continuously emerging and evolving, interpreting these and the mediation effects they have on actors' behaviour is crucial if well-rounded, fine-grained accounts of trusting across cultures are to be produced.

To summarize this section, we have discussed three important issues that conceptualizing trust as a social construction raises, and which we believe have not been adequately addressed in the literature. First, trust is a narrative process that is constituted through actors recounting and listening to stories that form certain discourses. Through understanding discourse the role of power in trusting and trust research is made more explicit, as being aware of the dominant discourse alerts us to the knowledge that certain ways of talking about trust across cultures are privileged over others that are suppressed. It is for this reason that constructionists reject any notion of a neutral language, as all talk represents power.

Next, trust occurs in temporal flows of existence. To better represent the 'ongoingness' of trust and to differentiate its use from a noun, we suggest it is used in its verb form, 'trusting', to get closer to the continual and evolving process it really is. Trusting is enacted in the present by people who are influenced by the meanings they assign to past experiences, and who focus their actions on what may happen in the future. This interplay of pasts, futures and presents guides all encounters, but unevenly so; different people may have varying orientations influencing their behaviours. One may be trusting more strongly based on her/his past experiences, while another may be trusting more in the expectation of what that may produce for her/him in the future.

Third, the social construction of trusting always takes place within and constitutes contextualizing. Acontextual trust research separates it from human experience, as when humans are becoming they are also contextualizing. Trusting and contextualizing evolve together as people accomplish their organizing. The task for the researcher is not to stop what is happening, remove trusting from its contextualizing and ignore the narrating of trusting but to find ways of developing insight into how actors practise trusting and how this shapes their organizing. This is the subject we move on to next when we discuss implications for research and suggest a possible research agenda for trusting across cultures.

## Researching trusting

As has been identified from within the trust community, the dominant discourse among trust researchers is positivistic (Kramer, 1999; Möllering *et al.*, 2004). It is through the language of normative science that the concepts, models and theories of trust have been created and promulgated by trust researchers. This discourse is itself a social construct: it does not represent the reality of trust across cultures, it creates it, therefore it is performative. No dominant research discourse represents reality. Therefore it can only ever constitute it; dominant discourses produce that which they claim to represent. The language trust researchers use when constructing their accounts is not neutral, it betrays the epistemological assumptions of the researchers and legitimates a view of knowledge that privileges a particular ontological stance. So when trust researchers speak of how agents 'win trust', 'invest trust', 'ground trust', 'exchange trust', 'breach trust', 'grant trust', 'destroy trust', 'drive trust', and when they conceptualize it as a 'mechanism' that can be 'absent' from relationships, but when it is present can be 'measured', they are creating a discourse and normalizing how trust is researched. Through use of such terms scholars have constructed trust as a commodity, separated from the humans of which it is part, which raises doubts about the relevance for practitioners of much trust research.

In this chapter we have drawn several analogies with sensemaking, and have argued that trust and sense share many ontological and epistemological properties, not least that trust, like sense, is better understood as a verb rather than a noun. If we carry this forward and ask how helpful to our understanding of sense it would be to talk of how actors 'win sense', 'invest sense', 'ground sense', 'exchange sense', 'breach sense', 'grant sense', 'destroy sense', 'drive sense', and suggest that sense can be 'absent' from relationships, we must surely question the usefulness of commodifying this narratively constituted social construct. Our point here is that researchers talk an academic field into being, and how it is talked about constructs the norms through which progress in the field is made. Generally speaking, to progress in that field scholars would be best advised to adopt the dominant discourse and use this as a means of socializing themselves into that specific research community.

What we are arguing for is not the suppression of positivist research into trusting, or for its dominant position to be supplanted by a dominant social constructionist ontology. Much like John van Maanen (1998: xii) we do not see quantitative research as qualitative research's 'evil twin'. What we call for is a pluralist approach to all academic topics, so that social phenomena are examined from multiple perspectives that offer alterative conceptualizations, adding richness to the academic debate. The social constructionist research agenda we offer next is intended to enable and guide a pluralist approach to sit alongside others, advancing our knowledge of how trusting across cultural contexts is achieved.

## Trusting across cultural contexts: toward a social constructionist agenda

Before articulating a possible research agenda for examining trusting across cultural contexts, we will address some of the criticisms frequently levelled at this approach to research. Social constructionism is often criticized along three fronts: for allowing an 'anything goes' approach to research and its findings, for not holding relevance for practitioners because generalizability is not claimed and for leading to academic navel-gazing through over-reflexivity.

First, traditional notions about what constitutes valid research have to be reappraised. Issues of validity transferred from the natural sciences simply do not apply to constructivist research that takes place within social worlds. Evaluations of social constructionist research reports are made in terms of their authenticity, usefulness, verisimilitude, criticality, hegemony and for their plausibility and credibility. The reader makes a subjective judgment of the quality of the account, which Phillips (1995) summarizes by saying that through reading such a script the reader should learn something new about him/herself.

Second, the objective is to produce rich or thick descriptions about actors' lived experiences of organizing that 'speak' to the reader, but the task of generalizing is not one for the author, but the reader (Czarniawska, 2003: 354). The transfer of knowledge from one context to another requires under-standing of both contexts; at best, the social constructionist researcher can claim partial knowledge of the context of the original site of his/her research, but none of the context of the reader. This does not mean such research is of no relevance to practitioners, but that relevance is co-constructed between reader and the text as he/she engages in a virtual dialogue with the script.

Third, while over-reflexivity can indeed paralyse, leaving researchers unable to act (Czarniawska, 2003), an absence of reflection can lead to them failing to consider how the assumptions they bring to the research task influence what they see. Unreflective research leads to the objectification of the research act that constructs researchers as distant, privileged observers, who deny that their presence influences what they see. Cunliffe (2003: 994–5) provides an excellent analysis of reflexivity and persuasively argues that 'research is as much about the world of the researcher (our experience, culture, language, and writing conventions) as it is about the world we are studying'.

As with all research perspectives, constructionist researchers hold certain assumptions about the world that influence how they approach their research activity. Chief among these is that social phenomena have no 'essence' to be discovered as they are constantly being made and remade (Czarniawska, 2001). The implication of this for research into trusting across cultures is that there is no ultimate element at the heart of trust to be revealed through deductive inquiry. For this reason the pursuit of antecedents, from a social constructionist perspective, is a misguided journey. Trusting is too fluid and open ended to have a central feature that is fixed and consistent across contexts. Mir and Watson (2000) encapsulate this view when they speak of research as sculpting rather than excavating. Sculpting suggests the creation of something that didn't previously exist; excavating implies the role of the researcher is to seek out and uncover something that is hidden. Any constructionist research agenda is predicated on the belief that by researching we are creating that which we are investigating, so any agenda setting is also an attempt at establishing a discourse, and by doing this we recognize we are inevitably seeking to marginalize other possible alternative agendas.

We now offer four questions, which echo those from Chapter 1, that may help guide and advance research into trusting across cultures. These are explicitly 'social constructionist' in tone, which means they are intended to guide only rather than be definitively answered. First, *how do individuals from different cultures construct trust in their day-to-day interactions?* This broad question can be further refined to focus on specific instances that involve actors from differing cultures coming together to accomplish their organizing. Second, *how do practitioners from different cultures assign trust to non-human material objects, such as texts?* This question acknowledges trusting as a narrative process that involves more than human talk; by focusing on texts insight into how non-face-to-face encounters can still influence how trusting is construed. Next, actors in cross-cultural exchanges are creating hybrid cultures while contextualizing their environments; to develop our understanding of how hybrid cultures and contextualizing influence trusting, researchers need to bring the multiple roles and contributions of third parties to the forefront. A helpful question could be, *how do those involved in cross-cultural interactions draw from external sources to construct their trust and make sense of their organizing?* And fourth, *how do actors in unfamiliar cultures present themselves as trustworthy?* This could be followed up with supplementary questions that focus on how those practitioners react when they then act out their roles. So, if their attempts at appearing trustworthy are successful, how does this affect their actions; alternatively, how do they respond when they find their efforts to appear trustworthy have not been successful?

The rich descriptions these questions help to generate would, gradually, help to build up a canon of specific accounts of trusting across cultures. The temptation when studying a relatively unresearched field is to make claims to generalization based on the findings researchers construct. As indicated earlier, we caution against this and advise that, when studying trusting and contextualizing, the task for the researcher is to produce an authentic, engaging narrative that speaks of the lived experiences of actors. Through this practitioners can connect with the stories produced, relate their own experiences to those of others and learn from the critical accounts scholars produce. This approach will help trust research regain its relevance for practitioners that ahistorical, acontextual and dehumanizing research has lost. James G. March encompassed this view when he identified the researcher's job as being 'to make small pieces of scholarship beautiful through rigor, persistence, competence, elegance and grace, so as to avoid the plague of mediocrity that threatens to overcome us' (2007: 18).

## Research methods

Following on from the above, we now describe some common principles of social construction that researchers of trusting need to be aware of when they are preparing their research strategies. These ideas are drawn from the ontological perspective that conceptualizes trusting as dynamic and forever becoming, as opposed to static and fixed, and highlights methods of inquiry that are sensitive to its uneven flow within social contexts.

First, research of this type should be longitudinal, as cross-sectional research can only ever represent a snapshot in time. Longitudinal research, on the other hand, recognizes the temporal nature of social activity, and allows for the possibility of different contextual and mediating factors shaping human activity at different times. Cross-cultural trusting encounters are likely to involve actors who, at different times during this interaction, are being oriented in their actions by complex combinations of contextual forces. Longitudinal research is sensitive to these temporal changes, and part of the task of producing authentic, rich descriptions of cross-cultural trusting is to include these contextual ebbs and flows in research accounts.

Second, primary data are best understood as a co-construction between researcher and subject. This operationalizes the principle that trusting has no essence that is hidden and fixed (Czarniawska, 2001), but holds that social phenomena are constantly made and remade. The interview act, for example, is a site of social interaction where knowledge is co-constructed (but not evenly constructed) between two or more parties. Put simply, what the interviewer asks influences what the interviewee says, and how the interviewer behaves influences how the interviewee behaves, and vice versa. Interviews are social exchanges, not talking questionnaires. Interviews are locations where knowledge is sculpted, not excavated. It is a legacy of positivist, scientific thinking, that perpetuates the myth of researcher objectivity, to speak of data *collection* through interviewing. Data are not collected but construed, involving more than one person. Therefore it is a co-construction. It is for this reason that cross-cultural trusting research must also contain researcher reflexivity. This is because researchers are influenced by what they see and how research subjects respond to their inquiries. The two authors of this chapter are a German female and an English male; each of us brings different gendered and cultural baggage to research encounters, and elicits different reactions from our subjects. This is not something that should be ignored or suppressed, but embraced; our alternative cultural contexts are generative for research as they help open up the possibility of insight being created that would be missed by researchers of similar cultural backgrounds.

Third, constructionism assumes that actors are working within social environments, which, from a narrative perspective, have been described as complex, storytelling milieu (Currie and Brown, 2003). Within such surroundings individuals are exposed to many different discourses, both formal and informal, dominant and competing, which influence behaviour in unknowable ways. However, such complexity should not just be ignored. Researchers need to include in their forays in the field the mediating effects of multiple third parties, who could be casual acquaintances as much as peers. Researchers need to consider how discourses are power-filled, and how legitimacy and authority are claimed for certain discourses over others. While it may not be possible to focus on all contextualizing aspects at once, because of the restrictions of length when writing for academic journals, a decision to narrow inquiry to only one or two characteristics is acceptable. This is one of the reasons why, no matter how rich or thick their research reports, social constructionists should only ever claim to tell a partial story of trusting across cultures, not *the* story.

## Conclusion

In this chapter we have argued for the dominant discourse on trust to accept an alternative one focused on 'trusting' and 'trust-in-the-making'. Trusting across cultures emerges in contexts that themselves are not fixed and to understand better how actors create trusting relationships a social constructionist perspective is needed. Analogies have been drawn with sensemaking, which supports the case for conceptualizing trust as a narrative process. Talk is never neutral, so the role of power is recognized as constitutive of trust; in short, trusting does not exist without the presence of power. Our discussion of trust research has highlighted the assumptions that have become taken for granted and unchallenged. We have shown how trust research itself is a social construction constituted by scholars who have developed a way of speaking about trust that has become normalized. In response to this, we have proposed a research agenda to take our knowledge of trusting across cultures forward and have supplied advice on how researchers can be guided by constructionism in their fieldwork.

## References

Alvesson, M. 2003. 'Beyond neopositivists, romantics, and localists: a reflexive approach to interviews in organizational research'. *Academy of Management Review*, 28, 13–33.

Astley, W. G. 1985. 'Administrative science as socially constructed truth'. *Administrative Science Quarterly*, 30, 497–513.

Atkinson, S. 2004. 'Senior management relationships and trust: an exploratory study'. *Journal of Managerial Psychology*, 19, 571–87.

Berger, P. and Luckmann, T. 1966. *The Social Construction of Reality: a Treatise in the Sociology of Knowledge*. London: Penguin Books.

Bird, A. and Osland, J. S. 2006. 'Making sense of intercultural collaboration'. *International Studies of Management and Organization*, 35, 115–32.

Brown, A. D. 2000. 'Making sense of inquiry sensemaking'. *Journal of Management Studies*, 37, 45–75.

  2004. 'Authoritative sensemaking in a public inquiry report'. *Organization Studies*, 25, 95–112.

Burt, R. S. and Knez, M. 1996. 'Trust and third-party gossip'. In R. Kramer and T. Tyler (eds.) *Trust in Organizations: Frontiers of Theory and Research.* Thousand Oaks, CA: Sage, 68–89.

Chao, G. T. and Moon, H. 2005. 'The cultural mosaic: a metatheory for understanding the complexity of culture'. *Journal of Applied Psychology*, 90, 1128–40.

Child, J. and Möllering, G. 2003. 'Contextual confidence and active trust development in the Chinese business environment'. *Organization Science*, 14, 69–80.

Cunliffe, A. L. 2003. 'Reflexive inquiry in organizational research: questions and possibilities'. *Human Relations*, 56, 983–1003.

2008. 'Orientations to social constructionism: relationally responsive social constructionism and its implications for knowledge and learning'. *Management Learning*, 39, 123–39.

Currie, G. and Brown, A. D. 2003. 'A narratological approach to understanding processes of organizing in a UK hospital'. *Human Relations*, 56, 563–86.

Czarniawska, B. 1997. *Narrating the Organization: Dramas of Institutional Identity.* University of Chicago Press.

2001. 'Is it possible to be a constructionist consultant?' *Management Learning*, 32, 253–66.

2003. 'Forbidden knowledge: organization theory in times of transition'. *Management Learning*, 34, 353–65.

2004. *Narratives in Social Science Research.* London: Sage.

Dietz, G. and den Hartog, D. N. 2006. 'Measuring trust inside organisations'. *Personnel Review*, 35, 557–88.

Dyer, J. H. and Chu, W. 2003. 'The role of trustworthiness in reducing transaction costs and improving performance: empirical evidence from the United States, Japan, and Korea'. *Organization Science*, 14, 57–68.

Emirbayer, M. and Mische, A. 1998. 'What is agency?' *American Journal of Sociology*, 103, 962–1023.

Ferres, N., Connell, J. and Travaglione, A. 2004. 'Co-worker trust as a social catalyst for constructive employee attitudes'. *Journal of Managerial Psychology*, 19, 608–22.

Kramer, R. M. 1996. 'Divergent realities and convergent disappointments in the hierarchic relation: trust and the intuitive auditor at work'. In R. Kramer and T. Tyler (eds.) *Trust in Organizations: Frontiers of Theory and Research.* Thousand Oaks, CA: Sage, 216–45.

1999. 'Trust and distrust in organizations: emerging perspectives, enduring questions'. *Annual Review of Psychology*, 50, 569–98.

Kroeber, A. and Kluckhohn, C. 1952. 'Culture: a critical review of concepts and definitions'. *Anthropological Papers No. 4*, Peabody Museum, Cambridge.

Latour, B. 2005. *Reassembling the Social: An Introduction to Actor-Network-Theory.* Oxford University Press.

Lewicki, R. J. and Bunker, B. B. 1996. 'Developing and maintaining trust in work relationships'. In R. Kramer and T. Tyler (eds.) *Trust in Organizations: Frontiers of Theory and Research*. Thousand Oaks, CA: Sage, 114–39.

Lewis, J. D. and Weigert, A. 1985. 'Trust as a social reality'. *Social Forces*, 63, 967–85.

van Maanen, J. (ed.) 1998. *Qualitative Studies of Organizations: the Administrative Science Quarterly Series in Organizational Theory and Behavior*. Thousand Oaks, CA: Sage.

March, J. G. 2007. 'The study of organizations and organizing since 1945'. *Organization Studies*, 28, 9–19.

Mayer, R. C., Davis, J. H. and Schoorman, F. D. 1995. 'An integrative model of organizational trust'. *Academy of Management Review*, 20, 709–34.

Mir, R. and Watson, A. 2000. 'Strategic management and the philosophy of science: the case for a constructivist methodology'. *Strategic Management Journal*, 21, 941–53.

Möllering, G. 2001. 'The nature of trust: from Georg Simmel to a theory of expectation, interpretation and suspension'. *Sociology*, 35, 403–20.

2006. *Trust: Reason, Routine, Reflexivity*. Amsterdam: Elsevier.

Möllering, G., Bachmann, R. and Lee, S. H. 2004. 'Understanding organizational trust – foundations, constellations, and issues of operationalisation'. *Journal of Managerial Psychology*, 19, 556–70.

Osland, J. S. and Bird, A. 2000. 'Beyond sophisticated stereotyping: cultural sense-making in context'. *Academy of Management Executive*, 14, 65–79.

Phillips, N. 1995. 'Telling organizational tales: on the role of narrative fiction in the study of organizations'. *Organization Studies*, 16, 625–49.

Rousseau, D. M., Sitkin, S. B., Burt, R. S. and Camerer, C. 1998. 'Not so different after all: a cross-discipline view of trust'. *Academy of Management Review*, 23, 393–404.

Schwegler, U. 2006. 'Trust building processes within German–Indonesian cooperation'. Paper presented at the 22nd EGOS Colloquium, 6–8 July 2006. Bergen, Norway.

Triandis, H. C. 1989. 'Intercultural education and training'. In P. Funke (ed.) *Understanding the USA. A Cross-Cultural Perspective*. Tübingen: Narr, 305–23.

Vaara, E., Kleymann, B. and Seristö, H. 2004. 'Strategies as discursive constructions: the case of airline alliances'. *Journal of Management Studies*, 41, 1–35.

Weick, K. E. 1995. *Sensemaking in Organizations*. Thousand Oaks, CA: Sage.

Williamson, O. E. 1993. 'Calculativeness, trust and economic organization'. *Journal of Law and Economics*, 36, 453–86.

Yamagishi, T., Cook, K. S. and Watabe, M. 1998. 'Uncertainty, trust, and commitment formation in the United States and Japan'. *American Journal of Sociology*, 104, 165–94.

Zaheer, S. and Zaheer, A. 2006. 'Trust across borders'. *Journal of International Business Studies*, 37, 21–9.

# PART II

# Trust across different 'cultural spheres': inter-organizational studies

# 5 | Examining the relationship between trust and culture in the consultant–client relationship

STEPHANOS AVAKIAN, TIMOTHY CLARK AND
JOANNE ROBERTS

## Summary

This chapter examines the dimensions of inter-organizational and interpersonal trust as they are manifested in the consultant–client interaction, viewed within the 'cultural spheres' framework (Schneider and Barsoux, 2003). The chapter argues that the alignment or misalignment of culture(s) helps foster or hinder the presence of trust in the consultant–client relationship. We support our argument by demonstrating how culture becomes an important informative resource from which consultants and clients manage their expectations and risk taking. In inter-organizational contexts, trust is developed through artifacts and formal procedures that are shared by both parties. In interpersonal contexts, trust is developed through the mutual sharing of cultural values, as manifested in the interpersonal qualities of integrity and benevolence. Cultural values are not necessarily part of the parent consulting firm but can be unique to the people working in partnership on a project. Examples of behavioural cultural values include forms of communication, constructive criticism, displays of ability, benevolence and integrity and an unhesitating voicing of opinions that can lead to a realignment of attitudes, feelings, motives and objectives.

## Introduction

In a service relationship where business advice is consumed over the course of a series of interactions, the presence of ambiguity creates uncertainty (Clark, 1995). Management consulting is an example of a complex service activity whose success is dependent on the nature of the interaction between the actors (Clark, 1995; Fincham, 1999; Lowendahl, 2005; Nachum, 1999). The organizational actors involved are placed in a challenging position without, in many cases, having adequate prior knowledge on which to establish their mutual expectations and interests. Consultants undertake the risk of designing a service that will meet the client's interests without full knowledge of the client's requirements and expectations. Clients undertake the risk of entering into a business contract without full knowledge of whether the consultants will meet their full expectations/needs.

The parties' interdependence is a compelling social force: both consultant and client are in need of common grounds of interest and mutual alignment (Sturdy, 1997). Clients are in need of the consultants' services for responding to an array of organizational and institutional needs, and consultants are in need of the client's contract for maintaining their own business presence in the market (Sturdy, 1997). This creates mutual vulnerability and fear of loss. As such, the corporate and personal dynamics that emerge during client–consultant interactions are highly instrumental to how satisfaction or dissatisfaction is produced (Roberts, 2003). Specifically, the consultants' production of knowledge and its presentation to the client is thought to take place through staged interactions involving information gathering and analysis (Czerniawska, 1999). Management methods and tools are employed in order to provide problem-solving frameworks that are believed to correspond to the client's needs. The consultant's success or failure to legitimize the value of their service is, therefore, dependent on their management of the client's expectations and uncertainty, as well as on the consultant's instrumentality in positioning/adjusting their service to meet the client's perceived needs (Czerniawska, 2002). For their part, clients need to be aware how their expectations of consultants responding to a business problem might be different from how the consultants think, design and seek to deliver their service.

Clearly, the consultant–client relationship is one in which trust is highly significant as a concept for helping us understand the mechanisms by which these risks and interdependencies are managed (Das and Teng, 1998; Roberts, 2003; Sheppard and Sherman, 1998). However, the notion of trust has been only partially discussed in the management consulting literature. Indeed, although the consultant–client relationship has been broadly discussed in light of the transfer of information and knowledge, little is known about the nature of the partnership (Sturdy, 1997).

The stages by which consultants detect and respond to the client's needs take place in a fluid social context where the qualities of credibility and value are intertwined with the meeting of expectations (Glückler and Armbrüster, 2003). The inter-organizational and interpersonal relationships between consultant and client involve a host of complex social, political and economic dynamics. Although these have generated much attention in the literature (Berglund and Werr, 2000), there is little understanding of the *social* dimensions contributing to the management of inter-organizational and interpersonal partnerships (Bhattacharya *et al.*, 1998; Bigley and Pearce, 1998).

This chapter aims to address this gap by exploring how representations of cultural 'spheres' (Schneider and Barsoux, 2003) or 'tiles' (Chao and Moon, 2005) shape the development of trust in the consultant–client relationship (see also Dietz *et al.*, this volume). We examine the implications of these processes for the credibility and value of the consulting service that is produced and consumed. The chapter argues that the alignment/misalignment of cultural spheres has implications for how trust/distrust is generated and maintained in consultant–client relationships at the inter-organizational and/or interpersonal levels.

The next section provides an overview on how culture and trust are discussed in the management consulting literature. The chapter then moves on to the method used in our empirical study and an analysis of findings. It concludes by arguing that at the inter-organizational level trust is maintained through the sharing of similar corporate values and ideology, and at the interpersonal level trust is maintained through the specific interaction between actors and the exercise of personal attributes like integrity, benevolence and ability.

## Cultural spheres between consultants and clients

Even though consultant–client practices have been discussed in the context of knowledge attributes, the nature of the interaction is heavily dependent on the consulting and client firms' *cultures*. The study of culture is an important tool for understanding the development of trust in the consultant–client relationship because each party's perceived level of risk and interdependence is embedded to some extent in the different sets of cultural values and artifacts that each party brings to the relationship. Understanding the cultural dimensions that influence the design and delivery of business advice can help us understand the interpretative framework from which both parties structure their expectations of each other.

In line with the treatment of the term 'culture' in this book – as being separated into different 'cultural spheres' or 'tiles' (Chao and Moon, 2005; Schneider and Barsoux, 2003) – we see consultants' and clients' multiple cultural spheres as representing sources of social identity and knowledge, from which the actors draw meaning in order to sustain and manage their mutual expectations. Parties' cultural spheres can also provide an important locus of information and knowledge from which each is able to manage their expectations of the other. In this sense, different cultural spheres provide a medium of information from which both parties are able to manage the mutually existing uncertainty.

We can delineate the 'multiple cultural memberships' that consultants encounter in themselves and in their dealings with their clients. 'Culture' in the consultant–client relationship is multifaceted. It is represented in forms of organizational structures, policies and procedures as well as in values and assumptions that are embedded and justified in the belief system of organizational actors. For consultants, cultural spheres can be expressed in the corporate identity of their employer. Such a corporate identity might extend to being known for a specialized line of business services (e.g. strategy, change management, business methodology or client ideology), or with a particular sector (manufacturing, services, public sector). This identity may be seen as setting the consulting firm apart from similar consulting players. Consultants' corporate cultural sphere may extend to their modes of designing and delivering a service in client organizations; for example, culture may determine the extent to which consultants grow into an understanding of whether they should be the dominant party or delegate the decision making to the client. In sum, consultants are equipped with the ideology, guidelines and methodology of the parent consulting firm which provide the *lens* through which the clients' needs are interpreted. Their corporate cultural sphere can exert a very powerful influence on individual consultants' thinking, values and behaviours. Other potentially influential cultural spheres include the national culture of the consulting firm, and of the individual consultant; the 'professional' cultural sphere of the sector or specialism the parties work within, and even workplace subcultures.

Similarly, clients' cultural spheres may extend to their personal anticipations of how consultants should address a given business situation. Sectors may have particular values and norms; for example, the public sector's priorities and modes of operating may differ markedly from those found in commercial enterprises. Furthermore, a client's 'personal' cultural sphere might differ according to whether consultants are seen as a positive asset from a 'corporate' culture, or as an unnecessary cause of expenditure to be avoided. Equally, client workplaces may have idiosyncratic 'cultures'.

Trust can be fostered or hindered through the way in which cultural spheres and their limitations are managed between the two parties. Consultants need to be aware of how their service needs to be tailored to the assignment but also of more general, related demands of the client. The consultant's process of entering into the client's culture and creating legitimacy requires the competency to address a host of issues that concern: a) the appreciation of the business problem and how it is interpreted by the client, b) the design of a consulting service that is able to address the problem while at the same time managing to generate the targeted revenues for the parent consulting firm, and c) the ability to address the interpersonal issues between the organizational actors and the emergence of conflict during the delivery of the business assignment.

Another source of cues regarding the parties' trustworthiness is institutional frameworks (Zucker, 1986) which can become instrumental in reducing levels of corporate risk and allowing the establishment of a cooperative relationship (Doney and Cannon, 1997). Legal frameworks also help outline the scope of responsibilities enclosed in such a business transaction (Ring and Van de Ven, 1992; Williamson, 1985). However, the management consulting industry does not have a formal system of knowledge that is commonly shared (Kieser, 1997). Although extant regulative frameworks can provide the institutional context in which the partnership can be manifested, the quality of the interpersonal relationship between actors is dependent on interpretive social mechanisms. As Glücker and Armbrüster (2003) argue, the presence of such bureaucratic frameworks is not enough to explain the continuing legitimacy of consulting firms in the market, because administrative structures cannot help explain the process of reducing social uncertainty in the interaction itself. Furthermore, Glücker and Armbrüster (2003: 270) argue that: 'personal experience that evolves from interaction between clients and consultants becomes most important in reducing uncertainty and controlling for opportunistic behaviour'. Trust and culture constitute such social mechanisms because their exploration reveals the micro-interpretive processes by which such interaction is produced, managed and maintained.

The implication of the above is that consultants and clients can find themselves in a kind of 'interpretive tension'. They try to reconcile a) the application of the corporate values as communicated by their employer firm with b) the client's expectations or 'ambiguous' requirements. Extant cultural values at a corporate level can influence how consultants think and deliver their assignment. Yet consultants often experience a sense of 'corporate rigidity' when they want to deviate from the instructions/culture of the parent firm. Such tension can have direct implications for the generation of trust in the consultant–client relationship. Figure 5.1 depicts these tensions.

Since each sphere 'may shape a person's thinking or conduct independently or simultaneously with another sphere' (Dietz *et al.*, this volume), understanding the alignment or misalignment of cultural spheres is about clarifying the meaning mechanisms by which the two parties communicate (Hatch,

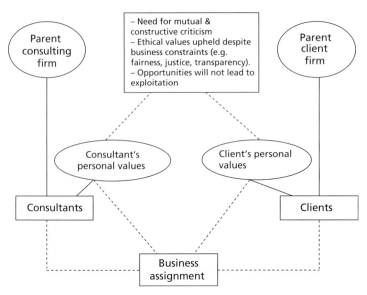

**Figure 5.1** Levels of interaction in the consultant–client relationship

1993; Schein, 2004). Culture constitutes a powerful informative resource from which actors craft their understanding and expectation about the other party. Our argument is that trust is embedded in the alignment of cultural spheres that helps reduce the perceived uncertainty of the transaction.

## Study of trust in the consulting literature

Glücker and Armbrüster argue that trust is not dependent on the institutional structures through which consulting firms position their services in the market but rather, economic transactions are deeply embedded in types of social networks that help reduce the perceived degree of risk and uncertainty. Consultants are able to maintain their popularity and presence in the industry through the use of 'networked reputation' (Glücker and Armbrüster, 2003). This term encapsulates two dimensions: first, public reputation as contained in claims of regulative acceptability, compliance with professional bodies and marketing practices; and second, transactional personal experience, as embedded in the temporalities of the business assignment. Networked reputation can be used to understand the shared qualities of these dimensions. Instead of being viewed as separate practices, networked reputation indicates that public reputation is really exemplified through interpersonal interactions. The transactional personal experience between consultants and clients comes to be equally embedded in the firm's reputation.

The personification of the firm's reputation by its actors creates a path of legitimacy that is missed when corporate reputation and experienced transaction are viewed separately. This means that consultants seek to make use of their firm's reputation in the interaction with clients in order to add credibility to the prospects of their service. Moreover, consulting partners seek to channel and utilize the success of an individual assignment to the overall firm's reputation (Maister, 1993, 1997). Thus, the use of 'networked reputation' argued by Glücker and Armbrüster is intended as a metaphor to exemplify a dualistic function in the context of organizational trust as it is demonstrated through forms of institutional legitimacy *and* personal social networks. In this context, Glücker and Armbrüster argue: 'networked reputation conveys a far more personal and reliable credibility, since word-of-mouth discloses "thick information" about potential transaction partners' (2003: 280).

Even though the work by Glücker and Armbrüster has helped widen our understanding of organizational trust in consultancy settings, the conclusion of their findings is mainly drawn from economic institutional trust which focuses on the macro-practices of management consulting firms. Moreover, their argument of networked reputation is based on the prominent role that informants play for potential clients. Informants represent third parties that provide testimonies to others and who can influence future clients out of their personal positive or negative experiences. Glücker and Armbrüster argue that a client's experience with a consultant becomes a source of information from which other clients come to shape their ideas about a particular consulting firm. However, in making this argument, Glücker and Armbrüster do not explain how this process takes place, but rather assume that the creation of positive testimonies becomes a powerful legitimatory force. Hence, risk and uncertainty are reduced as new clients base their decisions on the positive/negative experience from other clients to which they have access (i.e. a reputation effect from third parties).

Clearly, further research is needed to establish the nature of network practices between consultants and clients at a micro-level of analysis (Salaman, 2002). This is necessary to identify the more specific forms of trust building, not only by looking at how consultants personify their public reputation in the transactional experience with clients, but also how clients may react and influence how this process takes place. In this sense, we argue that there is a clear need to identify the establishment of personal and organizational trust from a discursive and practice perspective. We argue that by eliciting the forms of consultant–client interaction at a micro-level of analysis, and through the lens of culture, we will be able to reveal the role of cultural spheres through which trust is not only generated but also maintained. By exploring trust through the parties' cultural lenses we can learn how the mechanisms of trust emerge in the relationship.

## Methodology

The types of consulting firms ranged from small firms (under 10 employees) to medium (50–100 employees) to larger corporations (over 100 employees). Taking into account the diversity of consulting firms, we approached consultants where the nature of their service required a personal interaction with the client, and where business knowledge was the main input into the final service. Such consulting firms provided services related to strategy, human resources, operations, knowledge management and general management advice. We excluded firms that specialized in IT services or similar technical consulting firms whose mode of service was mainly expressed through outsourcing and with minimal involvement from the client. The client interviews also range between public and private organizations.

Data were collected through semi-structured interviews with twenty consultants and twenty clients in the UK. The interviews lasted between sixty and ninety minutes. The interviews were digitally recorded and transcribed and a copy of the interview transcript was sent back to each interviewee for corrections, additions or modifications before agreement was given to its content and a finalized version produced. Strict confidentiality and anonymity was provided for the protection of the personal and strategic information disclosed and all names have been replaced. The difficulty of gaining access to consulting and client firms limited our ability to interview parties engaged in the same assignment. Consequently, the clients that consultants referred to are not the ones we have interviewed and vice versa.

Our questions concern three main themes that can be summarized as follows: 1) the nature of inter-organizational and interpersonal trust in the consultant–client relationship; 2) the context of inter-organizational and interpersonal culture and the different ways in which it is demonstrated; 3) different organizational and personal forms of culture and trust manifestation in the consultant–client relationship during the course of an assignment.

Our categorization and analysis of the data is based on using thematic analysis techniques drawn from the work of Boyatzis (1998), Auerbach and Silverstein (2003), and Miles and Huberman (1994). Our focus concentrates on the variables emerging from the consultants' testimonies and the interrelationship between key concepts. Since the phenomena we are studying are personal testimonies recorded in text, the use of thematic codes helps group together ideas while questioning the relevance of the messages expressed.

We use thematic analysis not as a means of validating a predetermined hypothesis but rather to identify the significance of traces of trust in the available empirical findings. By examining the commonalities and differences between such themes, we analyze the qualities of validity within the linguistic context of the interviewees' interpretations of experience (Silverman, 2000). The nature of the assignment and dynamics of the projects certainly differ, but there are distinct similarities in the broader managerial context of organizational needs and proposed advice. For example, two clients that may have worked with two different consulting firms on different projects are asked to reflect on the degree of personal trust in the individual consultant during the course of the assignment, while consultants working in different firms were asked to comment on characteristics of trust displayed by clients.

Below we present selected testimonies, focusing particularly on comments made about culture and trust. Although our presentation of findings is limited in terms of its representation of all the varied and nuanced experiences of the participants, the themes we discuss are representative across the participants' experiences. In this sense, we have selected the quotations that most clearly help capture the overarching thematic trend between inter-organizational and interpersonal culture and trust.

## Cultural spheres – consultants and clients

Our findings indicate that, in the context of inter-organizational trust, culture is exemplified through forms of power structures, identity symbols and communicative procedures that become formalized and mutually shared between the two parties. The sharing of a corporate culture is not only about showing agreement with procedures, it is about sharing the deeper meaning and intentions attached to them (see Dietz *et al.*, this volume; Smircich, 1983).

We also find that the corporate cultural sphere of the client most often dominates the partnership with the consultant. Consultants reflect the client's organizational aspirations by contributing to the thinking and emotions expressed between members. At times, it is debatable whether the consultants' 'code-switching' (see Molinsky, 2007) to the client's culture is genuine or superficial. Nevertheless it is perceived to be an important quality for how and why their service is legitimized.

In addition, we find that the way in which consultants endeavour to align their corporate values with the client becomes an interpretative process that itself contains ambiguity and uncertainty. Often, consultants find themselves in a state of tension trying to reconcile the values attached to the parent consulting firm with their own personal values.

## Clients and inter-organizational trust

The following interview excerpt is drawn from a director with much experience in using management consulting firms. The client is representative of a large firm and he refers to the nature of his working partnership with the consulting firm at a strategic level. The client firm's activities are closely linked to the motor vehicle industry. The client director illustrates how the close corporate ties with the consulting firm have been instrumental in recent years for the firm's ability to adapt to environmental change and to enhance employee performance.

Part of the client firm's long-term plan has been the unusual integration of the consulting firm into the board of directors. Interestingly, the representative consultant has been given an equal degree of authority and responsibility as other directors. The rationale behind this move has been the alignment of culture between the two firms. This development of inter-organizational trust does not aim at generating short-term solutions, but rather, an equal share of commitment and responsibility for the long term. This is well expressed in the following statement from the client:

[The consultant] has an equal influence in many respects to all the other directors. So I don't think that we're in the situation that he has any more undue influence than any of the other 7 directors. And if he's voted down he's voted down. But at least he is there and he can help to make sure that ABA and the contract are focused on helping, because, he fully understands what the business drivers are and what the strategies are to make sure that they've put in the right sort of support arrangements to make sure that we actually get to them. But it is a contradiction and it's a balance. It's trying to get those two things working in harmony.

But our partnership was about the sharing of information from both sides of the organization from ourselves and our supplier, and the integration of all parts of the organization, again, at different parts of the layer. So, that goes all the way up to the board, so you have things like open book accounting, there's honesty about business benefits, there's honesty about the costs which are coming up, where they come from. And we have links at all different levels of the organization to try to work in more of a partnership rather than a customer supplier. We're trying to move along things like joint estimating, so that ABA and our partners actually work together on estimating what the costs of a new proposal might come up to, rather than let our suppliers go away for three months or a month and come up with a figure and then I'm spending 6 to 8 weeks asking them well where do you get this from? Why do you think it's going to take you 1,000 days to do that? They're actually part of the process and to see the build up these figures to actually make the proposal evaluation a lot quicker and more effective. So it is about trust and it's about letting the suppliers in closer to us and then letting us in closer to them and that goes all the way up to the level of the board.

The underlying notion of the consultant's 'inclusion', while at the same time retaining his status of being 'external' to the firm, is particularly interesting. The identity of the consultant is placed in a context of *transition* between being an 'insider' and yet at the same time remaining an 'outsider' (Sturdy *et al.*, 2009). It is through this ambiguity of the consultant's status that the client party believes they will be able to maximize the added value from their relationship with the consulting firm. However, the consultant's belonging to the parent consulting firm indicates a specific cultural sphere that is represented by the identity of the firm's corporate objectives and the need to maintain the continuation of the consulting contract. The consultant becomes a representative of the parent firm's desire to demonstrate an image of knowledge and expertise that will appeal to the client. The consultant is under pressure to uphold an image of service.

By having equal status of power and influence the consultant is being given an important sense of 'ownership'. The consultant is expected to express an equally strong sense of concern and care for the business issues that matter to the directors. The consultant becomes part of the corporate cultural sphere of the client by being allowed to sit on the board of directors. However, the consultant does not share their years of experience in the firm, nor is he part of the everyday working environment. He does not share that part of the client's culture, but is nevertheless expected to subscribe to their values. The consultant is required to envisage and *enact* a sense of ownership where he is believed to share the burden and vision of what needs to be achieved.

The client firm assumes that the consultant's contribution will not be driven by possible unwanted business motives influenced by the aspirations of the consulting firm to maintain the business contract or generate short-term revenues, for example. The client firm believes that the consultant's accountability to the firm becomes a lot more *transparent* by sharing an equal level of seniority and power. Such transparency is not simply produced at the interpersonal level, but also at the inter-organizational level, where the consultant is asked to reinforce the business mission of the client firm. The alignment or misalignment between the corporate cultural spheres is institutionalized in formal procedures that are mutually binding between the two parties. In addition to the above, the duration of the consultant's involvement in the board aims at the accumulation of experience that is believed to mature over time. The client firm believes that it can get added value out of the consulting firm through the consultant's depth of integration and experience. This is based on the assumption that the achieved maturity will further assist the making of decisions that do not simply seek to produce results for the short term.

The development of trust becomes possible out of the above sharing of cultural spheres because it contributes to nurturing the qualities of 'ability', 'benevolence' and 'integrity', all of which are necessary for the emergence of trustworthiness (Mayer *et al.*, 1995). The directors are able to detect the consultants' ability to provide input to the board's decision making concerning the future direction and strategy of the firm. If the directors detect that the consultant does not show the competency to appreciate the issues that concern them they will dispute his ability to be a channel of new knowledge and information.

Second, the consultant's context of manifesting his input in the client takes place by indications of benevolence, as the consultant is perceived to act in the interests of the trustor. The duration of the consultant's involvement creates the 'space' for the directors to *verify* the consultant's motives and intentions. As a result, the consultant is able to legitimize his service for the client by demonstrating that he is acting in their best interests.

Finally, and as the excerpt above indicates, the client firm is able to develop trust in the consultant because of the consultant and consulting firm's integrity to the client. The client discusses the consultant's integrity in the context of honesty and the quality of openness in the communication between the two parties. The client firm shows its commitment to trusting the consultant by allowing him to be part of its formal decision-making process. Such behaviour creates the need for an equal behaviour of reciprocation through which the consultant must demonstrate that he is able to live up to their expectations.

The client directors are well aware of the possible disadvantages of such a close partnership: namely that it prevents the client firm from having the scope of self-reflection and self-criticism. The long-term ties have clear organizational implications in the client in terms of not being exposed to alternative consulting suggestions as well as outside competition. Having entered into this partnership the client firm is 'compelled' to act on the consultants' recommendations. However, the internal decision making between members of the client firm aims to ensure that recommendations are well examined before being acted upon. There exists an inevitable degree of bias which can have disadvantages as the client firm does not have equal access to other consulting firms. This rather 'monopolized' type of partnership brings risk and uncertainty as to whether the consultants will endeavour to produce the best they can for the client. Despite the close and long-term relationship the client firm continues to make a strategic choice to trust that the consultants will continue to provide them with innovative insights. The client's sense of risk and uncertainty are clearly captured in the following statement:

Certainly within the client firm we have some get-out-clauses if we need to use them. But yeah I think that's a conscious decision that I think we made when we decided to go on this partnership approach. Yeah, you do have potentially more options available to you if you don't have a partnership if it's very much a customer-supplier relationship, but then you have the downside to that relationship as well. You don't always get the buy-in from your IT supplier about where you're going. You don't always expect your IT supplier to put a bit of skin into the game in terms of what we're trying to achieve. You miss out a little bit on some of the advice and guidance. But similarly you also don't get an idea of where that company is going and it's a difficult one.

Inter-organizational culture is institutionally embedded in the formalized authority and participation given to the consultant within the client board of directors. The frame of reference that governs this interaction is embedded in policies and procedures which might be expressed through explicit formalized statements of agreement. These are used to ensure transparency and open transfer of information. Organizational culture is situated within statements of agreement which also have consequences for the rest of the client member's practices at an operational level. It is the mutually shared *intention* and desire for a strategic partnership, at the corporate level, that creates meaning for the policies and procedures which in turns help sustain the corporate culture. We argue that the *co-created* culture from which organizational trust is manifested acts as a kind of information and experience resource. Risk and uncertainty are being 'managed' because of an implicitly achieved equilibrium of the positive expectations situated within the dimensions of organizational culture.

## Consultants and inter-organizational trust

The relationship between inter-organizational trust and culture is also evident from the consultants' testimonies and from working with clients. We argued earlier that the consultant's process of entering into the client's culture and creating legitimation for their services requires them to be competent in: a) appreciating the business problem and how the client sees it, b) designing a consulting service that can address the problem while at the same time generating targeted revenues for the parent consulting firm, and c) addressing any interpersonal issues between the organizational actors and the emergence of conflict during the delivery of the business assignment. There is mutual endeavour to develop common grounds of understanding, so that consultants are able to communicate and deliver their service according to the client's specific requirements.

The key theme that emerges out of the following analysis is the consultants' way of seeking to manage their personal and corporate cultural spheres/tiles. Consultants often have to modify their behaviour so that they can appear to 'fit' the culture of the client, despite the fact that they may not themselves represent the values that they seek to project. Consultants experience tension in having to accommodate the requirements of the parent consulting firm in relation to their own *and* those of the client. Such tension brings to the fore a clearer depiction of the coexisting and co-conflicting 'tiles' that consultants try to align, successfully or unsuccessfully.

In an interview with a management consultant who has extensive experience in the industry reference is made to his time of working with Arthur Andersen before its demise. The consultant held a high managerial position in the firm as a UK director. In discussing his experience the consultant argues that the corporate culture influenced how the consultants realized their role and objectives in relation to the client. In particular, the creation of corporate revenue targets and performance-related structures had implications for the consultant's engagement with the clients. Consultants were encouraged by the parent firm to find ways of promoting the impression that the consulting services would be competent to address the clients' organizational needs:

People very often are pulled in to working with those firms when they do have a calling, but the problem is when you're in that environment it's a very subtle process over which over time, and I was in the 'A' firm and 'B' firm for 18 years, and, over that period of time there's a process of osmosis where certain corporate values get taken on board. You don't realize they're not your values, you've taken them in from your environment and for me it was only in 2001 I got out of that environment. It was not probably until 2003/2004 before I really could say 'Wow, I don't have to do that, I can be me and I can do this.' Very difficult to do that in a big consulting firm because you're expected to follow a particular trajectory, your career progress is very clear, there's up or out.

The corporate values that consultants needed to communicate to the client firm represent one cultural sphere. The particular consultant's personal agreement or disagreement with the consulting behaviour represents a second cultural sphere. The client's identity and specific organizational problems against which the consultants seek to communicate their advice represent a third cultural sphere. Creating trust with clients arises from the way consultants are able to show that their corporate cultural sphere is in alignment with the client's corporate cultural sphere. The fact that consultants might not genuinely believe that such an alignment is possible brings to the fore Molinsky's (2007) argument of 'code-switching', where the consultants modify their behaviour so that it *appears* to be in alignment with the client. According to the quotation above the consultant's ethical consideration created unrest at the time of selling a service because the consultant knew the advice was 'disguised' with promises that could not be delivered. The ability of the consultants to 'switch' their behaviour does not itself assure the creation of a mutually shared ground of agreement. The personal cultural tile, represented in the consultant's moral assumptions, education or personal philosophy, became the principal factor by which the consultant sought to develop his own consulting firm over the years. Also, it became the reason he wanted to change the whole of his approach to working with clients.

The clash between the consultant's own belief systems and the parent consulting firm becomes even more apparent in the context of the financial targets consultants needed to achieve. The profit-seeking strategy of the firm was designed around performance measurement and career progression. According to the interviewee, the opportunity to achieve a promotion was partly dependent on the targets they achieved over the year. The parent firm seemed to require consultants to win the contract or deliver a business assignment successfully *without* appreciating how such corporate pressure might affect its people at an operational level. As a result, even though consultants might want to achieve the fulfilment of specific performance targets they might still find themselves unable to go against their personal ethical values.

It can be argued that the clients did not realize how and why the consultants managed to deliver a set of additional but unnecessary services in order to meet their own business revenue targets. It is certainly possible for consultants to develop trusting relationships with clients whether or not they exploit the relationship. The client's perceived trust in the consultant might not be dependent on the corporate targets set by the parent consulting firm. However, we argue that the client's possible perception of the consultants as exploiting a business opportunity may have a detrimental effect on whether a business proposal is viewed as credible. Clients may accept or reject the consultants' knowledge service because of the perceived fear of manipulation. Such perceived fear or uncertainty needs to be seen separately from the fact-based credibility of the information/knowledge proposed by the consultants. The consultants feel the need to project a positive image to the client so that they can win the client's trust. However, as the quotation below indicates, the consultant's personal frustration about how this might be possible does not seem to be appreciated by the parent consulting firm:

Yeah, I think there, there was a very strong feeling that if you went to a client meeting and you didn't come away with either an order [or something] then you'd sort of, failed. Whereas the people that I work with now, and the work that I do now, is very much a case of you develop relationships.

The interviewee succinctly expresses the essence of corporate culture by making reference to the firm's internal climate. The failure to produce a business order after a client meeting was not explicitly associated with poor performance yet consultants had internalized an association of such failure with poor performance. Furthermore, corporate culture also shaped the consultants' perceptions about their own performance and that of their colleagues. It is possible that the consultants' successes or failure to win a client assignment had broader implication for the power relationship between colleagues.

Even though the above statement can be interpreted as a personal internal struggle that is not representative of other consultants and which might not affect other consultants' trusting relationship with clients, it is clear that the corporate cultural sphere has a strong influence on how individuals perform at an operational level. The point of tension is not just the self-consciousness of the particular consultant, it is rather the wider struggle for the consultants to reconcile their corporate culture with their own and the expectations of the client. The phrases used by the consultant to describe his experience support our argument that the alignment of inter-organizational trust is dependent on the alignment of culture between parties. The consultant argues for 'a process of osmosis' where corporate values are internalized often without the actors being consciously aware of it. The corporate culture creates a powerful social setting where actors create meaning relations about their identity and role dealing with clients.

The exercise of corporate culture as represented in the form of power structures, corporate identity and communicative procedures makes up the cultural spheres between the consultant and client firm. The alignment or misalignment of culture is about the mutual sharing of the meaning attached to the above artifacts. The information produced from the cultural factors, we argue, plays an important role for managing the features of uncertainty and risk. For example, we have seen that clients are able to trust the consulting firm because of the commitment that the firm has made to contribute to the decision making of the board of directors. When the consultant shares an equal degree of power, authority and responsibility with the client, positive client expectations are created which also foster corporate trust. The above argument has clear implications for how and why *distrust* might develop in the relationship between consultants and clients, especially at the inter-organizational level. Clients seek to detect information about consultants which can inform their decision to allow themselves to become vulnerable.

## Interpersonal levels of trust

In the previous section we discussed the manifestation of inter-organizational trust in the context of the consultants' and clients' experience. We argued that trust may be understood from the alignment/misalignment of culture underpinning the structure of the consultant–client partnership. In this section, we turn to trust at the interpersonal level. From the trust literature we find that interpersonal trust is dependent on the personal attributes of the organizational actors (Sheppard and Sherman, 1998; Whitener *et al.*, 1998). This is in contrast to organizational trust which is situated in managerial frameworks of interaction that are mutually accepted prior to the business engagement (Gambetta, 1988).

## Clients and interpersonal trust

In an interview with a senior client from the public sector, reference is made to his experience of interaction with a particular consultant on a project. The project was part of a consortium between different local authorities in the North East of England. One of the challenges for this combined collaboration was the level of partnership and agreement. The client talks about the early stages of the project where initial drafts were made about the corporate objectives and the degree of commitment each party should show. In the following statement the client refers to the consultant's effort to create a sense of collectivism between the client members by discussing their support of local football teams, and to distract his client audience from the fact that he came from the polar opposite of the country, in regional culture terms. Football might have been felt to be irrelevant to the business topic but it clearly made an impression on the interviewee and also on the project:

A young chap – talking about relationships and about personalities – a young guy from Surrey, educated in Surrey, a very much South of England born and bred, first thing he did when he came into the town where he was doing this particular project, was learn who supported which football teams. And he found out who the Sunderland supporters were and he found out who the Newcastle supporters were [two bitter local rivals], and he got some information and some local information about the place, and talked about that. And I remember seeing him at the first meeting, and you can argue about whether he meant it or it was just his job, but his first 15 minutes of his presentation was talking about local themes, and it was a very much, a sort of, 'How does he know that? Maybe he's not so bad for a Surrey lad', so there was a sort of, not an acceptance, but there was a recognition that he was trying to involve . . . Rather than coming in and saying 'I'm the consultant, I know about these things, now you listen to what I've got to tell you'; [it's] how you manage the process, how you manage the relationship.

In the above excerpt we note a number of different cultural spheres/tiles that helped reduce the level of uncertainty in the client. The consultancy firm and its approach to tackling the organizational issue represent one cultural sphere. The client firm and its belonging to the public sector with its sensitive internal political issues represent a second cultural sphere. The use of sport and the football teams represents a further cultural sphere. We would note that it is not only the number of cultural spheres that might exist in the partnership that is important but how they are used in order to build trust in the relationship. The use of a shared cultural sphere specific to the client helped to reinforce the impression that the consultant was capable of delivering in the project. Reference to football teams became a metaphor through which the consultant tried to trace some common ground of interest between the actors. It is clear that this did not just happen on the day of the meeting. The consultant went through the process of identifying the Sunderland and Newcastle supporters and the geography of the region. The social context from which the client members could identify common grounds of interest helped reduce the actors' perceived uncertainty about the project itself. Identifying a common ground of interest within *football* (itself a unique cultural sphere, especially in the North East of England) became a point of information where the client members could demonstrate that they were able to share some form of agreement elsewhere, especially if organizational adversaries supported the same team outside of work. The above practice sent a clear message to the participants that the consultant was an individual who had the competency to facilitate a discussion, while showing a personal sense of interest towards the members themselves (benevolence). The members' association with football teams clearly signifies a sense of identity which the consultant also used to associate himself with the business project. In the above context, it can be argued that the existence of a shared identity concerning football created a disposition of trust towards the consultant who was seen as able to facilitate the discussion and accommodate their differences. Put differently, the cultural tile of sport came to dominate over the members' corporate consultant and client tiles and differences.

Even though the consultant's interest or commitment shown in the above approach might be regarded as superficial, temporary and irrelevant, it influenced the participants' perceptions of the consultant. The interpersonal trust was not based on the qualities of the managerial framework itself but on the interpersonal common grounds of interest. Certainly, we cannot assume that the client members' potential agreement about the project was merely dependent on their association with the football teams. However, it can be argued that the consultant had taken the time and trouble to find out about the client members and managed to create a climate or disposition to trust out of a relaxed atmosphere of *familiarity*. As argued by Dietz *et al.* (this volume), trust is gradually developed out of 'cues' individuals construct about each other. Even though the use of sport might seem a minor metaphor, it nevertheless helped create a sense of collectivism and this is the characteristic we seek to underline.

A further factor that created positive impressions in the client was the fact that the consultant showed the ability to manage a non-familiar social setting while having knowledge of the differences of interests between its members. The consultant showed a sense of benevolence by seeking to engage with the different groups even though this was perceived to be outside his own comfort zone. Thirdly, from the interview it may be said that the consultant demonstrated a sense of integrity by attempting to find new ways of engaging and communicating his ideas with particular members of the client party despite the fact that they exercised resistance and criticism over his propositions. The consultant went to some lengths to appreciate the different reasons why the client members disagreed with him, without exercising judgment against the clients or bypassing their implicit and explicit concerns.

The progress of the meeting and the success or failure of the project outside this area of agreement can only be subject to speculation. We do not seek to make conclusive statements about the broader implications of the achieved alignment of interpersonal culture. However, we can see from the client's reaction that the consultant's efforts made an impression. Interestingly, this became a tactic for the specific interviewee in a separate project where his team needed to make a presentation to a different public sector audience.

## Consultants and interpersonal trust

Consultants also place an equal degree of emphasis on their interpersonal qualities of trust with clients. Consultants argue that the personal cultural elements are situated around qualities of communication, expression of emotions and the process of making sense of the other party's expectations. In discussing the different reasons that might jeopardize the development of a client assignment, the consultant quoted below points to the interpersonal interaction of relationships at a subjective level. That is, the consultants' style of delivery might not be appropriate or desirable for the client. The consultant also mentions the dimension of timing, pace and misalignment of personal expectations that have to do with the client's understanding of the consultant's intentions.

I think that there are several. One is that you have a *mismatch* between the people that you have put on the project from the consulting company, and, their style in the client's environment. You may send someone that's quite aggressive and they're looking at a job in a client organization that has a very soft or passive culture. He/she will then have problems with the client's people. So that may go wrong. Another one is where you may try to recommend to change things too quickly. You've got to be able to choose the pace of the client. The third one which I keep mentioning is when you go in and the consultancy firm, whoever they are, ignore the recommendations made by the other parts of the organization. That's the reason why most of the [consulting interventions] go wrong.

The above statement encapsulates the interpersonal cultural spheres as residing within individuals who might not be aware of them until they are in some kind of conflict with the partners. The consultant's style of delivery of an assignment is subjectively ingrained in his/her personality, judgment and also sensitivity to accommodating other ideas before defending a point of view. This represents one cultural sphere that is outside the corporate cultural sphere of the parent firm. Furthermore, such a behavioural approach is not made mutually explicit until the point of the interaction with the client party. In this sense, the pace at which the client expects the consultant to make decisions or negotiate a point of view cannot be known a priori. The consultant's attempt to comply with the client's culture has to do with a state of transition between how they want to deliver a business assignment in contrast to how the client envisages it being satisfied. This is clearly an implicitly subjective process of sensemaking (see Weick, 1993). The client's corporate culture may signal a clear sense of direction to which the consultant needs to adapt. However, the client's manifestation of a personal cultural fabric is not necessarily represented by the corporate culture. As a result, the consultants enter into an arena of interaction where they have to build trust on the grounds of shared personal behavioural traits.

The process of 'thinking alike' or displaying a 'consulting style' that is in harmony with the client's expectations helps reduce the degree of uncertainty and risk in the relationship. This is because the signalled information helps actors manage the other party's anticipations, thereby reducing uncertainty. However, the creation of such a working relationship 'match' can be explained through the emergence of the personal cultural tiles that *happen* to be alike at the time of the interaction. Since the consultant is not in a position to know in advance what style might fit the client's culture he/she is trying to develop cues from which to adapt his/her behaviour. From the above it follows that consultants can find themselves in a state of a mutual working relationship 'match' with the client, because of their similar personal cultural spheres. At the same time, such personal cultural spheres might be very different. As a result, the consultant might need to make an effort to understand the consulting style they need to develop in order to be aligned with the expectations of the client: to 'code-switch', in other words (Molinsky, 2007).

From the analysis it is also clear that the behavioural qualities of benevolence and integrity are crucial for the building of trust. This is because they help create a safe and credible moral ground of communication in which the vulnerability of each party can be manifested without criticism or manipulation (Dietz *et al.*, this volume). This theme is illustrated in an interview with a senior management consultant who discusses aspects of her communication with the client and the reasons for building trust. The consultant is the HR manager for one of the four large consulting accounting firms with extensive experience in the industry. Elaborating upon the dynamics of a successful client project she makes reference to the context of her interpersonal interaction with the client: in particular, the importance of openness and quality of communication from which both parties can challenge each other, and freely express their views and emotions. For the interviewee the lack of hesitancy in being able to become vulnerable to each other without fear of being misunderstood is a critical factor in the success of the project. From the following statements there is clear acknowledgement that if the client does not make their views clear to the consultant, and the consultant does not take action to rectify a position, there is a high possibility of distrust endangering the continuation of the contract. According to the interviewee, the mutual constant feedback should not take place only at the time of disagreement, but should also become a constant feature of the relationship. By not hesitating to become vulnerable to each other, both parties manage to reduce perceptions of risk and uncertainty, which helps strengthen the degree of trust. What the client perceives to be the reality of the situation is often misunderstood by the consultants. Assumptions are made, consciously or unconsciously, that can lead to undesirable actions.

There'll be things I do that people love, and things that I do they think, 'oh God, I wish she didn't do that'. And you have to basically provide them with a forum to air those views. And once they air those views you have to commit to action, the ones you feel you can action, and change. Because one approach doesn't work for all. Now you'll have asked some of the questions along the time, maybe you didn't ask them in a way that they realized you were asking the question and at that point it challenges how do you turn it around and you can only get that from what they say, start feedback at that point and it might be: I hate the consultant, I can't work with her because I don't think she listens to me. Or it could be, she doesn't understand my business and then you would draw on the team. OK, I'll put somebody else in there.

Which is why I said to you, you know, when things go wrong and when things go well, why you have to get constant feedback from the client to make sure that you're all on the same track to ensure that the partnership works.

Now if you do that on a regular basis, you tend to either be able to mould the team, or, change the team, or, recognize it before it becomes an issue. But, as we both know, sometimes you don't get that feedback on the regular basis you should. Because you're in the project, you've got time restraints, you're running along, and then you know, they scream at the eleventh hour because: 'aagh, this isn't what I wanted, this isn't what I meant'.

The qualities of interpersonal interaction as confined within the transparency of communication and trust to air one's views without fear of being misunderstood needs to be part of the culture of the partnership. Although corporate values might not promote mutual openness in the manner expressed by the above interviewee, the success of a trusting relationship is situated in the way that such interpersonal dynamics are managed. Hence, these interpersonal cultural spheres that can promote qualities of integrity and benevolence become important building blocks for achieving trust.

The consultant's willingness to be challenged by the client is related to the personal cultural perception of the consultant as the 'knowledge provider' or expert. The consultant's personal culture is exemplified through the implicitly upheld notions of status and identity which also carry an inherent sense of credibility or correctness. The process of admitting that a suggested course of advice has not achieved the expected outcome is not only expensive for the client but also damaging for the consultant's reputation. However, the interpersonal nature of this relationship means that it is possible through mutual endeavour to create a culture of mutual vulnerability. Such vulnerability is possible when consultants and clients are able to express constructive criticism for each other's position.

What the clients and consultants really think of each other often remains hidden in the course of the interaction. However, the accumulation of feelings of resentment is likely to threaten the relationship unless they are made explicit and dealt with. According to the literature, trust becomes possible because of the positive expectations that one party is willing to uphold for the other (McKnight *et al.*, 1998). Creating an interpersonal culture in which actors are not hesitant to listen and adjust their positions against the criticism of the other party helps reinforce the accounts of positive expectations (Sheppard and Sherman, 1998). This is because both parties have a better mutual awareness about the motives, interests and way of thinking of the other party, with the result that it allows them to sense possible misalignments and avoid misinterpretations. Such behavioural cultural spheres promote the presence of integrity and benevolence in the relationship that in turn helps to foster the emergence of trustworthiness.

A strong theme that is reiterated in the interview, and which helps further support the above argument, centres on the term 'trusted advisor' (Maister *et al.*, 2002). The consultant argues that the point of becoming a trusted advisor to the client means that the interaction does not reside in the operational framework of the business assignment only. The trusted advisor is the individual against whom the client members are able to allow themselves to be vulnerable, that is, without feeling fear of being exploited by the consultants.

The process of becoming a trusted advisor does not seem to depend on a mere number of practices or 'unique' personal characteristics. To be a trusted advisor implies a state of communicative condition where the consultant has established clear interpersonal links that allow criticism and dialogue. To what extent such an objective can be achieved by the firm's consultants is not clear from the interview. Clearly, to become a trusted advisor is not dependent solely on the consulting party but also on the client. We do not conclude that an interpersonal trusting relationship can be achieved merely because of the consultants. What is clear, however, according to the HR manager, is that in the process of building mutual trust, the attention needs to shift from what the parent consulting firm represents at a corporate level, to the *individual* consultant on the project, and his/her relationship with the client:

> When something goes wrong on one of your projects, I mean it goes wrong on the project, it may cost your client money and it will cost you money because you probably won't bill for it in quite the same way. But if you are really that trusted advisor and in that partnership there is also self esteem that thinks: 'oh God, I did that so wrong'. And you beat yourself up, and you learn your lessons, and, if you are a true trusted advisor, you walk up to them and you say: 'you know, we got that wrong'. I've sat back and I've thought about it and I've beaten myself up about it and actually you know when I think about it on reflection, we should have done this that and the other. Tell me your way forward and we'll tell you ours. And often then you get quite a lot of synergy.

One of the functions the trusted advisor fulfils is by becoming more than just a conduit of information. The client's trust in the consultant provides an important social context of legitimation that has clear implications for why business advice might be accepted or rejected. In this sense, the client is able to accept a set of consulting recommendations without having clear knowledge of the outcome or implications of their implementation. Trust in the consultant provides a point of reference of meaning and experience that can be thought of as somehow conditioning the client's existing perceived uncertainty/risk. An interpersonal dynamic of trust is dependent on the underpinning assumptions and values of what makes the successful cooperation possible. Here the issue of perceived identity and exchange of power are dimensions that can influence how the individuals interpret their personal interaction with others. The above interviewee alludes to the consultant's willingness to admit that they do not have the answers or that they make mistakes.

To some extent, the consulting role has been idealized with features of 'accuracy', or 'solutions', creating an image of 'expertise' that is used to justify the charging of high fees (Clark, 1995; Fincham, 1999; Sturdy, 1997). In this context, the interviewee argues that such an image does not reflect the reality of a business assignment, and the effort to idealize such an image can produce a negative effect because by being reluctant to acknowledge mistakes or the limitations of their knowledge consultants may lose the client's trust, thereby jeopardizing the business relationship. According to the above reasoning, clients are keen on developing an interpersonal trusting relationship when consultants allow themselves to become vulnerable to the client.

This idea might seem contradictory to the image of expertise often projected by the parent consulting firms. Consultants seem to move into a state of transience between a) representing the corporate culture and identity of the firm, while at the same time, b) being able to respond to the client's specific expectations/needs. As we have seen, the psychodynamics of interpersonal trust are not just based on information and knowledge but also emerge from ability, integrity and benevolence (Mayer *et al.*, 1995). In our view, this is why the consultant supports 'constant feedback', so that she can know how the other person views and feels about the project.

## Conclusion

The aim of this chapter has been to examine how inter-organizational and interpersonal trust is produced, maintained or threatened between management consultants and clients. We examined trust through the lens of multiple cultural 'spheres', or 'tiles'. The alignment or misalignment of cultural spheres can help foster or hinder the development of inter-organizational or interpersonal trust because trust is developed from the way risk and uncertainty are managed in the consultant–client relationship.

At the inter-organizational level we argue that culture is demonstrated through the types of formal structures and strategic action plans with which consultants manage their intervention in the client firm. An alignment of culture is about sharing areas of agreement about how the service needs to be deployed. This is represented in formal decision making and reporting but also in informal discussions. We find that consultants find themselves in a state of flux between: a) having to uphold the culture of the parent firm, while at the same time, b) having to meet the different client needs and c) their own values. Deviating from the culture and corporate values of the parent firm can cause the consultant some degree of internal struggle when they are expected to meet expectations in a way that goes against their personal values.

Consultants can lose the clients' trust when they are not perceived to be committed to fulfilling the clients' interests. We argue that the corporate cultural sphere provides an important source of knowledge from which both parties draw information and experience about the other party in order to manage their sense of risk and uncertainty in the relationship.

At the interpersonal level, we argue that trust is managed through traits of culture as represented in behavioural qualities that match the client's anticipation/emotions. In contrast to inter-organizational trust, which can be seen as calculative and rational, personal trust is dependent on the features of ability, benevolence and integrity (Mayer *et al.*, 1995). The consultant's commitment to be caring towards the client is not necessarily confined within the boundaries of the business assignment. However, the consultant's frequent unwillingness to compromise their connection with clients can indicate a personal sense of commitment into the relationship.

Our study raises questions about the degree to which consultants and clients create some form of hybrid culture that is similar to or distinct from their corporate or personal cultural spheres. On the one hand it is clear that consultants and clients are both restricted by their corporate as well as personal cultural spheres in terms of making decisions that contradict the values represented in them. On the other hand, our study also indicates how both parties often seek to develop accounts of shared meaning and agreement by stretching the interpretation of what their corporate and personal values stand for. For example, consultants realize that manipulating a client's understanding in order to sell more consulting work could jeopardize the business relationship. Hence, the individual's role and influence in shaping the dynamic of an assignment may be driven by corporate objectives but also by personal values that often can be in tension with each other. It is difficult to identify how a hybrid culture is generated between the two parties because of the complex structure and fluidity with which values, aspirations and corporate demands are simulated and channelled within the consultant–client interaction to sustain the business relationship.

## References

Auerbach, C. F. and Silverstein, L. B. 2003. *Qualitative Data: an Introduction to Coding and Analysis*. London: New York University Press.

Berglund, J. and Werr, A. 2000. 'The invincible character of management consulting rhetoric: how one blends incommensurates while keeping them apart'. *Organization*, 7(4), 635–55.

Bhattacharya, R., Devinney, T. M. and Pillutla, M. M. 1998. 'A formal model of trust based on outcomes'. *The Academy of Management Review*, 23(3), 459–72.

Bigley, G. A. and Pearce, J. L. 1998. 'Straining for shared meaning in organization science: problems of trust and distrust'. *The Academy of Management Review*, 23(3), 405–21.

Boyatzis, R. 1998. *Transforming Qualitative Information: Thematic Analysis and Code Development*. London: Sage.

Chao, G. T. and Moon, H. 2005. 'The cultural mosaic: a metatheory for understanding the complexity of culture'. *Journal of Applied Psychology*, 90(6), 1128–40.

Clark, T. 1995. *Managing Consultants. Consultancy as the Management of Impressions*. Buckingham: Open University Press.

Czerniawska, F. 1999. *Management Consultancy in the 21st Century*. London: Macmillan Business.

2002. *Management Consultancy: What Next?*. Basingstoke: Palgrave.

Das, T. K. and Teng, B. S. 1998. 'Between trust and control: developing confidence in partner cooperation in alliances'. *The Academy of Management Review*, 23(3), 491–512.

Doney, P. M. and Cannon, J. P. 1997. 'An examination of the nature of trust in buyer–seller relationships'. *Journal of Marketing*, 61(2), 35–51.

Fincham, R. 1999. 'The consultant–client relationship: critical perspectives on the management of organizational change'. *Journal of Management Studies*, 36(3), 335–51.

Gambetta, D. 1988. *Trust: Making and Breaking Cooperative Relations*. New York: Basil Blackwell.

Glücker, J. and Armbrüster, T. 2003. 'Bridging uncertainty in management consulting: the mechanisms of trust and networked reputation'. *Organization Studies*, 24(2), 269–97.

Hatch, M. J. 1993. 'The dynamics of organizational culture'. *The Academy of Management Review*, 18(4), 657–93.

Kieser, A. 1997. 'Rhetoric and myth in management fashion'. *Organization*, 4(1), 49–74.

Lowendahl B. R. 2005. *Strategic Management of Professional Service Firms*. Copenhagen: Copenhagen Business School Press.

Maister, H. D. 1993. *Managing the Professional Service Firm*. New York: Free Press.

1997. *True Professionalism – The Courage to Care about Your People, Your Clients, and Your Career*. New York: Simon & Schuster.

Maister, H. D., Galford, R. and Green, C. 2002. *The Trusted Advisor*. London: Simon & Schuster.

Mayer, R. C., Davis, J. H. and Schoorman, F. D. 1995. 'An integrative model of organizational trust'. *Academy of Management Review*, 20(3), 709–34.

McKnight, D. H., Cummings, L. L. and Chervany, N. L. 1998. 'Initial trust formation in new organizational relationships'. *Academy of Management Review*, 23(3), 473–90.

Miles, M. B. and Huberman, A. M. 1994. *Qualitative Data Analysis: An Expanded Sourcebook*, 2nd edn. Thousand Oaks, CA: Sage.

Molinsky, A. 2007. 'Cross-cultural code-switching: the psychological challenges of adapting behaviour in foreign cultural interactions'. *Academy of Management Review*, 32(2), 622–40.

Nachum, L. 1999. 'Measurement of productivity of professional services: an illustration on Swedish management consulting firms'. *International Journal of Operations & Production Management*, 19(9), 922–49.

Ring, P. S. and Van de Ven, A. 1992. 'Structuring cooperative relations between organizations'. *Strategic Management Journal*, 13, 483–98.

Roberts, J. 2003. 'Trust and electronic knowledge transfer'. *International Journal of Electronic Business*, 1(2), 168–86.

Salaman, G. 2002. 'Understanding advice: towards as sociology of management consultancy'. In T. Clark and R. Fincham (eds.) *Critical Consulting*. Oxford: Blackwell, 247–60.

Schein, E. 2004. *Organizational Culture and Leadership*, 3rd edn. San Francisco: John Wiley & Sons.

Schneider, S. C. and Barsoux, J.-L. 2003. *Managing Across Cultures*. London: Prentice-Hall.

Sheppard, B. H. and Sherman, D. M. 1998. 'The grammars of trust: a model and general implications'. *The Academy of Management Review*, 23(3), 422–37.

Silverman, D. (ed.) 2000. *Doing Qualitative Research: A Practical Handbook*. London: Sage.

Smircich, L. 1983. 'Concepts of culture and organizational analysis'. *Administrative Science Quarterly*, 28(3), 339–58.

Sturdy, A. J. 1997. 'The consultancy process – an insecure business?' *Journal of Management Studies*, 34(3), 389–413.

Sturdy, A. J., Clark, T., Fincham, R. and Handley, K. 2009. *Management Consultancy in Action – Relationships, Knowledge and Power*. Oxford University Press.

Weick, K. E. 1993. 'The collapse of sensemaking in organizations: the Mann Gulch Disaster'. *Administrative Science Quarterly*, 38, 628–52.

Whitener, E. M., Brodt, S. E., Korsgaard, M. A. and Werner, J. M. 1998. 'Managers as initiators of trust: an exchange relationship framework for understanding managerial trustworthy behavior'. *The Academy of Management Review*, 23(3), 513–30.

Williamson, O. E. 1985. *The Economic Institutions of Capitalism*. New York: Free Press.

Zucker, L. G. 1986. 'Production of trust: institutional sources of economic structure, 1840–1920'. In B. M. Staw and L. L. Cummings (eds.) *Research in Organizational Behavior*. Greenwich, CT: JAI Press, 8, 53–111.

# 6 | Checking, not trusting: trust, distrust and cultural experience in the auditing profession

MARK R. DIBBEN AND JACOB M. ROSE

Corporate culture [is] one of those ink-blots in which we see what we want to see.

Charles Hampden-Turner, 1990: 11

## Summary

This chapter explores the interaction of trust and distrust with the associative cultural tiles of organizational and professional values, operating within individual auditors in accounting firms. Building on recent research into trust and culture in healthcare management, the authors consider the way in which this particular professional context (i.e. cultural sphere) affects trust, and at how trust and distrust can exist co-terminously in the same auditor. The chapter shows how an auditor's trust and distrust in their clients affects their professional judgments and decisions, and how sound auditing judgments may run counter to the accounting firm's needs. Findings include the revelation that less effective, highly trusting auditors tend to stay within the profession but more effective, less trusting auditors leave.

## Introduction

Although there is an extensive literature in management studies examining organizational cultures and their influence on firm performance (e.g. Barney, 1986; Pheysey, 1993; Sackman, 1997), little is written in the accounting literature about the role of culture in accounting practice. To this end, a very recent synthesis in *Behavioural Research in Accounting* (Jenkins *et al.*, 2008) of accounting-firm culture and governance concludes that there is a 'paucity' of research in all areas of accounting culture (2008: 49). Such a relative lack of interest in the accounting literature is in spite of the fact that accounting regulators themselves view sound organizational culture as critical to protecting the public good (PCAOB, 2004), because it helps prevent intentionally fraudulent misstatement. In this chapter, we make a step towards

156

answering Jenkins *et al.*'s call for more research. In particular, we focus on their call for greater understanding of the role of ethics and its impact on individual auditor behaviour, in the context of conflicts between individual and organizational goals as a function of the goals of differing subcultures within audit firms.

To do this, and in addition to the novel accountancy setting, we explicitly adopt an interdisciplinary approach that not only adopts an understanding of confidence as something quite different from trust itself, but also brings to bear upon the topic recent research in healthcare management that has explicitly made the link between trust and professional and organizational culture. This approach provides an alternative insight into the workings of trust, distrust and cultural experience in organizations.

In particular, we consider the extent, prevalence and effect of distrust as a corporate reality. We ask whether trust should be seen as a constructive or destructive factor in auditing culture and consider whether, and to what extent, the concept of distrust may be an even more helpful construct for understanding auditing decisions and intra-firm subcultures than that of trust. We begin the chapter with an examination of cultural spheres as these might apply in the auditing profession.

## Cultural spheres within audit firms

An organization's culture inherently involves both an organization's identity and stakeholder perceptions of the organization (Barney and Hansen, 1994; Hatch, 1993; Hatch and Schultz, 2004). Jenkins *et al.* (2008:69) argue that the concept of organizational identity is particularly relevant to accounting firms, where culture has been closely guarded by the accounting profession as 'unique and proprietary, the very essence of the firm'. Each firm has a particular, largely unchanging and thoroughly entrenched cultural corner-stone that is difficult to directly measure for the purpose of empirical research. Many argue that recent and widespread monitoring failures are the result of accounting firms' entrenched organizational identities that promote cultures of greed and profitability, rather than cultures of professional service and protection of the public good (see e.g. Wyatt, 2004).

In this regard, therefore, the accounting firm may be said to exhibit a number of cultural spheres/tiles, manifest in a tension experienced by individual auditors who are beholden both to organizational imperatives and professional codes of conduct, and yet at the same time are required to respond to the client's requirements as well. The auditor's cultural mosaic therefore appears to be dominated by the associative tiles (Chao and Moon,

2005) of profession, employer and avocation, since the auditor works for Company A and is auditing Company B, but is beholden – in theory – to profession C's norms, values and practices.

The cultural conflict that arises from this inherent tension, where entrenched accounting organizational identities and governance mechanisms have ultimately been seen, for example in ENRON, to overcome inherent professional values (Jenkins et al., 2008; Wyatt, 2004), is indicative of a possible need for cultural change to avoid future accounting reporting failures. This leads us to ask the question, is cultural change possible in such circumstances? While a substantive body of research into change resistance has yet to emerge in accounting, recent analyses of healthcare institutions, such as the National Health Service in the United Kingdom, reveal professional culture to be one cause of change resistance.

Healthcare research has sought explicitly to explore the reasons for the lack of change in healthcare institutions, in terms of 'entrenched organizational culture' (Davies et al., 2000; Hyde and Davies, 2005; Mannion et al., 2005; Marshall et al., 2003). Here, the lack of change is explained by the argument that considerable structural reform has had little effect on health service realities and performance because the beliefs, values, attitudes and norms of behaviour of the professionals working in the organizations remain the same (Davies, 2002a; 2002b). The cultural context, in turn, influences the trust that exists in colleagues for others based upon shared professional understanding (Dibben, 2000; Dibben and Davies, 2004). Rather than an organizational attribute, therefore, the cultural sphere exists as a result of the historical interaction of individuals (Chao and Moon, 2005: 1132–35; Hampden-Turner, 1990: 12–14). An organizational culture is an attempt to describe something of the dynamic and unstable processes and multiple perspectives that make up the 'life-worlds' (Schutz and Luckmann, 1974) of individuals going about their daily work. In this sense, the idea of one culture shared across an organization as an attribute of it may be somewhat simplistic (Scott et al., 2003a; 2003b).

With this understanding, we can now re-examine the inherent tension observed in the cultural sphere of financial auditing. As a group of individuals within an organization having a professional association – a distinctiveness network (Chao and Moon, 2005: 1136) – the subcultural sphere of auditors within an accounting firm is shaped by competing pressures to maintain healthy relationships with clients on the one hand (i.e. auditors need to acquire and retain clients in order to earn profits), and pressures to enforce regulations and reporting standards on the other hand (e.g. Bazerman et al., 2002; Cohen and Trompeter, 1998; Hooks et al., 1994).

Auditors are required to remain completely independent of their clients (e.g. AICPA, 2005a) and are thereby entrusted to evaluate evidence with objectivity. However, they also desire to avoid loss of revenues resulting from disagreements with clients, and they have profit motives (see Farmer *et al.*, 1987; Schuetze, 1994; Wyatt, 2004).

Prior empirical research indicates that auditors' judgments and decisions are indeed influenced by their relationships with clients. For example, auditors are willing to accept more aggressive reporting practices from their existing clients than they are willing to accept from new clients (Cohen and Trompeter, 1998); client-retention concerns promote auditor acceptance of more liberal interpretations of accounting standards (Hackenbrack and Nelson, 1996); and auditors who identify more with their clients are more likely to accept their clients' aggressive reporting choices than auditors who identify less with their clients (Bamber and Iyer, 2007).

There is clear evidence that building close relationships with clients can threaten auditor independence and the effectiveness of monitoring systems designed to promote accurate and reliable financial reporting. However, auditors must grow their businesses to remain profitable, and cooperation with client management is essential to acquiring the information needed to complete the audit process. Further, professional standards explicitly require that auditors become familiar with their clients so that they can understand the business and appropriately plan the audit (AICPA, 2005b). Thus, current auditing culture favours trust between auditors and clients, but this trust may erode the reliability of financial reports. In this culture requiring trust, there also appears to be a potential for acculturation (Kelman, 1972) and selection biases, where trusting individuals thrive and internalize the corporate culture, but sceptical individuals have difficulties complying with the values of their peers and may struggle to succeed in career terms against the standards set by their employer.

## Reconciling trust with competing cultural norms in accounting practice

Previous research (Rose, 2007; Rose and Rose, 2003) has examined the effects of contextually induced scepticism and dispositional trust on practising auditors' attention to aggressive financial reporting practices and assessments of financial fraud during the audit process.

Rose (2007) employed Wrightsman's (1974; 1991; also 1964) trust scale to measure dispositional trust in an experimental analysis using 125 practising auditors.[1] He found that auditors who are less trusting of others attend more to evidence of aggressive reporting than do more trusting auditors, and higher levels of induced scepticism also increase attention to aggressive and potentially fraudulent reporting. Further, auditors who pay more attention to evidence of aggressive reporting are more likely to believe that intentional misstatement has occurred. Finally, dispositional trust explained more of the variation in auditor judgments than did induced scepticism or even prior auditing experience.

The implications of this study for our understanding of the role and effect of trust in the auditing process and any decision context involving assurance are manifold. Far from being merely an experimental control mechanism, a simple psychological trust scale was more predictive of auditor judgment than either the decision context or prior experiences (Rose, 2007; Rose and Rose, 2007; Rose *et al.*, 2010). These results suggest that a deeper understanding of trust within the cultural sphere (Schneider and Barsoux, 1997) of the auditing profession is essential to unpacking the decision processes associated with the detection and prevention of corporate fraud and the promotion of financial reporting reliability.

Furthermore, within the cultural context of auditing and assurance firms, ongoing investigations by the authors (Rose and Rose, 2007; Rose *et al.*, 2010) indicate that auditors' dispositional trust levels, as measured by Wrightsman's scale, differ according to their position in the profession. In order to overcome many of the validity threats associated with employing mail or Internet-based methods of collecting questionnaire data, the Wrightsman (1974; 1991) trust questionnaire was provided to 216 practising auditors at Big 4 firms in the south-western United States directly and under controlled conditions during national training sessions or one-on-one sessions at their offices. The Wrightsman questionnaire consists of fourteen statements concerning honesty and trust, and participants indicate their agreement with each statement on a six-point Likert scale. The trust score produced by the questionnaire is the sum of the fourteen questions, where the trusting end of the scale for each question is scored as 3 and the non-trusting end is scored as -3 (Wrightsman, 1991). The score can range from -42 to +42, where lower scores represent lower levels of trust. The Cronbach alpha for the trust scale in the study was 0.724, which is consistent with the Cronbach

---

[1] The Wrightsman scale is a well-established control instrument in behavioural research, and is taken to indicate the dispositional trust of the respondent as a function of the judgment she instinctively makes regarding other people's trustworthiness, i.e. their expected behaviours or intentions.

alpha (0.78) obtained during large sample validation of the trust instrument (Wrightsman, 1974).

The average trust scores for newly appointed seniors (2.96) and also new staff (-1.58) are consistent with Wrightsman's (1974) own findings for the general population (1.45). Wrightsman (1974) and subsequent studies of dispositional trust have found that individuals vary widely in their levels of dispositional trust, and average trust levels for the general population tend towards the mid-point of the scale. That is, there is no general propensity in the population to be trusting or not trusting. We find that less experienced auditors also exhibit widely varying trust scores on both the trusting and non-trusting ends of the scale (much like the general population). In contrast, however, trust scores for partners (11.09) and managers (6.27) were significantly higher, and very few partners or managers possess trust levels on the not-trusting (i.e. below zero) end of the scale. In short, those auditors who choose to remain in the profession and are successful in advancing through the ranks are more trusting than auditors who leave the profession or fail to move into higher levels of the profession's hierarchy (Rose and Rose, 2007; Rose *et al.*, 2010). This situation may represent a significant threat to the integrity of the assurance systems designed to monitor the accuracy of financial reporting and provide reliable information to stakeholders in the capital markets. Experimental and survey evidence indicates that those in charge of preventing and detecting irregularities in financial reporting are highly trusting; assurance providers who are less trusting leave the profession or fail to achieve status in the profession; more trusting assurance providers are poor detectors of financial fraud and aggressive financial reporting practices (Rose, 2007; Rose and Rose, 2003; Rose *et al.*, 2010). Taken together, these findings indicate that those who are truly in charge of the assurance process are not naturally disposed to detecting and preventing fraud and other irregularities.

Related research further finds that those with ultimate responsibility for overseeing financial reporting processing and monitoring the effectiveness of auditors and other assurance mechanisms (i.e. audit committees of boards of directors) perpetuate the problems associated with the need for trust in auditor–client relationships. Directors are, on average, very trusting individuals (mean trust score = 14.78), and their high levels of trust make them extremely susceptible to management attempts to deceive them during the financial reporting process (Rose and Rose, 2007). Thus, a disturbing pattern emerges. Auditors who are highly trusting advance to high ranks in assurance firms because of their effectiveness in acquiring and maintaining clients. Yet, these auditors seem to be inherently poor at detecting and preventing fraudulent financial reporting. This indicates that the auditor-as-employee's organizational sphere of the cultural mosaic is dominant over the auditor's professional sphere.

To explore this further in terms of the interaction between trust and organizational cultural imperatives, corporate directors who oversee the financial reporting process operate in a culture where the development of high levels of interpersonal trust with key strategic actors at the top of one's own firm and among client firms is necessary to acquire and retain director-ships. As directors, these inherently highly trusting individuals are more likely to accept management explanations for financial reporting choices, even when explanations are designed to deceive board members and perpetuate financial reporting practices intended to overstate financial performance (Rose and Rose, 2007). From this chain of effects, we can see that the importance of trust in the upper echelons of business operates against effec-tive monitoring of financial reporting at all levels. Regulators recommend that audit partners reward their staff for exhibiting professional scepticism (POB, 2000), that is, they argue that firms should encourage the dominance of the professional sphere. However, in practice, the organizational culture of audit firms ultimately punishes those who are sceptical.

In the remainder of this chapter we consider the issue of professional scepticism and the effect of trust and distrust on the behaviour of individual auditors operating in the culturally complex environment of accounting firms. We do this, in the absence of a substantive literature on trust and culture in accounting, by returning to the healthcare management literature and, within this, we examine analyses of the rationale for and impact of performance measurement on trust. The literature suggests that the drive for explicit accountability in healthcare scenarios has superseded a profes-sional culture of trust to the detriment of the individual patient. We adopt the established argument in healthcare management that accountability systems are designed to allow managers to be confident in (as opposed to merely 'trusting of') the performance of practitioners[2] and that these systems erode the interpersonal trust required for effective (as opposed to efficient) health-care. We apply this argument to the case of auditing to explore the effects of trust and distrust on individual auditor behaviour, and finally link this back to the notion of tensions within the cultural mosaic.

---

[2] In essence, managers and their political masters need to be able to state publicly that they have confidence in the performance of their hospital. After numerous worrisome failures, such as one NHS hospital's retention without parental consent of a deceased child's body parts, managers and politicians can no longer simply trust that all is well and that the profession is maintaining standards. Rather, they need to be confident of it; there needs to be explicit and demonstrable evidence of performance.

## The 'confidence' problem

The complexity of the accounting cultural sphere, coupled with the risk-laden nature of audit decisions in practice, has led us to re-evaluate our understanding of trust as manifest in human interaction. While at the heart of much research, the nature and role of confidence as a key component of trust (often associated with Lewicki and Bunker, 1996; Luhmann, 1990), in terms of an association with willingness to confide in another, or have a positive belief about another party, has recently been implicitly called into question through a quite different interpretation of the concept. This reinterpretation brings with it an understanding of the statement of risk as a confidence interval within a bell-curve normal distribution, and is derived from the need to achieve clinical governance and public sector accountability. In brief, it suggests that the search for confidence is indicative of – at best – insufficient trust in the other party (Smith, 2001). More likely, it is indicative of the need to check rather than trust, i.e. explicitly and critically compare the performance of others for accountability purposes (Davies and Mannion, 1999) instead of taking their word for it; this seems more akin to distrust.

We understand that this represents a different interpretation of confidence than that presented by Lewicki and Bunker (1996), for example, who view confidence as a strength threshold for different types of trust (e.g. knowledge-based as opposed to calculus-based), and thus see confidence as synonymous with trust. Nevertheless, we can discern three main interpretations of confidence in the trust literature. First, confidence as concerning a trust of another party sufficient to be willing to confide in that party (e.g. Lewicki *et al.*, 1998). Second, confidence as being confident in one's own decision to place trust (or distrust) in another (e.g. Boon and Holmes, 1991). Third, confidence as self-assuredness to the extent of acting without consideration for risk (Luhmann, 1990).[3] These various approaches to the notion of confidence lead us to question whether there may be some new means by which to clarify the distinction between trust and confidence.

One contentious, but potentially helpful, way of understanding the difference has been proposed by Carole Smith (2001) as a result of studying social work and the public sector accountability of such activity. Research in public policy and management has revealed the need to comprehend better how trust sustains well-functioning organizations, especially those agencies in the

---

[3] A fourth has been noted by Dibben (2000), who suggests confidence in oneself as an agent, based on one's own assessment of one's own competence, as a conceptual proxy for self-trust.

public sector that lack market discipline (Cvetkovich and Lofstedt, 1999; Davies, 1999; Waren, 1999; Waterhouse and Bellof, 1999). The effect of public trust comes to the fore in such circumstances because it has influenced the nature and extent of the accountability systems put in place (e.g. Davies and Lampell, 1998; Mechanic, 1996). Such accountability systems are intended to provide appropriate reassurance to the public through the establishment of institutional trust (Anheier and Kendall, 2002; Zucker, 1986; also Lynch *et al.*, 2007) and enable effective corrective action to be taken by regulators to ensure public safety. These accountability systems, however, rely largely on explicit measurement of individual performance and organizational outcomes to establish a degree of confidence, i.e. within professionally understood and accepted limits, that they can be proven to be an accurate account of the organization and the work of its employees.

The establishment of confidence through explicit and often numeric measurement of performance is intended to ameliorate the effects of personal judgment based on one's trust of another. This downplays the moral component of decision making, based solely on the trust of another person, through so-called 'evidence-based' decision making (Davies and Nutley, 2000). This, in turn, places the focus on the probability of an outcome (as opposed to explicit guarantees about the certainty of an outcome) based upon objective performance measures, such that management can be 'confident in' (as opposed to merely trusting) the performance of the departments and individuals they are responsible for. In this sense, according to Carole Smith (2001), interpersonal trust is largely removed from confidence-building accountability systems in practice, which are more akin to institutionally based trust reliant on professional certification and legal systems (Zucker, 1986 in Anheier and Kendall, 2002: 350–1; also Lynch *et al.*, 2007). However, we distinguish between institutional-based trust and confidence-building systems since they are not imposed by institutions governing the sector. Rather they are put in place by hospital managers at the behest of politicians to provide empirical data in support of their hospital's activities, to evidence performance in an era of a lack of trust in the medical profession.

Such intense focus on performance measurement, however, coupled with a range of potential indictments for any failure to meet organizational objectives has, Smith (2001; also O'Neill, 2002) argues, eroded the interpersonal trust between employees and managers necessary for effective professional relationships. This is particularly true when the monitoring is seen by the professional culture as intrusive and interfering, countering the profession's view of its purpose (Chao and Moon, 2005). In this sense, the drive for public accountability through the establishment of explicit quantitative measures of performance standards (i.e. the drive for the establishment of public confidence) is in direct conflict with interpersonal trust (Dibben and Davies, 2004). This is certainly the case in healthcare; a doctor becomes a doctor because she wants to make people well, not because she wants to constrain access to healthcare on the basis of potential costs incurred to her department for the treatment. Yet, the requirement for performance measures leading to management being able to declare public confidence in the department's performance, regardless of whatever trust may or may not exist between the individuals, has the tendency to shift the focus away from culturally shared professional values of quality towards managerial estimates of quality through the measurement of quantity and efficiency.

We have also seen this conflict in our investigations of the role of trust in auditing firms, where the trusting nature of auditors and boards of directors creates norms and values that facilitate business activities and transactions but is at odds with mechanisms designed to measure and monitor performance accurately. Thus, efforts to create public confidence through strict enforcement of standards can fall flat when the mechanisms designed to promote confidence in financial reports must work against practitioner subcultures in the firm, subcultures that favour strong interpersonal trust between the members.

## Checking, not trusting

We suggest Huw Davies' arguments (1999; 2002a; 2002b; Davies and Lampell, 1998; Davies and Mannion, 1999, Davies *et al.*, 2000; Dibben and Davies, 2004) about cultural change in healthcare being impeded by the contradiction inherent in 'checking not trusting' (i.e. the interpersonal need for trust being countermanded by the organizational need for explicit accountability) hold true in auditing also. To unpack this problematic, we build on Smith (2001) to draw a stark conceptual distinction between what is involved in 'trusting' and what is involved in 'checking'. We use these phrases in order to circumvent the somewhat semantic problem rehearsed above, concerning just exactly what is meant and not meant by the word 'confidence' as opposed to the word 'trust'.

Trusting concerns uncertainty about outcomes, an ambiguity of objective information and the exercise of discretion about action. It is also an internal attribution, a moral exercise of free will that assumes most significance in situations where there is a lack of regulation or means of coercion. Checking, on the other hand, concerns the establishment of explicitly predictable outcomes, the availability of objective and standardized information, and little opportunity or even need to exercise discretion about action. Systemic checking is therefore seen as an external objective act that assumes most significance in situations where there are extensive regulatory mechanisms and/or opportunities for coercion of individuals. In sum, according to Carole Smith (2001), the institutional or managerial drive for accountability through perpetual checking mechanisms is indicative of a lack of trust, perhaps even genuine distrust. Further, such checking may in fact have a tendency to instil distrust among professional colleagues, as a result of the increased sense of scrutiny and critical peer comparison (O'Neill, 2002).

When seen from the perspective of the relationship between trust and control (Costa and Bijlsma-Frankema, 2007; Poppo and Zenger, 2002), Smith's trust–confidence distinction as outlined above favours the substitution thesis in respect of individual practitioners. This is because the presence of control mechanisms manifest in the checking activity erodes interpersonal trust, which cannot be present if one imposes controls, and indeed renders it superfluous as the controls obviate any risk (Schoorman *et al.*, 2007). However, when seen from the perspective of public trust in healthcare or accounting systems, the explicit controls evident in the checking are a source of trust; the public may trust the profession precisely because of the existence of controls. We suggest, however, that the 'public-trust-in-the-profession as a result of controls-within-the-firm complementarity' is ironically a result of a lack of trust within the firms for the professionals that work within them and consequently a perceived need within the firms for explicit control mechanisms. In this sense, we see controls as a substitute for trust; they are the means by which checking occurs in place of trust.

From the perspective of auditing and assurance providers, Smith's (2001) distinction suggests that the act of checking involves distrust, rather than trust. Regulation of accounting disclosure results from a need for standardized, objective, and measurable financial information that is materially free from management biases to present information that paints their decisions in a favourable light. The financial reporting process is heavily regulated, yet there are myriad incentives for managers (as well as auditors and directors) to misbehave and succumb to external pressures and coercion, and auditors have valid reasons to distrust their clients. As such, the auditing environment represents a culture where trust and distrust are likely to operate together (Lewicki *et al.*, 1998), and we posit that the level of distrust present in the auditing environment may serve to mitigate some of the threats posed by high levels of trust amongst auditors, managers and directors.

## Trust and distrust in accounting

Substantial evidence indicates the existence of threats to the effective monitoring of financial reporting posed by trust and auditors' incentives to maintain trusting relationships with clients (e.g. Bazerman *et al.*, 2002; Cohen and Trompeter, 1998; Farmer *et al.*, 1987; Hooks, *et al.*, 1994; Rose, 2007; Rose and Rose, 2003; Schuetze, 1994). Yet, existing empirical evidence for the influence of trust on financial statement assurance processes is based entirely on manipulations of situational trust and measures of dispositional trust using the Wrightsman scale, thereby viewing human exchange as a broadly positive experience. That is, in Lewicki *et al.*'s (1998) terms, an experience characterized by hope, faith, confidence, assurance and initiative in all circumstances. Furthermore, there is an implicit assumption that a low score is indicative of distrust (i.e. low trust and distrust are corollaries).

Rather than being indicative of trust, however, interactions between individuals in auditing culture may be more suggestive of what Lewicki *et al.* (1998) have characterized as distrust – fear, scepticism, cynicism, wariness and watchfulness, and vigilance (and such a perspective also aligns with Smith's (2001) description of confidence that we have expressed as an act of checking). Such distrust, they argue, is best considered as a disposition to be contrasted with trust, and indeed may be one that can work in concert with trust. Thus, rather than merely being the low-end of the trust scale, distrust can be considered a separate dimension of the human-exchange experience. In this way, they suggest that alternative social realities combining trusting and distrusting dispositions may operate in organizational scenarios: High Trust–Low Distrust (characterized by high value congruence, the promotion of interdependence, the pursuit of opportunities and the development of new initiatives); High Trust–High Distrust (characterized by a tendency to trust but verify, relationships that are highly segmented and bounded, and the continual monitoring of downside risks and vulnerabilities); Low Trust–Low Distrust (characterized by casual acquaintances, limited interdependence, bounded and arms-length transactions and professional courtesies); and Low Trust–High Distrust (characterized by the expectation and fear of undesired eventualities, an assumption of harmful motives, close management of interdependence, pre-emption as an active strategy where 'the best offence is good defence' and paranoia).

An indication of an active distrust (i.e. a negative expectation concerning the behaviour of another party with respect to oneself in a situation entailing risk to oneself) would provide further credence for the increasing reliance both in the private and public sector on evidence-based policy (Nutley and

Webb, 2000). That is, active distrust suggests the need for development of checking systems, as opposed to trusting-reliant systems. These checking systems seek to 'explicitly and critically compare the performance of others rather than take their word for it' (Marsh and Dibben, 2005: 28).

The importance of such a rendering of trust and distrust as coexisting to our understanding of auditing may lie in the practical importance of building and maintaining trust relationships with clients (as well as other senior auditors and partners), while at the same time treating with suspicion at least some of the financial information they provide. Indeed, one might argue that such distrust is manifest in the professional scepticism that is a requisite of auditing (e.g. AICPA, 2002 Statement on Auditing Standards No. 99). However, an alternative reading would posit that engaging in diligent checking may be seen as that party's trustworthiness, i.e. their ability to audit correctly, their benevolence towards investors and employees and their integrity in the production of true and accurate accounting reports. Thus, depending on one's perspective, trust and distrust may be seen in the same scenario.

Nevertheless, Lewicki *et al.* argue that dysfunction in relationships arises not from distrust, but rather from trust without distrust and from distrust without trust. It is the 'dynamic tension' between trust and distrust that allows relationships between actors to be productive, in the best interests of both confiding parties and as a source of long-lasting stability for relationships (Lewicki *et al.*, 1998: 450). The current focus in accounting research on trust alone has ignored this tension. However, such dynamic tension may be prominent in auditor–client relations, where the auditor's faith in a client's financial literacy, competence and honesty are replaced – often after trust violation – with what has been termed in medical contexts as a relationship of 'guarded alliance' (Mechanic, 1996; Mechanic and Meyer, 2000). This is one in which the auditor recognizes the limitations of the client but works with them to both maintain the relationship and manage a successful audit. From the perspective of the auditor's cultural mosaic, we recognize this process as a compromise, one in which the organizational cultural demands may supersede the auditor's professional cultural values; the impact of such compromises, and of feeling compromised, is an issue we shall return to later in the chapter.

### New research into the effects of trust and distrust on auditor judgments

New research by the authors has taken some of the first steps towards understanding the differential effects of trust and distrust on auditing judgments.

Based upon the results of an experiment with 126 professionals, findings indicate that distrust can be measured with an inverse of the Wrightsman trust scale and that trust and distrust have distinct and predictable effects on assessments of financial statement fraud risk. That is, trust and distrust are not merely opposite ends of the trust scale, but they are indeed discrete constructs.

Participants first read background information about a hypothetical firm and then reviewed a list of fraud cues associated with that firm's financial reporting. In line with previous research (Rose, 2007; Rose and Rose, 2003; Wilks and Zimbelman, 2004) participants in the experiment were randomly given one of two pre-validated texts containing fraud cues about a hypothetical company, one with six fraud cues (classified as low fraud risk), the other with thirteen (classified as high fraud risk). Participants assessed the risk of financial fraud for this realistic case scenario using the following Likert scale: *What is the overall risk of financial statement fraud?* (where 0 = Low Risk, 5 = Moderate Risk and 10 = High Risk). Half of the participants analysed the low-risk case (i.e. fewer fraud cues), and half of the participants analysed the high-risk case (i.e. more fraud cues). Based upon extensive evaluations of these decision cases by fraud risk assessment experts, the risk of financial fraud should be assessed at a low level in the low-risk case and at a high level in the high-risk case. Such assessments of fraud risk are critical to the audit process as they can influence the nature and extent of audit tests throughout the audit. As a result, assessments of fraud risk have major implications for audit effectiveness and efficiency. Understated risk assessments result in under-auditing and increase the likelihood that fraud will not be detected. Overstated risk assessments result in over-auditing and increased costs.

After reviewing the fraud cues, participants assessed the level of fraud risk. Following the risk assessment, all participants completed either the Wrightsman (1974) measure of trust, or a scale derived from the Wrightsman questionnaire that was designed to measure distrust.

The distrust questionnaire was designed to be the inverse of the Wrightsman questionnaire. Study of the Wrightsman questions reveal that they each signify one or a number of Lewicki *et al.*'s (1998) characteristics of trust (i.e. hope, faith, confidence, assurance and initiative). In writing the distrust scale, attention was paid to retaining the underlying topic of each question, while at the same time introducing Lewicki *et al.*'s characteristics for distrust (i.e. one or a number of fear, scepticism, cynicism, wariness and watchfulness). Thus, the Wrightsman questionnaire and our distrust questionnaire each consist of fourteen statements, and participants indicate their agreement with each statement on a six-point Likert scale. The trust score and

Table 6.1 *Assessments of risk by risk level and trust*

| Risk Level | Trust | N | Mean | S.D. |
|------------|-------|-----|------|------|
| Low | Low | 16 | 5.13 | 1.41 |
| | High | 15 | 4.53 | 0.99 |
| | Total | 31 | 4.84 | 1.24 |
| High | Low | 19 | 6.58 | 1.07 |
| | High | 12 | 5.50 | 1.09 |
| | Total | 31 | 6.16 | 1.19 |
| Total | Low | 35 | 5.91 | 1.42 |
| | High | 27 | 4.96 | 1.13 |
| | Total | 62 | 5.50 | 1.38 |

Table 6.2 *Assessments of risk by risk level and distrust*

| Risk Level | Distrust | N | Mean | S.D. |
|------------|----------|-----|------|------|
| Low | High | 14 | 5.43 | 1.09 |
| | Low | 18 | 4.94 | 1.47 |
| | Total | 32 | 5.16 | 1.32 |
| High | High | 12 | 5.58 | 1.24 |
| | Low | 17 | 6.71 | 1.21 |
| | Total | 29 | 6.24 | 1.33 |
| Total | High | 26 | 5.50 | 1.14 |
| | Low | 35 | 5.80 | 1.61 |
| | Total | 61 | 5.67 | 1.42 |

the distrust score are calculated as the sum of the fourteen questions, where the high-trust (low-distrust) end of the scale for each question is scored as 3 and the low-trust (high-distrust) end is scored as -3 (Wrightsman, 1991). Scores for each scale can range from -42 to +42, where lower scores represent lower levels of trust (higher levels of distrust).

Descriptive statistics for the dependent variable (fraud risk assessments) are shown in Tables 6.1 and 6.2, which provide means, standard deviations and sample sizes. The mean assessments of fraud risk are organized by the risk-level manipulation and the level of trust (distrust). To prepare the tables, trust and distrust scores are converted to dichotomous variables using median splits in order to produce the high versus low categories. With regards to individuals given the Wrightsman scale (Table 6.1), risk assessments are lower for individuals who are more trusting (4.96) than for individuals who are less trusting (5.91). With regards to individuals given the distrust scale (Table 6.2) risk assessments are slightly higher for individuals who are less distrusting (5.80) than for individuals who are more distrusting (5.50). Thus, it appears that trust and distrust influence professionals' assessments of fraud risk. More critical to our current discussion, there is also evidence of differential effects of trust and distrust on fraud risk assessments.

Comparison of the participants in the trust versus distrust measurement conditions (Tables 6.1 and 6.2) reveals that low distrust and high trust (fraud risk assessments of 4.94 and 4.53 respectively) and high distrust and low trust (fraud risk assessments of 5.43 and 5.13 respectively) provide near-identical results in regard to participants' mean assessments of risk in the low-fraud-risk scenario (i.e. when there are only six fraud cues). That is, assessments of the risk of financial statement fraud for a company do not vary significantly between individuals of high trust and low distrust or between individuals of low trust and high distrust when the decision context suggests low levels of fraud risk. However, low distrust and high trust (fraud risk assessments of 6.71 and 5.50 respectively) and high distrust and low trust (fraud risk assessments of 5.58 and 6.58 respectively) provide starkly contrasting results in regard to mean assessments of risk in the high-fraud-risk scenario.

To more formally analyse these findings, we employ ANOVA models where the dependent variable is the overall assessment of fraud risk, and the independent variables represent the manipulations of risk level (high versus low) and the trust measure (or distrust measure). In these models, there is a significant main effect of trust ($p<0.000$) on risk assessments, but there is no significant main effect of distrust ($p = 0.211$). Further, while there is no main effect of distrust on fraud-risk assessments, there is a statistically significant interaction between distrust and risk level ($p<0.000$). Unlike the results obtained for measures of trust, distrust interacts with the decision context.

In regard first to trust (Table 6.1), it appears that trust consistently reduces attention to indicators of financial fraud and aggressive accounting practices, regardless of contextual factors, such as the number of fraud indicators. Trusting individuals trust others to the extent that evidence of wrongdoing is often discounted, and high levels of trust result in less attention to evidence of financial fraud and consistently lower assessments of the probability of financial fraud relative to lower levels of trust (Rose, 2007).

The effects of distrust (Table 6.2), however, change with the decision context. We propose that the interaction of distrust and context (i.e. risk level) occurs because individuals having a high propensity for distrust are predisposed toward expecting fraudulent behaviour. At first glance, such distrust may appear desirable, as it suggests appropriate professional scepticism and proper intentions to verify financial disclosures and monitor risks.

The 'checking not trusting' distinctions articulated by Smith (2001) also suggest that the professional activities of auditors should select for individuals with simultaneously trusting and distrusting dispositions. Our experimental analyses, however, indicate that high levels of dispositional distrust do not lead to increased attention to indicators of fraud risk. Individuals with high levels of distrust were desensitized to financial fraud risks, and their assessments of financial fraud risk did not increase as the number of fraud risk indicators increased.

From Table 6.2, we observe that the mean assessments of fraud risk for high distrusting individuals are very similar in the low-fraud-risk and high-fraud-risk conditions (fraud risk assessments of 5.43 and 5.58 respectively, which are not significantly different). Bearing in mind the different perceptions of trusting and distrusting individuals in high apparent risk situations, we can surmise that those individuals having a high propensity for distrust are inherently predisposed toward expecting fraudulent behaviour. As such, they may be desensitized to its increase. Taking an inherent expectation of fraudulent behaviour coupled with a lack of sensitivity together, it appears that the presence of many indicators of fraud risk is insufficient to raise distrusting individuals' perception of risk significantly beyond their standard expectation of the presence of fraud. Highly distrusting decision makers simply expect fraud because they are distrusting. Indeed, to observe fraudulent behaviour appears normal to them and, in contrast to low-distrusting individuals, they do not respond in an exceptional way to its increase; in other words, the 'checking' did not take place.

Low-distrust individuals were far more sensitive to evidence of fraud, because such evidence violated their expectation that management would not commit financial fraud. That is, low-distrust individuals were sensitive to evidence of fraud, while high-distrust individuals were not sensitive to such evidence. As such, under experimental conditions, high-distrust individuals and low-distrust individuals behaved differently: high-distrust individuals did not recognize the dangers of a high-risk scenario, whereas low-distrust individuals did. Planned comparisons confirm that these differences are statistically significant (p<0.01).

Those individuals having a low propensity for distrust are not naturally inclined towards expecting fraud cues. Rather, they are inclined towards expecting an absence of fraud cues. As a result, these individuals are sensitive to an increase in fraud cues, in a manner that is identical to naturally low trusting individuals, in high-fraud-cue scenarios (fraud risk assessments of 6.71 and 6.58 respectively). This suggests that low trust and low distrust are contiguous with each other. That is, low distrust individuals, like low trust individuals, experience a 'violation' of their expectations regarding fraud cues, with a consequent rise in their sensitivity to fraud-cue increase. This leads to their high mean risk assessments in high-fraud-cue scenarios, in comparison with individuals who are inherently predisposed to high distrust (fraud risk assessments of 6.71 versus 5.58). Furthermore, a comparison of the mean risk assessments of high-trust and high-distrust individuals in the high-fraud-cue scenario (fraud risk assessments of 5.50 and 5.58 respectively) suggests that both high-trust and high-distrust individuals are resilient to expectation 'violation' (be this a positive expectation in the case of trust, or negative expectation in the case of distrust) as a result of high-fraud cues.

In high-trust individuals, the individual's inherently resilient trust is not violated, with the result that mean risk assessment is low. In high-distrust individuals, the level of fraud cues observed is not regarded as abnormal and thus no violation of expectation occurs, with the result that mean risk assessment is similarly low. In this sense, therefore, we can conclude that although trust and distrust are observable as *different constructs* operating at the same time to produce different effects in high-risk situations, the *nature of their operation* appears similar.

## Discussion

In sum, if trust and distrust operate simultaneously, and their effects are separate and distinct, then perhaps auditors exhibit both trust and distrust of their clients. Trust would facilitate cooperation with management and allow for business growth, while concurrent distrust of clients' financial reporting motives could lead to a tendency to trust but verify and continually monitor downside risks and vulnerabilities. From this perspective, effective auditors could be those who exhibit high levels of trust and high levels of distrust. Thus, understanding the nature of trust and distrust in the auditing environment may represent a key to understanding how auditors can maintain the requisite relationships with clients *and* provide reliable assurance for our capital market participants.

While highly distrustful auditors may act appropriately in low-risk scenarios, their judgment may be less effective in high-risk scenarios. One practice-oriented implication of such an analysis is that high-risk scenarios should be the preserve of more senior auditors or partners whose time in the profession may mitigate against such dispositional effects and make them more likely to accurately assess the implications of the fraud cues. From a recruiting perspective, the ideal auditor may be someone who, in Lewicki *et al.*'s (1998) terms, has high trust *and* high distrust dispositions. That is, they are characterized by a tendency to trust but verify, they seek relationships that are highly segmented and bounded, and yet they actively monitor downside risks and vulnerabilities. Such individuals may be able to maintain a client relationship yet at the same time work effectively within the regulatory requirements of the audit task. Identification experimentally of both sets of dispositions in the *same* individuals, is the subject of further research.

Our findings are in contrast to the presumption (based on the understanding that distrust is the corollary of low trust) that highly distrusting people would be expected to make very effective auditors. High-distrust auditors may react incorrectly to an absence of fraud cues, becoming unduly suspicious because the fraud cues they expect to see are not present (i.e. the evidence is too good to be true). In such cases, high-distrust individuals may be less efficient as auditors since their distrust leads them to unnecessarily question the validity of financial disclosures when there is little evidence of wrongdoing. In addition, the finding that trust and distrust act independently suggests that trusting auditors, who are needed to effectively maintain client relationships, may simultaneously possess varying levels of distrust. In sum, we suggest that low levels of distrust (not high levels of distrust) may act to increase auditors' sensitivity to fraud risk.

We are now in a position to return to our earlier discussion of trust and career advancement (Rose and Rose, 2007; Rose *et al.*, 2010). The study of auditors at Big 4 accounting firms (Rose *et al.*, 2010) found, in addition, that audit managers and partners need to be trusting in order to successfully manage client relationships, but their trusting nature makes them less effective detectors of financial fraud. However, since client relationships are the key to the survival of the firm, they are more likely to advance up the hierarchy, not for their ability as professional auditors but for their ability as professional managers of clients. In other words, competent auditors who are excellent relationship managers are more likely rise to partner status than those juniors whose less trusting disposition makes them simply excellent auditors. Highly trusting auditors tend to stay within the profession but less trusting auditors tend to leave.

The organizational cultural expectations of seniors to maintain client relationships and earn profits in addition to, or perhaps even above and beyond, carrying out effective audit practice, mitigates against less-trusting auditors succeeding. This is because the focus of the business at the partner level is not on the day-to-day tasks of auditing; to be able to audit one must first have clients. Thus, the nature of the business at the junior and partner levels is quite different. Distrusting auditors, having their focus on the detail of the particular audit, appear less able to cultivate and maintain client relationships, and this prevents them from progressing up the corporate ladder in comparison with their more trusting colleagues. The ultimate measure of success for an audit firm (and thus for a firm partner) is the maintenance of client relationships. The organizational cultures that have been established and maintained to promote audit firms' success, therefore, can conflict with the very purpose of the audit profession (i.e. protection of the public good), and we readily see such conflict operating when we examine auditor trust and distrust. In short, the organizational sphere appears to overcome the professional sphere, and individuals who are unable (or unwilling) to reconcile themselves to the client-maintenance values of the audit firm over and above the auditing-practice values do not advance and may ultimately leave the profession.

We conclude that the perfect audit manager/partner would appear to need to possess simultaneously high levels of trust and low levels of distrust. Low distrust would allow them to be competent enough as auditors to detect fraudulent and overly aggressive reporting, while their high-trusting nature as relationship managers would win them promotion (either within the firm or to another firm) to management – and beyond the subcultural sphere of auditing itself.

## Concluding comments

In this chapter we have begun to answer Jenkins *et al.*'s (2008) call for more research into accounting firm culture. We have argued that the act of trusting is conceptually quite different from the act of checking, and that the phenomenon of trust is quite different from that of distrust. This has allowed us to explore, in particular, the issues of conflicts between organizational and individual goals, and the role of professional subcultures on auditor performance, consultation, ethical behaviour and ultimately promotion.

Serious threats to practice result from high levels of trust among experienced auditors because managers and partners tend also to be highly trusting, and high levels of trust result in poor detection of fraud and aggressive reporting; the checking that is a prerequisite of accountability is less likely to take place when those in charge of the audit process possess high levels of trust. In this regard, professional accounting brings with it different expectations of the role of its practitioners than does professional management, with implications for the promotion of accountants from accounting juniors to managing partners. And in some respects these appear to be very different subcultural expectations, to the extent that the trust and distrust traits exhibited by accountants as individuals lead to them being able (or not) to transcend the accounting professional subcultural sphere within an accounting firm and move (or not) into the management one. That is, moving from checking a client firm's accounts with all the responsibility this entails to securing and maintaining client relationships, with all the different responsibilities that this entails.

We conclude by returning to national-values cross-cultural research, and posit that what we have observed in this chapter is a corporate cultural version of Molinsky's code-switching (2007; also Dietz *et al.* Chapter 1 of this volume). Molinsky argues that code-switching is:

the act of purposefully modifying one's behaviour, in a specific interaction in a foreign setting, to accommodate different cultural norms for appropriate behaviour ... [forcing] an individual to consciously override her [dominant], ingrained cultural response ... and [entailing] deviation from accustomed behaviour in one's native culture in order to engage in behaviour appropriate to a foreign culture (2007: 623).

The overriding presumption here is that trust emerges from an acceptance of, and possibly adaptation toward, the other's dominant culture (Dietz *et al.*, Chapter 1 this volume).

The research presented in this chapter suggests, in contrast, that the interaction of trust and cross-cultural code-switching within organizations may operate in a very different way to that across national boundaries described by Molinsky (2007). That is, trust does not necessarily emerge from, nor is the result of, corporate cultural adaptation, but seems in audit firms to *determine* the extent to which an individual may be able to adapt to a differently dominant cultural sphere/tile within the firm. Further, we suspect trust and distrust affect whether and to what extent individuals are in fact able to modify their behaviour in the specific auditing interactions that take place within accounting firms to accommodate the different cultural norms of management that are dominant. We suggest an individual's level of trust and/or distrust will determine whether or not they can 'code-switch' from a predominantly professional culture of scepticism to a firm culture of client-friendly values whose increasing influence emerges the higher up the firm they progress. Different levels of trust and distrust in individuals may in some cases be preventing those individuals from consciously overriding their ingrained auditing professional cultural response, such that they are not able (be this practically or morally) to engage in behaviour appropriate to the organization's management-level culture, as determined by the partners in the firm. However much their distrust-oriented professional scepticism ensures their quality as auditors, it prevents such individuals from being culturally acceptable to the firm; they are passed over for promotion and in some cases leave the profession.

Our argument, therefore, is not that trust and distrust emerge from the profession or the firm but that the trust and distrust that is inherent in individuals will play a considerable part in career progression, or otherwise, as the organizational cultural sphere becomes more dominant the further up the hierarchy one advances; trust is manifested in behaviour, culture is a manifestation of behaviour. In sum, on the evidence of the research presented in this chapter, cross-cultural code-switching occurs at the organizational level as well as the national-values level, but its *modus operandi* may be quite different. And in the case of auditing, it seems, the consequences of intra-organizational code-switching from professional culture to organizational culture are not always positive, either for the career of individual auditors or for the reliability of an audit firm's work.

## References

American Institute of Certified Public Accountants (AICPA). 2002. *Consideration of Fraud in a Financial Statement Audit*, Statement on Auditing Standards No. 99. New York: AICPA.

2005a. *AICPA Code of Professional Conduct*. New York: AICPA.

2005b. *AICPA Professional Standards. Section AU311 Planning and Supervision*. New York: AICPA.

Anheier, H. and Kendall, J. 2002. 'Interpersonal trust and voluntary associations: examining three approaches'. *British Journal of Sociology*, 53(3), 343–62.

Bamber, E. M. and Iyer, V. M. 2007. 'Auditors' identification with their clients and its effect on auditors' objectivity'. *Auditing: A Journal of Practice and Theory*, 26(2), 1–24.

Barney, J. 1986. 'Organizational culture: can it be a source of sustained competitive advantage?' *Academy of Management Review*, 11(3), 656–65.

Barney, J. B. and Hansen, M. 1994 'Trust as a source of competitive advantage'. *Strategic Management Journal*, 15(S1), 175–90.

Bazerman, M., Loewenstein, G. and Moore, D. 2002. 'Why good accountants do bad audits'. *Harvard Business Review* (November), 96–103.

Boon, S. D. and Holmes, J. G. 1991. 'The dynamics of interpersonal trust: resolving uncertainty in the face of risk'. In R. A. Hinde and J. Groebel (eds.) *Co-operation and Prosocial Behavior*. Cambridge University Press, 190–211.

Chao, G. T. and Moon, H. 2005. 'The cultural mosaic: a metatheory for understanding the complexity of culture'. *Journal of Applied Psychology*, 90, 1128–40.

Cohen, J. R. and Trompeter, G. M. 1998. 'An examination of factors affecting audit practice development'. *Contemporary Accounting Research*, 15(4), 481–504.

Costa, A. C. and Bijlsma-Frankema, K. 2007. 'Trust and control interrelations: new perspectives on the trust-control nexus'. *Group and Organization Management*, 32(4), 392–406.

Cvetkovich, G. and Lofstedt, R. E. (eds.) 1999. *Social Trust and the Management of Risk*. London: Earthscan.

Davies, H. 1999. 'Falling public trust in health services: implications for accountability'. *Journal of Health Services Research and Policy*, 4, 193–4.

2002a. 'Cultural change and healthcare performance'. *British Journal of Healthcare Management*, 6, 558–60.

2002b. 'Understanding culture in reforming the NHS'. *Journal of the Royal Society of Medicine*, 95(3), 140–3.

Davies, H. and Lampell, J. 1998. 'Trust in performance indicators?' *Qualitative Health Care*, 7, 159–62.

Davies, H. and Mannion, R. 1999. 'Clinical governance: striking a balance between checking and trusting'. In P. C. Smith (ed.) *Reforming Markets in Health Care: An Economic Perspective*. London: Oxford University Press.

Davies, H. and Nutley, S. 2000. 'Healthcare: evidence to the fore'. In H. Davies and S. Nutley (eds.) *What Works? Evidence-based Policy and Practice in Public Services*. Bristol: The Policy Press, 43–67.

Davies, H., Nutley, S. M. and Mannion, R. 2000. 'Organizational culture and quality of health care'. *Quality in Health Care*, 9, 111–19.

Dibben, M. R. 2000. *Exploring Interpersonal Trust in the Entrepreneurial Venture*. London: Macmillan.

Dibben, M. R. and Davies, H. 2004. 'Trust-worthy doctors in confidence-building systems'. *Quality & Safety in Health Care*, 13, 88–9.

Farmer, T., Rittenberg, L. and Trompeter, G. 1987. 'An investigation of the impact of economic and organizational factors on auditor independence'. *Auditing: A Journal of Practice and Theory* (Autumn).

Hackenbrack, K. and Nelson, M. 1996. 'Auditors' incentive-compatible application of professional standards'. *The Accounting Review*, 71(1), 43–59.

Hampden-Turner, C. 1990. *Corporate Culture*. London: Hutchinson.

Hatch, M.-J. 1993. 'The dynamics of organizational culture'. *Academy of Management Review*, 18, 657–93.

Hatch, M.-J. and Schultz, M. 2004. 'The dynamics of organizational identity'. In M.-J. Hatch and M. Schultz (eds.) *Organizational Identity*. Oxford University Press, 377–406.

Hooks, K. L., Cheramy, S. J. and Sincich, T. L. 1994. 'Methods used by Big 6 partners in practice development'. *Auditing: A Journal of Practice and Theory*, 13, 101–14.

Hyde, P. and Davies, H. 2005. 'Service design, culture and performance in health services: consumers as co-producers'. *Human Relations*, 11, 1407–26.

Jenkins, J. G., Dies, D. R., Bedard, J. C. and Curtis, M. B. 2008. 'Accounting firm culture and governance: a research synthesis'. *Behavioral Research in Accounting*, 20(1), 45, 74.

Kelman, H. C. 1972. 'Process of opinion change'. In T. D. Beisecker and D. W. Parson (eds.) *The Process of Social Influence*. Prentice Hall, 202–11.

Lewicki, R. J. and Bunker, B. B. 1996. 'Developing and maintaining trust in working relationships'. In R. M. Kramer and T. R. Tyler (eds.) *Trust in Organizations: Frontiers of Theory and Research*. Thousand Oaks,CA: Sage, 114–39.

Lewicki, R. J., McAllistair, D. J. and Bies, R. J. 1998. 'Trust and distrust: new relationships and realities'. *Academy of Management Review*, 23(3), 438–58.

Luhmann, N. 1990. 'Familiarity, confidence, trust: problems and alternatives'. In D. Gambetta (ed.) *Trust*. London: Blackwell, 94–107.

Lynch, P., Johnson, P. and Dibben, M. 2007. 'Exploring relationships of trust in 'adventure' recreation'. *Leisure Studies*, 26(1), 47–64.

Mannion, R., Davies, H. and Marshall, M. N. 2005. 'Cultural attributes of high and low performing hospitals'. *Journal of Health Organizations Management*, 19(6), 431–9.

Marsh, S. and Dibben, M. R. 2005. 'Trust, untrust, distrust and mistrust: an exploration of the darker side'. *Springer Lecture Notes in Computer Science* (LNCS), 3477, 17–33.

Marshall, M., Mannion, R., Nelson, E. and Davies, H. T. O. 2003. 'Managing change in the culture of general practice: qualitative case studies in primary care trusts'. *British Medical Journal*, 327, 599–602.

Mechanic, D. 1996. 'Changing medical organization and the erosion of trust'. *Milbank Quarterly*, 74(2), 171–89.

Mechanic, D. and Meyer, S. 2000. 'Concepts of trust among patients with serious illness'. *Journal of Social Science and Medicine*, 51, 657–68.

Molinsky, A. 2007. 'Cross-cultural code-switching: the psychological challenges of adapting behavior in foreign cultural interactions'. *Academy of Management Review*, 32(1), 622–40.

Nutley, S. and Webb, J. 2000. 'Evidence and the policy process'. In H. Davies and S. Nutley (eds.) *What Works? Evidence-based Policy And Practice In Public Services*. Bristol: The Policy Press, 13–41.

O'Neill, O. 2002. *A Question of Trust*. Cambridge University Press.

Pheysey, D. C. 1993. *Organizational Cultures: Types and Transformations*. London: Routledge.

Poppo, L. and Zenger, T. 2002. 'Do formal contracts and relational governance function as substitutes or complements?' *Strategic Management Journal*, 23(8), 707–25.

Public Company Accounting Oversight Board (PCAOB). 2004. 'An Audit of Internal Control over Financial Reporting Performed in Conjunction with an Audit of Financial Statements'. Standard No. 2.

Public Oversight Board (POB). 2000. *The Panel on Audit Effectiveness: Report and Recommendations*. New York: Public Oversight Board.

Rose, J. 2007. 'Attention to aggressive and potentially fraudulent reporting: effects of experience and trust'. *Behavioral Research in Accounting*, 19, 215–30.

Rose, A. and Rose, J. 2003. 'The effects of fraud risk assessments and a risk analysis decision aid on auditors' evaluation of evidence and judgment'. *Accounting Forum*, 27(3), 312–38.

2007. 'Management attempts to avoid accounting disclosure oversight: the effects of trust and knowledge on corporate directors' governance ability'. *Journal of Business Ethics*, 83(2), 193–205.

Rose, J., Rose, A. and Dibben, M. R. 2010. 'The implications of auditors' dispositional trust and career advancement opportunities for the detection of fraud.' *Journal of Forensic and Investigative Accounting.*

Sackman, S. A. 1997. *Cultural Complexity in Organization: Inherent Contrasts and Contradictions.* Thousand Oaks, CA: Sage.

Schneider, S. C. and Barsoux, J.-L. 1997. *Managing Across Cultures.* London: FT/ Prentice Hall.

Schoorman, F. D., Mayer, R. C. and Davis, J. H. 2007. 'An integrative model of organisational trust: past, present and future'. *Academy of Management Review*, 32(2), 344–54.

Schuetze, W. 1994. 'A mountain or a mole hill?' *Accounting Horizons*, 8, 69–75.

Schutz, A. and Luckmann, T. 1974. *The Structures of the Life World.* London: Heineman.

Scott, T., Mannion, R., Davies, H. T. O. and Marshall, M. N. 2003a. 'Implementing culture change in health care: theory and practice'. *International Journal for Quality in Health Care*, 15(2) 111–18.

2003b. 'The quantitative measurement of organizational culture in health care: a review of the available instruments'. *Health Services Research*, 38(3), 923–45.

Smith, C. 2001. 'Trust and confidence: possibilities for social work in "high modernity"'. *British Journal of Social Work*, 31, 287–305.

Waren, M. E. 1999. *Democracy and Trust.* Cambridge University Press.

Waterhouse, L. and Bellof, H. 1999. 'Trust in public life'. *Hume Papers on Public Policy*, 7(3), Edinburgh University Press.

Wilks, T. and Zimbelman, M. 2004. 'Decomposition of fraud-risk assessments and auditors' sensitivity to fraud cues'. *Contemporary Accounting Research*, 21(3), 719–45.

Wrightsman, L. 1964. 'Measurement of philosophies of human nature'. *Psychological Reports*, 14, 328–32.

1974. *Assumptions About Human Nature: A Social-Psychological Approach.* Monterey, CA: Brooks/Cole Publishing Company.

1991. 'Interpersonal trust and attitudes toward human nature'. In J. P. Robinson, P. R. Shaver and L. S. Wrightsman (eds.) *Measures of Personality and Social Psychological Attitudes: Vol. 1: Measures of Social Psychological Attitudes.* San Diego, CA: Academic Press, 373–412.

Wyatt, A. 2004. 'Accounting professionalism – they just don't get it'. *Accounting Horizons*, 18(1), 45–53.

Zucker, L. G. 1986. 'Production of trust: institutional sources of economic structure, 1840–1920'. In B. M. Staw and L. L. Cummings (eds.) *Research in Organizational Behavior*. Greenwich, CT: JAI Press, 8, 53–111.

# 7 | Trust barriers in cross-cultural negotiations: a social psychological analysis

RODERICK M. KRAMER

## Summary

This chapter reviews theory and evidence regarding the barriers to trust that arise within the context of cross-cultural negotiations. The chapter provides an overview of how trust has been conceptualized in the domain of cross-cultural negotiations. It also provides a discussion of the psychological and social barriers to trust common to cross-cultural negotiations. The chapter then discusses approaches to attenuating or overcoming the deleterious effects of these psychological and social barriers. The chapter concludes by discussing some practical implications of the findings, as well as some directions for future research.

## Introduction

A central and recurring question in the study of cross-cultural relations has been how best to resolve the unavoidable conflicts that arise between interdependent groups and nations (Kahn and Zald, 1990; Messick and Mackie, 1989; Pruitt and Rubin, 1986; Stephan and Stephan, 1996; Taylor and Moghaddam, 1987). Given the obvious importance of the problem, it is hardly surprising that a variety of approaches have been proposed for dealing with such conflicts, ranging from complex structural interventions to elaborate procedural remedies (Davis *et al.*, 1990; Mares and Powell, 1990). Despite the numerous creative approaches advanced to deal with this problem, negotiation remains one of the most basic and reliable mechanisms for conflict resolution in cross-cultural contexts (Garling

I am extremely grateful to Roy Lewicki and Mark Saunders for their detailed and thoughtful suggestions for improving this chapter. I wrote the first draft of this chapter while visiting the London Business School. I am grateful for the receptive scholarly environment and support its faculty offered. I would also like to acknowledge the support of the William R. Kimball Family and a Stanford faculty fellowship.

182

*et al.*, 2006; Gelfand and Brett, 2004; Kahn and Kramer, 2006; Leung, 2006).

Negotiation can be described as a process involving 'discussion between two or more parties with the apparent aim of resolving a divergence of interest and thus escaping social conflict' (Carnevale and Pruitt, 2000: 2). When applied to cross-cultural contexts, negotiation can be defined more narrowly in terms of the distinctive cultural characteristics that define the relationship between the negotiating parties, including the important differences associated with their cultural origins and locations. In his early and influential analysis, Sherif (1966) proposed that 'whenever individuals belonging to one [social or cultural] group interact, collectively or individually, with another group or its members in terms of their group identification, we have an instance of intergroup behaviour' (p. 12). Integrating these two definitions, we propose that when two or more individuals negotiate with each other as representatives of a cultural group, and in terms of their cultural backgrounds and identifications, we have an instance of cross-cultural negotiation.

This simple definition of a cross-cultural negotiation, of course, conceals many layers of complexity. Cross-cultural negotiations assume many forms, ranging from the relatively simple situation where two individuals negotiate on behalf of their respective cultural groups, to more complex negotiations involving multiple, large negotiating teams whose members have diverse expertise, multiple and often conflicting agendas, and divergent and potentially incompatible expectations (Gelfand and Brett, 2004; Kramer, 1991). Moreover, the broader social, organizational and institutional contexts within which such negotiations are embedded can exert a profound influence on the dynamics of a bargaining process (Allison, 1971; Kahn and Zald, 1990).

Researchers have also appreciated, however, that the effectiveness of a negotiation process depends, in no small measure, on the level of trust that exists between the negotiating parties (Blake and Mouton, 1986; Carnevale and Pruitt, 1992; Pruitt and Kimmel, 1977; Ross and LaCroix, 1996; Webb and Worchel, 1986). In particular, trust has been shown to facilitate attainment of more satisfactory negotiation outcomes, while the absence of trust typically results in suboptimal outcomes, stalemate or, worse, even destructive escalation (Butler, 1995; Larson, 1997; Lewicki and Bunker, 1995; Pruitt and Rubin, 1986).

However desirable trust may be, it is unfortunately often hard to come by in many negotiations, especially when a long history of distrust and suspicion exists between the disputants. This is especially true when trust involves individuals who are representing different cultural groups, where strong national, regional and religious differences may obtain. In such situations, individuals may feel intense pressure to fully represent their group's interests, leading them to adopt a stance of presumptive suspicion and wariness. But why is trust so difficult to create and sustain in cross-cultural contexts? What impedes the development of trust in the first place? And why does trust seem so fragile and easily undermined? A primary aim of this chapter is to explore such questions. In particular, I aim to review some of what we know about the barriers to trust that arise in negotiations that cross cultural divides. In doing so, I focus special attention on identifying social psychological barriers to trust in cross-cultural contexts.

A few words about the specific level of analysis and approach I take in this chapter seem in order before proceeding. First and foremost, I focus in this chapter on dyadic negotiations involving representatives from different cultural groups. I do so for two reasons. The first is simplification. But second and more importantly, the topic of multi-party negotiations and their dynamics has been treated elsewhere (e.g. Garling *et al.*, 2006; Kolb, 1999; Kramer, 1991). Second, I focus in this chapter primarily on common or shared features of cross-cultural negotiations (i.e. I do not attempt to discuss specific cross-cultural negotiations, while fully recognizing that the precise character of a negotiation will reflect idiosyncratic features of the specific cultures involved). Again, these cultural-specific negotiation dynamics have been treated elsewhere, most often by political scientists and historians (see, e.g. Larson, 1997; Rubin, 1981). With these caveats in mind, the chapter is organized as follows. I first discuss briefly how trust has been conceptualized in the context of cross-cultural negotiations. I then elaborate on some of the specific psychological and social barriers to trust development that arise in such contexts. I conclude by suggesting some implications of the analysis for trust building and restoration, as well as directions for future research.

## Conceptualizing trust in cross-cultural negotiations

Because the issue of how best to define trust and distrust has been treated so thoroughly elsewhere (see, e.g. Lewicki *et al.*, 1998; Lewis and Weigert, 1985; Mayer *et al.*, 1995; Pruitt and Rubin, 1986), I offer only a very brief overview here, choosing to focus down quickly on a preferred working definition.

Trust has been viewed as a psychological state or orientation of one social actor (a trustor) toward other people (a prospective trustee or trustees) within the context of specific situations in which they find themselves (Hardin,

1992). As a psychological state, moreover, trust entails awareness on the part of the trustor of perceived vulnerability or risk that derives from uncertainty regarding the motives, intentions, and/or prospective actions of others with whom they are interdependent. As Lewis and Weigert (1985) suggested in this regard, trust can be characterized as the 'undertaking of a risky course of action on the confident expectation that all persons involved in the action will act competently and dutifully' (p. 971). Along similar lines, Mayer *et al.* (1995) defined trust as 'the willingness of a party to be vulnerable to the actions of another party based on the expectation that the other will perform a particular action important to the trustor, irrespective of the ability to monitor or control that other party' (p. 712).

Within the context of cross-cultural negotiations, trust entails a variety of bargaining-specific perceptions, including the belief that the other party is expected to cooperate in exchanging information, is motivated to coordinate offers and counter-offers in moving toward a solution, is open-minded and is prepared to engage in earnest and constructive problem solving (Carnevale and Pruitt, 2000). Thus, when trust is present, the presumption is that one negotiating party is ready to engage in cooperative behaviour if the other party manifests a like readiness. This type of trust does not refer narrowly to a perception of the other's character or enduring attitude toward oneself but only of the other's orientation in the current situation.

Extrapolating from these various distinctions, I conceptualize trust in cross-cultural negotiation contexts as the set of assumptions, beliefs and expectations held by a negotiator (or negotiators) from one cultural group regarding the likelihood that the actions of a negotiator (or negotiators) from another cultural group will act beneficially, favourably, or at least not detrimentally to their interests.

## Benefits of trust in cross-cultural negotiations

Trust has been viewed as important in negotiation contexts primarily because of evidence that it facilitates the achievement of mutually beneficial or integrative outcomes (Butler, 1995; Larson, 1997). Negotiation scholars have long been aware that integrative potential is inherent in most conflict situations, and have identified numerous strategies negotiators can utilize to reach integrative solutions (Pruitt, 1981). For example, the strategy of compensation entails providing some sort of payment or other benefit to offset a loss or inconvenience. This strategy can be employed when one party suffers as a result of the other party's demands or actions – the party who suffers is indemnified for their loss by the other. However, the success of the strategy requires trust between the parties that the compensation will actually be delivered. Along similar lines, one can argue that, to fully realize the integrative potential within a negotiation, it is essential that negotiators exhibit considerable cognitive and behavioural flexibility (Carnevale and Probst, 1998). Among other things, they often must be willing to seek useful information about the other party's interests, preferences and concerns (Thompson, 1998). Additionally, they often must be willing to reveal information regarding their own interests, preferences and concerns. Finding the integrative potential in a negotiation depends, therefore, on negotiators' willingness to both assume personal risks themselves, and their effectiveness at persuading the other party to incur such risks as well.

Support for the general proposition that trust facilitates both integrative bargaining processes and outcomes comes from a variety of studies. There is evidence, for instance, that trust encourages the exchange of information about negotiators' respective values and priorities (Kimmel *et al.*, 1980). Trust also makes it easier to reach agreements on proposed offers (Lindskold and Han, 1988). Other research has demonstrated that individuals are much more likely to engage in cooperative behaviour when they trust others with whom they are interdependent to reciprocate such cooperation (Deutsch, 1986). Such expectations are related to negotiators' beliefs about the other party's motives and intentions, and also their predictions about the probable behaviour of the other party.

Trust can also affect behaviour during negotiation. To see how, it is helpful to recognize that negotiation is a form of social influence, in which each party attempts to shape or modify the attitudes, goals, values, feelings, beliefs, preferences and/or behaviours of the other through their strategic and tactical choices (Greenhalgh and Kramer, 1990; Solomon, 1960). Such influence strategies and tactics vary considerably along such dimensions as their positivity or negativity. Rothbart and Hallmark (1988), for example, drew a distinction between conciliatory and coercive bargaining strategies used in inter-group negotiations. Conciliatory strategies entail the use of positive inducements to elicit cooperative responses from a negotiation opponent. Coercive strategies, in contrast, entail the use of threats and deterrents and are aimed at inducing compliance from a presumably recalcitrant opponent. More recently, Nye (2008) has argued that negotiators have a choice between soft- and hard-power strategies, and that the effectiveness of a given power strategy depends on its fit with the context.

Negotiators' trust in the other party plays an important role in strategic choice because the selection of an influence strategy will be affected by a negotiator's assumptions regarding the other party's receptiveness or responsiveness to a given influence strategy. Negotiators are likely to employ cooperative or conciliatory influence strategies, for example, when trust in the other's responsiveness is high. In contrast, they are likely to resort to more coercive strategies if their trust is so low that they believe the other party will exploit cooperative or conciliatory gestures (Lindskold, 1978).

One of the most potent presumptive trust rules is trust predicated on social distance. As Macy and Skvoretz (1998) put it, 'trust neighbours, but not outsiders' (p. 651). On the basis of such logic, one might expect that negotiations involving individuals from very close or highly similar cultures might enjoy an advantage with respect to the trust-building process, whereas those involving individuals from very different cultures might be at a greater disadvantage. Yet recent research suggests that the picture may be somewhat more complex than this simple argument suggests (Yamagishi and Yamagishi, 1994). In particular, there may be cultural variations in how strongly individuals from different cultures respond to in-group-out-group distinctions. For example, in a recent review, Brewer and Yuki highlight evidence suggesting that 'East Asians discriminate between in-group and out-group distinctions more so than Americans do' (2007: 317).

Having briefly suggested some ways in which trust can usefully be conceptualized in cross-cultural contexts, and having described some of the benefits of such trust, I turn now to considering why such trust may be hard to achieve.

## Barriers to trust in cross-cultural negotiations

Social psychologists have noted the substantial evidence that trust matters in cross-cultural interactions (Ferrin and Gillespie, Chapter 2 of this volume). They have also documented the considerable difficulties that attend the creation and maintenance of trust within cross-cultural contexts (Lindskold, 1986; Morris and Gelfand, 2004; Sherif *et al.*, 1961; Webb and Worchel, 1986). Why is trust between negotiators from different cultures so difficult to create and sustain? Researchers interested in this general question have focused on a variety of factors that impede trust development and stability. These factors can be grouped in terms of 1) psychological barriers and 2) social barriers to trust. I consider each of these factors in turn.

### *Psychological barriers to trust*

Behavioural scientists have afforded considerable attention to identifying psychological processes that impair negotiator performance, including understanding how trust develops or fails to develop (Lewicki *et al.*, 2006). Some recent work on this topic has attempted to demonstrate the existence of cognitive biases that adversely impact integrative bargaining (e.g. Neale and Bazerman, 1991; Thompson, 1998). In terms of identifying basic cognitive processes that undermine trust development between groups, perhaps the most extensive research to date has examined the deleterious effects of social categorization on social perception and judgment in inter-group situations (Brewer and Brown, 1998; Messick and Mackie, 1989). Early ethnographic research on in-group bias demonstrated the existence of a robust and pervasive tendency for individuals to display favouritism toward other in-group members (Brewer, 1981; Brewer and Brown, 1998). Individuals tend, for example, to hold relatively positive views of their own group and its members (the in-group) and comparatively negative views of other groups and their members (the out-group).

Subsequent laboratory research showed that even the process of 'mere' categorization of individuals into arbitrary but distinct groupings resulted in systematic judgmental bias (Tajfel, 1970). Brewer and her associates (Brewer, 1979; Brewer and Silver, 1978), for example, demonstrated that categorization of a set of individuals into two distinct groups resulted in individuals viewing others outside the group boundary as less cooperative, honest, and trustworthy compared to members of their own group (Kramer *et al.*, 1993; Polzer, 1996; Probst *et al.*, 1999; Robert and Carnevale, 1997; Thompson *et al.*, 1995). On the basis of such evidence, Messick and Mackie (1989) concluded that this phenomenon of inter-group bias seems well established and its effects pervasive. In their related research on the discontinuity effect, Insko and Schopler have provided evidence regarding the existence of a negative out-group schema, which, in negotiation contexts, can lead negotiators to be distrustful and suspicious of out-group members and also to expect competitive behaviour from them (Insko and Schopler, 1997). According to Brewer and Brown, this out-group schema has two important components. The first is schema-based distrust which represents 'the learned belief or expectation that intergroup relations are competitive and therefore the out-group is not to be trusted and the in-group's welfare must be protected' (1998: 569). Second, this anticipated competition generates a self-fulfilling dynamic. As Brewer and Brown note, 'when one believes that the other party has competitive intent, the only reasonable action is to compete oneself in order to avoid potential loss' (p. 569).

Another manifestation of diminished expectations surrounds the negotiating parties' beliefs regarding the responsiveness of the other party to specific cooperative or conciliatory gestures. Rothbart and Hallmark (1988) found that one consequence of 'mere' social categorization processes is that individuals tend to believe that in-group members will be more responsive to conciliatory influence strategies, whereas out-group members will be more responsive to coercive strategies. Such presumptions are likely to lead negotiators in inter-group contexts to opt for overly coercive strategies when trying to influence a presumably resistant opponent.

By far the most systematic and conceptually sophisticated applications of cross-cultural psychological barriers to effective negotiation processes have been provided by Morris and his colleagues (e.g. Morris and Gelfand, 2004; Morris and Peng, 1994). In a recent overview of the state of our knowledge regarding these processes, Morris and Gelfand (2004) identified three major negotiator biases which may be culturally variable. One of these is the so-called '*zero-sum*' mindset or '*fixed-pie*' construal of conflict. Morris and Gelfand note, for example, research by Gelfand *et al.* (2001) showing differences in construal such that, 'Japanese negotiators tended to construe conflict in terms of mutual blame and cooperation, whereas Americans construed the same conflict in terms of a win–lose frame in which one party is right and the other wrong' (p. 5). In addition, they concluded, Americans tended to 'focus attention on the nature of individual rights in the conflicts, whereas Japanese focused their attention on duties, obligations, and violations of face' (p. 50).

A second bias that may be susceptible to cross-cultural variation, they argue, is the *egocentric bias* associated with fairness judgments. For instance, North American negotiators characteristically tend to be self-serving when making fairness assessments of their own versus another's behaviours, a result consistent with the primacy of self in cognitive processing among Westerners. Because individuals from Asian cultures place comparatively less emphasis upon the self and more upon relationships, this bias might be expected to be attenuated – an expectation supported by findings reported by Gelfand *et al.* (2002).

Finally, there may be similar asymmetries existing with respect to *dispositional biases* when judging negotiators' intentions and traits. The strong form of the dispositional bias is the so-called fundamental attribution error, whereby social perceivers tend to attribute an actor's behaviour to internal, dispositional factors, while minimizing or neglecting situational causes for that behaviour. Westerns have been found to make stronger individual dispositional attributions compared to Asians, who display more sensitivity to contextual causes (Morris and Peng, 1994).

All else equal, it might seem as if these various judgmental distortions would be difficult to sustain, especially as disconfirming evidence becomes available to negotiators. A considerable body of theory and research on history-based forms of trust suggests that, when making judgments about others' trustworthiness, people act much like intuitive Bayesian statisticians who recalibrate or update their judgments on the basis of their personal experiences. From this perspective, one might expect that such misperceptions and errors should, over time, be self-correcting. Unfortunately, there are a number of psychological dynamics that may contribute to difficulties in correcting such misperceptions, especially in inter-group negotiations. These self-sustaining characteristics of distrust and suspicion arise, arguably, from both the distrustful perceiver's difficulty in learning from trust-related experiences, as well as their difficulty in generating useful (diagnostic) experiences.

One problem that the suspicious negotiator confronts is that, because of the presumption that the other party is untrustworthy and that things may not be what they seem, the perceived diagnostic value of any particular bit of evidence regarding the other's putative trustworthiness is, from the outset, tainted. As Weick (1979) noted in this regard, all diagnostic cues are inherently corruptible. He cites an interesting historical example to illustrate this problem. The day before the Japanese attack on Pearl Harbor, an American naval attaché had informed Washington that he did not believe a surprise attack by the Japanese was imminent because the fleet was still stationed at its home base. As evidence for this conclusion, he noted that large crowds of sailors could be observed casually walking the streets of Tokyo. What the attaché did not know was that these 'sailors' were in actuality Japanese soldiers disguised as sailors to conceal the fact that the Japanese fleet had already sailed. From the perspective of the Japanese, this ruse was a brilliant example of what military intelligence experts call strategic disinformation. Such strategic misrepresentations can be used in negotiation and other conflict situations to mislead an adversary about one's capabilities or intentions (Kramer *et al.*, 1991).

In elaborating on the implications of this incident, Weick noted that the very fact that the attaché had searched for a foolproof cue made him, ironically, more vulnerable to exploitation. Quoting a passage from Goffman (1969), Weick reasoned that the very fact that the observer finds himself looking to a particular bit of evidence as an incorruptible check on what is or might be corruptible is the reason he should be suspicious of this evidence: 'for the best evidence for him is also the best evidence for the subject to tamper with ... when the situation seems to be exactly what it appears to be, the closest likely alternative is that the situation has been completely faked' (p. 172–3). For the already suspicious or distrustful negotiator, of course, the attaché's experience dramatically illustrates what happens when one is too relaxed about others' presumed trustworthiness.

Other research suggests additional cognitive barriers to trust that may plague inter-group negotiators. Slovic (1993) has noted, for example, that it is easier to destroy trust than create it. To explain this fragility of trust, he suggested that a variety of cognitive factors contribute to asymmetries in the trust-building versus trust-destroying process. First, he proposed that negative (trust-destroying) events are more visible and noticeable than positive (trust-building) events. Second, he proposed that trust-destroying events carry more weight in judgment than trust-building events of comparable magnitude. To provide evidence for this general principles of asymmetry, Slovic evaluated the impact of hypothetical news events on people's trust judgments. In support of his general thesis, he found that negative events had more impact on trust judgments than positive events. Slovic noted further that asymmetries between trust and distrust may be reinforced by the fact that sources of bad (trust-destroying) news tend to be perceived as more credible than sources of good news. In the context of inter-group negotiation, and especially those in which a climate of distrust or suspicion already exists, good news (evidence of the other side's trustworthiness) is likely to be discounted, whereas bad news (confirmatory evidence that distrust is warranted) is augmented.

## Social barriers to trust

In addition to these basic psychological factors, there are a number of social factors that can contribute to asymmetries in judgments regarding trust and distrust in inter-group negotiation. For example, several intra-group dynamics may impede trust development. Insko and his associates investigated the effects of in-group discussion on trust-related judgments (Insko *et al.*, 1990). In their study, judges coded tape-recorded discussions for both explicit and implicit statements of distrust. The results showed that there were significantly more distrust statements in discussions between groups compared to discussions between individuals. There was also a strong negative correlation between the level of distrust recorded in these conversations and subsequent cooperative behaviour.

Third parties involved in inter-group negotiation may further exacerbate such tendencies. Burt and Knez (1995) examined how social network structures, and the social dynamics they create, affect the diffusion of distrust information and its effects of trust judgments within the managers' networks. They found that, although both trust and distrust were amplified by third-party disclosures, distrust was amplified to a greater extent than trust. As a result, judgments about distrust had, as Burt and Knez put it, a 'catastrophic' quality to them. In explaining these findings, Burt and Knez posited that third parties are more attentive to negative information and often prefer negative gossip to positive information and gossip. Consequently, indirect connections amplify the distrust associated with weak relations much more than they amplify trust among strong relations.

Another potential social barrier to generating trust-building experiences derives from various self-presentational predicaments that negotiators, as representatives for their groups, face. As Kressel noted, 'negotiators may be pressured by their constituents into presenting the constituents' demands vehemently and without backing down, while their opposite numbers across the bargaining table may expect these same negotiators to adhere to norms of moderation and compromise' (1981: 227). Thus, when individuals feel accountable to others, they are more likely to be concerned not only about the objective outcomes they obtain, but also how those outcomes are perceived and evaluated by those to whom they feel accountable (Carnevale, 1985). Negotiators are accountable to constituents to the extent that their constituents are perceived to have power over them. If the other party is viewed as being accountable to a tough constituency, the other is unlikely to be trusted. Kimmel *et al.* (1980) found that trust and information exchange were both lower when negotiators did not know what instructions the other had received than when they knew that the other had received problem-solving instructions.

Research on the effects of perceived accountability on negotiator judgment and decision shows that such self-presentational concerns exert an important influence on negotiator judgment and behaviour. Carnevale *et al.* (1981) reported that accountability to constituents engenders a competitive atmosphere in between-group negotiation, which then diminishes the use of explicit information exchange and increases the likelihood of poor agreements. Interestingly, under high accountability, negotiators who did well tended to rely on indirect information exchange, such as the use of heuristic trial and error tactics (e.g. making and then remaking offers within a close range of value).

The interactive or dynamic complexity between trust and constituent accountability is further illustrated by Adams (1976). Adams noted that representatives who are trusted by constituents are frequently given considerable autonomy, and thus are freer to develop good relations with outsiders with whom they must negotiate. However, if those same constituents observe their representative cooperating with the other side, they may become suspicious and concerned that their interests are not being vigorously defended or represented. Accordingly, they will engage in greater monitoring of their negotiator's behaviour. This may be seen by the representative as a signal to stop cooperating with outsiders. In more complex inter-group negotiation situations, where negotiators are representing multiple constituencies with diverse concerns, these self-presentational predicaments become even more difficult to navigate (see Ginzel *et al.*, 1991).

## Discussion: implications for trust building

The numerous barriers to trust I have identified in the previous section might leave both researchers and practitioners pessimistic regarding the prospects for building or restoring trust in cross-cultural negotiations. To be sure, the problem of creating and sustaining trust, especially against the backdrop of a long history of mutual enmity or wariness, has proven daunting both in practice and theory. Although formidable, however, there is evidence that the barriers to trust are not insurmountable. Accordingly, I briefly turn to a discussion of the literature that addresses the question of how trust can be created, and the knot of distrust, if not untied completely, can be at least loosened. After discussing these implications for practice, I turn to a brief discussion of some directions future research might take. I then conclude the chapter by offering some summary comments.

## *Implications for practice*

This discussion of implications for practice is organized in terms of 1) behavioural approaches to trust building and 2) structural approaches to trust building. I discuss each in turn.

### Behavioural approaches to trust building

Negotiators can attempt to influence each other's perceptions and behaviours in ways that facilitate trust. This can include efforts to create a climate of mutual trust both by 1) trying to elicit cooperative behaviour from the other party, and/or (2) attempting to communicate their own trustworthiness and willingness to cooperate. Much of the literature on this trust-building process has been motivated by recognition of the circular relation between trust and cooperation (Deutsch, 1973): trust tends to beget cooperation, and cooperation breeds further trust. Therefore, if a cycle of mutual cooperation can be initiated and sustained, trust will develop (Lindskold, 1978). This trust, in turn, will spur further cooperative acts.

Perhaps the simplest and most direct way to initiate such constructive change in the relationship between two wary negotiating groups is for one of the negotiators to make a gesture which interrupts the usual relationship between them. Such an effort is direct in that it immediately alters the pattern of interaction and simple in that it requires no third-party interventions or elaborate structural changes. Early studies pursuing this idea examined the use of unconditional pacifism to elicit cooperative responses. The experimental evidence regarding the efficacy of this strategy was discouraging. At least in the context of laboratory settings, unvarying or unconditional cooperation is puzzling to recipients and the tendency is to exploit it (Deutsch, 1986; Shure *et al.*, 1965; Solomon, 1960).

Although the empirical evidence suggests that strategies of unconditional cooperation yield disappointing results, initiatives that involve contingent cooperation have proven more effective in eliciting and sustaining cooperative behaviour. Early studies on this issue involved simple mixed-motives games in which a confederate made an initial cooperative move, inviting a reciprocal act of cooperation (Deutsch, 1973). Subsequent studies in this vein identify specific patterns of reciprocation that are efficacious in such situations. Osgood's (1962) strategy of graduated reciprocation in tension reduction (GRIT) was early model of such patterns. Osgood's core insight was that a sequence of carefully calibrated and clear signals might initiate a sustainable process of mutual trust and cooperation. One of the appeals of this strategy, and perhaps one reason it attracted so much attention, was that it seemed to offer a mechanism for reducing distrust and suspicion between the nuclear superpowers. Thus, Etzioni (1967) used the GRIT framework to interpret the series of progressively conciliatory exchanges between President Kennedy and Premier Khruschev in the early 1960s.

Drawing on this theory, Lindskold and others undertook a sustained programme of laboratory-based research on the dynamics of trust development (see Lindskold, 1978; 1986 for reviews). Several practical recommendations have emerged from this work. First, it is useful for negotiators to announce what they are doing ahead of time, and to carry out the initiatives as announced. During the resolution of the Cuban missile crisis, both American and Soviet leaders worked to demonstrate that they were enacting the agreed-upon steps to reduce tensions between them. In addition, it has been suggested that conciliatory initiatives should be irrevocable and noncontingent, so that they will be understood as efforts to resolve the conflict rather than to gain a quid pro quo. Also, they should be costly or risky to oneself, so that they cannot be construed as a cheap trick or trap. They should be continued for a period of time so as to put pressure on the other party to reciprocate and to give the other party time to rethink its policy. Two other pieces of advice are added by the current authors: unilateral initiatives should be noticeable and unexpected so that they will provoke thought. Their users should try to demonstrate a good and lasting reason for wanting to change the relationship; otherwise such initiatives may be viewed as a flash in the pan.

The GRIT strategy proceeds from a logic of starting small in order to 'jump start' a trust-building process. An alternative strategy involves an attempt by one party to 'break the frame' of distrust and suspicion by making a large, dramatic conciliatory gesture. Because it entails such obvious and severe political costs to the negotiator making the initiative, its significance is hard to discount or ignore. An example is Egyptian President Anwar Sadat's trip to Jerusalem in 1978, which paved the way for peace between Egypt and Israel. Sadat stated the purpose of the trip was to improve Israeli trust in Egypt. Kelman (1985) has reported that most Israelis viewed this event as a genuine effort to improve relations. This strategy is not, however, unconditionally effective and may produce other than intended effects. Such initiatives risk alienating important constituents and may undermine a negotiator's credibility and effectiveness with constituents. And, as Sadat's experience demonstrated, sometimes this estrangement may even have fatal consequences.

Other studies indicate that cooperation leads to improved interpersonal and inter-group relations. In early studies on this topic, Sherif and his associates first produced animosity between two groups of boys in a summer camp by having them compete with and exploit each other. They were then able to dispel this animosity in a second phase by having them cooperate on 'superordinate goals' (Sherif *et al.*, 1961). Additional research suggests that even the anticipation of cooperation can also lead to improved interpersonal and inter-group relations (Ben-Yoav and Pruitt, 1984). There are many possible explanations for the positive trust-building effects of cooperation on relationships. Cooperation may lead to reward at the hands of the other party. It may provide favourable information about the other party that would not otherwise be available. It may enhance perceived similarity and break down the conceptual boundary between groups (Gaertner *et al.*, 1989). Helping the other party may induce positive attitudes, another dissonance-resolving effect.

Such findings suggest that another route negotiators can employ to build trust through their own actions is via relationship-building activities. Most experienced, professional negotiators recognize that it is often useful to attempt to build a positive personal bond with another party, even if doing so entails some scrutiny by constituents (Friedman, 1994). This approach builds on recognition of the fact that trust is a central characteristic of mature and secure relationships, where people are likely to exhibit a combination of problem solving and concession making, which can lead to mutually beneficial, win–win agreements.

Carnevale and Pruitt (2000) have termed these sorts of relationships 'working relationships'. Working relationships are often found between people with emotional ties, such as friends, relatives or married couples. Working relationships also are common between people with instrumental ties, such as colleagues whose jobs require them to cooperate, and negotiators in counterpart relationships. An example of the latter would be a salesperson and a regular client. Working relationships involve three related norms for dealing with mixed-motive settings: a) a norm of problem solving, which specifies that if both parties feel strongly about an issue, they should try to find a way for both of them to succeed; b) a norm of mutual responsiveness, which specifies that if only one party feels strongly about an issue or if problem solving fails, the party who feels less strongly should concede to the other's wishes; c) a norm of truth in signalling, which specifies that the parties should be honest about the strength of their feelings. Truth in signalling is a necessary adjunct to the norm of mutual responsiveness, preventing people from exaggerating the strength of their needs. In the absence of this norm, neither party will trust the other's statements about issue importance, and the norm of mutual responsiveness will collapse. Weingart *et al.* (1993) found evidence of the latter two norms in a study of multilateral four-party negotiation groups.

**Structural approaches to trust building**
There is a large body of theory and research, mostly sociological, on institutional approaches to creating and sustaining trust (Granovetter, 1985; Yamagishi, 1986; Zucker, 1986). The Standing Consultative Commission (SCC) provides one illustration as to how institutional structures can be used to potentially improve and stabilize trust in complex, recurring, high-stakes negotiation, and especially when the parties are highly distrustful of each other (see Kahn, 1991 for history and overview). The SCC was a product of the Strategic Arms Limitation Talks between the United States and Soviet Union begun in 1969. Thus, its creation was a direct result of a specific negotiation (the ABM treaty of 1972), but its aim was more general – the commission was to contribute to the continued viability and effectiveness of negotiated agreements by resolving questions of interpretation and concerns about compliance if and as they arose. It thus created an institutional mechanism for allowing the parties to reach an initial agreement, even though many details had not been worked out to the parties' respective satisfaction.

## Directions for future research

As this chapter has hopefully demonstrated, social scientists have made considerable progress in identifying psychological and social barriers to trust in cross-cultural negotiations. They have also made impressive inroads in designing interventions to attenuate the deleterious impact of such processes. Much research remains to be done, however. One important direction for future research is the development of multi-level models of cultural antecedents and consequences. In a thoughtful assessment of the state of the literature just a few years ago, Gelfand and Brett noted that 'there is a critical need to examine the role of national culture vis-à-vis other contextual and individual differences in negotiation' (2004: 421). These contextual factors include potentially significant differences in institutional and organizational forms that arise between different cultures.

Another important direction for future research is to examine institutional and structural solutions to trust barriers (see, e.g. Davis *et al.*, 1990; Fukuyama, 1995; Kahn, 1991; Kahn and Zald, 1990). Another is to investigate the role third parties can play in conflict resolution (e.g. Keashly *et al.*, 1993; Kressel and Pruitt, 1989). Finally, another fruitful direction for future research would be to investigate individual differences in effectiveness at trust building and negotiating in cross-cultural contexts. Earley and Ang's (2003) recent and important work on cultural intelligence implies the strong likelihood of significant individual differences in negotiators' cognitive sophistication and behavioural competence as a function of their cultural intelligence. In particular, we might expect that individuals high in cultural intelligence would be able to achieve higher levels of empathy and perspective-taking on the cognitive side, and display more nuanced responsiveness in their bargaining behaviour.

## Concluding comments

A primary aim of this chapter has been to review social psychological theory and research on the barriers to trust that arise in cross-cultural negotiation contexts. I suspect the research pessimist or dispirited practitioner might be likely to perceive the glass as half empty when it comes to theory and knowledge. Clearly, more can and needs be done in terms of developing a comprehensive and integrative theory regarding the role of trust in cross-cultural negotiations. A concerted effort to develop a more sophisticated and truly interdisciplinary conception of trust in cross-cultural negotiations would help push the boundaries of current psychological theory and research in fruitful directions. Such a conception would encompass not only the sort of psychological and social factors that social psychologists traditionally are enamoured by, but also trace the impact of sociological and political considerations. Imaginative work by Earley and Ang (2003) on the complexity of cultural intelligence sets an example of how motivated and creative researchers might gain some traction on this problem.

The research optimist, noting the large and rapidly growing literature might just as easily argue the glass is half full. Negotiation researchers and inter-group relations theorists interested in trust can draw on a much broader set of ideas regarding the origins and bases of trust than were available even a few years ago. And on the methodological front, recent experiments are employing more complex and realistic simulations of inter-group negotiation processes than early work in this area. Whereas past studies often used relatively simple binary-choice mixed-motive games as proxies for negotiation situations, more recent studies attempt to capture the flavour and complexity of real-world negotiation. Thus, substantial progress can be charted on both conceptual and methodological fronts.

# References

Adams, J. S. 1976. 'The structure and dynamics of behavior in organizational boundary roles'. In M. D. Dunnette (ed.) *Handbook of Industrial and Organizational Psychology*. Chicago: Rand McNally.

Allison, G. T. 1971. *The Essence of Decision: Explaining the Cuban Missile Crisis*. Boston: Little, Brown.

Ben-Yoav, O. and Pruitt, D. G. 1984. 'Resistance to yielding and the expectation of cooperative future interaction in negotiation'. *Journal of Experimental Social Psychology*, 34, 323–35.

Blake, R. R. and Mouton, J. S. 1986. 'From theory to practice in interface problem solving'. In S. Worchel and W. G. Austin (eds.) *Psychology of Intergroup Relations*. Chicago: Nelson-Hall, 67–82.

Brewer, M. B. 1979. 'In-group bias in the minimal intergroup situatuion: a cognitive motivational analysis'. *Psychological Bulletin*, 86, 307–24.

  1981. 'Ethnocentrism and its role in interpersonal trust'. In M. B. Brewer and B. Collins (eds.) *Scientific Inquiry in the Social Sciences*. San Francisco: Jossey-Bass, 345–59.

Brewer, M. B. and Brown, R. J. 1998. 'Intergroup relations'. In D. Gilbert, S. Fiske and G. Lindzey (eds.) *Handbook of Social Psychology*, Vol. II. Boston: McGraw-Hill, 554–94.

Brewer, M. B. and Silver, M. 1978. 'In-group bias as a function of task characteristics'. *European Journal of Social Psychology*, 8, 393–400.

Brewer, M. B. and Yuki, M. 2007. 'Culture and social identity'. In S. Kitayama and D. Cohen (eds.) *Handbook of Cultural Psychology*. New York: Guilford, 307–22.

Burt, R. and Knez, M. 1995. 'Kinds of third-party effects on trust'. *Journal of Rationality and Society*, 7, 255–92.

Butler, J. K. 1995. 'Behaviors, trust, and goal achievement in a win–win negotiating role play'. *Group and Organization Management*, 20, 486–501.

Carnevale, P. J. 1985. 'Accountability of group representatives and intergroup relations'. In E. J. Lawler (ed.) *Advances in Group Processes: Theory and Research*, Vol. II. Greenwich, CT: JAI Press.

Carnevale, P. J. and Probst, T. 1998. 'Social values and social conflict in creative problem solving and categorization'. *Journal of Personality and Social Psychology*, 74, 1300–9.

Carnevale, P. J. and Pruitt, D. G. 1992. 'Negotiation and mediation'. *Annual Review of Psychology*, 43, 531–82.

  2000. *Negotiation in Social Conflict*, 2nd edn. Buckingham, England: Open University Press.

Carnevale, P. J., Pruitt, D. G. and Seilheimer, S. 1981. 'Looking and competing: accountability and visual access in integrative bargaining'. *Journal of Personality and Social Psychology*, 40, 111–20.

Davis, G. F., Kahn, R. L. and Zald, M. N. 1990. 'Contracts, treaties, and joint ventures'. In R. L. Kahn and M. N. Zald (eds.) *Organizations and Nation-States: New Perspectives on Conflict and Cooperation*. San Francisco: Jossey-Bass, 55–98.

Deutsch, M. 1973. *The Resolution of Conflict*. New Haven, CT: Yale University Press.

  1986. 'Strategies of inducing cooperation'. In R. K. White (ed.) *Psychology and the Prevention of Nuclear War*. New York University Press.

Earley, P. C. and Ang, S. 2003. *Cultural Intelligence: Individual Interactions across Cultures*. Palo Alto, CA: Stanford University Press.

Etzioni, A. 1967. 'The Kennedy experiment: unilateral initiatives'. *Western Political Quarterly*, 20, 12–23.

Friedman, R. A. 1994. *Front Stage, Backstage: the Dramatic Structure of Labor Negotiations*. Cambridge, MA: MIT Press.

Fukuyama, F. 1995. *Trust: the Social Virtues and the Creation of Prosperity*. New York: Free Press.

Gaertner, S. L., Mann, J., Murrell, A. and Dovidio, J. F. 1989. 'Reducing intergroup bias: the benefits of recategorization'. *Journal of Personality and Social Psychology*, 57, 239–49.

Garling, T., Backenroth-Ohsako, G. and Ekehammar, B. 2006. *Diplomacy and Psychology: Prevention of Armed Conflicts after the Cold War*. London: Marshall Cavendish.

Gelfand, M. J. and Brett, J. M. 2004. *The Handbook of Negotiation and Culture*. Palo Alto, CA: Stanford Business Books.

Gelfand, M. J., Higgins, M., Nishii, L., Raver, J., Dominquez, A., Yamaguichi, S., Murakami, F. and Toyama, M. 2002. 'Culture and ego-centric biases of fairness in conflict and negotiation'. *Journal of Applied Psychology*, 87, 833–45.

Gelfand, M. J., Nishii, L., Dyer, N., Holcombe, K., Ohbuchi, K. and Fukumo, M. 2001. 'Cultural influences on cognitive representations of conflict: interpretations of conflict episodes'. *Journal of Applied Psychology*, 86, 1059–74.

Ginzel, L., Kramer, R. M. and Sutton, R. 1991. 'Organizational impression management as a reciprocal influence process: the neglected role of the organizational audience'. In B. M. Staw and L. L. Cummings (eds.) *Research in Organizational Behavior (Vol. 15)*. Greenwich, CT: JAI Press, 227–66.

Goffman, E. 1969. *Strategic Interaction*. Philadelphia: University of Pennsylvania Press.

Granovetter, M. 1985. 'Economic action and social structure: the problem of embeddedness'. *American Journal of Sociology*, 91(3), 481–510.

Greenhalgh, L. and Kramer, R. M. 1990. 'Strategic choice in conflicts: the importance of relationships'. In R. L. Kahn and M. N. Zald (eds.) *Organizations and Nation-States: New Perspectives on Conflict and Cooperation*. San Francisco: Jossey-Bass, 181–220.

Hardin, R. 1992. 'The street-level epistemology of trust'. *Annals der Kritikal*, 14, 152–76.

Insko, C. A. and Schopler, J. 1997. 'Differential distrust of groups and individuals'. In C. Sedikides, J. Schopler and C. Insko (eds.) *Intergroup Cognition and Intergroup Behavior*. Mahwah, NJ: Erlbaum, 75–108.

Insko, C. A., Schopler, J., Hoyle, R., Dardis, G. and Graetz, K. 1990. 'Individual-group discontinuity as a function of fear and greed'. *Journal of Personality and Social Psychology*, 58, 68–79.

Kahn, R. L. 1991. 'Organizational theory'. In PIN (Processes of International Negotiations) Project (ed.) *International Negotiation: Analysis, Approaches, and Issues*. San Francisco: Jossey-Bass, 148–63.

Kahn, R. L. and Kramer, R. M. 2006. 'Diplomacy and de-escalation: insights from social psychology'. In T. Garling, G. Backenroth-Ohsako and B. Ekehammar (eds.) *Diplomacy and Psychology: Prevention of Armed Conflicts after the Cold War*. London: Marshall Cavendish, 207–25.

Kahn, R. L. and Zald, M. N. 1990. *Organizations and Nation-States: New Perspectives on Conflict and Cooperation*. San Francisco: Jossey-Bass.

Keashly, L., Fisher, R. J. and Grant, P. R. 1993. 'The comparative utility of third party consultation and mediation within a complex simulation of intergroup conflict'. *Human Relations*, 46, 371–93.

Kelman, H. C. 1985. 'Overcoming the psychological barrier: an analysis of the Egyptian–Israeli peace process'. *Negotiation Journal*, 1, 213–35.

Kimmel, M., Pruitt, D. G., Magenau, J., Konar-Goldband, E. and Carnevale, P. G. 1980. 'The effects of trust, aspiration, and gender on negotiation tactics'. *Journal of Personality and Social Psychology*, 38, 9–23.

Kolb, D. M. 1999. *Negotiation Eclectics: Essays in Memory of Jeffrey Z. Rubin.* Cambridge, MA: PON Books.

Kramer, R. M. 1991. 'The more the merrier? Social psychological aspects of multi-party negotiations in organizations'. In M. B. Bazerman, R. J. Lewicki and B. H. Sheppard (eds.) *Research on Negotiation in Organizations* (Vol. III). Greenwich, CT: JAI Press, 307–32.

Kramer, R. M., Meyerson, D. and Davis, G. 1991. 'How much is enough?' *Journal of Personality and Social Psychology*, 58, 984–93.

Kramer, R. M., Pommerenke, P. and Newton, E. 1993. 'The social context of negotiation: effects of social identity and interpersonal accountability on negotiator decision making'. *Journal of Conflict Resolution*, 37, 633–54.

Kressel, K. 1981. 'Kissinger in the Middle East: an exploratory analysis of role strain in international mediation. In J. Z. Rubin (ed.) *Dynamics of Third Party Intervention: Kissinger in the Middle East.* New York: Praeger.

Kressel, K. and Pruitt, D. G. (eds.) 1989. *Mediation Research: the Process and Effectiveness of Third Party Intervention.* San Francisco: Jossey-Bass.

Larson, D. W. 1997. *Anatomy of Mistrust: US–Soviet Relations during the Cold War.* Ithaca, NY: Cornell University Press.

Leung, K. 2006. 'Effective conflict resolution in intercultural disputes'. In T. Garling, G. Backenroth-Ohsako and B. Ekehammar (eds.) *Diplomacy and Psychology: Prevention of Armed Conflicts After the Cold War.* New York: Marshall Cavendish, 254–74.

Lewicki, R. and Bunker, B. 1995. 'Trust in relationships: a model of trust development and decline'. In B. B. Bunker and J. Z. Rubin (eds.) *Conflict, Cooperation, and Justice.* San Francisco: Jossey-Bass, 131–45.

Lewicki, R. J., McAlister, D. and Bies, R. 1998. 'Trust and distrust: new relationships and realities'. *Academy of Management Review*, 23, 439–58.

Lewicki, R. J., Tomlinson, E. C. and Gillespie, N. 2006. 'Models of interpersonal trust development: theoretical approaches, empirical evidence, and future directions'. *Journal of Management*, 32, 1001–22.

Lewis, J. D. and Weigert, A. 1985. 'Trust as a social reality'. *Social Forces*, 63, 967–85.

Lindskold, S. 1978. 'Trust development, the GRIT proposal, and the effects of conciliatory acts on conflict and cooperation'. *Psychological Bulletin*, 85, 772–93.

1986. 'GRIT: Reducing distrust through carefully introduced conciliation'. In
S. Worchel and W. G. Austin (eds.) *Psychology of Intergroup Relations*.
Chicago: Nelson-Hall, 305–22.

Lindskold, S. and Han, G. 1988. 'GRIT as a foundation for integrative bargaining'.
*Personality and Social Psychology Bulletin*, 14, 335–45.

Macy, M. W. and Skvoretz, J. 1998. 'The evolution of trust and cooperation
between strangers: a computational model'. *American Sociological Review*,
63, 638–60.

Mares, D. R. and Powell, W. W. 1990. 'Contracts, treaties, and joint ventures'.
In R. L. Kahn and M. N. Zald (eds.) *Organizations and Nation-States: New
Perspectives on Conflict and Cooperation*. San Francisco: Jossey-Bass,
19–54.

Mayer, R. C., Davis, J. H. and Schoorman, F. D. 1995. 'An integrative model of
organizational trust'. *Academy of Management Review*, 20, 709–34.

Messick, D. M. and Mackie, D. M. 1989. 'Intergroup relations'. *Annual Review of
Psychology*, 40, 45–81.

Morris, M. W. and Gelfand, M. J. 2004. 'Cultural differences and cognitive
dynamics: expanding the cognitive perspective on negotiation'. In
M. J. Gelfand and J. M. Brett (eds.) *The Handbook of Negotiation and
Culture*. Palo Alto, CA: Stanford Business Books, 45–70.

Morris, M. W. and Peng, K. 1994. 'Culture and cause: American and Chinese
attributions for social and physical events'. *Journal of Personality and Social
Psychology*, 67, 949–71.

Neale, M. A. and Bazerman, M. H. 1991. *Cognition and Rationality in Negotiation*.
New York: Free Press.

Nye, J. 2008. *Powers to Lead*. New York: Oxford University Press.

Osgood, C. E. 1962. *An Alternative to War and Surrender*. Champaign, IL:
University of Illinois Press.

Polzer, J. T. 1996. 'Intergroup negotiations: the effects of negotiating teams'.
*Journal of Conflict Resolution*, 40, 678–98.

Probst, T., Carnevale, P. J. and Triandis, H. C. 1999. 'Cultural values in intergroup
and single-group social dilemmas'. *Organizational Behavior and Human
Decision Processes*, 77, 171–91.

Pruitt, D. G. 1981. *Negotiation Behavior*. New York: Academic Press.

Pruitt, D. G. and Kimmel, M. J. 1977. 'Twenty years of experimental gaming:
critique, synthesis, and suggestions for the future'. *Annual Review of
Psychology*, 28, 363–92.

Pruitt, D. G. and Rubin, J. Z. 1986. *Social Conflict: Escalation, Statement and
Settlement*. New York: Random House.

Robert, C. and Carnevale, P. J. 1997. 'Group choice in ultimatum
bargaining'. *Organizational Behavior and Human Decision Processes*, 72,
256–79.

Ross, W. and LaCroix, J. 1996. 'Multiple meanings of trust in negotiation theory: a literature review and integrative model'. *International Journal of Conflict Management*, 7, 314–60.

Rothbart, M. and Hallmark, W. 1988. 'Ingroup-outgroup differences in the perceived efficacy of coercion and conciliation in resolving social conflict'. *Journal of Personality and Social Psychology*, 55, 248–57.

Rubin, J. 1981. *Dynamics of Third Party Interventions: Kissinger in the Middle East*. New York: Praeger.

Sherif, M. 1966. *Group Conflict and Co-operation: Their Social Psychology*. London: Routledge and Kegan Paul.

Sherif, M., Harvey, L. J., White, B. J., Hood, W. R. and Sherif, C. W. 1961. *Intergroup Cooperation and Competition: The Robber's Cave Experiment*. Norman, OK: University Book Exchange.

Shure, G. H., Meeker, R. J. and Hansford, E. A. 1965. 'The effectiveness of pacifist strategies in bargaining games'. *Journal of Conflict Resolution*, 9, 106–17.

Slovic, P. 1993. 'Perceived risk, trust, and democracy'. *Risk Analysis*, 13, 675–82.

Solomon, L. 1960. 'The influence of some types of power relationships and game strategies on the development of trust'. *Journal of Abnormal and Social Psychology*, 61, 223–30.

Stephan, W. G. and Stephan, C. W. 1996. *Intergroup Relations*. Boulder, CO: Westview Press.

Tajfel, H. 1970. 'Experiments in intergroup discrimination'. *Scientific American*, 223(2), 96–102.

Taylor, D. M. and Moghaddam, F. M. 1987. *Theories of Intergroup Relations: International Social Psychological Perspectives*. New York: Prager.

Thompson, L. 1998. *The Mind and Heart of the Negotiator*. Upper Saddle River, NJ: Prentice-Hall.

Thompson, L., Valley, K. L. and Kramer, R. M. 1995. 'The bittersweet feeling of success: an examination of social perception in negotiation'. *Journal of Experimental Social Psychology*, 31, 467–92.

Webb, W. M. and Worchel, P. 1986. 'Trust and distrust'. In S. Worchel and W. G. Austin (eds.) *Psychology of Intergroup Relations*. Chicago: Nelson-Hall, 213–28.

Weick, K. 1979. *The Social Psychology of Organizing*, 2nd edn. New York: Addison-Wesley.

Weingart, L. R., Bennett, R. J. and Brett, J. M. 1993. 'The impact of consideration of issues and motivational orientation on group negotiation process and outcome'. *Journal of Applied Psychology*, 78, 504–17.

Yamagishi, T. 1986. 'The provision of a sanctioning system as a public good'. *Journal of Personality and Social Psychology*, 51, 110–16.

Yamagishi, T. and Yamagishi, M. 1994. 'Trust and commitment in the United States and Japan'. *Motivation and Emotion*, 18, 129–66.

Zucker, L. G. 1986. 'Production of trust: institutional sources of economic structure'. In B. M. Staw and L. L. Cummings (eds.) *Research in Organizational Behavior* (Vol. 8). Greenwich, CT: JAI Press, 53–111.

# 8 Trust development in German–Ukrainian business relationships: dealing with cultural differences in an uncertain institutional context

GUIDO MÖLLERING AND FLORIAN STACHE

## Summary

This chapter examines cultural differences and institutional uncertainty as important factors in the development of trust as a basis for successful international business relationships. The authors focus their investigation on the potential that actors have in becoming aware, and creatively responding to, institutional contexts, cultural differences and the challenge of trust development. Empirically, the authors look at German–Ukrainian business relationships and draw on a qualitative analysis of twenty-one field interviews and personal observations from the time of the so-called 'Orange Revolution'. They conclude that generally the trust dilemma in international business relationships can be overcome through reflexivity and creativity, and they give many practical examples of what this means.

## Introduction

The typical dilemma faced in international business relationships is that trust is particularly important and, at the same time, particularly difficult to achieve when the partners come from different cultures (Kühlmann, 2005; Zaheer and Zaheer, 2006). The positive expectations and willingness to be

For helpful comments on earlier versions of this chapter we thank Nicole Gillespie, Anna Kadefors, Albertus Laan, Olga Malet, Akos Rona-Tas, Mark Saunders, Martin Schröder and Lyudmyla Volynets as well as the many colleagues who gave us useful feedback at the EGOS Colloquium in Vienna, at the ESRC Seminar Series on Trust Across Cultures at Oxford Brookes University, at the Amsterdam Workshop on Trust Within and Between Organizations and at an informal seminar at the Max Planck Institute for the Study of Societies in Cologne. The German Academic Exchange Service (DAAD) kindly supported Florian Stache's fieldwork in Ukraine. Most of all, we are deeply indebted to the interview respondents for their time and openness which made this study possible.

vulnerable associated with trust (Rousseau *et al.*, 1998) are required even more, but are harder to produce, in business relationships where different cultural backgrounds increase the unfamiliarity and uncertainty between the partners. Successful cross-cultural business relationships may be jeopardized because the process of familiarization that they need to go through to build trust already requires some basic familiarity and trust to 'shift the boundaries of familiarity *from within*' (Möllering, 2006: 96, emphasis in original; see also Luhmann, 1988), which is more easily said than done. Slanted more positively, firms may have a competitive advantage in their international strategies if they manage to deal with cultural differences in a constructive manner. Research on trust development still emphasizes the obstacles resulting from cross-cultural differences (e.g. Nes *et al.*, 2007). In this chapter, we go beyond identifying obstacles and explore how they can be overcome in practice.

Empirically, we look at German–Ukrainian business relationships, where the challenge of dealing with cultural differences is amplified by institutional uncertainty. Experts describe the institutional uncertainty in Ukraine as marked by political instability, arbitrary red tape, obscure corruption networks and so on (Akimova and Schwödiauer, 2005; Meyer, 2006; Ögütçü and Kinach, 2002). These problems do not only put foreign investors off, they also upset the Ukrainian population and have contributed to large-scale protest and unrest culminating in the so-called Orange Revolution at the end of 2004. This 'revolution' was sparked by election fraud when opposition leader Viktor Yushchenko's electoral triumph was denied and incumbent Prime Minister Viktor Yanukovich was officially declared the winner. Peacefully enforcing Yushchenko's eventual rise to power, the Orange Revolution has become a symbol for the ongoing dramatic societal transformations in Ukraine, characterized by the clash of a still powerful yet also decrepit and self-serving elite with a far more progressive and ambitious population (for details see, e.g. Karatnycky, 2005).

This instability explains partly why relatively few German firms have established subsidiaries in Ukraine or relationships with Ukrainian business partners. However, Ukraine should also be a relatively attractive country for internationalization due to its low labour costs, favourable supply of raw materials, good level of education, great market potential and reasonable geographical and political proximity to Germany and, more generally, the European Union (Kohlert, 2006; Ögütçü and Kinach, 2002). And, indeed, success stories of German–Ukrainian business ventures do exist. Germany is Ukraine's most important trade partner after Russia; German investors have pumped hundreds of millions of euros into Ukraine; and major German firms have been operating in Ukraine for many years (Meyer, 2006; Ukrainian Embassy, 2008).

In our analysis, we focus on these successful cases and use qualitative data from interviews with experienced experts and practitioners, who explain, mainly from a managerial perspective, what is needed to build successful German–Ukrainian business relationships – and what needs to be avoided. Instead of simple recipes, however, we find that it takes reflexivity, sensitivity and curiosity. Managers cannot bypass the effort of getting to know their business partners and agreeing rules with them in the face of personal, cultural and economic differences. Hence we investigate the potential that actors have in creatively responding to institutional contexts, cultural differences and the challenge of trust development (Mizrachi *et al.*, 2007).

Adair and Brett (2005) argue that we need to take a closer look at what actors actually do in cross-cultural negotiations, and they show that actors can use communicative flexibility to overcome cultural distance. Swidler's (1986) concept of culture as a repertoire for action strategies equally suggests that reflexive actors are not 'cultural dopes' (Garfinkel, 1967) but can be very creative in how they use their cultural repertoires. Our emphasis on reflexivity is in line with an increasingly recognized need for more in-depth qualitative and interpretative research in international business (Marschan-Piekkari and Welch, 2004). What do international managers actually do when they need to build trust in the face of cultural differences and unfavourable institutions? This matches the 'trust repertoires' approach of Mizrachi *et al.* (2007) which portrays actors as knowledgeable agents who are not only passively affected by culture, but who can also draw on their cultural repertoires to apply different forms of trust purposefully.

In the next part of this chapter, we introduce briefly the main conceptual foundations and issues related to our research. This is followed by a short description of our data collection and analysis. In the main part of the chapter, we present our empirical findings from the German–Ukrainian business context. Finally, in the last part of the chapter, we discuss our findings and suggest implications for practice and directions for further research.

## Conceptual foundations: trust, culture and institutions

When studying cross-cultural relationships it would be absurd to conduct empirical research with narrowly defined concepts, simply because the meaning of the concepts is culturally variable and 'contextualization' (Tsui, 2006) is required of researchers as well as practitioners. Trust is culturally specific (Doney *et al.*, 1998; Johnson and Cullen, 2002) as shown, for example, in comparative studies (e.g. Burchell and Wilkinson, 1997; Fukuyama, 1995). Nevertheless, it is possible to agree on a baseline definition of trust as positive expectations in the face of vulnerability (Mayer *et al.*, 1995; Rousseau *et al.*, 1998) as long as we remain conceptually open to the various ways in which trust is produced and experienced in different cultures. Identifying cultural differences in trust is only the starting point for the more interesting question of what happens when different trust cultures meet (e.g. Child, 1998; Kühlmann, 2005; see also Ferrin and Gillespie in this volume).

We are particularly interested in the reflexivity of trust development (Möllering, 2006) and the notion of 'active trust' (Child and Möllering, 2003; Giddens, 1994; Mizrachi *et al.*, 2007). The crucial question is how a process of trust development can be started in initial encounters and later maintained as the relationship matures (see also Lewicki *et al.*, 2006; Williams, 2007). This is complicated by the proposition that trust is a matter of will but cannot be willed: it has to come naturally. Our qualitative research is designed to capture trust development as a creative learning process that is driven by the actors themselves and enabled by leaps of faith (Möllering, 2006) but also embedded in an economic, cultural and institutional context.

Analysing culture and cultural differences, we build mainly on the sociological literature and follow Swidler (1986) who argues that cultures and the differences between them are best understood in terms of the specific habits, skills and styles that people use, like a 'tool kit', in constructing 'strategies of action'. We assume that cross-cultural problems often result from difficulties in understanding signals rather than from incommensurable underlying values (see also Branzei *et al.*, 2007). It follows that actors need to be able to interpret the other's action correctly, which invokes another popular conceptualization of culture as a shared meaning system (Geertz, 1973). Meanings organize the cultural repertoire and indicate how it *can* be used, while values direct how it *should* be used.

Prior research on multinationals and international cooperation has shown very clearly that differences in national culture affect the way relationships are organized and the performance they achieve (e.g. Geringer and Hébert, 1991; Johnson *et al.*, 1996). For multinationals, Newman and Nollen (1996: 773) find that 'business performance is better when management practices are congruent with national culture', which includes the assumption and the conclusion that managers can deal productively with cultural differences by adapting their practices – in the way that is known proverbially as 'When in Rome, do as the Romans do'. This presumes that actors can adapt their cultural repertoires (Swidler, 1986). Accordingly, we suggest that researchers need to take a closer look at how cultures deal with culture. We advocate an autological perspective on cultural differences: what are the cultural differences in dealing with cultural differences?

From this perspective, generalized cultural stereotypes (or survey-based classifications à la Hofstede, 1980) are relevant only when respondents actually refer to them in their cross-cultural interactions at the micro-level. For example, Kühlmann (2005: 46) observes in some German–Mexican business relationships that 'both parties act as if they try to contradict the assumed heterostereotype of the typical German or the typical Mexican. German business partners attach great importance to close, friendly relationships whereas their Mexican partners demonstrate competence, reliability and honesty'. In other words, both sides are not trapped in their own cultures but can adapt their action strategies drawing on cultural resources from the *other* culture by reference to the cultural stereotypes that they actually seek to leave behind.

This notion of actors using culture in trust development, rather than merely reacting to it, has been elaborated on the basis of Swidler's (1986) repertoire theory into a 'trust repertoires' approach by Mizrachi *et al.*, (2007). Like our emphasis on reflexivity in active trust development their approach 'treat[s] the actor as the engine of trust' (Mizrachi *et al.*, 2007: 145) who uses culture as a resource to adapt trust to situational changes and challenges.

When a cross-cultural business relationship is formed in practice, the parties involved do not only bring their own culturally shaped strategies of action to the table, as it were, but their interactions are also embedded in an institutional context. According to Ayios (2004: 223), 'in cross-cultural business at least, the institutional context in which business takes place is an absolutely key variable'. However, it may not be clear to all parties what exactly the institutional context entails for them. Uncertainty in this regard has many sources which boil down to a lack of knowledge and/or agreement with regard to which rules, roles and routines can be taken for granted and which rights and obligations will be upheld. Such a lack of knowledge and/or agreement may not only be a subjective problem of the parties concerning a specific business relationship; it may exist 'objectively' when larger institutional frameworks are significantly absent, failing or changing, for whatever reason.

Zucker (1986) argues that trust can be based on institutions, especially between actors who have no history of prior interaction. Institutions are supposed to produce predictability through common rules and sanctions, substituting for prior interpersonal experience or membership of the same group or class. Accordingly, new relationships between German and Ukrainian firms would benefit from a reliable institutional context, but this presupposes that they trust those institutions (see Möllering, 2006 on the literature highlighting trust in institutions as a condition for institution-based trust). In as much as institutions are a source of trust (Zucker, 1986), an uncertain institutional context will generally impede trust in business relationships and may have to be compensated for by other ways of trust development (Child and Möllering, 2003; Radaev, 2005; Rose-Ackerman, 2001; Welter et al., 2003). Like culture, institutions shape the context and basis for trust development, but actors also exercise agency in the way they use, influence or make up for them.

In this paper, we are interested in both cultural differences and institutional uncertainty as important factors in the development of trust as a basis for successful business relationships. We look primarily at how national, rather than organizational, cultures and institutions are relevant for organizations that work across national borders. This is not to deny that issues of organizational culture and the institutionalization of organizations are relevant in inter-firm relations, too. Problems (and opportunities) may occur, for example, not just because one firm is Ukrainian and the other German and their exchanges take place in Ukraine or Germany, but also because one is a small, loosely structured service firm while the other is a big hierarchical manufacturing firm (on 'cultural fit' see, for example, Child and Faulkner, 1998).

Ukraine is one of the transformation economies and societies in Eastern Europe, which implies a very dynamic institutional context (Akimova and Schwödiauer, 2005; Ögütçü and Kinach, 2002; Rose-Ackerman, 2001). The main part of our fieldwork took place during the Orange Revolution at the end of 2004 when, to say the least, the Ukrainian institutional framework was put into question and forced to change with no reliable prospect of what would come next. If most Ukrainians do not have trust in their own country's institutions and the Germans or other foreigners do not trust Ukrainian institutions either, then it appears that they need to build trust largely without the support of institutions and also without prior experience with each other.

## Exploratory work: data collection and analysis

In order to find answers to the question of how trust can be developed in the face of cultural differences and institutional uncertainty, we draw on qualitative field data from exploratory interviews with actors who have substantial practical experience in German–Ukrainian business relationships. We talked to a restricted but balanced set of experts who are successful in this context, but who have also observed others fail. Interviews were not conducted for testing hypotheses but for generating rich new insights into our topic. Our case selection is justified, because Central and Eastern Europe is a region undergoing fundamental transformations that are relevant to the rest of the world; Germany is a leading industrial nation neighbouring this region; and Ukraine is a striking, yet under-researched, example of a large country torn between the old Soviet system and the new Western influences. Building on a two-month visit in 2003, one of us (Stache) used his contacts to carry out fieldwork in Ukraine in November and December 2004, which happened to coincide with the Orange Revolution.

The findings reported in this chapter are based on twenty-one interviews that were conducted and analysed specifically for research purposes (see also Stache, 2006). Their interpretation is facilitated by countless additional conversations and field observations in Ukraine and also back in Germany. Respondents were selected with the aim of obtaining the most authoritative and insightful viewpoints as well as a broad and fairly representative variety of perspectives. Aware of pronounced regional differences in Ukraine and their potential effect on levels of trust (e.g. Chepurenko and Malieva, 2005), we were careful to cover both the country's western regions (from Kiev) and the eastern regions (from Odessa). Our sample is biased in that almost all of our respondents were, at the time of the interview, still active in Ukraine and generally positive about the possibility of doing business there successfully. However, this bias is in line with our overall research design, since we seek to explore the positive, constructive ways out of the trust dilemma in cross-cultural business relationships.

Of the twenty-one interviews, fourteen were held with Germans (in German) and seven with Ukrainians (in Russian). The German sample consists of seven senior managers from different sectors (automotive, banking, engineering, logistics and textile), three consultants, two high-ranking commercial diplomats, a lawyer and a business professor. In the Ukrainian sample there were four specialists from professional service firms and consultancies (in accounting, marketing and human resources), a manager of an agency representing German firms, a radio station director and an economics professor. Each interview lasted between forty-five minutes and two hours. They were semi-structured, based on a five-page interview guide, and tailored to the diverse respondents (for details see Stache, 2006). Typical questions in relation to trust would be, for example, 'How do you deal with the fact that you cannot remove all uncertainty and vulnerability from a business relationship?' or 'Do Ukrainian/German business people mean different things by trust?' or 'How do you think trust develops in business relationships?' When trust is addressed directly in interview questions, social desirability effects (Crowne and Marlowe, 1964) cannot be ruled out, but this has been less of a problem in our interviews, because the trust questions were embedded in more general queries about relationship development, trust was a highly relevant topic to the respondents (no need for much prompting) and the perceptions of reality conveyed to us were quite balanced as to the potential and the limits of trust. Interestingly, cultural differences were not originally envisaged as a main theme of the interviews but were brought up regularly by the respondents.

While only one of us (Stache) performed the empirical fieldwork, the other (Möllering) gave key conceptual inputs, and together we engaged in an intensive process of interpreting the data. Our findings are the outcome of thorough iterations with mutual enrichment of theory and data, strong inter-researcher agreement and results solid enough to guide further research. Our main method of probing the validity of our findings has been to stay in touch with the field, including another visit to Ukraine in 2005. We arranged specific 'member checks' and presented our findings to experts on business in Ukraine, for example at the IHK Düsseldorf (Chamber of Commerce). We used their feedback to correct or confirm our own interpretations.

## Findings on German–Ukrainian business relationships

We describe our empirical findings, looking at the institutional context first, followed by cultural differences in trust development and action strategies for trust building across cultures. We also look at performance outcomes of the business relationships and the limits of trust development.

### Institutional context and trust

Institutions in Ukraine have been undergoing a vast transformation process since the beginning of the 1990s, most notably in the economic sphere. After the breakdown of the communist system, the change from a state-directed to a market-driven production system started off with virtually no production at all. Personal trust in business partners was the only way for directors of state companies to restart production and a prerequisite for their firms to survive. 'They were calling on the colleagues they trusted in order to get hold of, for example, some input factors in exchange for the promise of a certain amount of the finished good', as a professor of Ukrainian history and language at the State University of Odessa recalls. A German consultant in Odessa explains that 'under those circumstances of uncertainty, you are just much more dependent on each other. Without people you can rely on, you literally cannot survive in this country'. Personal bonds of trust and reciprocity substitute for institutional safeguards, and trust itself is very much a by-product of the very conscious mutual efforts to get by (see also Chepurenko and Malieva, 2005; Radaev, 2005; Rose-Ackerman, 2001).

The reliance on prior personal trust relationships coincides not just with the absence of reliable formal institutions but also with a deep mistrust towards the Ukrainian state shared by all Ukrainian and German interviewees alike (see also Akimova and Schwödiauer, 2005). However, informal institutions seem to take the place of the state and the formal institutionalized mechanisms provided by the state elsewhere. For example, as in Russia (Volkov, 2002), it is taken for granted in Ukraine that a company has a *krysha* (Ukrainian for roof) to protect its interests: 'This is formally only a company getting paid to arrange our security, with a security officer being there 24 hours' (German investor). The background of the companies offering these security services is somewhat obscure and dubious, but working with them is still 'much better than relying on the state', who 'won't help you anyway, even in case of a burglary, if you don't bribe them', as the Ukrainian head of a German radio station in Odessa points out. *Kryshas* are essentially criminal protection rackets, but have become highly institutionalized – with a kind of legitimacy based more on resignation than on approval – in the former Soviet Union as private power structures protecting their members' property based on the use of intimidation and violence outside of the law (see also Volkov, 2002). The *krysha* practice is appalling, but it is evidence of reflexive responses to institutional voids.

Bribery is another example of how relationships are built under institutional uncertainty. This is a paradoxical and pathological practice, because bribery seeks to reduce uncertainty but undermines the institutions that would reduce uncertainty and make bribes unnecessary. From the point of view of individual actors in Ukraine, the situation looks a little different though: on the one hand, using bribes can be part of a reflexive, bottom-up trust-building process; on the other hand, bribing in Ukraine has already become all but institutionalized. A Ukrainian tax specialist we interviewed was able to tell us the standard 'prices' for many 'state services' irrespective of the actual functionary performing them.

A further example of practices and organizations substituting for a well-functioning and trusted state is the so-called 'checking' of potential business partners, which the head of an international association strongly recommended to us. This 'checking' involves a thorough informal inspection of the target firm, its owners and business partners, which is partly done using connections to the secret service, as the representative of a German law firm in Kiev elaborates. According to him, it is 'a procedure the Ukrainians do themselves on a regular basis and taken as completely normal'.

These informal institutions and their capacity to make exchanges more efficient are rooted in a culture that has known a kind of unquestioned 'trust' routine of doing 'correct' business on the huge black markets, which stems from Soviet times when many formal institutions were in complete opposition to the needs of the population. This kind of routine is still part of the cultural repertoire that actors draw on when they form business relationships even though it contradicts some of the values that the actors espouse. As Rose-Ackerman (2001: 423) notes: 'Most people view corruption negatively even in countries where it is wide-spread.'

## Cultural differences in trust development

Following on from the institutional issues, another theme that emerged from our interviews concerns the different taken-for-granted meanings of trust and ways of trust building in different cultures. While a Ukrainian manager may find it completely normal to rely on informal institutions and to ignore the weak formal institutions, a German manager may be perplexed by this due to deep cultural differences in the action strategies on how business is done. A German consultant who works with German and Ukrainian firms in Ukraine stresses that 'in every community, be it in Germany or here in Ukraine, there are a number of mechanisms that one has learned from kindergarten onwards about how to build trust with others without falling flat on one's face'. According to him, trust building is the outcome of socialization and learning about a cultural repertoire, which implies that Germans who want to build trust with Ukrainians 'have to get deeper into the mentality and the ways of trust building that are customary here'. When asked if Ukrainians can be trusted as much as Western business people, this consultant replies: 'Ultimately the same but differently.' He explains that in Germany a handshake, a contract and a rough check of the other's creditworthiness are enough to give confidence. Not so in Ukraine where, according to him, 'a signed contract is not a signed contract. It takes more than the signature on the paper ... Here, you need to get to know the other and his background a little deeper, also personally, or you will not be able to build trust'.

Contracts have a different meaning in Ukraine and are seen more like internal rules in addition to a personal relationship, rather than as external safeguards substituting for personal relationships, simply because it is a very common view that 'the Ukrainian courts are corrupt' (Ukrainian Vice President of one of the world's leading accounting firms, see also Akimova and Schwödiauer 2005). Overall, the cultural differences in trust building in business are captured by a German consultant's talk of a clash of 'deal-oriented' and 'relationship-oriented' business cultures. Deal orientation is the predominant cultural style of Western managers who want 'a good deal, written down in a good contract'. Ukrainians do business in a 'relationship-oriented' way and rely on reflexive modes of trust production. Germans are used to very stable conditions, whereas the Ukrainians are used to high external uncertainty. Their cultural repertoires have developed in line with, and in response to, environmental conditions. If actors do not try to overcome their different action strategies for trust production, these can be culturally induced obstacles to international cooperation (Branzei *et al.*, 2007).

All our respondents expressed the view that trust development must not be left to chance – as a lucky by-product – but should be intentionally fostered through managerial action. In the Ukrainian context such action is seen as particularly important and should be targeted at building a relationship that allows for trust beyond narrow business issues. 'It is very important that not only the directors get to know each other step by step; all employees working together across borders should have the possibility to meet in person', states the German director of a management consultancy.

As described above, actors in Ukraine attach more importance to assessing specific managers and their background than to the details of the contract. One further reason for this may be that the understanding of what it means to be a manager is in flux in Ukraine as well. Interestingly, three different varieties of understanding the role of a manager appear frequently in talking to experts of the Ukrainian context, each variety associated with a different period of the Ukrainian transition and the cultural repertoires produced at the time (Stache, 2006: 73–9). First, some managers still work like 'general directors' in Soviet times, inefficiently and by personal command. Second, those managers who take advantage of the absence of reliable rules or who follow the spirit of free markets and capitalism excessively are often called 'cowboys'. Third, with the environment becoming less uncertain and with better knowledge in Ukraine about how capitalism works in other countries, German interviewees find more and more business people described as 'rational merchants' among Ukrainian managers who have adopted the predominant management style of mature market economies. The younger generation in particular espouses the Western business culture and distances itself from Soviet legacies and cowboy-type excesses, drawing on a new cultural repertoire that is less accessible to older generations.

Unsurprisingly, German firms interested in doing business in Ukraine will seek out the 'rational merchants' with whom they can build trust more easily thanks to a common understanding of the managerial role and a similar cultural repertoire, while they will avoid the 'general directors' and 'cowboys'.

Managers 'will seek partners for whom interpersonal approaches to business relationships represent their own choice of business behaviour', as Ayios (2004: 205) concludes referring to Russian businessmen. This makes choosing the right partner, as a first step of active trust development, a very important decision in Ukraine, which is something that German managers out of their usual experience in Germany do not seem to understand. And a German consultant frequently introducing foreigners to Ukrainian businessmen points out: 'At first I have to ask: Who is this? With whom does he work? And before he will really talk to me and tell me what he thinks, he needs to know who I am. If I don't pay attention to those things, I cannot do business here'.

In practical terms, taking the first steps in an unknown environment seems to be impossible without assistance. Organizations operating internationally with long experience in Germany and Ukraine can step in. The Düsseldorf Chamber of Commerce, for example, specializes in Eastern Europe and has a subsidiary in Kiev. Another example is the German Chambers of Industry and Commerce's office in Kiev, the *Delegation der deutschen Wirtschaft*. These organizations are well known and trusted by actors on both sides, as German and Ukrainian interviewees in Kiev agree. They take up the role of 'interpreting' trust. For example, they seek potential Ukrainian business partners as a service for German firms. They know those potential partners either directly or via their huge networks in the country. These organizations become institutionalized trust intermediaries and German managers are willing to pay for this.

## Active trust development across cultures

Interestingly, the German experts we interviewed in Ukraine often favour the Ukrainian business culture in many ways and mention more advantages than disadvantages compared to Germany. Especially those working in the western part of Ukraine in the Kiev area cite 'extremely motivated personnel' as an advantage, often even before geographical location, market size, market growth or low wages. 'I can call my employees day and night on the mobile phone. Imagine that in Germany!' highlights the director of the biggest German investor in the Odessa region. The German director of one of the biggest and fastest growing foreign companies in Ukraine asserts that 'since I have been working here, I sometimes don't understand anymore how they handle things in Germany'.

The high flexibility and motivation of Ukrainians can probably be explained by economic pressures and power asymmetries, too, but this does not contradict the fact that certain action strategies characterized by flexibility and responsiveness draw on cultural resources that have evolved in Ukraine over decades against the background of instability and uncertainty. German managers recognize – and appreciate – the different Ukrainian repertoire. Whether they will exploit it or make fair use of it is a different matter, but the questioning of one's own cultural coordinates and opening up to the foreign culture partly explains why some German companies are successful in the Ukrainian context while others fail. A German consultant says: 'In an environment where things do not work according to functioning rules, flexibility is a very important personal characteristic in everyday life as well.' Thus flexibility has to be part of the cultural toolkit due to the institutional context and because it is now a culturally expected skill.

While our respondents recognize the importance of dealing with cultural differences, they also see that the two cultures may not be that far apart. The director of the largest German consulting firm working in Kiev argues that 'cultural differences do exist, but they are by far not as great as between Germany and China. Compared to the latter, Ukraine is fairly similar to Europe'. This view is dominant among the German experts interviewed. When they name unfavourable differences – like less quality consciousness or a lack of willingness to take responsibility on the Ukrainian side – our respondents always manage to explain them very convincingly by differences in institutions and history. Thus another important point seems to be that successful German actors in Ukraine do not stop at the level of recognizing cultural differences. Even when they are unfavourable, they try to understand the reasons behind them, discuss the problems that arise openly, and try to work with them. All German experts agree that there is a big willingness to learn on the Ukrainian side which they attribute overall as going hand in hand with the vast changes the Ukrainians experienced during the past fifteen years and the flexibility that this required from them.

Ukrainian experts do reflect on their culture regarding openness and trust as well, but without always putting it in such positive terms. A Ukrainian professor of economic analysis and business at the State University of Odessa expresses it as follows: 'For reasons of history, we still have problems with plurality of opinion and that is a very important ingredient to trust in working relationships as well. If you are not tolerant towards differences, if you don't accept others as you accept yourself, there is no space for mutual trust.' Success might be connected to the ability to reflect on negative aspects of one's own culture when dealing with cultural differences. This is confirmed by a German lawyer working in Kiev: 'Generally, working with Ukrainians is not difficult. What they don't like is what we in Germany call *Besserwessitum* [Westerners' know-it-all manner].'

Starting with a basic attitude of openness and flexibility towards the other, the crucial point in building the relationship then seems to be to create internal stability and, most importantly, to 'find common rules, otherwise there will never be trust. If one plays soccer and the other handball, that is the same problem for building up trust as if they don't find a common aim to work towards', as a Ukrainian business professor puts it. Interestingly, German and Ukrainian experts often mention independently that trustful business relations first need a common goal and, second, common rules set out by both parties to achieve the goal under the given circumstances. This does not mean that in Ukraine everything has to be done the Ukrainian way. A German consultant in Odessa explains: 'You have to discuss what you see here and compare it to the way of work you are used to. What works better in Germany? What works better in Ukraine? How can we best work together under the circumstances here?'

Regarding the role of the manager, the president of a German bank in Ukraine gives the example of how he handled culturally different behaviour of the locals that was just not fitting as an efficient practice working in a market economy. He tells us:

> You always have to listen to other arguments, but sometimes you have to make things very clear. The problem was they never accepted responsibility and always asked me what to do. So I arranged a meeting with the highest executives working here with me and told them: 'It says 'manager' on your business card. You get paid like a manager. How do you think a manager should behave?' We went through this procedure a couple of times and now things are already a lot better.

Trust across cultures in business relations seems to emerge in interaction when, in situations that are also characterized by dependence and power differentials, people start to look beyond cultural differences and work on setting up common rules for their specific relationship. Those rules can then contribute to reflexive trust building by making each other's behaviour more understandable and less uncertain. A German lawyer observes:

> It is important to come here with a good amount of curiosity and interest for the country, and to look how the market works. You have to listen to the people when they tell you something. You have to go ways with them you would never go in Germany, open up your eyes and ears for completely different ways of handling business and sometimes go those ways.

Regular face-to-face meetings are required in order to learn about the unfamiliar context, get to know the personality of the business partner, define a common aim and develop rules for the relationship. In this regard, Ukrainian experts consider informal meetings as being more important than official business meetings. A Ukrainian business professor points out: 'To trust someone, you need to get to know him better in some informal atmosphere. That takes time. There is an old proverb saying you need to eat a centner [Russian unit of weight] of salt with him! It is very important to see how he behaves towards others, especially when he is in his natural environment and unforeseeable incidents occur.' Clearly, it takes many meals together to eat that much salt (about a hundred kilos). All German experts that we talked to in Ukraine are used to this business conduct. They say it is normal to bring their wives to business meetings in restaurants, for example. For them this cultural difference compared to Germany is something they even seem to enjoy. One respondent tells the story of how business partners cooked traditional dishes of their home country for each other. This is not only a very graphic and reflexive way of actively dealing with cultural differences, it is also a practice that goes much further than what would happen even in long-lasting business relations in Germany.

## Trust, culture and success

According to the German respondents, taking an interest in the foreign environment and being open to new ways different from the familiar ones in Germany is the key to success in Ukraine. Inversely, the most important reason for failure is said to be the unwillingness to do things differently than in Germany and to extend the cultural repertoire. We are actually surprised that our respondents put this cultural openness (or lack thereof) at the top of their list of reasons for success (or failure) in Ukraine. We asked them 'What do you see as the biggest trap for a foreign company starting to invest in Ukraine?' and anticipated that they would mainly talk about legal, political or technical difficulties. That they talked first and foremost about culture underlines the great practical relevance of this topic.

The notion of success in cross-cultural business relationships is somewhat diffuse among German and Ukrainian firms and their managers. However, in spite of this vagueness, they all agree that success is very much dependent on trust. The highest official representing German business in Ukraine expresses that, for her personally, trust is 'the very first priority. I have been in Ukraine for a long time and I know that trust is more important than any contract. Although I studied law, I can tell you once again: trust is the most important thing'.

We cannot claim that the twenty-one interviews we carried out give a fully representative picture. However, we find evidence in the accounts of our respondents that the success of cross-cultural business relationships depends significantly on active trust development activities which are undertaken from a position of openness to the other culture and a willingness to deal reflexively with cultural differences. We have analysed this empirically in an uncertain institutional context and we find that, overall, institutional uncertainty makes the cultural reflexivity and active trust development even more salient than in a stable context that offers much stability and certainty on which new relationships can draw.

## Limitations to trust-building strategies

Nevertheless, there are some caveats that became apparent during our research. Predominantly Ukrainian experts mention that active trust development loses its functionality when it is openly called that. As soon as the business partner feels that regular meetings are arranged just to build up trust in order to get a better deal, this will have counterproductive effects. There has to develop some real interest in the persons and, ideally, in the country if one wants to do good business in Ukraine. But if it is obvious that everything is *just* about the good business, then the issue of the cultural difference between 'deal orientation' and 'relationship orientation' returns. Two German respondents also mentioned that when trust builds up unnaturally quickly and a relationship gets too personal too quickly, this might be an early sign of the intention to abuse Western firms. Hence, managers must negotiate a terrain that lies conceptually between not forcing trust and not leaving it up to chance either, as well as between pursuing their own interest and contributing to the common interest in the relationship.

Finally, it must not be forgotten that things are still very much in flux in Ukraine and other countries of the former Soviet bloc. For example, Chepurenko and Malieva (2005) find in a survey of 400 small entrepreneurs in four Russian regions – much to their own surprise – that the importance of personal trust networks, *kryshas*, local milieus and intermediaries has declined and that business partners do rely on institutions even though they still say that they very much distrust those institutions. This is a very different picture compared to the 1990s and we may observe similar changes, perhaps even reversals, in Ukraine and other transforming economies and societies of Eastern and Central Europe.

Even against the background of the Orange Revolution, Ukrainian and German experts agree that, as in Russia (Chepurenko and Malieva, 2005), overall stability in Ukraine has increased in a noticeable way since about 2001. Whereas, before, enormous uncertainty prevented trust production outside of existing networks, because 'at that time, everyone would have taken as much money as possible, as you did not know what would happen tomorrow', people now value the new relative stability and 'nowadays might sometimes behave particularly correctly towards the foreign company, because it is seen to be something very special to work with foreigners who can supply a little stability, which is still a very scarce resource here' (both quotes by the Ukrainian director of a German radio station). This is supported by other respondents, too, and can be taken as evidence for agency in applying and adapting cultural repertoires in changing situations and cross-cultural interactions.

## Discussion

The research reported here confirms previous findings on the influence of cultural differences on trust and, subsequently, relationship performance (Ayios, 2004; Child, 1998; Doney *et al.*, 1998; Johnson and Cullen, 2002; Zaheer and Zaheer, 2006). Using a qualitative methodology, we have been able to look beyond abstract, superficial indicators and identify specific meanings and action strategies. We also contribute new insights by reporting specifically on business relationships involving Germany and Ukraine, which have not as yet been the object of much systematic study, despite the size and significance of the two countries (Kohlert, 2006). The experiences in the German–Ukrainian context that we relay in some detail in this chapter will be useful to managers and researchers planning to go into this context or comparable ones.

Our main contribution in this chapter has been to highlight the role of reflexivity in relationship building and the analytical and practical value of adopting what we call an autological perspective on cultural differences. By this we mean that we do not merely look at whether differences in the cultural repertoires exist but also, more importantly, at how people deal with them in interaction (Kühlmann, 2005). We do not simply ask whether trust matters but also what people do to build it in difficult situations (Mizrachi *et al.*, 2007). Overcoming barriers requires a genuine interest in understanding the other, questioning one's own assumptions and searching for common aims and rules for initial interactions that produce positive mutual experience from which a trustful relationship can grow.

Besides culture, we have also considered the role of the institutional context for trust development. We can confirm the notion that the *absence* of reliable institutions as a possible basis for trust (Zucker, 1986) might be compensated for by other ways of trust development (see also Rose-Ackerman, 2001; Welter *et al.*, 2003). In particular, we find that actors engage in reflexive relationship building which produces 'process-based trust' (in Zucker's terminology). At the same time, by developing their own rules for the relationship, actors attempt a kind of micro-institutionalization at the inter-organizational level. This matches Hultén's (2006) notion of a 'cross-institutional setting' which implies the transfer of institutional rules across institutional boundaries, resulting in hybrid institutional forms.

## Implications for practice

More normative inferences in the sense of models predicting success or checklists containing the managerial 'dos and dont's' at different stages in a cross-cultural business relationship would go against a fundamental message that we received in our interviews. Managers should not assume that there is a fixed model or an explicit 'best practice' that they can simply emulate. The specific suggestions and examples we have reported in the empirical part of this chapter can be no more than a rough guideline and source of inspiration. For example, it is advisable to arrange personal meetings, to seek the help of trusted third parties, and to openly discuss profit motives, but such pointers do not release managers from finding out for themselves what works when, where and with whom.

In a nutshell, our message to practitioners is that they should follow a modernized version of the simple advice of 'When in Rome, do as the Romans do' that Saint Ambrose gave in the fourth century AD. We would recommend: When in Rome, get to know the Romans, get them to get to know you, and get to know yourself. And then you have to be open, look for common goals and set up common rules together that work best in the given context.

## Directions for further research

We have focused in this chapter on cultural differences because, by definition, they characterize cross-cultural business relationships compared to relationships within one culture. However, it is an intriguing question whether managers in cross-cultural encounters should be explicit about cultural differences and address them in their trust-building processes, as we have suggested. After all, any concrete setting involves not only cultural differences but also different personalities, business goals, organizational structures, et cetera, each carrying a degree of potential conflict. Further research can address this question and elaborate how international business relationships involve not only the cultural level but also other levels (personal, organizational, technical, financial, etc.).

More comprehensive studies than ours could take two forms. First, a structured survey of a large sample of international business relationships could be undertaken in the tradition of the positivist search for 'success factors'. We think that this would produce only very superficial insights with limited practical value, though. Second, and more in line with our approach in this chapter, researchers could do in-depth, qualitative case studies following a small number of international business relationships over several years and analysing relationship development at various levels and in various dimensions (see also Marschan-Piekkari and Welch, 2004). The outcome could be an empirically grounded process framework for the development of cross-cultural inter-organizational relationships. This would give a very useful orientation device for managers without any 'best practice' claims.

Moreover, we suppose that actors differ in their capability to be 'the engine of trust' (Mizrachi *et al.*, 2007: 145). Further research needs to find out what separates those who are able to deal creatively with cultural differences, an uncertain institutional context and the difficulties in trust building from those who fail to overcome the obstacles. At the individual level, is it a matter of personality or can managers learn to develop an open and constructive attitude? And is this a gradual learning process or a sudden insight or event that changes managerial attitudes? Another factor that has been suggested to us is the difference between older and younger generations. It should be investigated whether the cultural repertoires of younger Germans and Ukrainians overlap to a much larger degree than those of their older collea-gues, bosses and predecessors. At the organizational level, it needs to be asked what kind of settings enable or constrain managers to become open, self-critical and creative in business relationships. An organizational culture of mistrust and bureaucratic control is probably not a good condition from which to build trustful relationships outside of the firm across national cultures. Hence, we encourage further research to look at how trust building depends on individual and organizational conditions in boundary spanning across cultural divides (Perrone *et al.*, 2003).

## Concluding comments

It almost goes without saying that the generalizablity of our findings and conclusions is limited in as much as we have only studied the German–Ukrainian context, used a small but in-depth sample approach and focused on salient cultural and institutional factors with less emphasis on personal, economic, technical and network factors that are clearly also relevant and hardly separable from culture and institutions. From this exploratory project we conclude that the trust dilemma can be overcome through reflexivity and creativity, and we have given many detailed examples of what this means. Most importantly, we have shown: many actors are not paralysed by institutional voids; they engage in processes of familiarization; they develop their own rules; and they adapt to changing circumstances. We hope that future research on trust, culture and institutions will pursue similar research strategies and study not only the issues but also the successful managerial responses to these issues. This will help us to understand why some firms are more successful in international business than others, and it can help firms to become more successful by reviewing their own practices in the light of our findings.

## References

Adair, W. L. and Brett, J. M. 2005. 'The negotiation dance: time, culture, and behavioral sequences in negotiation'. *Organization Science*, 16, 33–52.

Akimova, I. and Schwödiauer, G. 2005. 'The effect of trust in courts on the performance of Ukrainian SMEs'. In H.-H. Höhmann and F. Welter (eds.) *Trust and Entrepreneurship: a West–East Perspective*. Cheltenham: Edward Elgar, 156–75.

Ayios, A. 2004. *Trust and Western–Russian Business Relationships*. Aldershot: Ashgate.

Branzei, O., Vertinsky, I. and Camp, R. D. 2007. 'Culture-contingent signs of trust in emergent relationships'. *Organizational Behavior and Human Decision Processes*, 104, 61–82.

Burchell, B. and Wilkinson, F. 1997. 'Trust, business relationships and the contractual environment'. *Cambridge Journal of Economics*, 21, 217–37.

Chepurenko, A. and Malieva, E. 2005. 'Trust-milieus of Russian SMEs: cross-regional comparisons'. In H.-H. Höhmann and F. Welter (eds.) *Trust and Entrepreneurship: a West–East Perspective*. Cheltenham: Edward Elgar, 136–55.

Child, J. 1998. 'Trust and international strategic alliances: the case of Sino-foreign joint ventures'. In C. Lane and R. Bachmann (eds.) *Trust Within and Between Organizations*. Oxford University Press, 241–72.

Child, J. and Faulkner, D. O. 1998. *Strategies of Co-operation: Managing Alliances, Networks, and Joint Ventures*. Oxford University Press.

Child, J. and Möllering, G. 2003. 'Contextual confidence and active trust development in the Chinese business environment'. *Organization Science*, 14, 69–80.

Crowne, D. P. and Marlowe, D. 1964. *The Approval Motive: Studies in Evaluative Dependence*. New York: Wiley.

Doney, P. M., Cannon, J. P. and Mullen, M. R. 1998. 'Understanding the influence of national culture on the development of trust'. *Academy of Management Journal*, 23, 601–20.

Fukuyama, F. 1995. *Trust: The Social Virtues and the Creation of Prosperity*. London: Hamish Hamilton.

Garfinkel, H. 1967. *Studies in Ethnomethodology*. Englewood Cliffs: Prentice Hall.

Geertz, C. 1973. *The Interpretation of Cultures*. New York: Basic Books.

Geringer, J. M. and Hébert, L. 1991. 'Measuring performance of international joint ventures'. *Journal of International Business Studies*, 22, 249–63.

Giddens, A. 1994. 'Risk, trust, reflexivity'. In U. Beck, A. Giddens and S. Lash (eds.) *Reflexive Modernization*. Cambridge: Polity Press, 184–97.

Hofstede, G. 1980. *Culture's Consequences: International Differences in Work-Related Values*. Beverley Hills, CA: Sage.

Hultén, P. 2006. 'Transfer of management practices in a cross-institutional setting: a case study on a Western firm's subsidiary in the Ukraine'. *International Journal of Commerce & Management*, 16, 197–211.

Johnson, J. L. and Cullen, J. B. 2002. 'Trust in cross-cultural relationships'. In M. J. Gannon and K. L. Newman (eds.) *The Blackwell Handbook of Cross-Cultural Management*. Oxford: Blackwell, 335–60.

Johnson, J. L., Cullen, J. B., Sakano, T. and Takenouchi, H. 1996. 'Setting the stage for trust and strategic integration in Japanese–U.S. cooperative alliances'. *Journal of International Business Studies*, 27, 981–1004.

Karatnycky, A. 2005. 'Ukraine's Orange Revolution'. *Foreign Affairs*, 84, 35–52.

Kohlert, H. 2006. 'From risk to opportunity. Russia and Ukraine in the focus of medium-sized machinery builders and automotive suppliers from the state of Baden-Württemberg, Germany'. *Problems and Perspectives in Management*, 4, 4–11.

Kühlmann, T. M. 2005. 'Formation of trust in German–Mexican business relations'. In K. M. Bijlsma-Frankema and R. Klein Woolthuis (eds.) *Trust under Pressure: Empirical Investigations of Trust and Trust Building in Uncertain Circumstances*. Cheltenham: Edward Elgar, 37–54.

Lewicki, R. J., Tomlinson, E. C. and Gillespie, N. 2006. 'Models of interpersonal trust development: theoretical approaches, empirical evidence, and future directions'. *Journal of Management*, 32, 991–1022.

Luhmann, N. 1988. 'Familiarity, confidence, trust: problems and alternatives'. In D. Gambetta (ed.) *Trust: Making and Breaking Co-operative Relations*. Oxford: Basil Blackwell, 94–107.

Marschan-Piekkari, R. and Welch, C. (eds.) 2004. *Handbook of Qualitative Research Methods for International Business*. Cheltenham: Edward Elgar.

Mayer, R. C., Davis, J. H. and Schoorman, F. D. 1995. 'An integrative model of organizational trust'. *Academy of Management Review*, 20, 709–34.

Meyer, H. 2006. *Wirtschaftsstruktur und Chancen – Ukraine*. Cologne: BFAI.

Mizrachi, N., Drori, I. and Anspach, R. R. 2007. 'Repertoires of trust: the practice of trust in a multinational organization amid political conflict'. *American Sociological Review*, 72, 143–65.

Möllering, G. 2006. *Trust: Reason, Routine, Reflexivity*. Amsterdam: Elsevier.

Nes, E. B., Solberg, C. A. and Sikoset, R. 2007. 'The impact of national culture and communication on exporter–distributor relations and on export performance'. *International Business Review*, 16, 405–24.

Newman, K. L. and Nollen, S. D. 1996. 'Culture and congruence: the fit between management practice and national culture'. *Journal of International Business Studies*, 27, 753–79.

Ögütçü, M. and Kinach, J. 2002. 'Ukraine: A miracle in waiting?' *OECD Observer*, 234, 29–32.

Perrone, V., Zaheer, A. and McEvily, B. 2003. 'Free to be trusted? Organizational constraints on trust in boundary spanners'. *Organization Science*, 14, 422–39.

Radaev, V. 2005. 'Establishing trust in a distrustful society: the case of Russian business'. In H.-H. Höhmann and F. Welter (eds.) *Trust and Entrepreneurship: a West–East Perspective*. Cheltenham: Edward Elgar, 114–35.

Rose-Ackerman, S. 2001. 'Trust and honesty in post-socialist societies'. *Kyklos*, 54, 415–44.

Rousseau, D. M., Sitkin, S. B., Burt, R. S. and Camerer, C. 1998. 'Not so different after all: a cross-discipline view of trust'. *Academy of Management Review*, 23, 393–404.

Stache, F. 2006. *Kooperation mit osteuropäischen Unternehmen: Theorie und Praxis vertrauensvoller Zusammenarbeit*. Saarbrücken: VDM Verlag, Dr. Müller.

Swidler, A. 1986. 'Culture in action: symbols and strategies'. *American Sociological Review*, 51, 273–86.

Tsui, A. S. 2006. 'Contextualization in Chinese management research'. *Management and Organization Review*, 2, 1–13.

Ukrainian Embassy. 2008. 'Ukrainisch–deutsche Beziehungen: Wirtschaft und Handel'. www.mfa.gov.ua/germany/ger/publication/content/15288.htm, accessed April 21, 2008.

Volkov, V. 2002. *Violent Entrepreneurs: The Use of Force in the Making of Russian Capitalism*. Ithaca, NY: Cornell University Press.

Welter, F., Kautonen, T., Chepurenko, A., Malieva, E., Venesaar, U. 2003. 'Does trust matter? A cross cultural view of entrepreneurship in different trust milieus'. Paper to the 23rd Babson College – Kauffman Foundation Entrepreneurship Research Conference, Babson Park, USA, June 5–7, 2003.

Williams, M. 2007. 'Building genuine trust through interpersonal emotion management: a threat regulation model of trust and collaboration across boundaries'. *Academy of Management Review*, 32, 595–621.

Zaheer, S. and Zaheer, A. 2006. 'Trust across borders'. *Journal of International Business Studies*, 37, 21–9.

Zucker, L. G. 1986. 'Production of trust: institutional sources of economic structure, 1840–1920'. In B. M. Staw and L. L. Cummings (eds.) *Research in Organizational Behavior*, Vol. 8. Greenwich, CT: JAI Press, 53–111.

# 9 Culture and trust in contractual relationships: a French–Lebanese cooperation

HÈLA YOUSFI

## Summary

This chapter explores how national cultural differences between partners involved in a contractual relationship may interfere with the development of trust. This is illustrated through a case study of a management contract signed by a French private company (Promostate) and public Lebanese company (SONAT). Using an ethnographic approach and drawing on a qualitative analysis of field interviews, the author argues that the challenges faced by the French and Lebanese parties in developing a trusting relationship are due to classic issues of personal conflicts, differing organizational cultures and power asymmetries. Because their national cultural backgrounds were different, the parties had different conceptions of what 'good cooperation' should be that shaped their expectations of trustworthy behaviour and hindered the process of resolving the difficulties they encountered.

## Introduction

Contracts are recognized as universal management mechanisms that provide an efficient solution to the problem of coordinating expectations and interactions between economic actors from different nationalities. However, the impossibility of designing complete, explicit and easily enforceable contracts may restrict their effectiveness as a management mechanism (Macaulay, 1963). Trust is supposed to form a viable alternative or complement to contracts. Trust can reduce uncertainty and lead to more efficiently negotiated agreements (Koenig and van Wijk, 1992).

I would like to thank French Development Agency AFD, which kindly supported our fieldwork in Lebanon. I am also grateful to Denise Skinner, Mark Saunders and Nicole Gillespie for their detailed and insightful comments on earlier drafts. Special thanks are due to Philippe d'Iribarne and Alain Henry for their intellectual contribution to this paper.

Research on the development of trust in contractual relationships has focused largely on the question of how trust and formal contracts are related. At the same time, culture has been considered a factor in the trust-development process in many ways. There are three main perspectives, anchored in various disciplines, which provide different points of view on how national culture may interfere in the dynamic interaction between contracts, trust and the trust-development process. Trust in contractual relationships is the outcome of either: 1) shared values amongst a community whose members put collective interests ahead of their individual interests (Burchell and Wilkinson, 1997; Fukuyama, 1995; Sako, 1992); 2) calculative processes (Dasgupta, 1988; Williamson, 1985); or 3) interactions that result in negotiated shared meanings, i.e. social constructions (Das and Teng, 1998). Other researchers suggest these perspectives are not mutually exclusive and may operate together at various stages of the relationship (Johnson and Cullen, 2002; Rousseau *et al.*, 1998). However, confusion remains on how national cultural differences influence the development of trust, and research on cross-cultural trust tends to report contradictory results.

This chapter draws on a case study about a Lebanese management contract signed by a French private company (Promostate) and a Lebanese public company (SONAT). It seeks to offer an alternative way of looking at the influence of national cultural differences and the development of trust between partners from different countries. In the next section, I give a detailed outline that shows how different perspectives on trust development provide different insights into the relationship between contracts and trust, leading to different views of the way national cultural differences may interfere in this process. Then, after pointing out the tension between culturally shaped expectations and individual agency in trust development, I introduce d'Iribarne's (1989) conceptualization of culture, showing its relevance in investigating the impact of cultural differences in the trust development process. A section describing the case study and the qualitative methodology follows. Finally, after presenting my empirical findings, I discuss the extent to which they challenge earlier ways of thinking about the impact of cultural differences on the trust development process.

## Different perspectives on trust development in contractual relationships

The three main perspectives described below provide different insights into how differences in national culture can influence the trust development process in contractual relationships. The label 'national' is applied to culture to distinguish the character of a society as 'a system of values and norms shared among a group of people' from other forms of culture that we do not directly address here (e.g. organizational culture). Even though few scholars would argue that shared values, calculative processes or social interactions alone explain the development of trust over time, I refer to these perspectives as starting points to highlight how the trust literature developed. Current research on trust development which attempts to integrate these different perspectives is also considered.

## Trust: a result of shared values

The concept of trust traditionally signifies and represents a coordinating mechanism based on shared moral values and norms that support collective cooperation. Ouchi (1980) suggests that clan membership is a basis for trust: it influences members' behaviour. Fukuyama (1995) views trust as the expectation of regular, honest and cooperative behaviour based on commonly shared norms and values. Trust is associated with the capacity to cooperate in a spontaneous way based on shared values rather than formal rules. Zucker (1986) defines such a set of shared and 'taken for granted' expectations as part of a 'world known in common' among certain members of society.

Drawing upon Hofstede's (2001: 5) definition of culture as 'the collective programming of the mind which distinguishes members of one human group from another', a vast body of literature has been developed specifically about the influence of national culture on trust. Since each culture's 'collective programming' results in different norms and values, the processes trustors resort to in order to decide whether and who to trust may be heavily dependent upon their society's culture. Accordingly, several researchers theorize that trust is culturally specific (Doney *et al.*, 1998; Johnson and Cullen, 2002). They argue that the meaning of trust and the ways in which it is developed vary across cultures (Burchell and Wilkinson 1997; Fukuyama 1995; Sako 1992).

For instance, Doney *et al.* (1998) propose that individualists use calculative processes in evaluating trustee incentives more than collectivists do. Similarly, Hagen and Choe (1998) argue that individualist societies rely more on contracts and regulations as a basis for trust development. In contrast, collectivists' trusting choices are predicated on the awareness of shared group membership (Kramer, 1999; Yamagishi and Kiyonari, 2000). Essentially, trust takes place by means of a very strong belief in the absorption of an individual's interests into common objectives. Accordingly, the role of contracts may vary across cultures. Contracts and trust may be seen as substitutes for each other (Zucker, 1986).

In cross-cultural encounters, 'a lack of convergence in cultural proclivities may result in a virtual collapse of the trust-building mechanism' (Doney *et al.*, 1998: 617). Branzei *et al.* (2007) argue that the cultural norms and values that are conducive to efficient trust in one society may be misleading and even damaging in another. This may lead to cross-cultural misunderstandings about what trusting and being trustworthy requires.

Yet this conception of trust is based on a deterministic view of culture understood as those customary beliefs and values that societies transmit from generation to generation fairly unchanged. This leads to downplaying individual agency in the trust development process and leads to seeing the influence of cultural differences as an obstacle for trust development.

## Trust: a calculative process

Taking sociological contributions into account, research on contractual relationships has focused on the role of trust in reducing opportunism. Many authors suggest that developing trust involves a calculative process (Buckley and Casson, 1988; Williamson, 1993). Individuals are described as opportunistic and only seeking to maximize self-interest rather than seeking to act in the community's interest.

According to these behavioural assumptions, trust is established through a calculative process whereby one party calculates the costs and/or rewards of another party cheating or cooperating in a relationship. To the extent that the benefits of cheating do not exceed the costs of being caught (factoring in the likelihood of being caught), the trustor infers it would be contrary to the other party's best interest to cheat, so that party can be trusted. For Dasgupta, trusting another 'implicitly means that the probability that he will perform an action that is beneficial or at least not detrimental to us is high enough for us to consider engaging in some form of coordination with him' (1988: 217).

In this framework, the social norms of trusting behaviour are reduced to self-serving behaviour. From this perspective, trust and contracts are used in a complementary way to mitigate opportunism. Trust develops only through a rational self-interest process that is radically different from a spontaneous process of adherence to a shared sense of community. Even though the influence of a variety of institutional and societal factors on trust development might be acknowledged, compliance with these norms is seen only as the result of calculation and a self-interest based process. Williamson (1993) recognizes that social approvals, sanctions and socialization are pertinent factors in influencing individual's calculations, without going so far as to allow that a specific social context will shape individual's expectations.

## Trust: a social construction

Several scholars (Elster, 1983; Möllering and Stache, 2007) suggest a third perspective on the trust-development process, based on an understanding of trust and culture as social constructions. Trust is achieved through interaction and communication involving all actors in the negotiation of shared meanings, and in the development of rituals and practices that establish and reinforce shared values, norms and beliefs (Das and Teng, 1998). Firms learn to trust each other over time. They experience the fact that a partner does not take advantage of dependencies, or constructively solves small conflicts. Trust is not only a product of successful interaction, but actively worked on by actors involved in the contractual relationship (Giddens, 1984).

Likewise, drawing on German–Ukrainian business relationships, Möllering and Stache (2007) show that the challenge in cross-cultural encounters is how to develop shared expectations over time and find common values behind different cultural repertoires. Similarly, Ring and Van de Ven (1994) advocate that negotiations enable the development of joint expectations, followed by a commitment stage, in which obligations and rules are agreed upon, leading to a build-up of trust. Therefore, new, shared meanings must be negotiated across institutional and cultural differences.

Similarly, Lorenz (1988) and Brousseau (1996) argue that contracts should offer a framework for negotiating mutual commitments rather than formal constraints. The implementation of contractual clauses should recognize that there will be unanticipated questions raised by day-to-day cooperation. Contracts accommodating mutual learning could provide a solid basis for effective cooperation as well as trust development. This perspective seeks to overcome a deterministic view of culture by actively emphasizing the actors' agency. Such an approach tries to accommodate the influence of social norms in the building of trust, but maintains the actors' autonomy in shaping trusting relationships and negotiating contract implementation.

## Integrating across perspectives

As Figure 9.1 shows, these perspectives differ in what they see as the key influences on trust development and provide various insights into how national culture influences trust development. Yet several researchers suggest these perspectives are neither exclusive nor opposed to each other, and that they can operate together at various stages of the relationship. For example, Rousseau *et al.* (1998) advocate the need to integrate and use aspects of each of these different perspectives to explain trust development and/or the basic

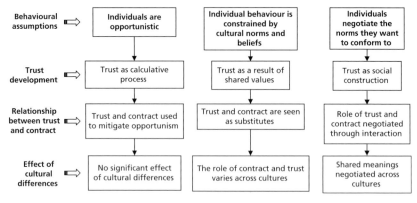

Figure 9.1  Trust, contract and cultural differences

forms of trust, i.e. relational trust, calculative trust and institutional trust. They argue that the amount of trust varies in a given relationship, and both the history and nature of the interaction between the parties shape the form that trust takes. Thus, a mix of formal and informal structures is often necessary to manage complex relationships (Das and Teng, 1998). According to Sitkin (2005), formal structures can simultaneously manage risk and uncertainty while furthering the development of trust.

That said, there is ambivalence regarding the extent to which trust development is influenced by stable, culturally shaped expectations, as opposed to individual agency. Resolving this ambivalence is critical to understanding how, and to what extent, national cultural differences may influence the trust-development process. This question calls for a new approach to understanding culture's influence on the development of trust. I argue that such an approach requires moving beyond the three traditional perspectives on trust, to identify how the term is used by those involved in contract implementation and the implications of these uses on the process of achieving cooperation. A complete understanding of the impact of cultural differences on trust development requires a deep analysis of the process and implementation of contracting. In the next section, I will introduce the conceptualization of culture used to address this question.

## Culture and trust: an alternative view

As I noted above, when the influence of national cultural differences is acknowledged, it is mainly seen as an independent variable that works on its own and could hinder trust development, i.e. trust as an outcome of shared values. The social construction perspective offers a different way of overcoming the deterministic relationship between cultural differences and trust development. Within the emergent, dynamic approach to culture, building on the social constructionist perspective, culture is seen as being made up of relations, rather than as a stable system of form and substance (Haastrup, 1996). Recent conceptualizations of culture highlight that individuals have multiple cultural memberships that arise from different social identities (Chao and Moon, 2005; Schneider and Barsoux, 1997). This implies national culture is one 'tile' or one 'sphere' of culture that is likely to work in concert with other aspects of culture (such as ethnicity, sector/industry, organization, profession, etc.), rather than singly.

The idea of cultural complexity suggests that every individual embodies a unique combination of personal, cultural and social experiences, and so ultimately any communication and negotiation is intercultural. In other words, people's cultural constructions and their social organizations of meaning are contextual. Trust development is therefore the outcome of individual agency and patterned social interaction that shape new common meanings and rules. This conceptualization leads to downplaying the understanding of culture as 'essence' in order to focus explicitly on individuals' interactions and negotiations with their various partners in overcoming cultural differences, as well as in developing trust. Any cultural stability, as implied by the previous perspective, seems inimical to trust development because it presupposes the absence of any kind of cultural learning or social transformation. Little progress has been made in understanding the extent to which stable, culturally shaped expectations influence individuals' interaction in trust development.

One possible way to overcome this hurdle is to change the way we look at the influence of culture on individual action. What is needed is not the privileging of culture as a variable that works on its own, but the integration of culture into a wider picture in which culture is seen as intimately connected to different aspects of the trust-development process. Culture must be seen as an element that shapes the expectations of a 'trustworthy' relationship as well as the means used to build a 'common interest'.

This invokes another conceptualization of culture. In this chapter, the notion of culture adopted is the 'framework of meaning' in each society that shapes conceptions of the way people should be governed (Geertz, 1973; d'Iribarne, 1989; d'Iribarne and Henry, 2007). In every country that has preserved its unity through the vicissitudes of history, one finds, for the most part, a shared conception of a well-ordered society. Across cultures, representations of relations between individuals and groups, legitimate means of exerting power and methods of cooperation vary noticeably. These conceptions, which are largely implicit, form the foundations of the image of a 'well-ordered society', but also serve as reference points for actors in their actions.

In every society, a specific network of real or mythical figures and narratives highlights the principles of classification through which society is made of separate groups. Words are associated with these classifications, such as 'impurity' in India, 'witchcraft' in Cameroon, the 'loss of freedom' in America, 'dishonour' in Algeria. These classifications provide interpretative systems that give meaning to the problems of existence, presenting them as elements in a given configuration that shape the relationship between individual autonomy and collective order.

In other words, I refer to culture not in terms of values and attitudes, but rather as implicit repertoires and guidelines that underlie the practices and discourses of people in terms of organization and cooperation. These implicit references underlie the way members of organizations belonging to a specific society give meaning to what they experience at work: hierarchical functioning, with the procedures of decentralization, control and performance evaluation; cooperation among different departments, decision making and conflict management; organization of relationships with customers, quality procedures, setting up codes of conduct, etc. The question is: to what extent could this conceptualization of culture help us move away from the tension between what is a matter of choice for individuals and what is constrained by national culture?

Within a society, attitudes and subcultures vary greatly. It is not just that individuals with a wide variety of attitudes can be found. It is, more radically, that the same individual can have sharply contrasting attitudes according to the circumstances. If national culture is seen as a 'framework of meaning', it implies that one would try to understand the interpretation culture proposes for particular events and situations, as well as for action strategies. The issue is not to try to find out how individuals from a specific culture are supposed to act in all circumstances, in compliance with inculcated attitudes. On the contrary, the focus will be on the fact that they change their attitudes and behaviours according to the meaning – provided by stable cultural guidelines – they give to particular events and situations.

From this perspective, national culture shapes expectations of a trustworthy relationship not as a set of internalized values and beliefs (Branzei *et al.*, 2007; Zaheer and Zaheer, 2006) but rather by the way in which national culture provides 'references' to interpret the other's action. The key distinction of this new conceptualization is that it allows individuals from the same societal background to vary in their beliefs, attitudes and 'cultural identities', but also recognizes that national culture shapes members' expectations and assumptions about specific situations and events, such as what constitutes 'good cooperation' and what constitutes 'trustworthiness' in the context of a cooperative relationship. This approach assumes some individual agency and choice, i.e. variation amongst individuals of the same culture. It also assumes cultural influence over underlying, and often unconscious, beliefs and expectations.

The merit of this perspective lies in its capacity to clarify the conditions for various representations and definitions of 'good cooperation' in each society and the way this affects a cross-cultural encounter. These definitions allow us to understand how different conceptions of an effective cooperation may interfere with developing joint expectations of cooperation or benevolence on the part of the trusted party.

## Data collection and analysis

I investigated a case study of a management contract in Lebanon signed by a French private company (Promostate) and a Lebanese public company (SONAT). For confidentiality, I have changed the organizations' names. AFD, the French Development Agency, funded the contract. The contract assigned Promostate the management of public service facilities. SONAT was to supervise the services provided, while retaining legal responsibility vis-à-vis their clients. The contracting and supervisory experience was intended to prepare Lebanese authorities for new modes of management, and to learn from positive or negative results, in order to improve public service management in Lebanon.

Research was conducted between 2002 and 2005, during which time I observed how the contractual relationship functioned from negotiation to implementation. When carrying out fieldwork, I used an ethnographic approach (Geertz, 1973; d'Iribarne, 1996). This consisted of conducting interviews in the field to understand how national cultural differences influence the trust-development process. This approach allowed me to analyse how the respondents interpret contractual clauses, and the way they implement them. I also aimed to highlight how French and Lebanese actors give 'meaning' to their actions when cooperating with their partner, and how both sides conceive an effective cooperation.

In order to do this, at various stages of the contractual relationship I conducted seventy interviews over three years with the five members of Promostate's management team as well as the four members of the SONAT management team. Twenty interviews were conducted with the Lebanese employees involved in the execution of the contract. In addition, I carried out ten interviews with representatives from AFD and the consultant who conceived the contract and supervised its implementation. I studied available documentation and attended meetings. As I am bilingual, I let the interviewees speak in their native languages, Arabic and French, to generate data with an authentic insight into people's experience of working on this project. I was introduced to the interviewees as a consultant working for AFD in charge of project follow-up. It should be noted that the representatives from the SONAT team are native-born Lebanese, whereas the five representatives of Promostate are half-Lebanese and half-French (that is, they were bilingual and bicultural). The AFD representatives and consultant are French.

The interviews were semi-structured with flexible interview guides that could be tailored to the interviewee and situation but typically covered the following themes: perceptions of technical and institutional difficulties affecting the implementation of the contract and/or the drivers of effectiveness; and how interviewees deal with situations that arise in day-to-day operations that were not anticipated in the contract. I also asked interviewees to comment on strategies and behaviours adopted by their partner at different phases of the partnership. Finally, I asked them to assess the partnership and to determine the conditions that would likely determine the success or the failure of their project. It is worth noting that cultural differences were not originally envisaged as a main theme of the interviews, but they were implicitly brought up in the way our respondents commented on various issues. The majority of the interviews were recorded and then transcribed literally, as per the comments below.

Discourse analysis was used to understand how interviewees used language to construct and convey their meaning of trust. It included identifying interviewees' use of metaphors to suggest what cooperation is or should be like, their use of words, expressions, repetitions and their emphasis on expressing and distinguishing desirable from undesirable motives and practices (d'Iribarne, 1996). Conflicts or misunderstandings faced by actors in the implementation of the contract provided us with a focal point around which to explore the different actors' representations of 'good cooperation' or conditions for 'trustful relationship'. Extracts from their interviews have been selected according to their relationship with trust. The words emboldened in the quotes below reflect the interviewees' emphasis.

The analysis presented in this document does not aim to establish all of the reference points that determine the French and Lebanese context of meaning in an exhaustive manner. Rather, it aims to show the way in which certain elements of cultural representations can influence the development of trust between partners from different countries.

## Findings

In this section, after examining the influence of French and Lebanese culture on work relations, I highlight how differences in national cultures influenced the development of cooperative relationships and hindered trust development.

## *Culture and management*

### France: the logic of honour

Using an ethnographic approach, d'Iribarne (1989) showed that when the life of a French factory is closely observed, the organizational model is embedded in a French framework of meaning. He explained that one finds a specific vision of a good way of living and working together in France. When the French speak of their work, reference to the rights and duties associated with the specific position one holds in the society, and to the rank associated to this position, is omnipresent. When hierarchical relationships and relationships with customers are at stake, the French speak of what seems normal to do in conformity with the customs of one's *métier* or profession. Without any reference to instructions from superiors or to a 'contract', these traditions define a 'good' way of working, what is 'normally' done and what one cannot stoop to, whether one is a production engineer, a plumber, an accountant or some other profession. Not respecting the norms of one's 'profession' through a lack of professional awareness, or through bowing to pressures from above to lower standards in the pursuit of profit, is considered an undermining of the 'honour' of the professional group to which one belongs. This can be seen as reflecting a society whose functioning is governed by a conception of freedom, quite different from the English or German conceptions, in that it is based on the rights specified by a given social position. The France of the Old Regime was marked by such a conception (Montesquieu, 1748; Tocqueville, 1856). Far deeper in history, such a conception already made medieval France distinctive (Bloch, 1939).

### Lebanon: a cultural 'mosaic' with a specific way of living and working together

The simple evocation of this small country, Lebanon, immediately brings diversity and contrasts to mind. The Lebanese people refer to their society as a 'cultural mosaic' to emphasize its diversity (Bahjat, 2001). The country is made up of eighteen communities, acknowledged by the constitution and very different in their cultural, ethnic and religious background. The major sects include Maronite, Sunni, Shiia, Greek Orthodox, Druze and Greek Catholic. As a result of its sectarian diversity, Lebanon created a unique political system in 1943, known as 'confessionalism', based on a community-based power-sharing mechanism. Individual Lebanese primarily identify with their family as the principal object of their loyalty. It is the basis of marriage and social relationships, as well as the confessional system. This, in turn, tends to clash with national integration and cohesion. The question is: is it relevant to talk about Lebanese culture at the national level and its impact on working relations?

The ideal of Lebanese society is marked by two tendencies that could appear antagonistic at first glance. On one side is the desire to preserve community membership and defend the community's solidarity. On the other side is the attempt to preserve the sensitive coexistence between different communities with respect of their diversity (Beydoun, 1984). This contrast is unravelled by a persistent reference to the duty of 'unity'. Reference to the importance of 'unity' in Lebanese discourse, framed also in terms of the 'union of hearts', tends to be as important as the challenge of diversity to the Lebanese. The resulting culture is distinctively Lebanese. If Lebanon allows people and groups who do not necessarily share the same beliefs and the same traditions to 'live together', it is because their 'hearts' unite the Lebanese. 'Their love for each other' and/or the common religious reference to 'love for God' are narratives used to transcend differences between people and communities, guaranteeing a minimum of integration and cohesion.

This specific conception of 'living together' has undoubtedly shaped the conception of 'a good working relationship' in Lebanon (Yousfi, 2008). When Lebanese speak of their work, reference to the importance of group unity is omnipresent. At the same time, the call for 'unity' is not dissociable from the attention that should be given to individual interests. A good working relationship should make it possible to take into account the specific contribution of each member in the cooperative effort. Allowing for individual contributions helps people to feel 'considered'. It also determines their involvement in enhancing the collective performance (Yousfi, 2008).

To sum up, a good working relationship in Lebanon is shaped mainly by the need to find a balance between the group's 'unity' and consideration for specific individual contributions. To ensure a good collective performance, the rule is to provide each person with the opportunity to express their point of view or to give their opinion on any given issue. The 'unity of hearts' metaphor takes on meaning through the attention given to individual interests, as well as the efforts to find a 'consensus' acceptable to everyone.

## Trust development in the face of what 'good cooperation' should be

For the two partners in our case study, the contract represents an important challenge. For the French company, it represents the opening of new markets, and for Lebanese authorities it is the first public–private partnership. On both sides, the building of trust is an essential condition to manage unanticipated questions in the contract and to guarantee the partnership's success. As a Lebanese interviewee declared: 'We need good will and good **intentions** to make the contract work.' A French interviewee commented: 'The contract is important, but we need to create a trusting relationship to work together.'

However, the relations soon turned sour when the director of SONAT wrote to the CEO of Promostate to ask that the project manager be replaced. Trust was never really established and the results were disappointing as regards the contract's objectives. According to the consultant who was in charge of monitoring the project, three main reasons could explain the disappointing results: first, institutional problems were caused by contradictions between public management rules and some of the contract's clauses, along with differences in public versus private organizational cultures. Second, personal conflicts and power asymmetries between partners complicated the contract's implementation. Third, a lack of communication between the two teams created misunderstandings concerning the interpretation of contractual obligations as well as the role of each partner.

When asked about their perception of the cooperation issues SONAT interviewees used expressions like 'Promostate's secrecy strategy' or 'Promostate hides its true intentions from us', to describe their relationship with Promostate. Promostate interviewees qualified the SONAT behaviour as 'two-faced' or 'intrusive', showing doubt about SONAT's commitment to make the contract succeed. But what exactly was the origin of these differences?

In their accounts of the difficulties encountered, the actors acknowledged the issues mentioned by the consultant, but implicitly emphasized two different visions of 'good cooperation', leading to different perceptions of what their role in the contract should be.

### Promostate: we want to be autonomous

The choice of Promostate to send 'bicultural' collaborators to Lebanon was motivated by the supposed ability of these people to adjust to the Lebanese culture. However, the findings presented below show that Promostate's representatives used the Lebanese repertoire only to ease communication problems. In commenting on their cooperation with SONAT as well as in interpreting the difficulties encountered, Promostate's representatives implicitly used the French repertoire. This was for two reasons: first, the French framework of meaning is embodied within the processes and the procedures of the organization. Second, all of Promostate's representatives had worked within a French company for their entire careers. It is hardly surprising that their accounts were influenced mostly by what good cooperation should be within the French framework of meaning.

For Promostate, a contract, in as much as it is the formal definition of a governance structure, underscores the role that should be played by each partner in implementing contractual commitments. According to this view, Promostate interviewees claimed 'autonomy' to execute their obligations and to honour their 'expert' status.

My hands are not free to execute my responsibilities ... There is a problem of the contract's interpretation ... They must understand that **we need autonomy**.

However, this implies that any questioning of their decisions by the Lebanese represented an obstacle to 'good cooperation'. On receiving suggestions or questions about something they did, they immediately felt their expertise was being scrutinized. Thus, any Lebanese involvement in their management was seen as an obstacle to the good implementation of the contract:

They should supervise the contract, but they mix supervision and surveillance ... Supervision should be on a quarterly basis, but they are supervising us on a daily basis ... For instance, they keep track of the material we are using; they have obliged us to buy a specific brand of screws that caused a delay. Then they accused us for being responsible for this delay ... This is not what supervision should be: it is an intrusion, they should free us to accomplish our mission.

These comments are based on the French context of a vision of 'good cooperation' as developed by d'Iribarne in 'Logic of Honour' cited above. From this perspective, Promostate actors act according to the responsibilities implied by their status rather than to conform to their customers' requests. It is considered an undermining of their honour as 'service provider' to be 'at the service of' SONAT. They want to be judged only on their capacity to honour the requirements of their 'status' in the contract.

I am a *'prestataire de service'* (service provider), not a subordinate. If I don't honor my commitments, they can fire me ... I want to be treated as a 'partner' and not as a 'subordinate'.

We are not considered partners, we are considered sub-contractors. We are service providers and they want to impose their rules on us. We don't feel we are responsible for our work; they keep complaining about our performance.

They should understand that we are a service provider. So, we are not here to work under their instructions, but to offer our services to them.

The Lebanese interpreted Promostate's particular vision of cooperation as a strategy of secrecy, while Promostate's vision underlined the importance of autonomy to achieve cooperation, within the framework limits of a contractual role.

### SONAT: we should work as 'one hand'

In contrast, SONAT interviewees stressed the importance of 'group unity' to achieve cooperation: 'we should work as one hand'. This metaphor is used to describe what their relation with Promostate should be, as well as to describe the way they consider procedural coordination. At first sight, this discourse may lead to the assumption that each individual sacrifices his/her own interests for the benefit of the whole community. However, many factors tend to show that individuals do not melt into the community and each individual remains strongly inclined towards his own personal interest. Individual suggestions occupy an important place. Each person should be able to express his/her point of view and deliver his/her opinion on any problem. Having their opinions taken into account in the course of the events is how the Lebanese can have their place of 'honour' in the partnership.

It's vital for Promostate that SONAT be able to understand Promostate's problems. I'm able to answer their questions; I can give support to the operator.

In the technical field, I try to facilitate Promostate's work, but **they have to consider my advice**. They should ask for my opinion: I gave them my comments, but they weren't taken into account.

From the perspective of our Lebanese respondents, the role of 'partner' in the contract implied that they should 'help' those whom they supervise by 'advising them' or by 'guiding them' in their work. To stress this role, they often quoted an extract from the contract that stipulated:

The management team of SONAT, should be, as much as possible, involved in the reorganization of the 'public' service. SONAT should allow Promostate to benefit from its thorough experience on the ground.

In this way, each partner can play an important role in the partnership and has an essential contribution to the success of the project. If their opinion is taken into account, they will not hesitate 'to solve' problems. As one of our SONAT respondents reports:

We are constrained by public rules. Promostate needs the signature of three people to order any kind of material; we are being cooperative, we close our eyes to this kind of procedure.

There is here a new combination of adherence to the same community and the defence of individual interests. This echoes the Lebanese-specific conception of 'living together' mentioned above. First, respect for differences between communities means everyone has a right to vigorously express their values and their feelings. Second, acknowledgement of differences between communities and individuals goes along with a passionate defence of 'unity' as the basis of cohesion in Lebanese society. This logic is what determined the Lebanese interpretation of the situations for the most part, as well as the strategies adopted. Consequently, when SONAT members felt their opinion was not considered, the group's unity was broken and formal rules had to prevail. The public rules referred to here are mainly financial. These rules are very bureaucratic and constraining for Promostate.

Some other difficulties came from the employees' status. Promostate was in charge of managing SONAT staff, but was limited by public rules as regards working hours as well as salaries and incentives

We did our best to help them, we tried to understand their problems but they didn't accept our help. So we are forced to apply the public rules.

### The influence of differences in French and Lebanese conceptions of cooperation

The differences between the two conceptions of 'cooperation' created an uneasy tension between the partners and made it difficult to develop 'trust'. Promostate perceived SONAT's interventions as a lack of respect for their status in the contract, as well as a lack of trust. Further, Promostate interpreted the oscillation of SONAT between two repertoires, i.e. 'we are here to help you' and 'we should apply the rules' as a sign of being 'two-faced'.

SONAT interviewees suggested Promostate employees wanted to keep them away.

I don't understand the source of their fear! I want the work to be well done; they don't want us to see what they are doing . . . They are hiding their true intentions!

Consequently, after many efforts to 'help Promostate' by modifying the public rules or by allowing exemptions, they decided to apply the public formal rules in a rigid way.

I tried to sort out the contradictions between the public rules and the contract to make the project succeed, but they didn't change their behavior, they didn't want to listen to us . . . So now we want to protect ourselves; we are applying the rules strictly.

The difference in what was understood to be 'good cooperation' implied different expectations of trustworthy behaviour. To be precise, when the interviewees drew on the idea of 'working together' to express praise, criticism or exhortation, they implicitly indicated the behaviour desired and expected from members. For Promostate's interviewees, one should simply trust the partner's technical skill. The status of 'expert' or 'professional' with a strong international reputation should be sufficient for SONAT to expect the partner would do his best to honour his obligations.

We are here to do a 'service provider's' job. They bought the services of an international expert, they must trust us.

From this perspective, each partner should have the autonomy to exercise their responsibilities in a climate of trust. Everyone's duty to honour their 'status' in the contract should guarantee the development of trust. Thus, Promostate's representatives perceived SONAT's checking on them and offers to help as a lack of trust. From the Lebanese point of view, technical skills are important but not sufficient to build a trusting relationship. The operator must be able to prove his good intentions by showing his ability to find consensual solutions which 'are convenient to' both parties in spite of constraints.

We need technicians, but also individuals who are capable of understanding us in order to collaborate.
  We did our best to help them but it didn't work out. We need people who are able to work 'as one hand' and to find solutions that work for all parties.
  Our mission is the success of the contract. If we say our role is to 'supervise' and we stick to a strict, 100%, application of the contract, we will ruin the contract. Right now, we are helping them to make this contract a success; they need our help.

To make the project a success, the operator should allow SONAT to contribute to it. These expectations, in a Lebanese context, are consistent with the need to reconcile the group's unity with the expression of individual contributions. They represent the prerequisites to developing trust.

According to Mayer *et al.* (1995), this case could be interpreted as evidence of differences in trustworthiness beliefs. For Promostate's interviewees, the 'ability/competence' dimension of trustworthiness was most important for building trust and evaluating trustworthiness, whereas for the Lebanese it was more about 'benevolence'. Analysis shows that the differences are far from being only differences in beliefs. Different conceptions of what 'good cooperation' should be imply different meanings given to concepts such as 'autonomy', 'working together', 'responsibility', etc. These differences determine the criteria used to assess the partner's behaviour. The French conception of the importance of 'honouring' the requirement of one's status gives meaning to 'competence'. The Lebanese conception of good cooperation where 'helping' or 'giving advice' is a way to have a place of 'honour' in the partnership is at the root of 'benevolence'.

Moreover, these findings help in understanding the relationships between trust, distrust and cultural differences. Lewicki *et al.* (1998) conceptualize trust and distrust as separate and potentially *coexisting* constructs with distinct determinants and effects. As far as cultural differences are concerned, the analysis reported here showed that both distrust – fear, scepticism and watchfulness – and trust – hope, faith and initiative – have the same basis. Trust and distrust depend on whether expectations of what good cooperation should be are met or not.

Even though both sides acknowledged the divergence in contract interpretation, it is worth noting that all respondents perceived power relations, personal conflicts and organizational differences as the only explanations for these divergences. A representative from AFD commented:

We notice the problem of different readings of the contract. Both parties are regularly accusing each other of not understanding the contract. I had to give a clear warning in order to push them to change their opportunistic behavior.

The consultant declared:

The supervision of SONAT is not effective because the SONAT team is unqualified to do it. Besides, personal conflicts between the two directors don't help solve the problems.

A representative from a Lebanese Ministry noticed:

The differences between private-company culture and the priorities of a public service were translated into difficulties in introducing the concept of public–private partnership into public sector in Lebanon.

It was difficult to grasp the implicit differences between the two partners in their conception of 'good' cooperation and the role these differences played in intensifying difficulties and undermining trust development. Analysis confirmed the consultant's view and revealed that power asymmetries, personal conflicts and differing organizational cultures were the main obstacles faced in this cooperation. Yet, as Figure 9.2 shows, cultural differences interfered in the process not as an independent variable to be juxtaposed with other obstacles, but in shaping the way partners perceived difficulties and envisaged solutions. Moreover, the action strategies of both partners were systematically and implicitly legitimized by different cultural repertoires. Cultural differences complicated the implementation of effective solutions by giving different interpretations of the problems encountered.

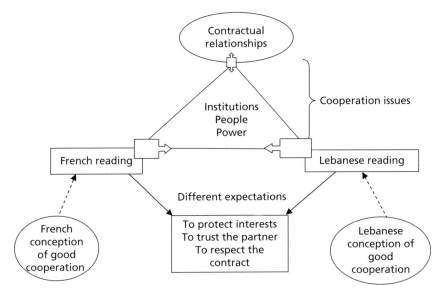

**Figure 9.2** Trust development in the face of what good cooperation should be
Cultural differences (different conceptions of good cooperation) provide different
interpretations of the cooperation issues faced in the contractual relationship as well
as different expectations for developing trust and thus influence the implementation of
effective solutions.

Regarding the difficulties in developing a trustful relationship, a representative of the Lebanese authorities declared:

I believe our mistake was that we believed that goodwill would prevail and allow the
contract to function smoothly.

In the face of persistent difficulties in finding practical means to cooperate, the
various stakeholders in the French and Lebanese organizations involved in
the partnership organized many meetings. The aim of the meetings was to
establish jointly agreed rules to smooth cooperation. The question is: to what
extent did the process of negotiating common rules help the partners to
overcome the obstacles to cooperation?

## Dealing with differences in interpreting the contract

Several meetings to mitigate the partnership's difficulties were organized, and
took place in the presence of the consultant who wrote up the contract. Two
strategies were adopted to work out misunderstandings and to establish a
trustworthy relationship. The first strategy focused on clarifying the contract

in order to build a homogeneous interpretation of each partner's contractual obligations. The second strategy, based upon the assumption that the cooperation problems were mainly 'relational', was to resort to a third party as a mediator or a conciliator to help ease the tension between the two sides. The task of this mediator was to seek consensus between the two partners.

### Clarifying the contract

Our respondents shared the view that the origins of the difficulties lay more in their failure to translate the contract into practical means of cooperation than in the contract itself. To manage these difficulties, the consultant suggested clarifying the contractual clauses. As he explains in one of his reports:

> The difficulties met from the beginning of the contract are not of a substantial nature and could be overcome within the contractual framework and the resolutions we reached in the meeting. These resolutions are subject to cooperation between the partners. The current situation does not justify an amendment to the contract.

The clarification process was simply a question of respecifying the responsibilities of each protagonist. Yet, a certain number of implicit divergences were not considered in spite of the explanations provided by the consultant. The actors agreed upon a presumably homogeneous 'reading' of the contract. But when it came to implementing the agreement they encountered difficulties due to their different ways of assessing behaviour on the ground.

The difficulty of implementing the supervision procedures is symptomatic of this type of obstacle. The two partners set up the supervision procedures together, but divergences appeared in the way they were put into practice. Their implementation was highly dependent on the perception of the other party's behaviour. One of Promostate's respondents pointed out that SONAT had exercised supervision as surveillance rather than a simple exercise of supervision. One of our Promostate's interviewee commented:

> The service provider should be autonomous and supervised from time to time. This week we were controlled three times. Mr. X sent me his assistant to check on the HR department three times; it is not supervision, it is surveillance.

Promostate reacted to this behaviour by sending a written correspondence to SONAT:

> We received Miss X's report and comments. We will check the reliability of the information reported and will recommend disciplinary measures for the people who did not meet their professional obligations in April. April was a transitional period for the staff. After that, we will contact you to specify the date on which Miss X could come to carry out her 'surveillance' although this is not in conformity with the spirit of the contract. Once again, I must insist on this last point.

At the same time, when relations with Promostate were good and SONAT members felt they were working with Promostate as 'one hand', the supervision procedures were applied in a flexible manner. SONAT members were willing to help Promostate carry out its work as long as they felt Promostate was considering their opinions. A SONAT member commented:

I am responsible for financial supervision of the contract. The relationship is getting better, they listen to us, so I am willing to approve Promostate's decisions without checking.

Therefore, the actors may have jointly set up procedures, such as supervision, but difficulties appeared when it came to implementing them. Implementation was highly dependent on the perception of the other party's behaviour. Even though the actors involved in the contractual relationship evoked divergences in interpreting the contract, they did not reach a point where they recognized the role of cultural differences in order to move beyond the simple task of clarifying the contract. The parties never realized that Promostate perceived SONAT's 'help' as a form of control, and that SONAT perceived Promostate's 'autonomy' as a lack of respect for their input and collaboration. The arguments 'we want to be autonomous' and 'we should work as one hand' were systematically perceived as ways to negotiate for more power. This cultural myopia hindered the process of cooperation and the actors were trapped in a bureaucratic routine that blocked the execution of the contract.

### Using relational mediation

The second strategy adopted to sort out the disagreements was mediation. The aim was to encourage the partners to find pragmatic compromises for specific issues. As a representative from AFD pointed out:

It seems to me it is important that we consider appointing a conciliator, or think seriously about introducing some sort of arbitration or conciliation element into the arrangement between SONAT and Promostate. As you are well aware, there is no way we can make the contract work unless the parties want it to work. There was no way we could have made the contract itself foolproof. It seems that we have reached the point of irreconcilable differences.

After a 'mediation' facilitated by the Lebanese Minister, the actors proved they were able to resolve a certain number of problems, indicating goodwill could help overcome unanticipated questions raised during daily cooperation. Moreover, Promostate's members used the Lebanese repertoire of the importance of 'good relationship' to ease communication problems. However, the negotiated agreements were fragile and did not last long. The question is: why didn't these agreements last?

The accounts of our respondents on both sides showed that relational mediation helped them reach consensus. One of the outcomes of this mediation was to convince both parties to leave room for a certain freedom in interpreting the contract in order to improve cooperation. We can see this in the following passage from a document presented by Promostate at a reconciliation meeting:

> The signed contract is defined as a management contract and not as a technical assistance contract. The rationale behind this is to give the service provider a certain freedom to carry out its mission.

Similarly, SONAT pointed out the importance of a certain freedom in interpreting the contract. In a document presented at the same meeting, they note:

> The contract should be regarded as a sort of pilot project and as such any changes to the contract that would improve it should be seriously considered.

Yet, whereas the principle of free interpretation of the contract adopted by both sides allowed them to reach consensus, respect for the negotiated solutions did not last long. In fact, the divergences over the criterion used to allow free interpretation weakened the durability of the agreed solutions. While for the French partner, free interpretation of the contract should have been constrained by the rights and duties associated with their specific 'mission' in the partnership, for the Lebanese these consensual solutions were motivated mainly by the will to strengthen the group's unity. The following extract from the minutes of a meeting organized with the Lebanese Minister well illustrates this:

> Promostate and SONAT should act as one entity and their aim should be to ensure the success of contract.

Thus, the partners showed they could work together, but their differences were far from being overcome. Trust was broken the first time one of the partners felt or perceived they were not being treated the way they should be in a good cooperation. The involvement of a third party helped them work together but failed to sort out the deep, implicit divergences undermining the cooperation process.

## Discussion

When the influence of national cultural differences is acknowledged, it is mainly seen as a set of values and attitudes – an independent variable – that works on its own and could hinder trust development (Doney *et al.*, 1998; Johnson and Cullen, 2002; Zaheer and Zaheer, 2006). New, shared culture negotiated over time and across national boundaries is perceived as the only way to tackle cultural differences (Möllering and Stache, 2007). The research reported here offers different insights into how differences in national culture influence trust development. At first glance, the case reported here could be interpreted as evidence for differences in trustworthiness beliefs that hinder the development of trust (Mayer *et al.*, 1995). However, the analysis shows the differences reflect more than just beliefs. Using d'Iribarne's conceptualization of culture as well as a qualitative methodology, we have been able to highlight the fact that, because of the parties' different national cultural backgrounds, they held different conceptions of what a 'good cooperation' is as well as different criteria for assessing the partner's behaviour. Different meanings were given to the partnership, and to autonomy, working together, responsibility, status and legitimacy. There were also different ways of interpreting and processing information about each other's trust and trustworthiness.

Thus, trust development across cultures should be incorporated in the way actors conceive of as 'good cooperation'. For the actors, a prerequisite to trusting their partner was feeling that they were being treated appropriately according to their role in the contract. However, different conceptions of what a 'good cooperation' is shaped different expectations of trustworthy behaviour. The patterns generally used by the partners to build trust in French or Lebanese culture created misunderstandings when in confrontation between two foreign cultures. Consequently, trust development broke down.

## Implications for practice

This paper has important implications for analysing how cultural differences and trust interact in cross-cultural encounters. I have demonstrated that the influence of national cultural differences on the trust-development process has to be analysed within the context of how actors interpret their contractual relationships, perceive their partner's behaviour and give meanings to cooperation issues as well as actions. Promostate and SONAT were mainly paying attention to the institutional dimension, such as laws and regulations, or the strategic dimension, rather than the cultural one. Obviously, local institutional conditions or power relations are taken into account in business operations in foreign countries. Yet culturally driven social customs, local frameworks of meanings and culture-specific societal mechanisms are often not taken into account. They are familiar to the local population, but cannot be identified by an outsider easily.

So knowledge about cultural differences is indispensable for partners to be able to shape a stable but adaptive action framework and see the role of the contract as a cooperative mechanism. Learning about the other party's interpretation of contractual obligations and principles of regulation within the framework of meaning in each society may provide an opportunity for the partners to facilitate the building of trust and adjust their behaviour as required. Taking the role played by cultural differences into account may be an efficient way to appease strained situations and handle conflicts. Moreover, by interpreting contracts in this dynamic cultural, as well as legal, fashion, the relationship between trust and a contract becomes less simple, yet closer to reality.

## Directions for future research

To understand the impact of national cultural differences on trust development, we should not seek to categorize trust development solely in terms of trustworthiness beliefs. Following Noorderhaven (1999), I argue it is more productive to explore and compare the meaning of trust in various cultures. As a first step, we should identify how trust or dimensions of trustworthiness, such as benevolence or competence, take on meaning in the accounts of contractual partners, and how they affect the process of achieving effective cooperation.

Second, the broader conceptualization of culture used in this chapter allows us to overcome the difficulty of the three perspectives usually used to understand the relationship between what is unconsciously shaped by national culture and what is accounted for by individual agency when developing trust. This research shows that French and Lebanese cultures had an important impact on trust development by implicitly influencing the particular direction of the strategies adopted by each partner rather than by imposing roles or standards of behaviours on each individual from which he or she could not escape. Culture also had an important impact on their expectations of others as partners defended both their interests and their convictions.

Third, as far as the relationship between trust and contract is concerned, the findings reveal that the issue is not to identify whether contracts and trust are substitutes or complements or how their role may differ across cultures. This study reveals that the contract was not only the mechanism used to regulate the cooperation but appeared also to be a source of identity. When Promostate asks: 'What's our role in the contract?' the question is clearly one of identity that will generate the type of behaviour which goes with it. It is the same when SONAT declares, 'we should work as one hand'. As soon as someone is convinced that the contractual relation gives them a particular role, a set of taken-for-granted assumptions shapes the way they see their actions and their partner's behaviour. Divergences in perceiving roles in the contract led to misunderstandings over contractual clauses and their implementation. It proved difficult to set up a durable cooperative relationship since each party felt they were not being treated as they should be, given their roles.

Fourth, the findings suggest that cultural differences do not have an independent influence on the problems faced in a partnership; culture is intimately connected to different aspects of cooperation. Analysis revealed the main obstacles to cooperation to be power asymmetries, personal conflicts and differing organizational cultures. However, the effect of differences in national cultures could not be disentangled from these obstacles. Cultural differences complicated the implementation of effective solutions and hindered trust repair by providing different interpretations of the problems encountered. If the two processes undertaken to facilitate exchange and understanding between the parties did little to build or sustain trust, it is because they addressed only the explicit, differing interpretations of the contract. These processes failed to help the partners recognize they had different methods of implementing contractual commitments, as well as different perceptions of their counterpart's behaviour. One of the main limitations of our research is that we were not able to share our empirical results with our respondents. This would have helped us to test whether an awareness of these implicit differences could have helped repair trust.

## Concluding remarks

The fieldwork findings indicate that it is necessary to increase awareness of the ways cultural differences influence and shape how partners perceive cooperation issues, and attempt to address those issues. This means national cultural differences should not be dealt with independently from other obstacles. An effective process to facilitate exchange and build or sustain trust between parties should not only address the explicit, differing interpretations about the contract or obvious cooperation problems. The process should also take into account that partners have to cooperate with groups who not only have different interests but also different interpretations of what is good cooperation and different means to achieve it. In this paper, we provide an analysis that begins to address these important issues. Future empirical work is needed to further describe how national culture is connected to other problems of cooperation, such as personal, organizational, institutional,

etc. in trust development and how to create effective processes to build or
maintain trust across cultures.

## References

Bahjat, R. 2001. '*L'identité pluriculturelle libanaise: pour un véritable dialogue des cultures*'. Paris: idlivre.com, Collection Esquilles.

Beydoun, A. 1984. *Identité confessionnelle et temps social chez les historiens libanais contemporains*. Beirut: Lebanese University Publications.

Bloch, M. 1939. *La Société Féodale*. Paris: Albin Michel.

Branzei, O., Vertinsky, I. and Camp, R. D. 2007. 'Culture-contingent signs of trust in emergent relationships'. *Organizational Behavior and Human Decision Processes*, 104, 61–82.

Brousseau, E. 1996. 'Contrats et comportements coopératifs : le cas des relations interentreprises'. In J. L. Ravix (ed.) *Coopération entre les entreprises et organisation industrielle*. Paris: Editions du CNRS, Collection Recherche et Entreprise, 23–51.

Buckley, P. J. and Casson, M. 1988. 'A theory of cooperation in international business'. In F. Contractor and P. Lorange (eds.) *Co-operative Strategies in International Business*. Lexington Books.

Burchell, B. and Wilkinson, F. 1997. 'Trust, business relationships and the contractual environment'. *Cambridge Journal of Economics*, 21, 217–37.

Chao, G. T. and Moon, H. 2005. 'The cultural mosaic: a meta-theory for understanding the complexity of culture'. *Journal of Applied Psychology*, 90(6), 1128–40.

Das, T. K. and Teng, B. S. 1998. 'Between trust and control: developing confidence in partner cooperation in alliances'. *Academy of Management Review*, 23(3), 491–512.

Dasgupta, P. 1988. 'Trust as a commodity'. In D. Gambetta (ed.) *Trust: Making and Breaking Cooperative Relations*. New York: Basil Blackwell, 47–72.

Doney, P. M., Cannon, J. P. and Mullen, M. R. 1998. 'Understanding the influence of national culture on the development of trust'. *Academy of Management Journal*, 23, 601–20.

Elster, J. 1983. *Sour Grapes*. Cambridge University Press.

Fukuyama, F. 1995. *Trust: the Social Virtues and the Creation of Prosperity*. New York: Free Press.

Geertz, C. 1973. *The Interpretation of Cultures*. New York: Basic Books.

Giddens, A. 1984. *The Constitution of Society: Outline of the Theory of Structuration*. Berkeley, CA: University of California Press.

Haastrup, K. 1996. *A Passage to Anthropology: Between Experience and Theory*. London and New York: Routledge.

Hagen, J. M. and Choe, S. 1998. 'Trust in Japanese interfirm relations, institutional sanctions matter'. *Academy of Management Review*, 23(3), 589–600.

Hofstede, G. 2001. *Culture's Consequences: Comparing Values, Behaviors, Institutions and Organizations across Nations*. Thousand Oaks, CA: Sage.

Iribarne (d') P. 1989. *La Logique de l'honneur, Gestion des entreprises et traditions nationale*. Paris: Edition de poche, Point-Seuil.

1996. 'The usefulness of an ethnographic approach to the international comparisons of organizations'. *International Studies of Management and Organization*, 26(4).

Iribarne, P. (d') and Henry, A. 2007. 'Successful companies in the developing world: managing the synergy with culture'. Notes et documents AFD.

Johnson, J. L. and Cullen, J. B. 2002. 'Trust in cross-cultural relationships'. In Martin J. Canon and Karen L. Newman (eds.) *The Blackwell Handbook of Cross-Cultural Management*. Oxford: Blackwell, 335–60.

Koenig, G. and van Wijk, G. 1992. 'Alliances inter-entreprises, le rôle de la confiance'. In A. Nöel (ed.), *Perspectives en Management stratégique*. Paris: Economica.

Kramer, R. M. 1999. 'Trust and distrust in organizations: emerging perspective, enduring questions'. *Annual Review of Psychology*, 50, 689–714.

Lewicki, R. J., McAllister, D. J. and Bies, R. J. 1998. 'Trust and distrust: new relationships and realities'. *Academy of Management Review*, 23(3), 438–58.

Lorenz, E. H. 1988. 'Neither friends nor strangers: informal networks of subcontracting in French industry'. In D. Gambetta (ed.) *Trust Making and Breaking: Cooperation Relations*. Oxford: Basil Blackwell, 194–210.

Macaulay, S. 1963. 'Non-contractual relations in business: a preliminary study'. *American Sociological Review*, 28(1), 151–75.

Mayer, R. C., Davis, J. H. and Schoorman, F. D. 1995. 'An integrative model of organizational trust'. *Academy of Management Review*, 20(3), 709–34.

Möllering, G. and Stache, F. 2007. 'German–Ukrainian business relationships: trust development in the face of institutional uncertainty and cultural differences'. MPIfG Discussion Paper.

Montesquieu, C. (de) 1748 (ed. 1979). *De l'esprit des lois*. Paris: Flammarion.

Noorderhaven, N. G. 1999. 'National culture and the development of trust: the need for more data and less theory'. *Academy of Management Review*, 24, 9–10.

Ouchi, W. 1980. 'Markets, bureaucracies and clans'. *Administrative Science Quarterly*, 25, 129–41.

Ring, P. S. and Van de Ven, A. H. 1994. 'Developmental processes of cooperative inter-organizational relationships'. *Academy of Management Review*, 19, 90–118.

Rousseau, D. M., Sitkin, S. B., Burt, R. S. and Camerer, C. 1998. 'Not so different after all: a cross-discipline view of trust'. *Academy of Management Review*, 23(3), 393–404.

Sako, M. 1992. *Prices, Quality, and Trust: Inter-firm Relations in Britain and Japan*, Cambridge University Press.

Schneider, S. C. and Barsoux, J.-L. 1997. *Managing Across Cultures*. London: FT/Prentice-Hall.

Sitkin, S. B. 2005. 'Managerial trust-building through the use of legitimating formal and informal control mechanisms'. *International Sociology*, 20(3), 307–38.

Tocqueville (de) A., 1856. *L'ancien régime et la revolution*. Paris: Gallimard.

Yamagishi, T. and Kiyonari, T. 2000. 'The group as the container of generalized reciprocity'. *Social Psychology Quarterly*, 63(2), 116–32.

Yousfi, H. 2008. 'Coopérer au Liban, l'idéal de l'unité à l'épreuve de la diversité des points de vues'. *Gestion en contexte interculturel*, February, CD Rom, Université de Laval, Canada.

Williamson, O. E. 1985. *The Economic Institutions of Capitalism*. New York: Free Press.

    1993. 'Calculativeness, trust and economic organization'. *Journal of Law and Economics*, 36, 453–86.

Zaheer, S. and Zaheer, A. 2006. 'Trust across borders'. *Journal of International Business Studies*, 37, 21–9.

Zucker, L. G. 1986. 'Production of trust: institutional sources of economic structure'. In B. M. Staw and L. L. Cummings (eds.) *Research in Organizational Behavior*, Vol. 8. Greenwich, CT: JAI Press, 53–111.

# 10 | Evolving institutions of trust: personalized and institutional bases of trust in Nigerian and Ghanaian food trading

FERGUS LYON AND GINA PORTER

## Summary

This chapter examines the processes of building cooperation in a context of sparse public-sector regulation. The Nigerian and Ghanaian food sectors are characterized by a highly dispersed and fragmented system of micro-entrepreneurs from diverse ethnic groups who both compete and cooperate in order to flourish. Drawing on ethnographic research, we consider the relationships and contracts that require an element of cross-cultural trust, how personal social relations and institutional forms are used to ensure trust and the role of cultural norms. Our empirical findings indicate that individuals draw on both personalized social relations and institutional forms of trust that are underpinned by culture-specific norms. Through personalized trust, traders have been able to operate across cultural boundaries, building common norms of behaviour over centuries, and shaping these into what are perceived essentially as professional, albeit personalized, codes of conduct and semi-formal institutional forms (such as associations) that function in parallel to the state.

## Introduction

The Nigerian and Ghanaian food sectors are characterized by a highly dispersed and fragmented system of micro-entrepreneurs from a range of ethnic groups who both compete and cooperate in order to survive and grow. The fragmented nature of the sector necessitates a range of cooperative forms in order for the enterprises to gain access to information, finance, quality products and market spaces. The traders involved are found to have a number of different types of bilateral relations (joint ventures and informal reciprocal arrangements) both within cultural groups and crossing cultural boundaries. These may be combined with multilateral forms of cooperation in powerful trader associations, some of which are of single ethnic groups while others cut across ethnic boundaries.

The issue of ethnicity is particularly interesting in the countries studied as both nations are made up of a large number of different ethnic groups, resulting in much of the long-distance trade between rural and urban areas taking place across cultural boundaries. There is thus a degree of unfamiliarity in early stages of relationships which requires a greater degree of trust because of the inherent risk and vulnerability. These boundaries have also been areas of contestation and tension in the past. While Ghana has a record for relative harmony between ethnic groups,[1] in Nigeria there have been sporadic outbursts of considerable violence, one such episode taking place in the middle of the longitudinal study reported here.

The process of building cooperation is particularly interesting in the two case countries as it occurs in a context with minimal legal recourse or regulation by the public sector. The role of the state is relatively weak in each case, with a large proportion of business being carried out without written contracts and/or other forms of formal institutional support. In response, traders have developed parallel systems to reduce the high degrees of uncertainty.

These two cases offer an opportunity to explore the following questions concerning issues of building trust and institutional forms in different cultural contexts:

- What are the relationships and contracts that require an element of trust across cultures?
- How are personal social relations and institutional forms used to ensure trust across cultures?
- What are the roles of cultural norms in the development of relationships across cultures?

## Theoretical grounding

The chapter draws on theoretical and conceptual insights from a range of social sciences, including anthropology (on how culture, social structures and social networks shape organizational forms), economic sociology and economics (on economic institutions, transaction costs and how economic activity is embedded in social relations and relationships of trust) and management studies (on how businesses operate and entrepreneurs behave).

Drawing on literature on the processes of economic development, the case studies demonstrate the social institutions that shape economic life (Hodgson,

---

[1] Ethnic troubles in northern Ghana continue to result in sporadic violence, but this rarely occurs on the scale evidence

1988) and allow us to consider the roles of traders as actors being shaped by the structural context in which they operate (Granovetter, 1985; Long, 1992). Culture plays a central role in how they carry out business and there is a need for greater understanding of how traders cross cultural boundaries. Culture is a nebulous and contested concept but for the purposes of this chapter can be defined as the collective programming of the mind distinguishing the members of one group or category of people from another (Hofstede, 1996), where the group/category may be a nation, region, profession, organization, department, gender or generation. For this study, we look at those aspects of ethnic culture that shape the way boundaries are crossed and collaboration and trust is built. These include social norms that steer behaviour, values, sanctions on others in the community and reward systems, which in turn shape the process of collaboration. In addition to ethnic cultural differences, the analysis of supply-chain relationships also demonstrates a range of professional cultural differences between traders of various kinds and positions in the marketing chain, as well as between farmers and traders (Eaton *et al.*, 2007; Masuku and Kirsten, 2003).

## *Relationships and contracts requiring an element of trust across cultures*

Cross-cultural relationships present an interesting avenue in which to explore trust. Trust can be defined as an expectation of others' behaviour (Gambetta, 1988: 217; Humphrey and Schmitz, 1996: 5; Zucker, 1986: 54) with confidence based on personal relationships or knowledge that there are institutions that can ensure or enforce expected behaviour. Trust also requires an element of willingness to embrace vulnerability and expectation that the other party will act responsibly (see Mayer *et al.*, 1995; Rousseau *et al.*, 1998). Well-placed trust is based on active enquiry, often extended through questioning and listening over time, rather than blind acceptance (O'Neill, 2002: 76). This may be a conscious action based on calculations of vulnerability, risks and rewards, or it may be more instinctive based on habitual action (Lyon, 2006; Möllering, 2006).

In an African context there is a limited literature about food-marketing organizations and their cross-cultural relationships, despite the fact that they play a major role in the national economy, as well as being central figures with regard to food security. With regard to finance, personalized trust-based informal sources are vital, as banks are unwilling to lend to small-scale traders (Lyon and Porter, 2007; Nissanke and Aryeetey, 1998). Informal sources of financing are vital to keep trade moving although they can be used

exploitatively if individuals become tied into debt relations over many years
(Bhaduri, 1986; Clough, 1981, 1985; Watts, 1987). Food market traders
often form associations which have a number of roles. These include providing welfare support for traders, building market infrastructure, sharing market information and lending to each other (Smith and Luttrell, 1994). They
may also be the arenas for setting prices and ensuring the rules of the market
are followed (Clark, 1994). They play specific roles in dispute resolution
(Lyon, 2003; Whetham, 1972) and are responsible for hiring private security
guards, often part of youth vigilante groups (Gore and Pratten, 2002).

Of particular interest in this study are the boundary-spanners and intermediaries who can cross ethnic and professional cultural boundaries. There
are considerable challenges to crossing cultural boundaries; what Zaheer
(1995) refers to as the 'liability of foreignness' and Child *et al.* (2002) as
'psychic distance'. These challenges include an unfamiliarity with the other
culture and potential cultural hostility.

## Personal social relations and institutional forms for ensuring trust across cultures

In terms of addressing the second objective of examining the social relations
that ensure trust, this chapter explores both the personal relationships and the
institutional bases of trust. Many relationships within and between organizations involve informal relationships of trust. These can be contrasted with
institutional forms of trust, where there is trusting behaviour because there
are institutions that can play a role in safeguarding any interaction and
limiting opportunism. However, in many cases there are elements of both
trust and contract-with-trust often preceding the development of contracts
(Klein Woolthuis *et al.*, 2005).

Personal trust is particularly important where 'transactions are so complex
that law cannot possibly cover all contingent circumstances' (Moore, 1994:
819), where legal mechanisms are hard to use and where there are no formal
systems of contracts available. In such cases, more informal personalized
relationships become increasingly important for reducing uncertainty.
Personalized trust is based on an assessment of the other party's actions and
characteristics, information from third parties, and from direct interactions
with them (Humphrey and Schmitz, 1996; Lyon, 2006; Zucker, 1986).

With personalized trust, cooperation is ensured through a balance of
wanting to act reciprocally and being coerced into action due to the sanctions
and control exerted by the other party. The outcomes of trusting for each
individual will depend in part on the specific balance of power achieved

between the parties. This supports Möllering's (2005) view of the duality of trust and control, in which both assume the existence of the other.

Trust can also be based on institutional forms whereby actors can build confidence without having a personalized relationship. The institutional forms allow one party to take action against another if an agreement is not honoured. Institutionally-based trust is built up through ensuring that those relying on these institutions perceive them to be trustworthy and able to sanction norm breakers. Institution-based trust is most frequently underpinned by state-developed and enforced legislation. In the food marketing context, the Food and Agriculture Organization (2001) and Cullinan (1997) divide these into enabling functions (laws of contract, property rights, exchange and security/collateral), economic regulatory functions (laws of unfair competition/cartels, weights and measures, quality and tax) and constraining functions to avoid socially undesirable consequences (consumer protection, urban planning, environmental protection).

As institution-based trust rests on the perception that the institutions themselves are trustworthy, it may operate best when these institutions are invisible or perceived to be inevitable (Searle, 2005). However, in a Nigerian context, government-related regulatory forms have been associated with widespread corruption and, in the food sector, a lack of capacity for enforcement (Mustapha and Meagher, 2000: 36). This has led to loss of trust in these forms of institutions. They have been abandoned, where possible, in favour of parallel non-state forms of regulation that encourage institution-based trust, such as trader associations and transport unions. These relationships may exhibit elements of both personalized and institution-based relationships as each party may draw on what they know personally, as well as on the safeguards of the institutions (formal and informal). Furthermore, there is not a clear distinction between institutional and personal trust. Personalized forms can include relationships between groups of people (as opposed to bilateral relationships between two people), which become more like institutions when operating at a larger scale. Examples of relationships based on personalized links include groups of friends or groups of individuals all well known to a trusted guarantor. Larger scale examples include trader or other business associations.

## The role of cultural norms in the development of relationships across cultures

The final research question relates to the cultural norms in personal relationships and institutions. Building trust is culturally specific as it involves norms and values (Gibbs *et al.*, 2007). Discussions on the nature and formation of norms underlying trust are restricted as they are intangible and difficult to observe. Norms define what actions are deemed to be right or wrong, and include customs of cooperation, reciprocity and interaction with strangers. Furthermore, norms cannot be produced at will and their creation and shaping depends on the cultural background to the relationship, including the market exchange context (Harriss-White 1996: 318).

For personal trust, the act of reciprocity is a norm of behaviour that involves an element of altruism or benevolence, and an ethical decision that is not solely based on self-interest (Sayer, 2004). Indeed, trustworthiness may be regarded a duty and part of being a good and honourable person. Trust is also based on sanctions for those breaking norms, with enforcement only possible with social consensus (Brennan and Pettit, 2004), as there are norms that dictate what are appropriate sanctions given the particular circumstance. Sanctions may take the form of peer pressure, shaming, damaging personal reputations and exclusion from economic or community activities, through to physical threats and actual bodily harm (Porter and Lyon, 2006).

The production of norms is based on what Platteau (1994: 536) refers to as 'historically-rooted cultural endowments', upon which norms of a more generalized morality can be encouraged when the right conditions arise. Portes and Sensenbrenner (1993: 1324–5) use the term 'bounded solidarity' which can lead to 'the emergence of principled group-oriented behaviour . . . If sufficiently strong, this emergent sentiment will lead to the observance of norms of mutual support, appropriable [sic] by individuals as a resource in their own pursuits'. Shared norms and organizational conventions support trust building. However, where trust is built across professional boundaries, these culture-specific values cannot be so easily drawn on. Nonetheless, it may be possible to build them up over time.

## Research method

The empirical work took an ethnographic approach and was carried out through two case studies. The Ghana case involved data collection in four urban markets between 1995 and 1999. The greatest attention was given to Kumasi market while shorter studies were undertaken in Sunyani, Techiman and Accra. These markets were selected because of their importance in national marketing systems for agricultural produce, especially tomatoes. A total of 200 interviews were undertaken in Ghana. The Nigerian case involved research conducted on the Jos Plateau in 2001 and 2004, but builds on earlier work conducted by the authors in this region and elsewhere. Eighty interviews were undertaken with vegetable farmers and diverse types of vegetable trader in rural, peri-urban and urban markets.

Open-ended questions were used that allowed respondents to describe specific experiences in their own words. The traders were interviewed in the markets and while they were visiting the farmers. Locating the traders when they had time to discuss their work was difficult and a random sample could not be taken. It was necessary to build up relationships with traders over several years. This was achieved by regular visits. Data collection also involved a considerable amount of observation of market transactions and dispute settlements; what Hollier (1986) refers to as 'lurking'. The rationale here is that collective action and the social relations of a particular context are best understood by following explanations of important events and disputes by traders themselves. Small focus groups were used to explore key issues in detail and took place in the market association sheds. These were informally organized and included between three and eight traders who were present at the time.

Interviews were conducted in English where spoken by interviewees or using interpreters. The researchers were sensitive to their position as outsiders and to potential influence of interpreters from different ethnic groups. These biases were minimized by ensuring a range of methods were used (interviews, observations, informal discussions) combined with a sampling of interviewees that allowed comparison and cross-checking of issues from multiple sources.

The 2001 Nigeria study occurred at a time of considerable tension, with severe conflicts taking place several months later. In early 2004 we undertook a follow-up study and were struck by the ease of access for researchers and the recovery of (urban and peri-urban) markets, post conflict, on the Plateau, though we were unable to access rural markets because of continuing unrest in remoter locations.

Data analysis drew on grounded theory with careful analysis of comments and the reaction of respondents, particularly in those cases where they were asked questions that related to habitual behaviour. Data from a questionnaire survey of 127 wholesale traders in Nigeria (2001) and 37 traders in Ghana (1999) are also drawn on. In each case, the informal nature of the marketing system meant that no adequate sampling frame could be established, since traders are constantly arriving or leaving the market and physical market boundaries in West Africa are commonly highly porous, being open to entry and exit from diverse points (Barrett, 1988: 14). Research assistants were consequently asked to interview each wholesaler they met as they progressed through the market concerned, until it closed for the day, i.e. our aim was to obtain responses from the full population of traders present on the day of the survey, but given the fluidity of the population concerned we cannot guarantee that our data refer to the full population. The response rate was remarkably high with only a handful of direct refusals (though traders not wishing to be interviewed may have simply moved away before we reached them).

## The cultural contexts of the case study areas

There is a diversity of market types ranging from village markets to bulking markets and large urban markets. The perishable nature of vegetables means that there are fewer intermediaries and produce may be bought from farmers by itinerant traders who take it direct to the urban centres where it is sold on to retailers. This can reduce the time taken to reach the consumers and the risk of losses.

One of the most striking aspects of the vegetable marketing system is the dominance of women in Ghana and southern Nigeria. This is reported in other sectors in Ghana, Nigeria and many other African countries (Attah *et al.*, 1996; Clark, 1994; Horn, 1994; Onyemelukwe, 1970; Trager, 1981, 1985). Trager found that the 'market place is historically the domain of women in Yoruba society. Beliefs and institutions recognize women's importance in the market' (Trager, 1985: 280). However, in Hausa and other Moslem-dominated markets in northern Nigeria, men are far more prominent, especially in the larger-scale perishables trade.

The Ghanaian case study involves the trading relationships between farmers growing vegetables in the Brong Ahafo Region and traders coming out of the large conurbations such as Kumasi and Accra. The area has a long tradition in commercial agriculture and private trading, particularly with the arrival of cocoa as a cash crop in the early twentieth century. A market system evolved based on historical approaches to trade and growing urban markets. This has been centred on self-employed independent traders building relationships with farmers.

There has been evidence of trade in Ghana for the past thousand years. This has led to dramatic social changes over time and the development of economic activity that involved long-distance trade and the development of trading networks that stretched throughout West and North Africa (Chamlee-Wright, 1997: 14; Hymer, 1970: 39; Lovejoy, 1974; Mikell, 1989). Trade was central to the colonial expansion, encouraging the development of trade routes and infrastructure. The state played an increasing role in the marketing of cocoa and staple food crops particularly in the post independence period (Hansen, 1989). Growing constraints were placed on the informal marketing system as market traders were seen as the cause of agricultural decline. The role of traders came under increasing pressure in the late 1970s and early 1980s as markets were destroyed and traders pushed out, most notably in Accra and Kumasi (Clark, 1994; Robertson, 1983).

Tomato producers are predominantly from the Brong ethnic group, who moved into the Brong Ahafo area with the expansion of cocoa production in the twentieth century. There are also many Ashantis who moved from Kumasi and Mampong areas (Hilton, 1960: 29–30). The traders are from the main urban areas to the south of the producing areas and include Ga traders from Accra, Ashantis from Kumasi and Fantes from the southern part of Ghana.

In the Nigerian case there is clear ethnic differentiation within the vegetable production and marketing system. In the Jos urban markets Hausa traders still dominate, so far as vegetables are concerned, because of their enormous experience in this trade and their extensive networks which reach across West Africa. Hausa farmers also dominated production until about ten years ago, when indigenous Berom expanded production, taking back land that had been rented to Hausa farmers (Porter *et al.*, 2003). However, the area has a wide range of other ethnic groups.

The Jos Plateau experienced considerable in-migration in the colonial period, associated with the importation of labour from other areas of Nigeria for tin production. Currently, there are immigrants who have lived on the Plateau for several generations, and therefore feel that the Plateau is their home state, although they are not indigenes. There are also newcomers (first-generation migrants), and temporary migrants who come to participate in the vegetable industry on a seasonal basis. For the most part, these immigrant groups – notably Hausa, Kanuri, Ibo and Yoruba – had managed to coexist alongside each other and with the indigenous Berom and other Plateau ethnic groups remarkably peaceably. However, friction has grown with the decline in tin production, the movement of settled immigrant populations out of mining into farming and the expansion of dry-season migrations of Hausa farmers to the Plateau. Thus, while religious tensions between Moslems and Christians were, ostensibly, the touchpaper which sparked serious riots in Jos city in August/September 2001 and again in November/December 2008, ethnic tensions around access to land and trade probably form an important backcloth to these disturbances in which many hundreds of people were reportedly killed.

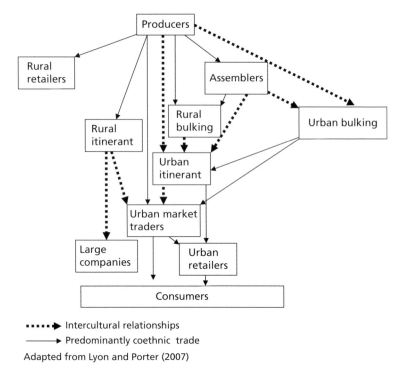

**Figure 10.1** Urban marketing chain and cross-ethnic cultural links (Adapted from Lyon and Porter, 2007)

## Findings: relationships and contracts requiring trust across cultures

The two case studies demonstrate a range of arenas where trust across cultures is central to the operation of the marketing system. While ethnic culture is most pronounced in the longer-distance relationships, the relationships between each type of actor in the marketing chain require the crossing of professional cultural boundaries as well. The marketing chain (set out in Figure 10.1) summarizes the range of avenues that are operating in both of the case studies. There are differences between the two cases, however, particularly in terms of the role of commission agents and rural bulking markets. These were found to be important parts of the Nigerian system with commission agents providing much funding for farmers. This was not found to the same degree in Ghana, where long-distance traders often form relationships with farmers directly. Common to both case studies were a range of arenas where trust was required to overcome the risk of opportunism. These are set out in Table 10.1.

Table 10.1 *Trust and opportunism in vegetable production and marketing*

| Trust arena | Potential opportunism |
| --- | --- |
| Farmers receiving credit from traders | Not repaying, diverting sales to other traders, not reducing price for trader as agreed |
| Bargaining | Farmers and traders withholding information on supply or prices from the other party |
| Paying for produce after harvesting | Traders reducing the price negotiated with farmers after they have harvested |
| Diverting harvested produce to traders with higher prices | Farmers negotiate a price to harvest for some traders and more traders come offering higher prices. Farmers can dump the earlier traders' boxes and harvest for the higher price |
| Low quality produce | Farmer hides grass, rocks and unripe or damaged tomatoes in the crate |
| Traders take on credit | Traders ask to take on credit and do not return. Traders return saying the price was low in the market and so cannot pay the full amount |
| Trader associations | Trader does not cooperate with association members. Stealing customers of other traders in the market |
| Sales to retailers | Retailers fail to pay later after taking goods on credit or cannot pay the full amount |

(Adapted from Lyon, 2000)

Where formal legal contracts and agreements cannot be enforced by a legal system, more informal personalized trust relationships become increasingly important in order to reduce uncertainty. For example 68 per cent of wholesale traders in Ghana and 56 per cent of traders in Nigeria were providing long-term credit to supplier farmers usually coming from different ethnic groups. Surveys of 159 Ghanaian farmers found that 10 per cent were receiving credit from traders (Lyon, 2000). No evidence of recourse to legal structures was found and interviewees reported that they were reliant on trust. The amounts of credit provided are considerable for the farmers, with the figure of £125 reported in Table 10.2 representing up to five months' income for a farm labourer. The money lent out is also a large proportion of the trader's capital, in a context where banks are unwilling to lend to either farmers or traders.

Credit systems in Ghana were found to flow both ways, with 68 per cent of farmers giving produce on credit to traders although there are considerable

Table 10.2 *Trader credit to farmers*

|  | Ghana case study | Nigeria case study |
|---|---|---|
| N | N = 37 | N = 127 |
| Percentage of traders giving credit to farmers | 68% | 56% |
| Average number of farmer customers being given credit | 4.6 | 4.0 |
| Average amount given (converted to pounds) | £125 | £50 |

Table 10.3 *Traders buying and selling goods on credit*

|  | Ghana case study | Nigeria case study |
|---|---|---|
| N | N = 37 | N = 127 |
| Percentage of traders receiving produce on credit | 68% | 57% |
| Percentage of traders selling produce on credit | 76% | 50% |

differences between villages. Table 10.3 above also shows a majority of traders taking produce on credit from producers and paying later. A majority of traders were also selling produce on credit in Ghana. A comparison with the Nigerian case shows a difference in the proportion of traders providing credit and receiving credit. The lower proportion of traders involved in these trust-based credit systems in Nigeria may be due to both the greater risks found in Nigeria, and the differences in the marketing chain allowing a greater amount of spot purchasing rather than long-term relationship building.

## Personal and institutional forms used to ensure trust

The empirical findings show that individuals draw on both personalized social relations and institutional forms of trust. Personalized trust is shown to be based on having information on the other party and the ability to sanction those that do not behave as expected. On the one hand this is a calculative process, but our data show that in many cases people based trust on instinct and reported that they had not thought about the issue until asked about it by a researcher.

Traders take considerable risks in lending to people who could disappear and the issue of personalized trust was often identified by interviewees as a way to reduce this risk. To build up trust, traders have to gather information about the farmers' prior behaviour and also have sanctions or potential ways of putting pressure on them if they try to avoid repaying. In this way they balance both controls and goodwill or benevolence (Nooteboom, 2004).

The types of relationships that are drawn on are existing relationships through kinship, community or church links, working relationships built up over time, friendships that come out of the working relationship and intermediaries who are known to both sides. Information leading to personalized trust is gathered on the competence of the person to repay by visiting the farm, assessing its size and asking others about their ability as farmers. By working together the farmers and traders learn more about each other. One (male) trader in Nigeria stated: 'I know him – in and out of season we are all together'. Information about the person's character and behaviour is also gathered from people in the recipient's community and traders may go to visit the village and the farmer's house. This allows traders to meet the family members and other villagers. If there is a problem with repayment, traders can use the family members, leading farmers in the village or the village head, to settle disputes and put social pressure on the farmer. Meeting family members also acts as a proof of giving the loan. In Nigeria, some farmers were additionally being asked to 'sign evidence before collecting' (i.e. put a signature or mark on a written statement confirming receipt of the loan before it is handed over).

The sources of information for personalized trust may also come from using intermediaries, particularly the elders of the different types of associations. These intermediaries are able to build on bilateral relationships and allow multilateral relationships to evolve through being a guarantor. In this boundary-spanning role they cross ethnic and professional boundaries and facilitate the building of trust based on their personal relationships. However, these personal relations become more institutional as the scale of the boundary crossing increases. This demonstrates the lack of a clear distinction between institutionally based and personalized trust, especially with respect to the role of intermediaries.

Institution-based trust is built on organizational forms that have regulatory roles and allow confidence in others' actions without personal relations. These include trader associations, traditional chieftaincy systems and community leadership and allow individuals to take action against others if an agreement is not honoured. These institutions tend to become parallel institutions to the state as public-sector-supported institutions are not perceived to be trustworthy because of the high degree of corruption.

The two case studies found no formal legal basis for any of the transactions but contracts are partly enforced by trader associations operating as parallel institutions to the state. These organizations also regulate the market place through settling disputes, regulating the activities of the intermediaries and controlling the use of the market space. In Nigeria they played a role in organizing private 'vigilante' security groups and in Ghana they were also providing forms of insurance. Trader associations were found to vary, with many markets having an umbrella association that included a wide range of other associations divided along commodity lines, which in turn might be subdivided into autonomous groups for retailers and wholesalers. The associations were therefore playing a boundary-spanning role between different professional cultures.

While power can be drawn from mutual action in the market associations (i.e. there is a collaborative side to power in the form of social solidarity which enables trust in the collective, Arendt 1958), it will not necessarily operate positively for all traders. In the Nigeria case, the expanding role of local Berom and other Plateau people in the vegetable trade has been achieved despite the evident dominance of Hausa traders in Jos urban vegetable markets. In this case the ability of smaller players to mobilize against a greater force (a possibility which Arendt also observes) was presumably feasible because of the collaborative, integrative (ethnic) resources of the less established Berom trader group.

## Cultural norms that influence relationships

Norms define what actions are considered acceptable or unacceptable and are therefore the basis of building and maintaining personalized trust and institutions in themselves. Norms of reciprocity are the most commonly referred to in this study, particularly with regard to customer relationships. These relationships, frequently between people from different ethnic groups, were found to be able to withstand the serious conflict between ethnic groups which occurred in Jos in 2001, even though the origin of the conflict was linked to resentment against traders of a particular ethnic group.

These norms of reciprocity were often referred to in terms of friendship and obligation to others. In Nigeria, cooperation in long-distance trading relationships is frequently cemented through landlord relationships whereby the trader of one ethnic group will reside with another ethnic group while their goods are being sold (Cohen, 1971; Hill, 1971; Mortimore, 1989: 131). This provides a sense of security, even if the landlord takes some advantage of his client's limited knowledge of local conditions and languages:

The [Ibo] dillali that takes you to his house personally has shown great concern. There are many thieves in the east. If you go to lodge and get attacked you won't return to him. So you are safe . . . You go back to him because of the relationship between you, even though he has cheated you. If you go to another place it could be even worse . . . he respects me because I help him earn a living (driver/farmer from Tudun Mazat, Barikin Ladi district, talking about the six-year business relationship with his Ibo dillali based in Onitsha, January 2004).

In Ghana, the forms of reciprocity and obligations were cemented through attending church together and, most importantly, through attending funerals of a family member of the other party. These are large events where the number of guests is a sign of status and financial contributions are provided for the cost entailed. In such cases the common norms of professional cultures overrode the ethnic cultural boundaries.

Other important professional cultural norms include keeping agreements, avoiding deception, not stealing customers or outbidding fellow traders. The studies also identified norms related to modes of interaction with strangers with an expectation on traders to welcome buyers and sellers and treat them fairly. However, the definition of what is considered fair was found to be open to interpretation in the different case studies, with further differences between markets, between commodities and changes over the season as goods become more or less abundant. The moral norms regarding the relationship between competitor traders are strongly enforced as this allows the markets to operate without descending into chaos and results in traders regarding those carrying out the same activities as colleagues rather than competitors.

Norms can be applied consciously and rely on altruism and benevolence, as well as social consensus to enforce sanctions on those that break them. The roles of associations in each case study demonstrate common forms of social consensus and punishment of norm breakers. The sanctions or motivations may also come in the form of shame, peer pressure and fear of a damaged reputation that would limit access to support from other traders in the future (for credit or for settling disputes, for example). Individual traders are therefore pressured into keeping to norms by those around them. This can be done by withdrawal of cooperation, disapproval and attaching social stigma to norm breakers.

Pressure can also be exerted through forms of authority. The strength of this authority is based on their own set of norms that include common beliefs, values, traditions and practice that result in the recognition of the authority's right to command. Norms of leadership are adapted from common forms of behaviour of those involved. Examples include the form of the trader associations, drawing on norms of leadership found in the chieftaincy system in Ghana. The Ghanaian associations, dominated by women traders, had market queens, referred to as *ohemma*. Their roles and operations draw on the Ashanti and Brong cultural-specific practices where a leading woman plays a key role in traditional chieftaincy.

While norms may be enforced through sanctions, there are also norms that determine which sanctions or forms of coercion are acceptable. The ability to make threats and carry them out is shaped by the norms of what is deemed acceptable behaviour. In Ghana's Central Region, individuals claimed they were restricted from taking forceful action against people from their own community as they did not want a confrontation and to 'get a bad name' (Lyon, 2000). On the Plateau we heard similar sentiments expressed: 'there have been a few cases [of stealing]. We send them away. We don't take them to the police station because we have been together. Maybe if you can recognize your mistakes and promise not to do it again ... if you repent you can stay' (Hussain, loader at Building Materials market).

Obligation to cooperate or reciprocate is also based on common norms to support family or fellow workers or community members. These norms may be very different from the accepted norms of how others are treated, as seen in the case of the loaders above. This demonstrates the importance of considering the plurality of norms dependent on the existing and emerging relationship of the two parties. Traders were found to draw on these obligations to follow norms by visiting a customer's house and getting to know other family members and community members who might be able to put pressure on the customer should there be any problems in the relationship.

In the Nigeria study area, the role of religion (both Islam and Christianity) has been increasing in importance. Traders suggest religion shapes their own moral approaches, but it does not appear to be substantially reshaping how and with whom the vegetable business is transacted since the 2001 crisis. The issue of Islamic sharia law, while very important in other parts of Nigeria, was not mentioned by anyone we interviewed, although this may be due to the sensitivity of the subject following the conflict and ongoing tensions.

## Discussion

### *Implications for practice*

This chapter has set out how trust can be built up between cultures in unpromising circumstances created by multiple cultural nodes and boundaries and a lack of formal institutions. The multiple cultural boundaries include those related to ethnicity, profession (different types of trader and position in the marketing chain) and gender that actors have to cross in order to participate in markets. In many regions a large proportion of traders are women who have specific cultural approaches to interaction and regulation of market places.

The ethnic cultural differences are particularly important in an African context as in most African countries there is considerable ethnic diversity. Markets are often the major points of interaction for these ethnic groups, and the trust-based relationships established in trading act as a means of creating ties and avoiding wider community conflict. However, where there is ethnic tension, market places have been found to be triggers for widespread ethnic conflict in Nigeria, while at the same time acting as a means of bringing conflicting groups together again to build peace (Lyon *et al.*, 2006). This suggests that attention could profitably be given to the dynamics of trader interactions in ethnic-conflict prone areas, since knowledge and understanding of local cross-cultural trading practices and associated points of tension and cooperation may be of value in developing broader initiatives to defuse conflict and build peace.

Lack of state-based formal institutions results in traders and farmers having to rely more on personalized relationships and the development of semi-formal institutions such as trader associations. Traders can draw on institutional forms of trust (such as enforcing contracts and uniform measures) in order to build confidence without having a personalized relationship. The institutional forms allow one party to take action against another if an agreement is not honoured. Institutional trust is built up through ensuring that those relying on these institutions perceive them to be trustworthy and able to sanction norm breakers. This demonstrates the importance of understanding both the personalized and institution-based relationships that occur in most examples of trust. These are identified in the case studies but can also be found universally (Bennett and Robson, 2004; Möllering, 2002; Zucker, 1986). This challenges approaches that present different cultures as being either 'high' or 'low' trust. The findings here demonstrate the importance of making a distinction between personalized and institution-based trust, each of which may vary between high and low in different contexts.

## Directions for future research

The cases presented in this chapter demonstrate high degrees of personal trust and low institutional trust. Nigeria and Ghana present relatively unique contexts for exploring the issues of trust and cultural norms, but the study can contribute to wider theoretical discussions of trust and control between organizations and within organizations. In other cultural contexts there may be high institutional trust and lower personal trust (often as a result of the higher institutional trust). In some African contexts such as Zambia and Tanzania, there is also some evidence of lower personal and institutional bases of trust (Porter *et al.*, 2007; Tillmar and Lindkvist, 2007). To explore this differential development of institutional and personal trust in different contexts, case-study research in a diverse set of African regions would be valuable. In such research a historical perspective is likely to be extremely important for learning how trust may be built, but also how it may be undermined or destroyed. Such a perspective on cross-cultural trust building will demonstrate the importance of cultural context while at the same time identifying those factors and conceptual frameworks that transcend culture.

There are considerable cultural differences across Africa, as in Europe, although there has been little research assessing these issues with regard to building trust. Lane and Bachmann (1996) found relatively high institutional trust in a German inter-firm supply context and relatively low institutional trust by comparison in the UK. Furthermore, there are differences within individual African countries, and within particular professions or sectors. This means that we cannot refer to an Africanist approach to trust building any more than we can refer to a European approach. Detailed research is therefore needed on the culture-specific or emic dimensions to building trust (Zaheer and Zaheer, 2006) operating at a national and sub-national level.

There is also a need for research to identify some generalizable findings that could contribute to a universalist theory of trust. While that is a larger project that has not been attempted in this chapter, this study shows that there are elements of trust production that can be found in all cultures, most notably the balance of personal and institution-based trust, the balance of wanting to act reciprocally and being coerced into cooperation, and the role of locally specific norms. These norms and the response to norm violation will vary from culture to culture and affect the development of trust in different ways.

## Concluding comments

With both personalized and institutional trust, cooperation is ensured through a balance of wanting to act reciprocally and being coerced into action due to the control exerted by the other party. The nature of reciprocity is based on norms of behaviour, customs and 'rules of the game'. In the case studies, control is based on peer pressure (shame within a community and reputation protection), the authority of informal organizations (penalties, exclusion from market spaces) and, in some cases, strength (physical or in numbers). There is evidence of both norms of cooperation (reciprocity, keeping agreements, friendship, etc.) and norms of sanctions (acceptance of authority, acceptable types and strength of sanctions). Furthermore, the way reciprocity and control are used is not just calculative, as people are found to act on instinct and out of habit.

Our case-study research emphasizes the importance of taking a historical perspective to understanding trust because norms may vary over time and be applied in different ways. This resonates with Lane and Bachmann's (1996) observation (in comparing trust relationships in a European industrial context) that structures are socially constructed in a long historical process. In Europe, as in an African context, for instance, there can be a rapid change when marketing systems are disrupted by conflict, by a changing political context or by changing technology (such as mobile phones). This plurality of norms in our case studies is seen when comparing relationships between community members and relationships with distant others. While norms of reciprocity may be expected to be stronger in local communities and amongst relatives, there are also more limitations on what sanctions can be applied in case of opportunism. This results in people preferring to do business with non-relatives.

There is, therefore, a central role for cultural norms to play. Incentives are necessary for trust-based relationships but are often not sufficient. Trust across cultural boundaries thus has to identify the common norms, and where norms of behaviour may be different, each party has to adapt to the other. In the two case studies, relationships across cultures were found to have been built on common norms of behaviour that had evolved over time and were perceived as professional cultural norms amongst similar types of traders. In both case studies, the norms have been built on a long history of intercultural exchange over long distances.

## References

Arendt, H. 1958. *The Human Condition*. Chicago and London: University of Chicago Press.

Attah, M., Apt, N. and Grieco, M. 1996. 'Expected to earn, constrained to trade: trading a customary role for Ghanaian women'. In M. Grieco, N. Apt and J. Turner, (eds.) *At Christmas and on Rainy Days: Transport, Travel and the Female Traders of Accra*. Aldershot: Avebury, 3–18.

Barrett, H. 1988. *The Marketing of Foodstuffs in the Gambia, 1400–1980: a Geographical Analysis*. Aldershot: Avebury.

Bennett, R. and Robson, P. 2004. 'The role of trust and contract in the supply of business advice'. *Cambridge Journal of Economics*, 28, 471–88.

Bhaduri, A. 1986. 'Forced commerce and agrarian growth'. *World Development*, 14(2), 267–72.

Brennan, G. and Pettit, P. 2004. *The Economy of Esteem*. Oxford University Press.

Chamlee-Wright, E. 1997. *The Cultural Foundations of Economic Development: Urban Female Entrepreneurship in Ghana*. London: Routledge.

Child, J., Ng, S.-H. and Wong, C. 2002. 'Psychic distance and internationalization: evidence from Hong Kong firms'. *International Studies of Management & Organization*, 32(1), 36–56.

Clark, G. 1994. *Onions are my Husband: Survival and Accumulation by West African Market Women*. Chicago and London: University of Chicago Press.

Clough, P. 1981. 'Farmers and traders in Hausaland'. *Development and Change*, 12, 273–92.

——— 1985. 'The social relations of grain marketing in Northern Nigeria'. *Review of African Political Economy*, 34, 16–35.

Cohen, A. 1971. 'Cultural strategies in the organisation of trading diasporas'. In C. Meillassoux (ed.) *The Development of Indigenous Trade and Markets in West Africa*. London: Oxford University Press.

Cullinan, C. 1997. 'Legal aspects of urban food supply and distribution programme FAO'. Approvisionnement et distribution alimentaires des villes. Série Aliments dans les Villes.

Eaton, D., Meijerink, G., Bijman, J. and Belt, J. 2007. 'Analysis of institutional arrangements: vegetable value chains in East Africa'. Paper presented at the 106th EAAE seminar, 25–27 October, Montpellier, France.

FAO [Food and Agriculture Organization] Agricultural Services Bulletin 139. 2001. 'Law and markets, improving the legal environment for agricultural marketing'. Food and Agricultural Organization of the United Nations.

Gambetta, D. 1988. 'Can we trust trust?' In D. Gambetta (ed.) *Trust: Making and Breaking Cooperative Relations*. Oxford: Blackwell, 213–37.

Gibbs, J. C., Basinger, K. S., Grime, R. L. and Snarey, J. R. 2007. 'Moral judgment development across cultures: revisiting Kohlberg's universality claims'. *Developmental Review*, 27(4), 443–500.

Gore, C. and Pratten, D. 2002. 'The politics of plunder: the rhetoric of order and disorder in southern Nigeria'. African Studies Association of the UK biennial conference, University of Birmingham, 9–11 September 2002.

Granovetter, M. 1985. 'Economic action and social structure: the problem of embeddedness'. *American Journal of Sociology*, 91(3), 481–510.

Hansen, E. 1989. 'The state and food agriculture'. In E. Hansen and K. Ninsen (eds.) *The State, Development and Politics in Ghana*. London: CODESRA, 184–221.

Harriss-White, B. 1996. *A Political Economy of Agricultural Markets in South India: Masters of the Countryside*. New Delhi: Sage.

Hill, P. 1971. 'Two types of West African house trade'. In C. Meillassoux (ed.) *The Development of Indigenous Trade and Markets in West Africa*. London: Oxford University Press.

Hilton, T.E. 1960. *Ghana Population Atlas: the Distribution and Density of Population in the Gold Coast and Togo Land under UK Trusteeship.* London: University College of Ghana/Thomas Nelson and Sons Ltd.

Hodgson, G.M. 1988. *Economics and Institutions: a Manifesto for a Modern Institutional Economic.* Cambridge: Polity Press.

Hofstede, G. 1996. *Cultures and Organizations, Software of the Mind: Intercultural Cooperation and its Importance for Survival.* London: McGraw-Hill.

Hollier, G.P. 1986. 'The marketing of gari in North-west Province Cameroon'. *Geographiska Annaler*, 68B(1), 59–68.

Horn, N.E. 1994. *Cultivating Customers: Market Women in Harare, Zimbabwe.* London: Lynne Rienner.

Humphrey, J. and Schmitz, H. 1996. 'Trust and economic development'. Institute of Development Studies, Discussion Paper 355. Brighton, IDS.

Hymer, S.H. 1970. 'Economic forms in pre-colonial Ghana'. *Journal of Economic History*, 30(1), 33–50.

Klein Woolthuis, R., Hillebrand, B. and Nooteboom, B. 2005. 'Trust, contract and relationship development'. *Organization Studies*, 26(6), 813–40.

Lane, C. and Bachmann, R. 1996. 'The social construction of trust: supplier relations in Britain and Germany'. *Organization Studies*, 17, 365–95.

Long, N. 1992. 'From paradigm lost to paradigm regained? The case for an actor oriented sociology of development'. In N. Long and A. Long (eds.) *Battlefields of Knowledge: the Interlocking of Theory and Practice in Social Research and Development.* London: Routledge, 16–46.

Lovejoy, P.E. 1974. 'Interregional monetary flows in the precolonial trade of Nigeria'. *Journal of African History*, 15(4), 563–85.

Lyon, F. 2000. 'Trust networks and norms: the creation of social capital in agricultural economies in Ghana'. *World Development*, 28(4), 663–82.

  2003. 'Trader associations and urban food systems in Ghana: institutionalist approaches to understanding urban collective action'. *International Journal of Urban and Regional Research*, 27(1), 11–23.

  2006. 'Managing co-operation – trust and power in Ghanaian associations'. *Organization Studies*, 27(1), 31–52.

Lyon, F. and Porter, G. 2007. 'Market institutions, trust and norms: exploring moral economies in Nigerian food systems'. *Cambridge Journal of Economics*, 33(5), 903–20.

Lyon, F., Porter, G., Adamu, F. and Obafemi, L. 2006. 'The Nigerian market: fuelling conflict or contributing to peace?' In J. Banfield, C. Gunduz and N. Killick (eds) *Local Business, Local Peace: the Peace Building Potential of the Domestic Private Sector.* London: International Alert.

Masuku, M.B. and Kirsten, J.F. 2003. 'The role of trust in the performance of supply chains: a dyad analysis of smallholder farmers and processing firms in the sugar industry in Swaziland'. 41st Annual Conference of the Agricultural Economic Association of South Africa, October 2–3, 2003. Pretoria, South Africa.

Mayer, R. C., Davis, J. H. and Schoorman, F. D. 1995. 'An integration model of organizational trust'. *Academy of Management Review*, 20(3), 709–34.

Mikell, G. 1989. *Cocoa and Chaos in Ghana*. New York: Paragon House.

Möllering, G. 2002. 'Perceived trustworthiness and inter-firm governance: empirical evidence from the UK printing industry'. *Cambridge Journal of Economics*, 26, 139–60.

2005. 'The trust/control duality: an integrative perspective on positive expectations of others'. *International Sociology*, 20(3), 283–305.

2006. 'Understanding trust from the perspective of sociological neo-institutionalism'. In R. Bachmann and A. Zaheer (eds.) *Handbook of Trust Research*. Cheltenham: Edward Elgar.

Moore, M. 1994. 'How difficult is it to construct market relations? A commentary on Platteau'. *Journal of Development Studies*, 30(4), 818–30.

Mortimore, M. 1989. *Adapting to Drought: Farmers, Famines and Desertification in West Africa*. Cambridge University Press.

Mustapha, A. R. and Meagher, K. 2000. 'Agrarian production, public policy and the state in Kano region, 1900–2000'. Crewkerne: Drylands Research, Working Paper no. 35.

Nissanke, M. and Aryeetey, E. 1998. 'Financial integration and development: liberalisation and reform in Sub Saharan Africa'. *Routledge Studies in Development Economics*, 11.

Nooteboom, B. 2004. 'Governance and competence: how can they be combined?' *Cambridge Journal of Economics*, 28, 505–25.

O'Neill, O. 2002. *A Question of Trust*. Cambridge University Press.

Onyemelukwe, J. O. C. 1970. 'Aspects of staple foods trade in Onitsha Market'. *Nigerian Geographical Journal*, 12(2), 121–39.

Platteau, J.-P. 1994. 'Behind the market stage where real societies exist – Part I: The role of public and private order institutions'. *Journal of Development Studies*, 30(3), 533–77.

Porter, G., Harris, F., Lyon, F., Dung, J. and Adepetu, A. 2003. 'Markets, ethnicity and environment in a vulnerable landscape: the case of small-scale vegetable production on the Jos Plateau, Nigeria, 1991–2001'. *Geographical Journal*, 169(4), 370–81.

Porter, G. and Lyon, F. 2006. 'Groups as a means or an end? Social capital and the promotion of cooperation in Ghana'. *Environment and Planning D: Society and Space*, 24(2), 249–62.

Porter, G., Lyon, F. and Potts, D. 2007. 'Urban food-supply in Sub-Saharan Africa in the twenty-first century: the role of trading intermediaries and market institution'. *Progress in Development Studies*, 7(2), 115–34.

Portes, A. and Sensenbrenner, J. 1993. 'Embeddedness and immigration: notes on the social determinants of economic action'. *American Journal of Sociology*, 98(6), 1320–50.

Robertson, C. 1983. 'The death of Makola and other tragedies'. *Canadian Journal of African Studies*, 17(3), 469–95.

Rousseau, D., Sitkin, S. B., Burt, R. S. and Camerer, C. 1998. 'Not so different after all: a cross-discipline view of trust'. *Academy of Management Review*, 23(3), 393–404.

Sayer, A. 2004. 'Restoring the moral dimension: acknowledging lay normativity'. Mimeo, published by the Department of Sociology, Lancaster University, www.comp.lancs.ac.uk/sociology/papers/sayer-restoring-moral-dimension.pdf.

Searle, J. 2005. 'What is an institution?' *Journal of Institutional Economics*, 1(1), 1–22.

Smith, H. M. and Luttrell, M. E. 1994. 'Cartels in an 'Nth-Best' world: the wholesale foodstuff trade in Ibadan, Nigeria'. *World Development*, 22(3), 323–35.

Tillmar, M. and Lindkvist, L. 2007. 'Cooperation against all odds: finding reasons for trust where formal institutions fail'. *International Sociology*, 22(3), 343–66.

Trager, L. 1981. 'Customers and creditors: variations in economic personalism in a Nigerian marketing system'. *Ethnology*, 20(2), 133–46.

 1985. 'From yams to beer in a Nigerian city: expansion and change in informal sector trade activity'. In S. Plattner (ed.) *Markets and Marketing*. Boston: Monographs in Economic Anthropology No.4., University Press of America, 259–86.

Watts, M. 1987. 'Brittle trade: a political economy of food supply in Kano'. In J. I. Guyer (ed.) *Feeding African Cities: Studies in Regional Social History*. Manchester University Press for the International African Institute, 55, 111.

Whetham, E. H. 1972. *Agricultural Marketing in Africa*. London: Oxford University Press.

Zaheer, S. 1995. 'Overcoming the liability of foreignness'. *Academy of Management Journal*, 38, 341–63.

Zaheer, S. and Zaheer, A. 2006. 'Trust across borders'. *Journal of International Business Studies*, 37, 21–9.

Zucker, L. G. 1986. 'Production of trust: institutional sources of economic structure, 1840–1920'. In B. M. Staw and L. L. Cummings (eds.) *Research in Organizational Behavior*, Vol. 8. Greenwich, CT: JAI Press, 53–111.

# PART III

# Trust across different 'cultural spheres': intra-organizational studies

# 11 | *The role of trust in international cooperation in crisis areas: a comparison of German and US-American NGO partnership strategies*

L. RIPLEY SMITH AND ULRIKE SCHWEGLER

## Summary

International and intra-national crises often require international cooperation for resolution. Cooperation is increasingly a function of international
partnerships among various levels of societal, non-governmental organizations (NGOs). The present study examines partnership strategies within and
between international development and humanitarian agencies based in
Germany and the United States.[1] Using in-depth interviews and content
analytic methods, the study looks at the trust-development criteria and processes across multiple levels of international organizational cooperation.
Culture-specific preferences in trust-building processes are identified which
can enable actors to build and maintain trust within and between international development and humanitarian agencies, but can also generate potential barriers. The study extends standard trust-building models to include
affective and progressive trust formation processes. Findings on cultural
differences in partnership-building strategies and trust development are presented as well as recommendations for improving best practice in strategic
NGO alliances.

The authors would like to thank the ESRC Seminar 6 participants for a generous grant
and helpful feedback on an earlier version of this chapter at the Oxford Brookes University,
seminar, 22 June 2007. Special thanks to Graham Dietz, Denise Skinner and Mark
Saunders for their thorough reading and helpful remarks throughout the writing process.
[1] The data and organizations from the United States of America will be referred to
variously in the chapter as 'US-American', or simply 'American' by convention and for
simplicity's sake without the intention of usurping the continental identity of North
America.

## Introduction

The last two decades have produced some of the most significant humanitarian crises in history. The natural disaster and conflict centres include Haiti, Southeast Asia, Pakistan, Sudan, Rwanda, the Balkans, West Africa, Afghanistan, Columbia, Iraq, Sri Lanka, East Timor and the United States. As crises tax the capacity of the United Nations and other international governmental organizations (IGOs), non-governmental organizations (NGOs) are asked to play an increasingly significant role in disaster relief, rehabilitation and development (Helton, 2002). Unfortunately, the response of the international community in providing food, shelter and medical care in the midst of these crises is often disjointed and inefficient (Bebbington and Farrington, 1993; Loescher and Helton, 2002) In part, the explanation for this less than optimal response lies in the complexity of the task to which these organizations apply themselves. However, inefficiencies in the partnering process are also to blame (Helton, 2002) and, as we shall argue, cultural differences play a role in hampering these partnership processes.

The demands being placed on NGOs in the twenty-first century highlight their complex and changing role (Teegen et al., 2004). NGOs are confronted with the confounding issue of acting in situations where other authorities, e.g. the nation state, do not have enough resources to respond (Fowler, 2002a; Shreve, 2006; Williams, 2003). That capacity-extension function is complicated by the multiplicity of roles NGOs occupy between different sectors as they build partnerships with and between different levels of agents, variously serving as negotiator, mediator, innovator, developer, and watchdog (Edwards and Fowler, 2002; Fowler, 2002b: 21). A variety of tensions exists in these relationships, including adversarial relationships between NGOs and corporations, NGOs' willingness to expose operations to an outside organization (Plante and Bendell, 1998), and divergent goals in collaboration (Bebbington and Farrington, 1993). According to Fowler (2002a), NGOs' major task in the future will be to foster cooperation and collaborative spirit. Few will disagree that 'the changing global context opens up a world of possibilities for NGOs to relate to each other through alliances between equals and networks based on synergy (not competition)' (Edwards and Fowler, 2002: 7). Unfortunately, effective NGO activities remain islands of success without level-spanning cooperation (Edwards and Hulme, 2002).

Trust, or lack of it, has been identified as a 'make-or-break' factor in partnerships and strategic alliances (Blomqvist, 2005; Gambetta, 1998) and lack of trust between NGOs is often a primary obstacle preventing their inter-organizational cooperation and coordination. Crisis conditions tend to stress 'trust indicators' such as committing to possible loss based upon another's actions, placing resources or authority in another's hands, task coordination, etc. Many of those interviewed for this study mentioned that trust is central to cooperation and coordination. One German executive noted that, 'If trust is there everything is easier.' Even though executives are aware of the relevance of trust, in practice they experience enormous difficulties in establishing and maintaining trust. Hence, trust becomes an effective but rarely implemented coordination mechanism (McEvily *et al.*, 2003).

A plethora of convincing studies has demonstrated the importance of trust for partnerships and long-term cooperation, but there is still confusion about the process of trust building between organizations, especially in an intercultural context. Despite the fact that the final goal of the Organization for Economic Cooperation and Development's (OECD) eight millennium development goals (MDG) is to develop a global partnership for development (Barbanti, 2003), it is clear that one of the obstacles is the diversity of partnership criteria across international organizations. The *cultural* dimension of the contexts facing NGOs is extremely complex. Not only do these organizations span national and cultural boundaries with home and foreign offices, but many of them also operate in multiple, distinct NGO sectors; for example, one organization may be involved in disaster response (relief), rehabilitation following a disaster and long-term development (e.g. AIDS prevention or human trafficking). Furthermore, the NGOs themselves reflect internal organizational cultures ranging from clan-based, consensual cultures to hierarchical, process-based orientations (Cameron and Quinn, 1999; Hofstede, 1983; Pacanowsky and O'Donnell-Trujillo, 1983). The result is an overlapping network of organizational, cultural and professional affiliations. Add to that an additional ideological, or faith, sphere which motivates many of the NGOs involved in this study, and the multidimensional nature of the trust environment begins to take shape. (It should be noted that even the notion of a faith-based organization is culture specific; the German faith-based organizations, while faith-based in motivation, maintain an objective neutrality in their operations, whereas many US faith-based organizations approach their operations with an evangelical mission.)

The challenge of establishing trust across these organizational, national and cultural boundaries is connected to various factors that make it difficult for an organization to adapt to a potential partner: the increasing risk because actors are not familiar with the other culture (ethnic, organizational, religious), or the increasing complexity of supervision and (hierarchical) control. Bijlsma-Frankema and Klein Woolthuis claim that it is especially in those situations that trust becomes relevant 'as it can enable a 'leap of faith' beyond that which reason alone would warrant... Building upon this conceptualization of trust,

trust appears to be of great importance in relationships that are staged within environments where a solid basis for control – for instance in well-developed institutional structures, complete contracts and hierarchies – is lacking' (2005: 3). These 'trust-relevant' conditions of uncertainty and inadequate organizational infrastructure tend to be typical of crisis intervention contexts in which many NGOs operate.

Helton (2002) calls for 'a new, more flexible mechanism' through which crisis management and relief organizations 'can organize and channel humanitarian action' (p. 75). The present study explores the role of trust in the partnership-building process within German and US-American NGOs, and the influence of culture on trust formation, in an effort to identify similarities and differences in partnering strategies that may improve our understanding of effective practice. We first review the relevant literature on trust in inter-organizational partnerships. We then present a comparison of trust mechanisms and partnership criteria identified in a content analysis of interviews with a sample of twenty-five executives from German and US-American non-governmental organizations.

## Partnership formation and trust

From military interventions to humanitarian assistance, partnerships, or inter-organizational relationships, are common mechanisms for addressing mutual concerns in international security, the environment, natural disasters, and humanitarian relief, reconstruction and development (Bebbington and Farrington, 1993; Fisher, 2003; Ring and Van de Ven, 1994). The reasons behind forming a strategic organizational alliance such as a partnership vary, but at the most basic level, the partnering organizations offer something to each other that could not be achieved from sporadic opportunism or by more formal organizational integration (Bachmann, 2001). A partnership or coalition is by definition a 'temporary alliance or partnering of groups in order to achieve a common purpose or to engage in joint activity' (Spangler, 2003: 1) and requires that certain factors be in place in order to successfully collaborate (Lipschutz, 1989; Spangler, 2003). Inter-organizational relationships operate on the basis of 'principles, norms, rules, and decision-making procedures around which actor expectations converge in a given issue-area' (Krasner, 1983: 1) for the purpose of achieving effectiveness and efficiency (Krasner, 1983: 1; Ring and Van de Ven, 1994). Koh (2000) refers to these collaborations as networks and sees them evolving 'out of communities of like-minded individuals who gather around shared interests and values' (p. 2). Unfortunately, the meaning and original idea of partnership has been stretched in many directions. While *authentic partnership* implies equality, mutuality, reciprocal obligations and balance of power, according to Fowler (2002b) these are not common relational conditions in most organizational settings.

Previous literature (Edwards and Fowler, 2002; Helton, 2002; Koh, 2000) has made it clear that a new, flexible mechanism is needed to facilitate coordination in the partnering process among NGOs. However, such a mechanism must be able to operate across cultural and organizational divides. Given the multiple cultural spheres in the partnership process, the path toward implementation can be rocky (Bouckaert *et al.*, 2006). As will be shown, some partnerships are made explicit through planned coordination and contractual provisions among members, while others emerge via spontaneous, informal agreements.[2] In both cases, the establishment of trust has been identified as an important antecedent condition (McKnight *et al.*, 1998) as well as a central mechanism in ongoing coordination between organizational partners (Bachmann, 2001). According to the interviews conducted for this study, there currently exists no global NGO partnership mechanism that facilitates coordination between funding agencies and implementation organizations with various capacities and expertise. In our approach we focus on trust as just such a flexible mechanism that mitigates the high levels of uncertainty that mark the NGO crisis context (Lewis and Weigert, 1985b).

## Organizational trust

Trust exists on both the interpersonal and the institutional level (McKnight *et al.*, 1998), but organizational-level trust emerges as a result of the micro-level interactions of individual actors (Ring and Van de Ven, 1994). Extant understanding on trust reflects different preconditions and bases of trust building: background expectations, constitutive expectations (Zucker, 1986), shared beliefs (Bachmann, 2001), reliable institutional norms (Child and Möllering, 2003), a set of shared values (Mayer *et al.*, 1995), etc. But these shared beliefs, shared values or familiarity are conditions which often do not exist within these cross-border or inter-organizational settings. Thus, the

---

[2] Because a partnership ordinarily comes together to manage some immediate, collective exigency, the long-term viability of the cooperative effort may not be relevant. In the formation of a partnership in the midst of crisis there are often recognized social conventions or supra-national organizations that guide coordinated action making it unnecessary to work out specific standards on a case-by-case basis (Lipschutz, 1989); though the protocols for these kinds of crisis partnerships clearly varied by organization in the present study.

inter-organizational and intercultural situation becomes a trust dilemma because the higher the uncertainty the stronger the need to trust occurs; but also, the higher the uncertainty the greater the difficulty there is in building trust (see Kühlmann, 2005).

Given the definition for trust put forward in this volume as a psychological state 'comprising the intention to accept vulnerability based upon positive expectations of the intentions or behaviour of another' (Rousseau et al., 1998: 395), we view the idea of vulnerability as both the personal and institutional exposure present in the organizational circumstance of a partnership decision. The expectation is that a specific other will act benevolently and not be harmful (see McKnight and Chervany, 2001), as well as competently, honestly and fairly (Mayer et al., 1995). Our conceptualization of trust involves the three dimensions of human behaviour, including a cognitive (expectation and experience), an affective (feeling relatively secure) and a behavioural component (acts of dependence or reliance) (see Schwegler, 2008). People might move from the cognitive analysis of evidence about the apparent trustworthiness of another person to the emotional sense of wellbeing and personal security until there is a willingness to make distinct behavioural choices in an attempt to establish trust with that person (McKnight and Chervany, 2001; cf. Schwegler, 2006).

An important component in our approach to trust is the cultural context in which it is developed. Cultural factors affect both the decision to trust and the way in which it is formed (Dietz et al., this volume; Doney et al., 1998). As an interpretive construct, trust is woven into the signifying universe of each specific cultural context and is only fully understood within that 'universe of discourse' (Geertz, 1973; Smith, 2005; Triandis, 1972). If it is true that culture creates and filters the cues and signals of trust in relationships, then it is essential to acquire cultural competence in the trust-building process. Doney et al.'s (1998) cultural framework focuses on five cognitive trust-building processes: a calculative process, a prediction process, an intentionality process, a capability process and a transference process. Because each of these trust processes calls upon differing behavioural norms, it stands to reason that their applicability will vary by culture. However, the Doney et al. (1998) framework specifically addresses only cognitive trust processes in trustors and targets who share in-group membership. Therefore, we are expanding the model in these two areas to explore the use of cognitive and non-cognitive trust processes within in-group as well as out-group relationships. We now turn to an examination of the five processes identified by the Doney et al. model.

Taking each in turn, the calculative process is based upon an assessment of the costs and rewards of trusting a specific 'target'. Doney *et al.* (1998) predict that more individualistic cultures with lower uncertainty avoidance will prefer the calculative trust process; for that reason we might expect US-American organizations with their relatively loose people bonds and tolerance for variation to exhibit calculative processes more often than German organizations. The prediction process is developed through prior experience and the ability to predict a target's behaviour. Therefore, given Germany's higher national cultural orientation toward collectivism and uncertainty avoidance, it is expected that they will prefer predictive trust processes more than the US-American organizations. The intentionality process is based upon shared values and insight into the target's motivations. Doney *et al.* (1998) attribute this process more to collectivistic, feminine, higher uncertainty avoidant and lower power distance cultures. While the USA and Germany are very similar in national culture scores on power distance and masculinity, German national culture fits three of the four predictors for intentionality processes whereas the USA only fits one predictor – lower power distance (Hofstede, 1983). Thus, we might expect the German trust processes to reflect more intentionality. Bachmann (2001) hints that just such a response is to be expected by German firms given their propensity to rely on institutional trust; 'trust finds no ground when there is no shared world of institutional arrangements' (p. 354). The capability process is predicated upon the perceived ability of the target to satisfy the relationship, and given the mixed cultural predictors suggested by Doney *et al.* (1998) both national cultures could prefer this trust process. The final trust process, the transference process, has its origin in reputation, or the transference of confidence from a third party. McKnight *et al.* (1998) suggest that '*initial* trust between parties will not be based on any kind of experience with, or firsthand knowledge of, the other party [but rather] on institutional cues' that provide the foundation for trust in the absence of firsthand knowledge (p. 474). German culture's relatively lower score on individualism might give us reason to expect more transference process than in US-American organizations.

## Empirical analysis: research questions and methods

Our empirical analysis emphasizes the challenge and process of cooperation and partnership building. As previously mentioned, the literature identifies trust as a critical factor within cross-cultural and cross-organizational cooperation strategies and processes. We believe that a cross-cultural analysis of partnership criteria and trust mechanisms can reveal important insights about effective international NGO collaboration. Therefore we look at the following research questions:

RQ1:   Are there cultural differences between US-American NGO and German NGO partnership-development criteria?

RQ2:   What are the preferred trust mechanisms in US-American NGOs and German NGOs in the partnership-development process?

RQ3:   What is the impact of NGOs' different cultural spheres on the trust-building process?

In order to access the partnership criteria and processes of international NGOs, twenty-five interviews were conducted with executives from sixteen US-American and German NGOs (a sample list includes organizations like World Vision, Diakonie Katastrophenhilfe, Opportunity International, Welthungerhilfe, Brot für die Welt, World Relief, Compassion International, Salvation Army, Médecins Sans Frontières, HCJB Hospital Voz Andes and the American Leprosy Mission). It was decided that the perspectives of upper-level management would best reflect the organizational approach, both in practice and philosophy. All interviewees held upper management positions (e.g. programme director, regional director, director of international coopera-tion, senior vice president for programmes, etc.). Most of the interviewees were primary influencers on partnership implementation within their organi-zations. Not only were they involved in setting organizational policy, but they had relevant, implementation-level experience in partnership development. The average age of the American respondents was 47; twenty per cent were female. The average age of the German respondents was 42; twenty-five per cent were female.

We used a seven-point interview protocol consisting of a semi-structured series of questions about the level of coordinated activity with other NGOs, Governmental Organizations (GOs), and the partnering process. In general the questions related to organizational positions and responsibilities in the area of partnering; criteria for establishing a project in a given area (e.g. What are the decision points that are commonly used when deciding to get involved in an international project?), and procedures for engaging in cooperative projects and relationships with other organizations (e.g. What strategies do you use to involve potential partners in a project?). Face-to-face and telephone interviews were used in order to provide greater depth in, and clarification of, responses as well as to create the rapport necessary to generate additional interview con-tacts. The interview data were supplemented by content analysis of organiza-tional mission statements and codes of conduct. The interviews were recorded, transcribed and then content-analysed for thematic units in order to identify differences and similarities in the message characteristics of the surveyed organizations. Content analysis is commonly used to investigate cultural aspects of organizations and societies (Weber, 1985). The classification categories, or thematic units, in this study were generated from high-frequency words and phrases present in the interview transcripts and notes and then assessed for fit with Doney *et al.*'s (1998) five trust process categories. Related thematic units were then aggregated to 'represent the intensity of concern with each category' in the interview data (Weber, 1985: 39).

## Empirical analysis: results

Our research revealed that partnership criteria not only differ from organization to organization, but evidence suggests that cultural tendencies may interfere with best practice or good intention (RQ1). Throughout the interview process it was clear that the participating organizations recognized the need for stronger partnerships. However, they also admitted to deficiencies in the intentional development of these strategic alliances. And as one NGO executive put it, the worst time to start thinking about your core values and principles for partnering is in the midst of a crisis situation. Table 11.1 presents the identified thematic units by culture relating to criteria for a partnership decision. Each of these constructs emerged during the interviews in reference to the antecedent conditions or characteristics necessary for a decision to enter into a partnership. The thematic units are grouped by type and frequency of direct references to the concepts during the interviews, though interpretive weight was accorded each concept due to indirect reference as well.

In total 14 different primary thematic units and 253 references to partnerships in the German interviews were identified. The primary thematic units with the highest grounded references in the German data set are capabilities and competencies (19 direct references), standards/principles (e.g. code of conduct) (18 direct references), institutional affiliation (17 direct references), experience/history (17 direct references), shared values (14 direct references), contextual factors (14 direct references), capacity and resources (13 direct references) and neutrality (13 direct references).

Out of 204 references to partnerships in the US-American interviews, strong co-occurrences were found with the terms capacity, mission, reputation, longevity and like-mindedness. The primary thematic units that emerged in the American data set related to mission and core values (combined 38 direct references), longevity in the field and reputation (combined 35 direct references), capacity (18 direct references), firsthand experience (14 direct references) and like-mindedness (13 direct references).

Table 11.1 *NGO partnership criteria by thematic unit (frequency) and culture*

| Theme/Culture | German Partnership Criteria | US Partnership Criteria |
|---|---|---|
| Values | Standards/principles (e.g. accept and act on principles like 'code of conduct' or 'agenda of basic principles') (18)<br>Institutional affiliation (17)<br>Shared values (14) | Common core values (18)<br>'Like-minded' (spiritual assessment) (13) |
| Competence/ Philosophy | Capabilities and competencies (19)<br>Credibility and integrity (<5) | Mission (20)<br>Core competencies (7)<br>Philosophy of development practice (7) |
| Familiarity/ Reputation | Experience and history (17)<br>Neutrality (13)<br>Independence (7)<br>Reputation/character reference (<5) | Reputation (17)<br>Firsthand experience (14)<br>Transparency (<5) |
| Partnership potential | Capacity and resources (13)<br>Synergy (<5) | Resources/capacity (18)<br>Synergy potential (7)<br>Combined expertise (<5) |
| Local awareness | Local knowledge (8) | Longevity in field (18) |
| Need/Benefit | Need/contextual factors (14) | ROI versus inconvenience of coalition (8) |
| Other | Participation of target group (7) | Stipulated Request for Proposals (RFP) (8) |

When trust was identified explicitly during the interview, it was coded as a 'trust component'. We coded thirteen trust components in the American data and fifteen trust components in the German data, with strong co-occurrences with each of the primary thematic units, thereby reinforcing their validity as trust-mechanism indicators.

Several preliminary observations can be made about the primary thematic units. First, several trust indicators emerge that have been described in previous models (e.g. McKnight *et al.*, 1998). For instance, the primary thematic units in the American data set of common core values and mission reveal an expectation of benevolence, but also a confidence in the structural assurances of the institution. Similarly, in the German data, the thematic unit of standards and principles (represented by codes of conduct) suggest common trust indicators on the institutional level, while integrity reflects an honesty belief (McKnight *et al.*, 1998).

The second initial observation from the thematic units is the confluence in practice of institution-based and cognition-based trust indicators (i.e. the cultural trust-building processes from Doney *et al.*, 1998). Several of the thematic units cross these conceptual boundaries. For example, the American thematic unit of longevity in the field reveals both a security in the durability of organizational structure and a predictability belief. More will be said about overlapping conceptual categories later in the analysis.

In order to determine the influence of culture on partnership-building processes (RQ2), the thematic units related to partnership criteria were classified using the trust-building process framework from Doney *et al.* (1998). The model allows us to look at the similarities and differences within and between German and US-American trust mechanisms and partnership criteria (see Table 11.2).

## *The calculative process*

As expected, calculative processes did not play a central role for the German interviewees. While German organizations don't describe their partnership activities in terms of 'return on investment' (ROI) like the American NGOs, they do mention coalition building as an important issue depending on various factors. Contextual factors (e.g. local need, urgency of action after a tsunami or an earthquake, etc.), as well as the specific expectations in a situation, influence the process of partnership selection. One executive put it this way: 'There is a difference whether we are looking for a partner who is just operating a project or whether we are looking for a long-term partnership where contents and values are transported.' Even when the German interviewees talked about different levels of investment in partnerships, they did not refer explicitly to exchange-theory-like assessments of costs and rewards or projections of risks involved if the target of trust were to prove untrustworthy.

In contrast, as might have been predicted, the calculation of benefits and costs is mentioned more often in the American interviews. From the US perspective, partnerships require a lot of work. Consequently organizations must perform due diligence to ensure a positive return on their investment of time and resources. As one US-American executive put it:

A partnership is strong only to the extent that both sides of the partnership contribute something and are allowed to make mistakes . . . building that comfort level takes some time, you don't just clap your hands and create it, it develops over contact and time and experiences . . . We start out projects pretty modestly and there are a lot of things projects can eventually do but we don't open all that up immediately, and we know that they're doing the same thing with us. They're sort of checking it out to see if it's

Table 11.2 *NGO partnership formation and trust-building processes*

| Trust-Building Process (after Doney, *et al.*, 1998) | German Thematic Units | US Thematic Units |
| --- | --- | --- |
| Calculative | Depending on framework and needs | ROI versus inconvenience of coalition |
| | | Stipulated RFPs/funding |
| Prediction | Long-term versus initial relationship | Need for long-term relationship/firsthand experience |
| | Coalition with other organizations | |
| | | Best-in-class organizations |
| Intentionality | Accept and act on basic principles and standards (e.g. code of conduct, agenda of basic principles, etc.) | Transparency |
| | | Common core values |
| | | Philosophy of development practice |
| | Common ground/shared values | Identity |
| | Participation of target group | |
| | Integrity | |
| Capability | Competencies, expertise, resources and capacity, capabilities running a project | Core competencies |
| | | Synergy potential |
| | | Combined expertise |
| | | Resources/capacity |
| | | Local/indigenous |
| Transference | Reputation | Longevity in field |
| | 'character reference' | Reputation |
| Other | Experience/common, long-term history | 'Like-minded' (spiritual assessment) |
| | 'private relationship' | Capacity for vulnerability/ risk |
| | | Mutual-ness |

really going to work. They want to know what kind of people we are and watch as we react to things and so it takes a bit of time to do that. Sometimes people want to have a partnership that benefits them, and sometimes it's better to think about a partnership as what am I going to be able to do for you instead of what are you going to be able to do for me; to the extent that there is that mutual discussion and attitude, then it works pretty well. But if one of the partners, one of the parties, just sees it as a cow to be milked, then you're in trouble.

This interviewee seemed to recognize that risk taking is best done in small increments; trust and vulnerability require a balance that takes time to develop (Bachmann, 2001; Ring and Van de Ven, 1994). Occasionally the return on cooperative investment was talked about in terms of mutual benefit by US NGOs: 'what makes [the partnership] a win–win?' But the win, or ROI, was most often discussed in terms of enhancing the organization's ability to fulfil its mission, not based upon whether the crisis objective was being met. Interestingly, several American executives used exchange-theory language in describing synergy potential, combined expertise and the return on investment versus the inconvenience of the coalition in the field. The fact that a strategic alliance is viewed by some as an inconvenience as opposed to an asset is an interesting cultural artifact in itself. As one American executive put it, 'We call it a partnership, but it's more a marriage of convenience.'

That US-American NGOs reflect more of the calculative trust process is not surprising given the somewhat more individualistic national culture relative to Germany (Hofstede, 1984, 1983). However, as opposed to conceiving the use of this trust process as a measure against self-serving opportunism (Doney *et al.*, 1998), it is more likely that the calculative basis for trust in this case is a function of evaluating the potential synergy available from a partnership. Interviews indicated that the calculation has to do with the thematic unit of networking capital, which comprises co-occurring concepts like capacity, overlapping programme areas and programme implementation. While the risk of self-seeking behaviour certainly exists, the dominant uncertainty that emerged in our data related to *operational capacity*. For example, one of the more practical external influences on the partnership process comes from funding aimed at coalitions. Several organizations noted that requests for proposals (RFPs) that stipulated collaboration were a primary motivation to form partnerships – a calculated motivation. One executive put it this way:

One of the other reasons people will coordinate has to do with [funding]. For instance if you're looking at rebuilding the house infrastructure in DRC Congo right now, your money is going to be coming primarily from three places; USAID, World Bank or EU. Now they will encourage not [necessarily] the people working in partnership in the field, but they're going to [encourage] coming together for meetings on policy practice, information sharing, best practice, that sort of thing.

Those initial relationships, initiated via a calculative process, are then often the basis for expansion into other partnership areas.

## The prediction process

To establish trust using the prediction process a variety of information about the partner's past actions is necessary. The greater the knowledge base, the more a target's behaviour becomes predictable (Doney *et al.*, 1998). Obviously, the established trust via the prediction process leads to a deeper

feeling of relative security (McKnight *et al.*, 1998) and captures the conceptualization of trust as a concept involving cognitive, affective and behavioural
components (see the foregoing discussion of trust). Given that the predictive
process is based on consistency with past actions, in many cases the NGOs we
examined did not have enough prior experience with partner organizations to
use this trust process. Whether the prediction process comes into play in the
German context depends partly on the length of cooperation. Trust building
via the prediction process requires shared experience, as one German executive mentioned: 'after several years of cooperation you really know your
partner, you know they do well, they are reliable, and cooperation in this
case is easy'. This statement reflects the idea of knowledge-based trust mentioned by Lewicki and Bunker (1996).

The US-American NGOs did not identify prediction-based processes very
often either. The exception came in the form of a reference to the need to work
with best-in-class organizations; '[we will only work with a partner if] the
partner is a global best-in-class organization in their field'. A 'best-in-class'
designation then serves as a basis for prediction. Of course, best-in-class is
also an assessment of the expertise and reputation of the organization,
suggesting a capability process. However, in this case, a best-in-class assessment was based upon past experience with the target and co-occurred with an
observation of common values; hence trust had emerged over a period of
time. Best-in-class then, is a response to evidence of consistent behaviour
(Doney *et al.*, 1998). Several US-American executives also noted that indirect
experience with another organization in a crisis context or working on a
similar project will occasionally lead to enough of an observational base to
warrant exploring a partnership, thus indicating the initial formation of trust
using a prediction process. In most US cases, the prediction process leading to
inter-organizational trust began with a unique instance of micro-level interpersonal, or 'qua persona' trust (Ring and Van de Ven, 1994); although as
expressed earlier the trusting behaviour is restrained by institutional factors.

## The intentionality process

The intentionality process is a central trust process for both German and
US-American NGOs. Although it is primarily a relational concept with
particular attention to benevolence, according to Doney *et al.* (1998), the
German respondents' depictions of their intentionality process referred more
to identified core values and being benevolent in general. Thematic units of
credibility, integrity, neutrality and adhering to common core values featured
prominently in the German interviews. Specifically, accepting and acting on

principles and standards was a critical issue for most interviewees. As an example of a culture-specific criterion, most German organizations base partnering decisions in large part on formal 'codes of conduct' defining the organization's basic principles and mission. The intentionality process for German NGOs is more about benevolence and integrity in general (toward other partners, organizations, etc.) and not specifically dependent on benevolence of the target directed toward the trustor. Accordingly, the 'code of conduct' is not about operational details. Rather it seeks to safeguard the standards of behaviour and to maintain the principles of independence, benevolence and effectiveness in general. The 'code' implies an obligation to provide humanitarian assistance wherever it is needed. Thus, giving humanitarian aid follows a humanitarian imperative and must not be a political act. Even though the 'code of conduct' is a voluntary code, German NGOs expect partner organizations to accept, maintain and act on these principles. The particular importance of the 'code' becomes apparent in the statement of a German executive: 'The "code of conduct" is our bible.' Aligning organizations via codes of conduct ensures that partners act on the same core values as the funding (donor) organization does. In addition, the German organizations were unique in describing 'participation of target groups' as partnership criteria. The involvement of the indigenous population in relief, rehabilitation and development is an important consideration, as is assistance without discrimination (ethnic, political, religious, etc.).

Attention to 'common core values' and 'mission' were also favoured trust processes by US-American NGOs. A strong thematic unit of sharing core values (including a common mission) emerged from the American interviews as a first principle in building trust-based inter-organizational relationships. Statements like, 'If the core values are different, then no matter what the other elements say at some point there will be a conflict' and 'the first thing we look at is just an absolute clear match on vision, mission, motivation and values' illustrate the importance of the intentionality-based trust process. However, the American sense of intentionality is subtly different from the German orientation. While the German organizations employ a more generalized concept of goodwill directed toward others and depend less on the relational dimension of intentionality, the American organizations emphasize a direct exchange of benevolence. Furthermore, for the American organization the object of the intentionality process is not assessing devotion to a code of conduct as in the German case, rather it is determining 'like-mindedness'. US-American NGO executives were in search of a shared cultural identity, both interpersonally and organizationally, that would provide the 'common frames of reference, values and behavioural expectations' that constitute the basis of trust across both national and institutional boundaries (Chao and Moon, 2005). Given the centrality of values as a cultural variable, the intentionality process is the most direct indicator of those values in that it is based on a mutual identification, therefore producing the most robust kind of trust (Doney *et al.*, 1998).

Trust was also directly linked to accountability, openness and transparency in US-American organizations. As one interviewee told us, 'they have to have complete trust in our quality standards; they have to trust us in doing what we say that we will do. Issues of transparency and accountability, those are often used words, but they're often used because it's so critical'. The product of intentionality processes, like accountability and transparency, often becomes the input into the transference process – reputation. A relief NGO's reputation is built on the local level in the crisis region; according to one NGO executive, 'In the field, in different countries it's very easy to find out the track record and the reputation of various partners . . . [that reputation] may even supersede their financial record'. The interplay between these two trust-building processes demonstrates the cycling 'sequence of negotiation, commitment, and execution stages' of partnership development (Ring and Van de Ven, 1994).

Intentionality trust processes appear to be a primary process in both American and German organizations with subtle differences in how and when the process is relied upon. German organizations rely upon the intentionality process as a matter of course, a first step in partnership building. American organizations rely on intentionality trust processes when the relationship is expected to be long-term and involve a greater degree of resource sharing or institutional vulnerability.

## The capability process

Subtle differences also emerged in the criteria of core competencies. German organizations tended to speak about capacity and expertise while US-American organizations primarily discussed philosophy of practice, though capacity did emerge as a strong thematic unit in the US data as well. Most German executives cited skills, competencies and the ability to run a project as the most important criteria for partnership building. The assessment of the capabilities of the potential partner depends on the various needs required within a specific situation, as one respondent noticed: 'the main issue is how do they deal with the situation there, we look at their abilities . . . we need to see how they address the crisis'. Capability is certainly a decision point for short-term crisis intervention partnerships for US-American NGOs, as evidenced by this representative statement from one interviewee: 'I think there are two ways to look at it: one is do they already have an on-ground presence [in the crisis region], meaning an in-country office or representation of some sort, and the other side would be do they have trusted partners with the capacity to get the job done so to speak'. US-American organizations not only viewed capability from a capacity basis in terms of networking, looking for overlapping programmatic areas and assessing the longevity of a potential partner's work in a particular area, but also framed it in terms of competence. One interviewee cited capability as a decision point in this way:

Are we involved in the countries that they are interested in or the regions or the sectors? Then of course they look at our track record. One of the things in seeking an implementing partner is they need an organization or a partner that they can just completely trust; that we will follow the best practices of development and rehabilitation and relief. In some ways we are an extension of . . . [their] programs, so they have to have complete trust in our quality standards; they have to trust us in doing what we say that we will do . . . both sides need to genuinely appreciate the other and really feel that the partnership allows them to do things that they could not do on their own, maybe the word synergy would be something to describe that.

These sentiments reflect the underlying individualism in US NGOs in that they view capability from a perceived competence perspective. Any change in that perception can jeopardize the trusting relationship, making this form of trust fragile (Doney *et al.*, 1998).

Another interviewee referred to capability processes that result from first-hand experience (predictive process): 'The most important is really if we've worked with them before and they've shown a good ability to develop a project and implement them properly.' And one US-American organization that was not as particular about the qualities of potential partners (and admitted that they are not often intentional about seeking out strategic partners) employs a serendipitous, or prima facie trust approach; rather than assessing the target's resources and ability to follow through, they fairly indiscriminately join with other organizations in order to respond to communities with pressing needs. Trust is extended on the basis of critical need. For example, the interviewee mentioned that the varying scope of partnership formality depended on the crisis conditions:

The biggest thing is to respond to the need . . . We don't like to duplicate efforts or do something that's not helpful to the people who are in charge of the community, because we look at ourselves as a community member that's helping the people who enact the government part . . . and we work with other agencies as well, and sometimes we have an actual memorandum of understanding; we have that with the Red Cross.

The capability trust-building process, then, is more pragmatic in the German organizational context, referring to competencies, expertise, resources and capacities as well as to the capabilities of running a project. The US-American organizations stressed potential synergies and core competencies from a partnership, generally requiring a higher degree of mutuality in philosophical approach to relief, rehabilitation and development.

## The transference process

Both cultural organization types displayed some degree of interest in transference, or reputation, of the potential partner. However, our data revealed that transference only plays a marginal role in the partnership-building process and trust formation in German NGOs. According to one German NGO representative, initial situations do require organizations to obtain reliable information on the reputation of the target. In some cases they gather information about the reputation and reliability of a potential partner through third parties, or even demand a *Leumundszeugnis* (character reference). In contrast, US-American organizations often operate on a more intuitive assessment of 'like-mindedness' in partnership decisions. The former articulates principles, while the latter evaluates values and 'an organic, kindred spirit'.[3] As one American executive put it, when it comes to partnering, 'I'd like to say it has to do with mission statements and all that, but I think a lot of it comes down to individuals and practicality and the "feel good index".' For several American organizations, reputation established the warrant for trust and was a result of transparency in the home office and longevity on the field. However, as the previous quotation implies, while transference is useful for taking initial steps in a partnership process, the ultimate decision often rests on the establishment of common identity in what he referred to as a 'feel good index'.

The location of the transference also emerged as an important condition to this trust process. American organizations emphasized that partnerships were most effectively initiated in the field. In response to the question, where do organizations initiate partnerships, one executive stated:

> [I]t depends on organizational culture because some groups will say we met so and so from this organization at a conference and they seem like nice people. Maybe that helps it happen but in most organizations where there's been any degree of devolution to the field it's going to be up to the field people because all organizations have good people and all organizations have [below average people]. So I think it's more of a field thing and a contextual thing because there are different flavors.

---

[3] Many of the organizations studied have an overt Christian mission. Consequently, expressions of 'like-mindedness' and 'kindred spirit' are believed to be, literally, spiritually based. The basis of trust decisions is not entirely rational, but is also metaphysical in nature.

In a related criteria to reputation, German organizations mentioned institutional affiliation and coalitions with other groups as important criteria in their partnering decisions.

## Affective processes

Several thematic units emerged in the coding process that are not captured by the cognitive trust-building processes mentioned by Doney *et al.* (1998), and may be attributable to the sample in the current study. Their model omits the identified affective criteria, such as like-mindedness or mutuality, which one interviewee from a faith-based NGO described as having 'a strong spiritual compound to it, overwhelmingly it's a spiritual measure'. Within empirical research settings this affective component is often neglected (e.g. Doney *et al.*, 1998; McKnight *et al.*, 1998). Specifically, the spiritual assessments and more 'reflexive aspects' of trust in our data are not accounted for by Doney *et al.*'s (1998) model. Referring to feelings of relative security some trust researchers do acknowledge that trust has an affective basis (Lewis and Weigert, 1985a; McAllister, 1995), or admit that affect and emotions come into play when trust is lost (Schwegler, 2008). We incorporate the attributed spiritual criteria that emerged in our data into the affective processes because they are associated with a sensory experience (feeling). Our argument is that cognitive processes alone are not sufficient to describe the complex and multifaceted process of trust building among different partners in that they fail to capture the metaphysical, sense-of-security criteria our subjects described in the trust-formation process. However, as long as we admit that trust is partially built upon the perception and evaluation of others' behaviours, intentions and motives (e.g. evaluations of other people's perceived trustworthiness), we need to accept that the process of this assessment has an affective basis (McAllister, 1995). In other words, we need to consider that the affective component plays a central role when trust becomes established. In short, the person who chooses to trust another party also feels comfortable about the prospect of willingly depending on that party. For many of the American organizations, trust is formed upon a confidence in knowing that the organizations are like-minded and that they will create a good fit on the operational level. One organization stated it definitively, '[It] would be very difficult for [*organization name omitted*] to have a strategic alliance with a non-faith-based organization. We might have an alliance in a certain area, but I don't think I would call it a strategic alliance'. The thematic unit of like-mindedness had strong co-occurrences with 'spiritual purpose', 'mission', 'mutual-ness' and 'relationship-based' as opposed to 'need-based' partnering criteria.

Having argued for an affective route in trust building, we also suggest that national and organizational culture will influence parties' preferences for these emotion-laden processes. Our research suggests that the intentionality process as enacted by German organizations is more 'rational', whereas the intentionality process for the US-American organizations is overlaid with more of an affective process. For the German organization, affective processes appear to be more relevant after the cognitive processes and expectations (e.g. maintaining the principles of 'code of conduct', meeting the expectations regarding the required competencies and abilities) are met. Thus, the inter-organizational relationships that primarily operate based upon the rational processes will experience lower levels of trust. Those partnerships that evolve through the affective stages earlier will more quickly develop a security-based relationship that represents a higher trust situation.

## A *hierarchy of trust processes*

It became clear during our study that NGOs do not approach strategic alliances by using one mutually exclusive trust-building process. The Doney *et al.* (1998) model 'suggests five different routes trustors may take to develop trust in a target', separate 'pathways' producing trust of varying durability (p. 615). However, in practice these processes are often combined and sequenced. The current model does not adequately capture the notion of progressive trust formation. Our data revealed that organizations often con-ceptualized a hierarchy of trust processes (see Figure 11.1).

The US-American interviews demonstrate that the first level consisted of intentionality processes, often referred to by interviewees as a philosophical or theological level. One executive listed the sharing of core philosophical values as the top criteria for entering into a partnership suggesting that, 'it's kind of like a marriage; you can have different habits and different interests but the core values have to be the same ... you really have to embrace and share together what's important and what's not'. The intentionality level is seen as distinct from the second level which consists of capability processes, 'are we involved in the countries that they are interested in or the regions or the [same] sectors?' Interviewees described this level as a strategic concern of assessing capacities and competencies. At the third level, the transference process is employed by assessing the potential partner's 'track record'. This

**Figure 11.1** US-American organization hierarchical trust-building process

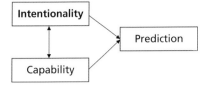

**Figure 11.2** German organization hierarchical trust-building process

'operational' level is only reached if the concerns on the philosophical and strategic levels have been satisfied. Combined, these three processes provide the organization with 'a partner that they can ... completely trust'.

The German organizations revealed a hierarchy of trust processes as well, but with subtle differences. The German process is illustrated by one executive's comment that, 'Trust is very important. At the very beginning we start with small steps only. Either trust will be established or not. If our partners stand to the agreements and standards and act upon the guidelines of the project, trust can be built'.

The dominant process for the Germans is the intentionality process, which is based on the identification of core values. But how these 'core values' are identified varies between the two cultures (see Figure 11.2). In contrast to the US executives' flexible and intuitive mechanisms, the German interviewees refer to their 'code of conduct' which is in a certain way a 'catalogue' of norms and values. And while we are able to distinguish between the first and second step of trust processes in the US data, these different steps don't emerge in the German data: the capability process is integrated at the first step of trust development and falls together with the intentionality process. As a further step, and in contrast to the American data, the prediction-based process is mentioned by the German NGOs. Here, the aspects of a common history and long-time experience with the partner come into play as a German executive put it: 'India for example, we cooperate for many years with our partner organization in India ... we have a MoU [memorandum of understanding] and they get a bigger grant, that's a trusting relationship'. Based upon agreement in shared basic principles and capability, the NGO will then base the relationship on a tighter ground and establish a different basis for cooperation and trust.

In summary, both the intentionality process and the capability process are instrumental for both cultural organization types analysed here, but the bases of these processes and the underlying criteria differ between the cultural groups. It may be that what we are observing are distinct, culture-specific prototypical trust-building processes (Schweer and Thies, 2003).[4]

## Discussion

### Implications for practice

Interview data from this study demonstrate clearly that coordination among and between NGOs is a multifaceted process, involving internal and external factors from the decision to form a partnership to the mechanism employed to operate and sustain the partnership. It is apparent that cultural preferences in trust processes inform our understanding of the procedures (mechanisms) used to establish a trusting partnership across cultural boundaries (RQ3). One of the interesting findings in our study was the emergence of *organizational* culture as a trust-inhibiting or trust-promoting factor. We found that organizational culture acts as a moderating variable on the culturally preferred trust mechanisms. Each organization's self-construal affects organizational factors like control and command systems, financial transparency, development philosophy, branding/imaging, etc. (see Figure 11.3). The five trust processes discussed above, calculative, predictive, intentional, capability and transference, all involve a tension between uncertainty and confidence, dependability and vulnerability. That tension identified in the partnering decision is, in part, a question of organizational face. Extending the concept of interpersonal face to the organization, we define organizational face as an extension of corporate mission (self-concept), a vulnerable, identity-based resource (after Ting-Toomey, 2005). Just as individuals have a projected image, corporate face is the projected image of the organization in a partnership situation. Two dominant self-construal types have been identified in the literature which we have adapted to the organizational context: an *independent self-construal* perceives the organization as stable, separate and autonomous, reflecting an individualistic orientation; an *interdependent self-construal*

---

[4] Schweer and Thies (2003) show that individuals possess an idea about a prototype of a trustworthy person. In a concrete situation the individual prototype of trustworthiness will be compared with the specific interacting person. In the case of a high correlation between the prototype and the 'real' person, a progressive trust-building process is possible. The German data show that the process of evaluating a specific trustworthy person, in the first step is based on the evaluation of the correspondence between the expected and actually displayed codes of conduct criteria. The preference of German executives for 'facts and regulations' seems to be a typical German cultural orientation and may reflect the higher uncertainty avoidant characteristic of the culture.

**Figure 11.3** Effect of organizational self-construal on preferred trust mechanism

perceives the organization as flexible, intertwined and contextual, reflecting a collectivistic orientation (Ting-Toomey, 2005, 1994).

Cultural characteristics, moderated by organizational self-construal (Ting-Toomey and Oetzel, 2003), then shape the trust processes employed and the resulting choice of trust mechanism. Organizations with a more independent self-construal will lean toward autonomy, perceiving their organization as a separate and stable enterprise, in need of little assistance in carrying out its mission. This attitude was very common in the American interviews, epitomized by the comment of this executive: 'We don't have a strong drive to seek partners. Our first instinct is, our first reaction is probably, what will [our organization] do in this situation...?'

Another US NGO referenced the impact of organizational culture on the decision to partner, revealing a calculative trust-building perspective that requires a flexible organizational self-construal:

[I]t depends a bit on the organizational culture and it depends a little bit on how the organizations learn; and then it depends on the individuals within the organization itself. So you take a group like [*organization name omitted*], which is almost hermetically sealed and they are not going to really coordinate with anybody. Then you would go to a [smaller] organization ... [they are] precisely the groups which, in my experience, are going to be more open to looking at partnership mechanisms because funding ebbs and flows ... and they may not be able to keep in-house expertise ... [it has] to do with their organizational openness, willingness to cooperate. Do they want to go it alone or are they willing to work with other people because of the need for expertise to sort of get back to the win/win exchange theory part of it.

In the case of the 'hermetically sealed' organization, risk to organizational face is controlled and minimized by avoiding coordination. The drawback is the opportunity cost of efficiencies and innovation. In contrast, the smaller organization with a flexible self-construal will be able to adapt to the culture (Chao and Moon, 2005) of a potential partner and build trust across cultural and organizational boundaries.

Many of the faith-based organizations interviewed for this study reflected independent self-construals. Yet that quest for autonomy represents an obstacle for a partnering process that calls for vulnerability, transparency and accountability. Several scholars point out that trust building requires familiarity or similarity, highlighting either the time required to develop a relationship or the necessity of identifying common or compatible 'cultural tiles' (Chao and Moon, 2005). In the case of NGOs, this often means extensive 'field visits' to create relationships that will not only build trust, but also test its durability. Many interviewees noted the time and effort required to establish a trusting relationship, founded on clear communication and transparency: 'there's a getting to know you phase which is very essential for a successful partnership' (American NGO) and again, 'communication is very critical and that's where transparency and openness is very important which is also tied to that level of trust that I talked about having' (American NGO).

Table 11.3 *Preferred NGO partnership mechanisms*

| German Approach | US-American Approach |
| --- | --- |
| 1. High-trust versus low-trust partnership | 1. Practical versus strategic<br>Field versus home office |
| 2. Procedure:<br>Written forms: reports<br>Fieldtrips<br>Local consultants | 2. Procedure:<br>Listening/introductions<br>Identify programme areas<br>Design logistics |
| 3. Principle driven | 3. Model driven |
| 4. Hierarchical versus egalitarian relationship | 4. Unintentional versus intentional |

A second complicating factor in building trust is the different bases used to establish partnerships across cultures and organizations. In US NGOs, trust was often dependent on the model used by a particular organization to develop partnerships. That is, if the model didn't prescribe trusting a particular type of organization, or if the model did not require trust at all, then partnership development as described here was considered unattainable or even undesirable. In the case of German NGOs, trust was often based on principles contained in codes of conduct. This complicates the establishment of partnerships with organizations that don't specify operational principles and philosophies precisely; or, in the case of American organizations, that base collaboration on conceptual models. Another complicating factor is the organizational complexity of many NGOs. Most NGOs operate in multiple cultural contexts with relatively autonomous development and fundraising divisions, not to mention a matrix of local organizations in the field (see Table 11.3). A simple partnership between two uni-national, integrated corporate structures with a single development focus is the exception, not the rule.

A final observation from our research pertained to the nature of the partnership being pursued. US-American NGOs distinguish between practical alliances and strategic alliances. In the case of strategic alliances, trust was a larger consideration. But if the partnership was a practicality, and therefore probably of shorter duration, then trust was not a necessary condition. In fact, in the latter case, the absence of trust might be something that was planned for and monitored. Furthermore, the German NGOs mention trust as a situation-specific variable. Depending on their mission and vision, the nature of crisis (or conflict), the scope, scale and urgency for action, trust may be a more or less relevant factor. In the case of high urgency for example, coalition-building strategies *can't* play a main role. One German executive put it this way: 'the point is, we go in and we deal with need, now. We want to save lives, now. Rather than coming up with training programs for long impact'. Therefore, whether or not trust plays a make-or-break role depends on situational factors.

## Concluding comments

This study examined trust-building processes in German and US-American non-governmental organizations facing the challenges of cooperation and partnership building in international crisis areas. We view this as an important area of research because the complexity of international humanitarian action increasingly demands coordinated intervention. We examined the demands being placed on NGOs and identify trust as a make-or-break factor in partnerships and strategic alliances. To avoid creating islands of success, NGOs need to engage and maintain relationships, and join what Bachmann (2001) called a global trend toward trans-organizational partnerships with trust as the 'central mechanism to allow for an efficient solution to the problem of co-coordinating' (p. 338).

Applying the trust-building framework from Doney *et al.* (1998), similarities and differences within and between German and American partnership development criteria and preferred trust mechanisms emerge. For both German and American NGOs the intentionality process and the capability process are favoured pathways for relationship development and trust building. Nevertheless, subtle differences become apparent regarding their relative meaning and how these pathways are applied.

Even though the model by Doney *et al.* (1998) provides a helpful framework to categorize our empirical data and advance our understanding of the differences and similarities of trust-building processes between national cultures, we recognize several limitations of applying the model. Firstly, the cognitive processes described by Doney *et al.* (1998) should be supplemented by the affective processes which played such an important role in our data. For the US organizations, the affective component already plays a role in the first step of trust building (intentionality and capability), whereas for the German NGOs the affective component comes into play at a second step of trust building (predictability) (see Figures 11.1 and 11.2). Future research should examine the role of affective trust processes in a range of cultural and organizational settings.

Secondly, the notion of progressive trust formation is not adequately captured by the Doney *et al.* (1998) model and can be expanded by our empirical data conceptualizing a hierarchy of trust processes. According to our data we can distinguish three different trust-building processes where the trusting partners move from an initial step of intentionality to capability and then to transference (US-American), or respectively, start with intentionality and capability and then move to prediction (German). Future investigations might look at progressive trust formation in other organizational sectors (i.e. for-profit organizations, military coalitions, or contract-for-services relationships) and cultural situations.

Thirdly, the construct of organizational self-construal was introduced to explain the (un)willingness to risk organizational image and reputation in a trust-based inter-organizational relationship. The NGOs' independent versus interdependent self-construal influences not only their decision to partner, but also the trust mechanism of choice. Because trust relationships operate within a dialectical tension between uncertainty and confidence, dependability and vulnerability, future research should explore the intersecting cultural spheres of national and organizational culture and their impact on the trust-building process.

Our conclusion is that a strong mechanism allowing NGOs to coordinate with each other, as well as with sponsoring GOs, is presently lacking. Our research has shown that NGOs currently lack the necessary flexible mechanism to partner effectively across cultural, organizational and hierarchical divisions. As we have shown, most NGOs lack the 'intentionality' necessary to form lasting, strategic alliances. Complex organizational structures, preferences for existing practice, diffused decision making and the mixture of implementing and non-implementing organizational foci stand in the way of partnership development. Lastly, NGOs lack the time, resources and supra-structures necessary to nurture the culture-specific trust required for effective partnerships.

If Koh (2000) was correct that international humanitarian work is increasingly dependent on networks of partnering organizations rather than on isolated agencies, then there is great incentive to further our understanding of partnership strategies and practices from a comparative vantage point. The challenge is to harness the combined social capital in the form of contacts and relationships with communities and other organizations that all NGOs possess and turn it into a coordinated resource. The goal should be facilitating coordination – and that will then become best practice.

# References

Bachmann, R. 2001. 'Trust, power and control in trans-organizational relations'. *Organization Studies*, 22, 337–65.

Barbanti, O. 2003. 'Global partnerships and development'. Conflict Research Consortium, University of Colorado.

Bebbington, A. and Farrington, J. 1993. 'Governments, NGOs and agricultural development: perspectives on changing inter-organizational relationships'. *Journal of Development Studies*, 29, 199–220.

Bijlsma-Frankema, K. and Klein Woolthuis, R. (eds.) 2005. *Trust Under Pressure. Empirical Investigations of Trust and Trust Building in Uncertain Circumstances.* Cheltenham, UK: Edward Elgar.

Blomqvist, K. 2005. 'Trust in a dynamic environment: fast trust as a threshold condition for asymmetric technology partnership formation in the ICT sector'. In Bijlsma- Frankena, K. and Klein Woolthuis, R. (eds.) *Trust Under Pressure*.

Bouckaert, G., Peters, G. and Verhoest, K. 2006. 'Coordination strategies in seven OECD countries from 1980 to 2005: Comparative findings'. *EGPA Study Group: Coordination of Public Sector Organizations in the Era of Marketization and Joined-up Government.* Milan, Italy.

Cameron, K. and Quinn, R. 1999. *Diagnosing and Changing Organizational Culture.* New York: Addison-Wesley.

Chao, G. T. and Moon, H. 2005. 'The cultural mosaic: a metatheory for understanding the complexity of culture'. *Journal of Applied Psychology*, 90, 1128–40.

Child, J. and Möllering, G. 2003. 'Contextual confidence and active trust development in the Chinese business environment'. *Organization Science*, 14, 69–80.

Doney, P. M., Cannon, J. P. and Mullen, M. R. 1998. 'Understanding the influence of national culture on the development of trust'. *Academy of Management Review*, 23, 601–20.

Edwards, M. and Fowler, A. 2002. 'Introduction: changing challenges for NGDO management'. In M. Edwards and A. Fowler (eds.) *NGO Management*. London: Earthscan.

Edwards, M. and Hulme, D. 2002. 'Making a difference: scaling-up the developmental impact of NGOs – concepts and experiences'. In M. Edwards and A. Fowler (eds.) *NGO Management*. London: Earthscan.

Fisher, J. 2003. 'Local and global: international governance and civil society'. *Journal of International Affairs*, 57, 19–40.

Fowler, A. 2002a. 'NGO futures – beyond aid: NGDO values and the fourth position'. In M. Edwards and A. Fowler (eds.) *NGO Management*. London: Earthscan.

　　2002b. 'Beyond partnership: getting real about NGO relationships in the aid system'. In M. Edwards and A. Fowler (eds.) *NGO Management*. London: Earthscan.

Gambetta, D. 1998. *Trust: Making and Breaking Cooperative Relations*. Oxford: Blackwell.

Geertz, C. 1973. *The Interpretation of Cultures*. New York: Basic Books.

Helton, A. C. 2002. 'Rescuing the refugees'. *Foreign Affairs*, 81, 71–82.

Hofstede, G. 1983. 'The cultural relativity of organizational practices and theories'. *Journal of International Business Studies*, 14, 75–89.

　　1984. *Culture's Consequences*. Beverley Hills, CA: Sage.

Koh, H. H. 2000. 'U.S. State Department report on human rights practices'. US State Department.

Krasner, S. D. 1983. 'Structural causes and regime consequences: regimes as intervening variables'. In S. D. Krasner (ed.) *International Regimes*. Ithaca, NY: Cornell University Press.

Kühlmann, T. M. 2005. 'Formation of trust in German–Mexican business relations'. In K. Bijlsma-Frankema and R. Klein Woolthuis (eds.) *Trust Under Pressure*.

Lewicki, R. J. and Bunker, B. B. 1996. 'Developing and maintaining trust in work relationships'. In R. M. Kramer and T. R. Tyler (eds.) *Trust in Organizations*. Thousand Oaks, CA: Sage.

Lewis, J. D. and Weigert, A. J. 1985a. 'Social atomism, holism, and trust'. *The Sociological Quarterly*, 26, 455–71.

　　1985b. 'Trust as a social reality'. *Social Forces*, 63, 967–85.

Lipschutz, R. D. 1989. 'Bargaining among nations: culture, history, and perception in regime formation'. *Workshop on Managing the Global Commons: Decision Making and Conflict Resolution in Response to Climate Change*. Knoxville, Tennessee.

Loescher, G. and Helton, A. C. 2002. 'War on Iraq: an impending refugee crisis?' Council On Foreign Relations.

Mayer, R. C., Davis, J. H. and Schoorman, F. D. 1995. 'An integrative model of organizational trust'. *The Academy of Management Review*, 20, 709–33.

McAllister, D. J. 1995. 'Affect- and cognition-based trust as foundations for interpersonal cooperation in organizations'. *Academy of Management Journal*, 38, 24–59.

McEvily, B., Perrone, V. and Zaheer, A. 2003. 'Trust as an organizing principle'. *Organization Science*, 14(1), 91–103.

McKnight, D. H. and Chervany, N. L. 2001. 'Trust and distrust definitions: one bite at a time'. In R. Falcone, M. Singh and Y.-H. Tan (eds.) *Trust in Cyber-societies*. Berlin/Heidelberg: Springer.

McKnight, D. H., Cummings, L. L. and Chervany, N. L. 1998. 'Initial trust formation in new organizational relationships'. *Academy of Management Review*, 23, 473–90.

Pacanowsky, M. and O'Donnell-Trujillo, N. 1983. 'Organizational communication as cultural performance'. *Communication Monographs*, 50, 127–47.

Plante, C. S. and Bendell, J. 1998. 'The art of collaboration: lessons from emerging environmental business-NGO partnerships in Asia'. *Greener Management International*, 24, 91–115.

Ring, P. S. and Van de Ven, A. H. 1994. 'Developmental processes of cooperative interorganizational relationships'. *Academy of Management Review*, 19, 90–118.

Rousseau, D., Sitkin, S. B., Burt, R. S. and Camerer, C. 1998. 'Not so different after all: a cross-discipline view of trust'. *Academy of Management Review*, 23, 393–404.

Schweer, M. K. W. and Thies, B. 2003. *Vertrauen als Organisationsprinzip: Perspektiven für komplexe soziale Systeme*. Bern: Huber.

Schwegler, U. 2006. 'Trust building processes within German–Indonesian cooperation'. *22nd EGOS colloquium: Trust within and across boundaries: Conceptual challenges and empirical insights*. Bergen, Norway.

  2008. *Vertrauen zwischen Fremden: Die Genese von Vertrauen am Beispiel deutsch-indonesischer Kooperationen*. Frankfurt am Main: IKO-Verlag.

Shreve, C. 2006. 'Non-governmental organizations research guide'. Perkins Library, Duke University.

Smith, L. R. 2005. 'The structural context of intercultural personhood: identity re-formation'. *International Journal of Communication*, 15, 89–112.

Spangler, B. 2003. 'Coalition building'. Conflict Research Consortium, University of Colorado.

Teegen, H., Doh, J. and Vachani, S. 2004. 'The importance of nongovernmental organizations (NGOs) in global governance and value creation: an international business research agenda'. *Journal of International Business Studies*, 35, 463–84.

Ting-Toomey, S. 1994. *The Challenge of Facework: Cross-cultural and Interpersonal Issues*. New York: State University of New York – Albany Press.

  2005. 'The matrix of face: an updated face-negotiation theory'. In W. B. Gudykunst (ed.) *Theorizing about Intercultural Communication*. Thousand Oaks, CA: Sage.

Ting-Toomey, S. and Oetzel, J. G. 2003. 'Cross-cultural face concerns and conflict styles: current status and future directions'. In W. B. Gudykunst (ed.) *Cross-cultural and Intercultural Communication*. Thousand Oaks, CA: Sage.

Triandis, H. C. 1972. _The Analysis of Subjective Culture_. New York: Wiley.

Weber, R. P. 1985. _Basic Content Analysis_. Beverley Hills and London: Sage.

Williams, M. 2003. 'Global civil society: expectations, capacities and the accountability of international NGOs'. 21st Century Trust.

Zucker, L. G. 1986. 'Production of trust: institutional sources of economic structures, 1840–1920'. _Research in Organizational Behaviour_, 8, 35–111.

# 12 Antecedents of supervisor trust in collectivist cultures: evidence from Turkey and China

S. ARZU WASTI AND HWEE HOON TAN

## Summary

The premise of much research on dyadic trust building within organizations has been framed around the relationship as it emerges in the work context. Such models, including the seminal Mayer *et al.* (1995) model of dyadic trust, have been applied to contexts outside North America without a careful understanding of the distribution of social practices and everyday situations in such contexts. This chapter examines culture-specific workways as a starting point for understanding subordinates' trust in their supervisors in collectivist cultures. Workways refer to the pattern of workplace beliefs, mental models and practices about what is true, good and efficient within the domain of work. Drawing from interviews with sixty organizational respondents from two countries, Turkey and China, we propose that the multiplexity of work relations needs to be taken into account as both personal and professional life domains are important for understanding supervisor–subordinate trust in collectivist cultures.

## Introduction

Dyadic trust, and in particular, trust between supervisors and their subordinates has been well documented and studied (e.g. Lewicki *et al.*, 2006). However, this body of work is limited largely to the North American context (e.g. from the meta-analysis of Dirks and Ferrin (2002)). Moreover, almost all research on dyadic trust in other countries or cultures employs quantitative methodologies (but see Mizrachi *et al.*, 2007; Saunders and Thornhill, 2004; Tan and Chee, 2005 as notable exceptions) with the questionable assumption (see Wasti *et al.*, 2007) that trust as

This research was supported by Sabanci University's Office of Research and Graduate Policy and by a research grant from the Singapore Management University.

conceptualized and operationalized in contexts such as that of North America is universal and hence transferable. The predominance of this approach to the investigation of organizational phenomena across contexts is undesirable because by design it is unlikely to uncover the differences in the meaning of constructs or to allow the discovery of consequential emic (culture-specific) constructs or relationships among constructs (e.g. Katigbak *et al.*, 2002; Rousseau and Fried, 2001). Not surprisingly, scholars are now urging greater use of inductive or qualitative research strategies in order to truly contribute to the growing cross-cultural organizational literature (e.g. Meyer, 2006). This chapter heeds these calls and, drawing from interview findings, explores the mechanisms of trust development in hierarchical dyadic relationships within large-scale organizations in China and Turkey.

## Culture-specific workways and trust

The literature on dyadic trust in organizations gathered momentum after the seminal paper by Mayer *et al.* (1995) where they proposed a parsimonious model of trust, distinguishing between trust and factors of trustworthiness. While no doubt capturing some universal attributes of trust formation, we argue that this and subsequent conceptualizations of interpersonal dyadic trust (e.g. McAllister, 1995) largely reflect American workways, i.e. the American signature pattern of workplace beliefs, mental models and practices about what is true, good and efficient within the domain of work (Sanchez-Burks and Lee, 2007). However, American workways emerge as an anomaly with respect to workplace relational styles in cross-national comparisons (Sanchez-Burks, 2005). Drawing on theories of individualism and collectivism (Hofstede, 2001; Triandis, 1995) as well as low- versus high-context cultures (Hall, 1976), American workways are described as being comparatively low in relational focus and high in task focus. Recently, Sanchez-Burks (2005) argued that American workplace norms are guided by Protestant Relational Ideology, which refers to a deep-seated sentiment that affective and relational concerns ought to be put aside at work in order to direct one's attention to the task at hand. Maintaining a task focus is not perceived as a way to suppress interpersonal harmony, but rather as an effective strategy for ensuring smooth interactions within the workplace by leaving personal issues and emotional sensitivity outside the office. Relatedly, social interactions are characterized by a separation of professional and personal domains: social cliques vary across activities and rarely bridge the work/non-work divide (Sanchez-Burks, 2005). This divide facilitates the maintenance of 'professionalism' at the workplace as there is little spillover from the personal life domain in terms of relational norms or expectations.

The cultural psychology of workways provides a frame of reference not only to organizational members, but also to organizational scholars in a given context (Hofstede, 1994). Indeed, critical reviews of the existing (i.e. mostly North American) trust literature note that prior theorization has treated the organizational context as an overarching condition that limits the relevance of the social/emotional/relational element of trust relations (Lewicki *et al.*, 1998). Furthermore, this literature has largely ignored the multiplexity of relationships that refer to whether or not personal friendships and instrumental resources are exchanged in the same relationship (Morris *et al.*, 2000). Not surprisingly, the operationalization of trust and factors of trustworthiness in the Mayer *et al.* (1995) model as well as other frameworks (see Dietz and Den Hartog, 2006) are largely work related, i.e. define the constructs of interest in terms of their 'professional' manifestation. Even scale items reflecting affect-based trust are limited to workplace interactions (e.g. 'I can talk freely to this individual about difficulties I am having at work and I know (s)he will want to listen'). In a similar vein, it has been proposed that interpersonal trust building starts with calculus-based trust, progresses to knowledge-based trust and finally to identification-based trust (Lewicki and Bunker, 1996). Lewicki and Bunker assert that most relationships at work stop at the knowledge-based stage, and never progress to the identification-based stage. Given the unique nature of American workways, whether these trust models and measures, which are generated and validated mostly in North America, are sufficient or relevant in other contexts emerges as an important question (Wasti *et al.*, 2007).

Indeed, evidence from collectivist, high-context cultures such as East Asian or Middle Eastern countries suggests that workways are characterized by a much greater emphasis on relational, affective components (e.g. Sanchez-Burks and Lee, 2007; Triandis, 1995). While these relationships are slow to develop, they permeate many facets of life and are difficult to break (Sanchez-Burks, 2005). For many Asian cultures, establishing a highly personal connection is a necessary precondition to working with others (Hampden-Turner and Trompenaars, 1993; Park and Luo, 2001). In such cultures, the prevalent leadership style is paternalism (Aycan, 2001; Cheng *et al.*, 2004). Paternalistic managers show holistic concern for subordinates' personal or familial wellbeing, attend the personal events of employees and intervene on behalf of their employees in personal problems. Similarly, an employee's sense of obligation to his or her boss extends the boundaries of the office or workday (Aycan, 2001; Sanchez-Burks and Lee, 2007).

These differences undoubtedly affect interpersonal trust development in organizational settings across cultures. In particular, we concur with Branzei *et al.* (2007) that differences between collectivist and individualist cultures elicit distinct 'grammars' for producing trust as a function of the dominant relational forms (Fiske, 1992; Sheppard and Sherman, 1998). Relational forms vary in terms of dependence and depth, the latter referring to the importance, range and number of points of contact among people (Sheppard and Sherman, 1998). Cross-cultural research on organizational commitment suggests difference in depth to be especially relevant with respect to employees' relationships with their supervisors (Chen *et al.*, 2002). Specifically, it is argued that the emphasis on submission to authority and personalized loyalty render the supervisor a more significant focus of commitment than the organization, and a more consequential antecedent to various job outcomes in collectivist cultures (e.g. Cheng *et al.*, 2003). Hence, while subordinates in individualist cultures tend to perceive their relationship with their supervisor as one of shallow dependence, in collectivist cultures subordinates are likely to perceive a greater depth of dependence (Branzei *et al.*, 2007; Cheng *et al.*, 2004).

The different dependence and depth perceptions that trustors have of their relationship with a trustee entail different risks, thus motivating different ways of producing trust (Sheppard and Sherman, 1998). For individualists who forge shallow dependence relationships, the risks involve unreliability and indiscretion, making the trustee's ability to accomplish specific tasks and honest intent to keep promises the primary antecedents of trust (Branzei *et al.*, 2007; Sheppard and Sherman, 1998). For collectivists who establish deep dependence, the risks involve cheating, neglect, abuse and harm to self-esteem, which suggest that trustee integrity and benevolence are paramount qualities of trustworthiness (Branzei *et al.*, 2007; Sheppard and Sherman, 1998). Thus, as argued by Branzei *et al.* (2007) collectivists are more likely than individualists to attend to signs that describe the nature, depth and quality of the connection with a trustee (e.g. similarity, familiarity, caring and empathy). Similar arguments have been made by Doney *et al.* (1998), who proposed calculative- and capability-based processes to be basic building blocks for trust formation in individualistic cultures while prediction, inten-tionality and transference (e.g. reputation, certification) processes to be pre-dominant in collectivistic cultures.

Several empirical studies support these contentions (e.g. Branzei *et al.*, 2007; Mizrachi *et al.*, 2007). For instance, Mizrachi *et al.*'s (2007) ethno-graphic research at an Israeli–Jordanian industrial site describe the Jordanians as associating trust with human motives and intentions rather than with evaluation of competence and reliability. They also characterize the Jordanian trust-building process to be holistic in terms of seeking to share personal information, time and space, thereby blurring the professional versus personal boundaries and expanding the bandwidth of trust. These observations also concur with Child and Möllering's (2003) findings in China, who note that active trust development via establishing personal rapport is very relevant for modernizing societies where the strong institutions commonly associated with modernity do not work reliably. However, evidence suggests that Chinese people's emphasis on socio-emotional ties in business transactions stems more from socio-cultural roots than from poorly regulated institutions (Chua *et al.*, 2005). It appears that in collectivistic, high-context cultures, where the professional/personal dichotomy is less clear, the foundations and sequence of interpersonal trust building may be different. In contrast to the accepted view in the North American literature (Lewicki and Bunker, 1996; McAllister, 1995), the basis of trust development may be primarily affective in nature, and cognitive bases may only develop subsequently. For instance, Chua *et al.* (2005) argued that in a workplace context, the Chinese tend to build trust from an affective foundation and mix personal and professional concerns, whereas Americans tend to build trust from a cognitive foundation and are less likely to mix socio-emotional concerns with instrumentality. In line with this argument, they found that the two dimensions of trust were more intertwined in the Chinese context than in the American context (Chua *et al.*, 2005).

In this chapter, we build on the research on interpersonal trust development in collectivist, high-context cultures. We use a qualitative approach to allow respondents to define the content and range of variables they consider relevant (see Kramer, 1996). Moreover, we focus on subordinates' trust in their supervisor. Specifically, we address two research questions. First, what are the antecedents of supervisor–subordinate trust and their operationalizations in these contexts in comparison to existing frameworks of trust? Second, how does supervisor–subordinate trust develop over time in these contexts? In tracking trust development, we pay particular attention to identifying if and how the supervisor–subordinate relationship straddles personal and professional life domains.

## Method

Semi-structured interviews were conducted with thirty Turkish and thirty Chinese employees in large-scale, mostly multinational organizations in Istanbul, Turkey and ShenZhen, China. While cultural effects are less likely

Table 12.1 *Sample characteristics*

|  | Turkey | China |
|---|---|---|
| Number of organizations | 10 | 2 |
| Represented in study | (2 Turkish MNC, 6 joint ventures or wholly owned subsidiaries, 2 companies of family-owned conglomerates) | (a Chinese multinational corporation and a Hong Kong joint venture) |
| Gender of respondents (subordinates) | Male – 17; Female – 13 | Male – 24; Female – 6 |
| Gender of supervisor | Male – 27; Female – 3 | Male – 28; Female – 2 |
| Same gender dyad | 18 | 24 |
| Different gender dyad | 12 | 6 |
| Length of relationship | ½ – 17 years | 1–18 years |

to emerge in large and/or multinational organizations due to institutionalized human resources practices (Aycan, 2005; Cheng *et al.*, 2004), they constitute a more valid comparison to the North American literature.

In both samples, the respondents were in their mid-thirties and highly educated (90 per cent with at least a university degree). The background characteristics of the participants and their companies are presented in Table 12.1. We note that the majority of the participants from both countries are male, reported to a male supervisor, and there are more same-gender supervisor–subordinate dyads in the sample than different-gender supervisor–subordinate dyads. The length of the supervisor–subordinate relationship ranged from one to eighteen years for the Chinese and six months to seventeen years for the Turkish sample. Only one respondent (in the Turkish sample) had a relationship with his supervisor prior to joining the organization.

Interviews were conducted on site by the authors in their respective languages (first author Turkish, second author Chinese). Respondents were asked to define trust and to identify a supervisor with whom they had developed a strong trust relationship. They were subsequently asked to discuss which characteristics or behaviours of the supervisor affected their trust development at early as well as the later stages of their relationship, including a critical incident that was a milestone event for trust formation. They were also asked how trust affected their behaviour towards the supervisor, both in and outside of the work context and whether they fully trusted their supervisor.

All interviews were tape-recorded and transcribed verbatim. The researchers read the transcripts in their native language and then jointly designed a coding manual to systematically summarize the data. For each country sample, two trained research assistants who were blind to the research questions coded the data in the native language. They coded background information (i.e. gender of trustor and supervisor, length of relationship) and as many factors as possible that contributed to trust development during the early and later stages of each supervisor–subordinate relationship. The coders concurrently developed a glossary of antecedents (Table 12.2), in which they labelled, defined and categorized each factor of trust identified. They further coded every distinct behavioural response by the subordinate towards the supervisor in the initial and later stages of the relationship, and further categorized these behaviours in terms of whether they pertained to the professional or the personal domain. They also coded whether the respondents expressed full trust towards their supervisor. After coding all transcripts independently, the two coders met to resolve discrepancies through extensive discussions. This process, which was moderated by the researchers, yielded a revised coding manual and a final glossary of antecedents, which was then provided to third coders, who independently coded all interviews. Discrepancies at this stage were resolved through a final discussion between the third coders and the researchers.

## Results

We developed our analysis strategy to answer the two research questions we have raised, namely; what are the antecedents of supervisor–subordinate trust? and how is this trust developed over time in the specific context of Turkey and China? We report our results accordingly.

### *Antecedents of supervisor–subordinate trust*

A total of nine antecedent categories were found in both Turkey and China: Ability, Professional Benevolence, Personal Benevolence, Integrity, Common Values, Reciprocity, Personality, Communication and Modesty. While the categories are similar across both countries, antecedents within the broad categories are sometimes manifested in different ways in each culture as can be seen in Table 12.2. We will refer to these different manifestations of an antecedent category as facets. For example, for the Integrity antecedent, respondents report four different facets in the Turkish sample; Reliability, Fairness, Being Responsible and Keeping Secrets. Only antecedent categories

Table 12.2 *Glossary and frequency of antecedents across Chinese and Turkish respondents*

| Antecedent category | Frequency (China) | China | China definition | Turkey definition | Turkey | Frequency (Turkey) | Antecedent category |
|---|---|---|---|---|---|---|---|
| Ability | 26 (86.7%) | Capacity | Trustee has ability related to work, in terms of decision making, execution and long work experience | Trustee has work-related ability in terms of decision making, execution, vision as well as experience, success, position | Capacity | 18 (60%) | Ability |
| Ability | 4 (13.3%) | Interpersonal Skills | Trustee has good interpersonal skills | Trustee has good interpersonal skills | Interpersonal Skills | 3 (10%) | |
| | | | | Trustee is self-assured, confident, able to persuade | Self-confidence | 2 (6.7%) | Ability |
| At least one facet (Ability) | 18 (60%) | | | | | 18 (60%) | At least one facet (Ability) |
| Professional Benevolence | 5 (16.7%) | Understanding | Trustee will take trustor's perspective and is tolerant | Trustee is tolerant, non-judgmental, forgiving in general or in a specific situation | Understanding | 3 (10%) | Professional Benevolence |
| Professional Benevolence | 22 (73.3%) | Guidance and Support | Trustee guides trustor in his/her development and growth, and supports the trustor in times of need | Trustee guides the trustor in solving his/her problems and provides encouragement | Guidance and Support | 11 (36.7%) | Professional Benevolence |

| Category | n (%) | Facet | Description |
|---|---|---|---|
| Professional Benevolence | 6 (20%) | Protection | Trustee protects interests of the trustor without necessarily being objective |
| Professional Benevolence | 2 (6.7%) | Cooperation | Trustee endorses a win–win approach |
| Professional Benevolence | 3 (10%) | Listening | Trustee listens to trustor's concerns and opinions, making the trustor feel cared for |
| At least one facet (Professional Benevolence) | 16 (53.3%) | | |
| Personal Benevolence | 3 (10.0%) | Intimacy | Trustee displays a desire to share personal life and build a close relationship |
| Personal Benevolence | 3 (10.0%) | Personalized Generosity | Trustee allocates 'extra' time, material support |
| At least one facet (Personal Benevolence) | 7 (23.3%) | | |
| Integrity | 14 (46.7%) | Reliability | Trustee is consistent in behaviour, words and deeds, and is honest |

| Category | n (%) | Facet | Description |
|---|---|---|---|
| At least one facet (Professional Benevolence) | 17 (56.7%) | | |
| Personal Benevolence | 2 (6.7%) | Intimacy | Trustee is concerned with trustor's personal life |
| At least one facet (Personal Benevolence) | 2 (6.7%) | | |
| Integrity | 12 (40%) | Reliability | Trustee is consistent in behaviour, words and deeds and is honest |

**Table 12.2** (*cont.*)

| Antecedent category | Frequency (China) | China | China definition | Turkey definition | Turkey | Frequency (Turkey) | Antecedent category |
|---|---|---|---|---|---|---|---|
| Integrity | 9 (30%) | Fairness | Trustee is objective, fair and able to separate work issues from person issues | Trustee is objective, fair, protective of everybody's rights, refrains from exploiting others | Fairness | 6 (20%) | Integrity |
| Integrity | 2 (6.7%) | Being Responsible | Trustee can be relied on to get work done and have high work standards | The trustee can be relied upon for successful completion of assigned tasks | Being Responsible | 2 (6.7%) | Integrity |
| | | | | The trustee keeps secrets | Keeping Secrets | 2 (6.7%) | Integrity |
| At least one facet (Integrity) | 20 (66.7%) | | | | | 19 (63.3%) | At least one facet (Integrity) |
| Personality | 3 (10%) | Charisma | Trustee is charismatic | Trustee is charismatic, including his/her physical attributes | Charisma | 1 (3.3%) | Personality |
| Personality | 7 (23.3%) | Affability | Trustee is able to relate well to others and is sincere and kind | Trustee is affable, pleasant, smiling | Affability | 2 (6.7%) | Personality |
| At least one facet (Personality) | 7 (23.3%) | | | | | 3 (10%) | At least one facet (Personality) |

| | | | | | | | |
|---|---|---|---|---|---|---|---|
| Reciprocity | 11 (36.7%) | Reciprocity | Trustee reciprocates perceived trust from trustor; including delegation and empowerment | Reciprocation of perceived trust | Reciprocity | 9 (30%) | Reciprocity |
| | | | | **Trustee shows his/her appreciation towards the trustor** | **Being Appreciated** | **3 (10%)** | **Reciprocity** |
| **At least one facet (Reciprocity)** | **11 (36.7%)** | | | | | **11 (36.7%)** | **At least one facet (Reciprocity)** |
| Communication | 10 (33.3%) | Communication | Trustee is open in communication, in exchanging opinions and in sharing expectations | Trustee is open and frank in communication, shares expectations, allows free exchange of ideas | Communication | 7 (23.3%) | Communication |
| Common Values | 7 (23.3%) | Congruence | Trustee has similar values, personality and interests as trustor | Approval of trustee's values and lifestyle particularly relating to family | Values | 7 (23.3%) | Common Values |
| Modesty / Humility | 2 (6.7%) | Respect Towards Subordinates | Trustee does not carry airs and treats subordinates with great consideration | Trustee does not look down on others in lower status, respects subordinates as individuals | Respect Towards Subordinates | 5 (16.7%) | Modesty |

and facets with a frequency greater than two (in at least one sample) are reported in Table 12.2. The frequency counts provided across each facet refer to the number of individuals who mentioned that particular facet at least once. The total count under each multifaceted antecedent category represents the number of individuals who mentioned at least one manifestation of that antecedent category.

### Comparison with existing frameworks

Broadly speaking, the majority of the antecedents (and their operationalizations) identified in both samples are compatible with Mayer *et al.*'s (1995) Ability-Benevolence-Integrity (ABI) framework. Under the Ability category, other than the facets labelled Capacity that refer to work-related ability, experience, etc. and Interpersonal Skills, there is an additional (but rarely mentioned) facet in the form of Self-confidence in Turkey.

For the Benevolence category in both countries, the majority of the antecedents are from the professional context (labelled as Professional Benevolence) and represent facets such as Understanding, which refers to being understanding in terms of work-related issues (e.g. forgiving a serious process-related blunder) and Guidance and Support, mainly in the form of career guidance and support in times of need. For the Turkish sample, other facets are Cooperation, Listening and Protection. Cooperation refers to the supervisor endorsing a win–win approach, while Listening involves paying attention to the subordinate's concerns. Protection refers to the defence of the subordinate's interests, but is not necessarily based on objective criteria. Thus it is different from Fairness (categorized as Integrity), being more about demonstrating concern. It should also be noted that whereas Guidance and Support, Listening and to some extent Protection are represented in existing operationalizations of Benevolence (Dietz and Den Hartog, 2006), Understanding appears to be culturally salient, and a defining characteristic of paternalistic leadership (Cheng *et al.*, 2004).

While most facets of Benevolence occur in the context of work, there are a few of a personal nature, which are labelled Personal Benevolence. This group of antecedents is not found in the existing trust frameworks. One facet of Personal Benevolence, common across both samples is Intimacy and denotes the supervisor's holistic concern for the subordinate's professional and personal life. Not surprisingly, respondents who identified such behaviours typically made analogies to familial life, describing their supervisor to be like a brother (sister) or a father (mother). Another facet of Personal Benevolence in the Turkish context is Personalized Generosity, which refers to the supervisor giving extra time or even financial resources (for personal need) to the subordinate as a demonstration of personalized, fatherly care (it is interesting to note that all supervisors in this category were male). Interestingly, the three respondents who narrated Personalized Generosity incidents were different from the rest of the sample. One was working with a supervisor who was already a family friend. The second narrated a critical incident from his previous work experience at a family firm. In this specific incident, the owner-manager had provided financial support for the respondent's marriage and had paid for his son's birth expenses. The third respondent was a relatively less educated (hence more traditional) female secretary working with a very elderly boss. Therefore, we were able to observe classic manifestations of paternalism in their stories. These cases suggest that in Turkey (and very likely China, see Cheng *et al.*, 2004), as the focus shifts from institutionalized organizations towards smaller family-owned firms, Personal Benevolence can take centre stage in the formation of trust in the supervisor.

Facets of Integrity common to both countries are Reliability, Fairness and Being Responsible. Reliability consists of behavioural consistency and integrity as defined by Whitener et al. (1998). Fairness refers to the trustee being objective, fair and protective of everybody's rights. Being Responsible includes being able to complete work successfully. For the Turkish sample, Integrity has one further facet reflected in being able to Keep Secrets.

In addition to the familiar trustworthiness antecedents of ABI, we found Reciprocity to be a common antecedent of trust. Reciprocity refers to the subordinate's perceptions of being trusted and appreciated, typically through sharing and delegation of control. While delegation has previously been found to lead to greater trust (Schoorman *et al.*, 1996), Reciprocity has not been explicitly examined (Schoorman *et al.*, 2007), despite having a long history (see Zand, 1972). Establishing Reciprocity as an antecedent of trust in the current study presents a rare piece of empirical evidence that initial delegation and empowerment, or an initial overture of closeness (Kramer, 1996) by the supervisor may be needed for trust to develop. The emergence of Reciprocity possibly indicates the relevance of mutual obligations in collectivist cultures as well.

Other antecedents identified that also exist in mainstream frameworks are Communication and Common Values. Communication is in line with Whitener *et al.*'s (1998) propositions and highlights the desire of respondents to engage in open sessions with supervisors where expectations and opinions are exchanged. Common Values refers to values or lifestyles that are shared by both trustee and trustor, as well as to similarity in terms of personality and interests. While this antecedent has been proposed by McAllister (1995) to affect cognition-based trust, Gillespie and Mann (2004) have found common values to be one of the strongest predictors of overall trust in a leader in a team environment. Of note, in the Turkish sample, Common values was mentioned regarding family life, which is in line with Tan and Chee's (2005) qualitative study in Singaporean organizations, where filial piety and family values, which do not concern the realm of work, emerged as important antecedents of trust.

What is also interesting is the antecedent category of Personality. While the leadership literature places importance on trait theories, trust theorists have tended to lump all personality traits of the leader into 'good character' (see Dirks and Ferrin, 2002). However, other than the Integrity antecedents, it is not clear what 'good character' consists of. We found that across both countries, Charisma and Affability are important in trust building. Last but not the least Modesty is another antecedent that is common across both samples, but different from the existing literature. Modesty denotes treating subordinates with respect and not looking down on them due to their status. We speculate that the salience of Affability and Modesty is due to the high power distance in the two societies. Indeed, these ideas are in line with the Chinese views on how superiors should treat those in inferior roles; with kindness, gentleness, righteousness and benevolence (Farh and Cheng, 2000).

### Most essential trust antecedents

As mentioned above, we calculated the number of respondents who mentioned each facet at least once as well as the number of respondents who mentioned at least one facet in each multifaceted antecedent category as an indicator of antecedent importance.

For the Turkish respondents, Capacity (Ability) is the facet that is mentioned most frequently (18 = 60%), followed by Reliability (Integrity) (14 = 46.7%) and Guidance and Support (Professional Benevolence) (11 = 36.7%). In terms of overall antecedent categories, however, Integrity has the highest frequency (19 = 63.3%), closely followed by Ability (18 = 60%), Professional Benevolence (16 = 53.3%) and Reciprocity (11 = 36.7%). Similarly, for the Chinese respondents, we found the Capacity (Ability) facet to have the highest count (26 = 86.7%), followed by Guidance and Support (Professional Benevolence) (22 = 73.3%) and Reliability (Integrity) (12 = 40%). In the overall antecedent categories, the pattern is the same as the Turkish sample, the highest antecedent category is Integrity (20 = 66.7%), followed by Ability (18 = 60%), Professional Benevolence (17 = 56.7%) and Reciprocity (11 = 36.7%). These results are in line with Kramer's (1996) observations

Table 12.3 *Most essential antecedents for trust in supervisor*

|  | China | Turkey |
| --- | --- | --- |
| Integrity | 8 | 10 |
| Common Values | – | 2 |
| Ability | 3 | 3 |
| Benevolence | 1 | 3 |
| Communication | 2 | 1 |
| Reciprocity | 1 | 2 |
| Modesty | – | 2 |
| Personality | 5 | – |
| Total | 20 | 23 |

*Note:* as only some of the respondents were able to single out one antecedent as being the most essential, the sample sizes for this analysis do not add up to 30.

that subordinates tend to ruminate their relationship with the supervisor, and take into consideration many factors of trustworthiness.

Given each respondent typically narrated multiple antecedents of trust, we asked respondents for the one that was most essential in their trust development (see Table 12.3). Among the respondents who were able to single out one antecedent, we found Integrity to be the most essential antecedent across both countries (8 in China and 10 in Turkey). The next highest count is Ability (3 in each country), followed by Communication (2 in China and 1 in Turkey) and Benevolence (1 in China and 3 in Turkey). In the Turkish sample, Modesty is also one of the essential antecedents (2 counts). Interestingly, for the Chinese sample, the Personality of the trustee merits a high count of five in being the most essential antecedent. As one of the Chinese respondents said (translated from Mandarin), 'it is more important to know how to "be a person" than to know how to get work done'.

Contrary to our literature review, the respondents' rankings in both countries highlight the importance of the cognitive bases of trust (i.e. competence and reliability) in high-context, collectivist cultures. This might be reflective of what has been labelled the 'deprivation hypothesis' by the GLOBE team (Javidan *et al.*, 2006), who propose that individuals value what they lack in their cultural context. Indeed, traditional paternalistic leadership in Turkey and China also involves centralizing authority, maintaining hierarchical distance with subordinates, keeping intentions ill-defined, implementing control tactics and nepotism (Cheng *et al.*, 2004). Thus, our respondents may be taking the affective bases of trust for granted, but expressing the importance of what is rarer and perhaps needed.

*Profiles and patterns of trust development*

To discern profiles and patterns of trust development, we first categorized all cases into two bases of trust formation: cognitive or affective. The respondents who identified Ability and/or Integrity (or Communication) antecedents and made no mention of Benevolence as the basis of their trust were coded as representing cognition-based trust (CBT). All other respondents who mentioned Benevolence as one of the trust antecedents were coded as representing affect-based trust (ABT) alongside CBT. Within the affective- and cognitive-based trust (A&CBT) group, we further categorized those who made reference to Personal versus Professional Benevolence. In sum, three profiles of trust formation were identified (i.e. CBT, Personal A&CBT, Professional A&CBT). (See Table 12.4.)

There were eight cases of CBT in the Turkish sample. There was no spillover to the personal domain in any of the CBT relationships; the relationship was strictly professional (an expression also used by the respondents). Put differently, perceptions of Ability, Integrity and/or Communication did not elicit sharing personal information, time or space from trustors. As the relationship progressed, respondents narrated that they knew more about their supervisor, respected him/her more, and shared more professional experiences (e.g. work-related problems, relations at work). Except for one case, no respondent expressed full trust in their supervisors. The exception was the only case who expressed Integrity as the sole basis of initial trust, suggesting that integrity-based trust may be stronger than competence-based trust even if it is not conducive to the development of affect or intimacy. Of note, three of the CBT cases mentioned the short relationship length as a factor in their lack of full trust. Others perceived a more competitive organizational context or stated that they did not trust anyone (perhaps other than family) fully.

There were nine cases of CBT in the Chinese sample. In contrast to the Turkish data, for seven cases, subordinates' response to trust was sharing both professional and personal life domains and gender composition did not

Table 12.4 *Frequency of trust profiles*

|  | Cognition-Based Trust (CBT) | Personal Affective- and Cognition-Based Trust (A and CBT) | Professional Affective- and Cognition-Based Trust (A and CBT) |
|---|---|---|---|
| Turkey | 8 | 7 | 15 |
| China | 9 | 0 | 21 |

appear relevant in terms of determining the basis or course of the relationship. The exceptions were two cases where one respondent was a very private person and the other had not yet had an opportunity. Irrespective of the nature of sharing, the majority of the respondents expressed full trust towards their supervisor. Thus, it appears that the divide between professional and personal domain is more porous in the Chinese sample than in the Turkish sample. However, for the Chinese CBT relationships that developed to a level of full trust, assessments of Integrity and Ability were typically accompanied by favourable evaluations in terms of Personality, Communication and Reciprocity, which was a pattern distinct from the Turkish sample.

While none of the Chinese respondents were categorized as Personal A&CBT relationships, there were seven cases in the Turkish sample. In all Personal A&CBT relationships, there were antecedents of initial trust other than Personal Benevolence (such as Ability, Integrity, Common Values, Modesty). However, there was no pattern as to their occurrence. The consistent pattern was that (except for one case) all perceptions of Personal Benevolence elicited sharing of both professional and personal domains of life from the subordinates. The exceptional case was that of a technical worker who had a relatively distant relationship with his supervisor, particularly in terms of socioeconomic differences. Four respondents in this group were able to differentiate between the initial and later stages of their relationship. As their relationship developed, the supervisor showed greater Intimacy and Professional Benevolence (typically in terms of protecting, guiding or supporting the subordinate), as well as sharing more information and control (i.e. Communication and Reciprocity). This in turn generated greater sharing of both personal and professional life domains, and typically led to a relationship characterized by full trust. It is also interesting to note that all except one of the Personal A&CBT relationships were characterized by same-gender dyads (five male dyads, one female dyad), and the exception was a female employee who referred to her supervisor as her father. This is in contrast to the Turkish CBT group, where five of the seven relationships were different-gender dyads.

Finally, fifteen Turkish and twenty-one Chinese respondents were categorized as Professional A&CBT relationships. For the Turkish sample, while all respondents narrated other antecedents of initial trust, there was no evident pattern as to their emergence. In eleven cases, subordinates responded by only sharing their professional domain, and this did not appear to be a function of the gender composition. Irrespective of subordinates' initial reciprocation, respondents narrated that the relationship typically developed by receiving more Reciprocity, Communication, Personal and/or Professional

Benevolence from the supervisor, upon which they shared personal and professional life domains to a greater extent. Interestingly, whether this led to full trust was mostly a matter of individual propensity to trust. That is, upon receiving Benevolence from the supervisor, if the respondents did not feel full trust, they typically explained it by 'excusing' it as their low propensity to trust. The interviews also suggest that the gender composition sets a boundary condition such that Professional A&CBT relations that are homogeneous are more likely to yield full trust relationships. Finally, although Professional Benevolence had a tendency to trigger spillover to the personal domain, Professional Benevolence without the spillover was able to generate full trust.

All Chinese Professional A&CBT relationships also involved other antecedents of initial trust such as Modesty and Reciprocity. However, there was no evident pattern as to their emergence or implications. Of the nineteen cases for which there was full information, twelve responded with sharing both professional and personal domains, out of which eleven respondents were of the same gender composition. Of the six respondents who were able to differentiate stages in their relationship, three narrated that the relationship developed by observing more instances of Ability from the supervisor, one mentioned Integrity but only one mentioned Intimacy. This was quite different to the Turkish case, where it was typically Benevolence which characterized trust development. A final observation was that there was no clear indication as to what led to full trust; nor was there much full trust. In fact, one respondent noted that one could never fully trust others; trust is already considered high if it is at 80–90 per cent. This was in line with the respondents' sentiments that Chinese people in general did not trust each other, a tendency attributed to both historical and economic reasons.

## Discussion

While indigenous research aims to uncover context- or culture-specific constructs or relationships, it also serves the invaluable role of establishing generalizability. Our qualitative inquiry on the development of supervisor trust in China and Turkey has revealed that antecedents identified in existing, typically North American, models are largely relevant across other contexts. In particular, the perceived ability, integrity and benevolence of the supervisor as observed in the professional context seem to be the major factors of trustworthiness in Turkish and Chinese employees' minds. However, in view of the fact that our sampling strategy, which involved large-scale organizations with institutionalized HR practices, was in effect a conservative test of cultural differences (Aycan, 2005), we consider the findings that depart from the existing literature to have important implications. We discuss these below.

First, our findings indicate that subordinate trust in supervisor has consequential affective bases in these contexts. In both samples, manifestations of benevolence are broader and deeper, encompassing behaviours such as magnanimity in terms of both the professional and personal welfare of the subordinate. Furthermore, benevolent behaviour is not saved to later stages of trust, but appears to be bestowed upfront in order to establish quick but firm trust. In both samples, perceptions of supervisor trustworthiness are reciprocated by sharing of both personal and professional information, time and space. This is particularly so for the Turkish sample when supervisor trustworthiness has strong affective bases. The Turkish sample also reveals that personal sharing in turn triggers benevolence in the professional context, particularly in the form of greater guidance, support and protection.

Second, our analyses speak to the relevance of the deprivation hypothesis in terms of understanding the influence of culture (Javidan *et al.*, 2006). The emergence of modesty, communication, affability and the importance of integrity and ability highlight the importance of studying what is rare in a culture as well as what is the norm.

Finally, our observations point to the role of the gender composition, propensity to trust and similarity in terms of socioeconomic status in trust development in subordinate–supervisor relations. Many respondents mentioned their personal propensity to trust to be a determining factor in trust development. Furthermore, the development of affect-based trust and spillover to the personal domain appear more probable in same gender dyads and when the subordinate and the supervisor belong to the same socioeconomic class. It is interesting to note that these factors are also informed by culture. For example, individual propensity to trust may be lower in countries characterized by higher levels of cultural cynicism (Leung and Bond, 2004). Similarly, more instances of trust development in the personal domain may be observed for different gender dyads in countries characterized by gender egalitarianism (House *et al.*, 2004) or across various hierarchies in low power distance cultures (Hofstede, 2001).

## Implications for practice

Our finding that the Ability-Benevolence-Integrity framework proposed by Mayer *et al.* (1995) is largely replicated in the present study suggests that managers should place importance on these three factors in building and maintaining trust within and across cultures. The caveat though, is that the manner in which such factors of trustworthiness are communicated may vary in the different cultures. For example, being benevolent appears to involve being forgiving in collectivist cultures. Perhaps more importantly, benevolence is communicated via both personal and professional domains. That is, managers should realize that boundaries such as work (professional) and non-work (personal) may be artificial in collectivistic cultures. Subordinate trust towards the supervisor can develop via different domains (professional versus personal) and in different order (affect followed by cognition or put differently, cognition coloured by affect). As observed by Mizrachi et al. (2007), trust established in the personal domain will generate expectations in the professional domain, which in instances will counter what is otherwise considered 'professional'. Although it is possible to avoid diffusion out of efficiency and fairness concerns, this stance may risk signalling distrust.

While such dynamics are particularly relevant for cross-national interactions, they have implications for transitional societies like China and Turkey, too. In the midst of rapid economic and social change, as argued by Kağıtçıbaşı (1997), the affective bases of collectivism are still salient; yet, the normative aspects such as submission to in-group authority are fading out. What exactly sets the conditions of trustworthiness in these turbulent contexts, where efficiency and performance concerns are also heightened, emerge as important leadership challenges.

## Limitations

While the strength of this study lies in the use of rich qualitative data focusing on specific points in the relationship, retrospective methodology raises alternative interpretations (Korsgaard et al., 2002). It is also possible that our methodology did not elicit some very salient antecedents simply because of their salience. Just like fish in the aquarium, unable to describe the water, perhaps common trust-building processes such as reputation were under-represented. Quantitative methodologies and more generally, longitudinal designs, will be fruitful extensions.

Secondly, we recognize that there are species of collectivism (Morris et al., 2000), as well as other cultural differences between the two countries (e.g. House et al., 2004). For instance, China and Turkey differ markedly with respect to performance orientation, and this might be reflected in the divergence observed regarding the implications of CBT. In addition, the Chinese sample is from ShenZhen, a special economic zone set up by the Chinese government to drive economic growth in the country. Hence, these samples may not be representative of respondents from other organizational types in these countries. There is certainly a need to undertake further investigations within each culture, particularly along the dimensions of organizational ownership and size (family firms versus large-scale corporations versus MNCs). Finally, the samples were not fully equivalent in China and Turkey and it is possible that the differences observed are in part due to the differences in samples drawn from each country.

## Directions for future research

Given the multiplexity of relationships and holistic trust-building processes in organizations in high-context, collectivist cultures, the first research direction is to devise methodologies and measures that capture this complexity. We advocate more qualitative work and social network analyses (e.g. Morris *et al.*, 2000), as well as the subsequent development of scales that operationalize culture-specific manifestations of antecedents of trust.

Second, the individual and group level implications of the professional–personal spillover need to be established. What does this diffusion imply in terms of work attitudes, citizenship and deviant behaviours, efficiency and group processes as well as wellbeing? Does it enhance cooperation and altruism among the parties or create a situation where trustees take advantage by perhaps shirking from work or being delinquent, knowing that the trustor will protect them? Does it foster organizational commitment, or undermine it as valuable workplace relationships are not bound by membership to the organization? Does it serve as a stress buffer amidst concerns to balance work and family life?

Finally, the boundary conditions of the professional–personal spillover need to be established. Would spillover be different in vertical relationships (i.e. between supervisor and subordinate) as opposed to horizontal relationships (i.e. between peers)? Male-to-male dyads versus female-to-female dyads? How would culture moderate these relationship dynamics?

## Concluding comments

Despite significant theoretical and practical relevance, our knowledge of the development of supervisor–subordinate trust in contexts such as Turkey and China remains limited. Our investigation has highlighted both universal and culture-specific aspects of supervisor–subordinate trust development in such contexts. We found the Mayer *et al.* (1995) Ability-Benevolence-Integrity framework to be generalizable to the Turkey and Chinese contexts.

However, we also found the manifestations of such antecedents to vary across cultures and particularly in the case of Benevolence, to straddle the professional–personal (work–non-work) divide. In terms of trust development, in the organizational context, the three trust-development profiles found in this study showed that trust can be developed in more than one way; via cognitive bases alone, via both cognitive and affective bases (that can be in the professional or personal domain) or it can develop with affective bases first, followed by cognitive bases. In sum, our investigation in effect yielded more questions than answers, and the findings in this chapter represent the first steps in understanding how trust is developed across cultures. We continue our research efforts in the directions this study has pointed.

## References

Aycan, Z. 2001. 'Human resource management in Turkey: Current issues and future challenges'. *International Journal of Manpower*, 22(3), 252–61.
  2005. 'The interplay between cultural and institutional/structural contingencies in human resource management practices'. *International Journal of Human Resource Management*, 16, 1083–119.
Branzei, O., Vertinsky, I. and Camp II, R. D. 2007. 'Culture-contingent signs of trust in emergent relationships'. *Organizational Behavior and Human Decision Processes*, 104, 61–82.
Chen, Z. X., Tsui, A. S. and Farh, J. L. 2002. 'Loyalty to supervisor vs. organizational commitment: relationships to employee performance in China'. *Journal of Occupational and Organizational Psychology*, 75, 339–56.
Cheng, B. S., Chou, L. F., Wu, T. Y., Huang, M. P. and Farh, J. L. 2004. 'Paternalistic leadership and subordinate responses: establishing a leadership model in Chinese organizations'. *Asian Journal of Social Psychology*, 7, 89–117.
Cheng, B. S., Jiang, D. Y. and Riley, H. J. 2003. 'Organizational commitment, supervisory commitment, and employee outcomes in Chinese context: proximal hypothesis or global hypothesis?' *Journal of Organizational Behavior*, 2, 313–34.
Child, J. and Möllering, G. 2003. 'Contextual confidence and active trust development in the Chinese business environment'. *Organization Science*, 14, 69–80.
Chua, R., Morris, M. and Ingram, P. 2005. *The Social Structure of Affect- and Cognition-based Trust in Chinese and American Managerial Networks*. Working Paper. Columbia Business School.
Dietz, G. and Den Hartog, D. 2006. 'Measuring trust inside organizations'. *Personnel Review*, 35(5), 557–88.
Dirks, K. T. and Ferrin, D. L. 2002. 'Trust in leadership: meta-analytic findings and implications for research and practice'. *Journal of Applied Psychology*, 87, 611–28.

Doney, P. M., Cannon, J. P. and Mullen, M. R. 1998. 'Understanding the influence of national culture on the development of trust'. *Academy of Management Review*, 23, 601–20.

Farh, J. L. and Cheng, B. S. 2000. 'A cultural analysis of paternalistic leadership in Chinese organizations'. In J. T. Li, A. S. Tsui and E. Weldon (eds.) *Management and Organizations in the Chinese Context*. London: Macmillan, 85–127.

Fiske, A. P. 1992. 'The four elementary forms of sociality: framework for a unified theory of social relations'. *Psychological Review*, 99,689–723.

Gillespie, N. A. and Mann, L. 2004. 'Transformational leadership and shared values: the building blocks of trust'. Journal of Managerial Psychology, 19(6), 588–607.

Hall, E. T. 1976. *Beyond Culture*. New York: Doubleday.

Hampden-Turner, C. and Trompenaars, F. 1993. *The Seven Cultures of Capitalism*. New York: Currency/Double Day.

Hofstede, G. 1994. 'Management scientists are human'. *Management Science*, 40, 4–13.

2001. *Culture's Consequences: Comparing Values, Behaviors, Institutions and Organizations across Nations*. Thousand Oaks, CA: Sage.

House, R. J., Hanges, P. J., Javidan, M., Dorfman, P. W. and Gupta, P. (eds.) 2004. *Culture, Leadership, and Organizations: The GLOBE Study of 62 Societies*. Thousand Oaks, CA: Sage.

Javidan, M., House, R. J., Dorfman, P. W., Hanges, P. J. and de Luque, M. S. 2006. 'Conceptualizing and measuring cultures and their consequences: a comparative review of GLOBE's and Hofstede's approaches'. *Journal of International Business Studies*, 37, 897–914.

Kağıtçıbaşı, Ç. 1997. 'Individualism and collectivism'. In J. W. Berry, M. H. Segall and Ç. Kağıtçıbaşı (eds.) *Handbook of Cross-Cultural Psychology*, 2nd edn. Boston: Allyn and Bacon, vol. III, 2–49.

Katigbak, M. S., Church, A. T., Guanzon-Lapena, M. A., Carlota, A. J. and del Pilar, G. H. 2002. 'Are indigenous personality dimensions culture specific? Phillipine inventories and the five-factor model'. *Journal of Personality and Social Psychology*, 82, 89–91.

Korsgaard, M. A., Brodt, S. E. and Whitener, E. M. 2002. 'Trust in the face of conflict: the role of managerial trustworthy behavior and organizational context'. *Journal of Applied Psychology*, 87, 312–19.

Kramer, R. M. 1996. 'Divergent realities and convergent disappointments in the hierarchic relation: trust and the intuitive auditor at work'. In R. M. Kramer and T. R. Tyler (eds.) *Trust in Organizations*. Thousand Oaks, CA: Sage, 216–145.

Leung, K. and Bond, M. H. 2004. 'Social axioms: a model for social beliefs in multicultural perspective'. *Advances in Experimental Social Psychology*, 36, 119–97.

Lewicki, R. and Bunker, B. 1996. 'Developing and maintaining trust in work relationships'. In R. M. Kramer and T. R. Tyler (eds.) *Trust in Organizations*. Thousand Oaks, CA: Sage, 114–39.

Lewicki, R. J., McAllister, D. J. and Bies, R. J. 1998. 'Trust and distrust: new relationships and realities'. *Academy of Management Review*, 23, 438–58.

Lewicki, R. J., Tomlinson, E. C. and Gillespie, N. 2006. 'Models of interpersonal trust development: theoretical approaches, empirical evidence, and future directions'. *Journal of Management*, 32(6), 991–1022.

Mayer, R. C., Davis, J. H. and Schoorman, F. D. 1995. 'An integrative model of organizational trust'. *Academy of Management Review*, 20, 709–34.

McAllister, D. J. 1995. 'Affect-based and cognition-based trust as foundations for interpersonal cooperation in organizations'. *Academy of Management Journal*, 38, 24–59.

Meyer, K. E. 2006. 'Asian management research needs more self-confidence'. *Asia Pacific Journal of Management*, 23, 119–37.

Mizrachi, N., Drori, I. and Anspach, R. R. 2007. 'Repertoires of trust: the practice of trust in a multinational organization amid political conflict'. *American Sociological Review*, 72, 143–65.

Morris, M. W., Podolny, J. M. and Ariel, S. 2000. 'Missing relations: incorporating relational constructs into models of culture'. In P. C. Earley and H. Singh (eds.) *Innovations in International and Cross-cultural Management*. Thousand Oaks, CA: Sage, 52–90.

Park, S. H. and Luo, Y. 2001. 'Guanxi and organizational dynamics: organizational networking in Chinese firms'. *Strategic Management Journal*, 22(5), 455–77.

Rousseau, D. M. and Fried, Y. 2001. 'Location, location, location: contextualizing organizational research'. *Journal of Organizational Behavior*, 22, 1–13.

Sanchez-Burks, J. 2005. 'Protestant relational ideology: the cognitive underpinnings and organizational implications of an American anomaly'. *Research in Organizational Behavior*, 26, 265–305.

Sanchez-Burks, J. and Lee, F. 2007. 'Cultural psychology of workways'. In S. Shinobu and D. Cohen (eds.) *Handbook of Cross Cultural Psychology*. New York: Lawrence Erlbaum.

Saunders, M. N. K. and Thornhill, A. 2004. 'Trust and mistrust in organizations: an exploration using an organisational justice framework'. *European Journal of Work and Organisational Psychology*, 13(2), 229–39.

Schoorman, F. D., Mayer, R. C. and Davis, J. H. 1996. 'Empowerment in veterinary clinics: the role of trust in delegation'. Paper presented at the 11th Annual Meeting of Society for Industrial and Organizational Psychology.

    2007. 'An integrative model of organizational trust: past, present, and future'. *Academy of Management Review*, 32(2), 344–54.

Sheppard, B. H. and Sherman, D. M. 1998. 'The grammars of trust: a model and general implications'. *Academy of Management Review*, 23(3), 422–37.

Tan, H. H. and Chee, D. 2005. 'Understanding interpersonal trust in a Confucian-influenced society: an exploratory study'. *International Journal of Cross-cultural Management*, 5, 197–212.

Triandis, H. C. 1995. *Individualism and Collectivism*. Boulder, CO: Westview Press.

Wasti, S. A., Tan, H. H., Brower, H. H. and Önder, C. 2007. 'Cross-cultural measurement of supervisor trustworthiness: an assessment of measurement invariance across three cultures'. *Leadership Quarterly*, 18, 477–89.

Whitener, E. M., Brodt, S. E., Korsgaard, M. A. and Werner, J. M. 1998. 'Managers as initiators of trust: an exchange relationship framework for understanding managerial trustworthy behavior'. *Academy of Management Review*, 23(3), 513–30.

Zand, D. E. 1972. 'Trust and managerial problem solving'. *Administrative Science Quarterly*, 17(2), 229–39.

# 13 | Trust in turbulent times: organizational change and the consequences for intra-organizational trust

VERONICA HOPE-HAILEY, ELAINE FARNDALE
AND CLARE KELLIHER

## Summary

This chapter explores trust in the context of significant corporate change. The context for the study is nine organizations experiencing significant amounts of corporate change. The chapter explores the levels of trust held by different cultural groupings. In particular, it examines trust in cultural groupings based on *job grading*, *age* and *length of service*, highlighting in particular how trust in the employer appears to decline based on length of service. The chapter also investigates the difference in trust levels between employees and managers within their local subcultures and the same employees' trust in their employer and senior management. The chapter explores whether local culture engenders a level of trust in line management which the broader organizational culture cannot deliver particularly at times of transformational change. The chapter interweaves illustrative qualitative material from three of the organizations researched with the overall survey results from the full sample.

We start the chapter by showing how critical trust is to the successful implementation of change programmes, before going on to argue that, despite this criticality, change-programme design fails to take account of varying attitudes and perceptions within different cultural groupings and at different cultural levels. We then present the research questions that guided our analysis before describing the methods we used to collect data, and then presenting and discussing the results.

We conclude that the prescriptive change-management literature, which had informed many of the practitioner approaches to implementing the organizational changes we were researching, needs to take account of two major aspects of trust. First, change-management programme designers need to consider that different levels of trust may be shown by certain employee groupings. Employees cannot, therefore, be treated as a homogeneous group. Groupings exhibiting lower levels of trust may need extra attention or care

336

during the change process to ensure minimal resistance and maximum collaboration.

Second, those responsible for the design of change implementation need to consider whether there are different levels of trust between the organization and the individual and the local line manager and the individual. If the impact of the local culture is stronger and, if the local line manager is more trusted than the senior management or employer, then the responsibility for leading change may need to be devolved to local managers rather than held as the preserve of senior managers. Overall these two findings point to a need for a more discriminating appreciation of the pivotal role of trust during change which may then result in greater effectiveness in organizational transition work.

## Introduction

### *The importance of trust in times of turbulent change*

Maintaining trust through change becomes all important because transition increases employees' sense of vulnerability due to perceptions about the uncertainty of the future and the loss of the past (Rousseau *et al.*, 1998: 395). If a corporate change requires individuals to change their attitudes or behaviours, then the employer is asking those people to discard old routines, perceptions and certainties and instead consider new ways of thinking, feeling and behaving (Bridges, 1991). In profound transformational change, such as privatizations or mergers and acquisitions, people's individual identities may be disrupted (Beech and Johnson, 2005). However, whilst experiencing that disruption at an individual level, people also cannot be sure that they are capable of making the change or whether the change means they will feel better or worse in the future (Beckhard and Harris, 1987). This only increases their sense of vulnerability. As soon as the organization starts to go into transition, the past starts to appear to be a place of security and safety, whereas the future represents a place of uncertainty and confusion (Adams *et al.*, 1976). Persuading people to make these transitions is a huge management challenge and we argue that it is one that is helped if 1) trusting relationships exist at all levels within the organization, but if not, 2) the design of the change implementation recognizes where trust relationships are weakest and manages the transition with that in mind.

Trust has been defined as the 'willingness to be vulnerable' (Mayer *et al.*, 1995) and so, in organizational change contexts, this would mean a willingness to test out new ways of working despite a feeling of vulnerability. The definition of trust assumed in this chapter includes both social and relational aspects of trust:

First and foremost, trust entails a state of perceived vulnerability or risk that is derived from individuals' uncertainty regarding the motives, intentions and prospective actions of others on whom they depend. (Kramer, 1999: 571)

Based on this assertion, trust exists provided that three elements are present in the relationship: first, the willingness to be vulnerable; in other words the individual must be willing to make themselves vulnerable to the actions of other people within the relationship (Rousseau *et al.*, 1998); second, that there is a level of uncertainty in the outcome of the interaction between the parties in the relationship; third, that there is a dependence between those individuals such that one individual is dependent upon the action of others to achieve a successful outcome.

In his paper on social embeddedness, Granovetter (1985) defines trust as emerging out of personal relationships within an organizational context:

Actors do not behave or decide as atoms outside a social context . . . Their attempts at purposive action are instead embedded in concrete, ongoing systems of social relations. (Granovetter, 1985: 487)

Therefore the relationships within an organization at a time of change, and the specific context of that organization, all shape the degrees of trust held at different levels of the organization.

Unlike other behavioural elements that are features of an individual's character, such as honesty, trust is a parameter which is dependent upon the relationship between two individuals: the trustor and the trustee (Bhattacharya *et al.*, 1998; Butler, 1991; Jones and George, 1998). Trust can only be assessed on the basis of the perception of the two individuals involved in the relationship. In other words, it is the link between the two that determines the type and level of trust – not the individual's propensity to trust per se. If trust is to improve the adaptive capabilities with which organizations and individuals react to change, it is the relationship between individuals, their managers and the organization that needs to be studied.

The related benefits of trust relationships within organizations include faster decision making and the acceptance of decisions. The latter is particularly relevant to a study of change. Uzzi's (1997) research demonstrated that where good trust relationships existed, the information required to make risky decisions was not, in fact, systematically compiled and analysed by individuals. Instead, with these high levels of trust existing, favourable interpretations were made of situations even if individuals had limited information and certainty. Uzzi suggests that trust acts as a heuristic: 'a predilection to assume the best when interpreting another's motives and actions' (Uzzi, 1997: 43) and this speeds up decision making even where full information is difficult to establish such as in times of organizational change.

## Different cultural contexts and their impact upon trust

We now examine the impact of different cultural groupings on trust levels within organizations. There has been a tendency within the prescriptive change literature to present culture as a single entity within organizations. Instead many other commentators have argued that it is important to see an organization's culture as an 'amalgam' of many cultures (Morgan and Ogbonna, 2008: 41; Sackmann, 1992) Whilst there may be shared values across different groups, thereby supporting an integrationist view of culture, there is also contestation and difference, thereby giving credence to the differentiation and fragmentation views of organizational culture (Martin, 1992).

Chao and Moon (2005) introduced the idea of a cultural mosaic whereby employees are seen not only as members of organizational cultures, but also as part of cultures based on demographic, geographic and associative groupings. Demographic cultures are defined as physical definitions and social identities derived from parents or ancestors such as age, ethnicity, gender and race. In this research analysis we examine age and length of service (see also Pfeffer, 1983). Geographic cultures are defined as natural or man-made features of a region that can shape group identities such as climate, location or temperature. These aspects of cultural groupings do not feature in the research presented here as all organizations were based in one country, the UK.

Associative cultures are defined as formal and informal groupings that an individual chooses to associate with such as their work group, or their profession, or their religion (Chao and Moon, 2005: 1130). Here we consider trust levels amongst different job gradings and also trust in local subcultures as distinct from corporate or organizational cultures. Subcultures are defined as organizational subsets with regular shared interaction, whose members see themselves as having a distinct identity and a common set of problems and understandings (Van Maanen and Barley, 1985). As this forms a major feature of our research we examine this in greater depth.

The importance of recognizing that attitudes to change may vary at different levels of the organization is well established (Corley, 2004). For instance, your job grading will determine your proximity to the strategic decision making that has prompted the change. In turn, your proximity to the change will increase your awareness and understanding of the reasons for the change and the intentions of the senior strategic decision making. The further away from the decision making, the more dependent the employee becomes on the communication and persuasion of their local manager. However, in change contexts the various actors and stakeholders have a multitude of interests and loyalties which means that loyalty and trust in the overall organization's change intentions may not be the primary motivator for either employee or managerial behaviour. Hallier and James (1997) argue that managers have difficulty representing their own and their employer's interests simultaneously as in effect they are participating in two employment relationships – one with those they manage and one with those who manage them. They also note that when middle- or lower-level managers feel aggrieved by their own losses within an organization, they may seek redress through their relationship with their subordinates. Sometimes local managers are against the changes themselves perhaps because they might lose status, power or even their own jobs (Sims, 2004). In effect, in communicating with their staff, these agents can make or break trust levels in the relationship that their subordinates have with both the employer and with senior management, particularly in times of turbulent change (Coyle-Shapiro and Shore, 2007).

Yet the prescriptive change literature also assumes that middle and line managers as agents of the organization will act in the interests of the organization (Coyle-Shapiro and Shore, 2007). Whilst some extant research has recognized the tensions implicit in the middle/local line management roles, as both advocates for employees and at the same time implementers of senior management's strategic plans (Balogun and Johnson, 2004), this research seldom seemed to influence the change-management plans of the senior managers in the organizations we researched. Local middle managers are often the 'shock absorbers' for the emotional turbulence generated by senior management strategies for the people they manage (Frost and Robinson, 1999). They also become buffers, shielding their teams from information and change pressures that are not essential for them to know. Moreover, as discussed above, middle managers are often as much the recipients of detrimental change as the implementers.

Therefore, the three-way relationship between the local line manager and the local employees and the organization as a whole is problematic. The relationship between local employees and the line managers in the local subculture may mediate between the trust relationship between the local employee and the overall organization. In addition, these relationships may be moderated by the trust levels within the cultural groupings such as age, length of service and job grading. These assertions form the basis of the data analysis which follows.

First, we set out the methods used to collect data before describing the context and the change scenarios we researched within the different organizations. We present our findings on trust levels across the whole sample, analysing the data by using both demographic and associative cultural groupings. We illustrate these findings with detail from three organizations, particularly focusing on the unique cultural and contextual factors that influenced the differences in results. We conclude the chapter by discussing the implications of these findings for practice in terms of the employer's deeper understanding of trust in the employee–organization relationship, and also for the implementation of strategic change in both private and public sector organizations.

Summarizing, this leads to the following research questions which are further addressed in this chapter. First, we consider the cultural mosaic. Specifically, we explore the impact of job grade, age and length of service on levels of trust in the local line manager and trust in the employer/senior management. Second, we take a comparative perspective and consider how levels of trust in the employer compare with levels of trust in local line managers across the different organizations. In particular, we also explore whether trust in the local line manager is an antecedent of trust in the employer. Finally, given the potential importance of the cultural mosaic, we explore whether job grade, age and length of service moderate the relationship between trust in the local line manager and trust in the employer.

## Methods

Data for this study were collected by the Change Management Consortium (CMC) in the UK. The CMC was set up in 2001 as a collaboration of practitioners and academics to share experiences and discuss recent research and development within the area of change management. This chapter focuses on research conducted from 2003 onwards which assessed change receptivity within the organizations.

### Quantitative data

Quantitative data were collected using questionnaires distributed within the nine organizations (see Table 13.1). These included four public-sector and five private-sector organizations, all of which, at the time of issuing the questionnaire, were undergoing major organizational change. For the purpose of anonymity, pseudonyms based on sector are used to identify organizations.

**Table 13.1** *Respondent organizations*

| Organization | Sector | Activities | Type of change | No. of responses included |
|---|---|---|---|---|
| AdviceCo | private | professional services | cultural change programme | 96 |
| EngineerCo | private | manufacturing | several mergers and acquisitions | 86 |
| FinanceCo | private | financial services | merger | 192 |
| FoodCo | private | food manufacturer | global centralization | 83 |
| HealthCo | private | healthcare manufacturer | restructuring due to automation | 171 |
| CommsCo | public | communication agency | merger | 163 |
| AdminCo | public | administration | merger | 202 |
| ProcessCo | public | sub-division of AdminCo | introduction of lean processing | 204 |
| RiskCo | public | sub-division of AdminCo | culture change and downsizing | 208 |

From the nine organizations a total of 5,032 responses were received; however, because more than half of these came from AdminCo and RiskCo, a random sample of 15 per cent and 7 per cent of the cases from these two organizations, respectively, have been included here to reduce bias in the data. This resulted in 1,405 usable cases. The spread of respondents across the cases is represented in Table 13.1.

## Measures

The questionnaire was designed to gain general data on how respondents felt about their organization and included, amongst others, questions relating to organizational commitment, trust and justice, clarity of strategy and receptivity to change. Two scales in particular are used further here: *trust in employer* and *trust in local line manager*. For each measure, participants provided responses based on a 5-point Likert scale (1 = strongly disagree; 5 = strongly agree). The data were analysed using principal components analysis (PCA), which resulted in two clear factors emerging corresponding with the two levels of trust identified (see Appendix). No items were removed from the analysis, as all loaded sufficiently onto the expected factors. Mean scores for each factor were calculated for the analyses which follow.

The measure for *trust in employer/senior management* includes four items from Cook and Wall (1980), which explored interpersonal trust by measuring faith in the intentions of management and confidence in the actions of management, and seven items from the 'bases of trust' work by Gabarro and Athos (1976). In total, eleven items were included, with example items being: 'I feel confident that senior management will always try to treat me fairly', 'Senior management is sincere in its attempts to take account of the employees' point of view' and 'Senior management can be trusted to make sensible decisions for this organization's future'. In each organization, it was first discussed what terms would best be understood internally. For example, in the professional services firm, the term 'senior management' was replaced by 'partners' as this was the most common phraseology in this setting. The scale's reliability is high (Cronbach's alpha = 0.943). No distinction emerged in the data differentiating between the items relating to the employer or senior management; therefore all items were included in this single measure.

Trust in the local line manager is measured using six items based on three items from Cook and Wall (1980) and three items from Unden (1996). These focus on how well employees feel supported by and have confidence in their manager. An example item is 'I get support from my line manager when I have a problem at work'. The Cronbach's alpha for this scale is good (0.899).

## Qualitative data

In addition to the questionnaire, we conducted approximately twenty-five interviews and focus groups within each of the nine organizations. Interviews and focus groups were designed to elicit data on how individuals had experienced the recent changes in their organization and also about engagement, voice and support. Interviews and focus groups were conducted in the workplace and lasted approximately one hour each. These were audio-taped and subsequently transcribed. In addition we collected documentary evidence on the change programmes and were invited to give feedback on the research at various senior management meetings. We use these qualitative data from three of the organizations here to illustrate our broader findings. One of these, AdviceCo, was examined in depth because it reported high levels of trust; in contrast, ProcessCo was a public-sector organization with poor levels of trust whilst FoodCo was examined because the trigger for change, the imposition of global reporting structures, was an interesting development causing a decrease in trust in the UK unit.

## Results: cultural mosaics of trust across organizations

This section refers to the combined data from the nine case organizations to illustrate the first question raised regarding cultural mosaics of trust, drawing out how different associative cultures (by job grade) and demographic cultures (by age/length of service) perceive levels of trust. We also make reference to some of the individual case organizations to illustrate our findings in more detail. Table 13.2 shows the descriptive data of the key variables. As can be seen, there is a high correlation between age and length of service (as could be expected), therefore only length of service is considered further here. Trust in employer and trust in line manager are both calculated based on the mean score of the factor items.

ANOVA tests were first carried out to check whether *trust in employer* varied significantly by the respondent's job grade or how long they had been with this employer. The results for both variables are significant: job grade $(F(4,1380) = 17.588$, $p<0.001)$; length of service $(F(3,1395) = 38.184$, $p<0.001)$. Based on post-hoc tests (Tukey HSD), the lower the grade of staff (administrative $[M = 2.87]$ and professional/technical $[M = 2.79]$), the more likely employees were to be reporting *low* levels of trust in their employer $(p<0.005)$ (compared to managers $[M = 3.21]$ and senior managers $[M = 3.34]$). For length of service, those with the shortest service (less than

Table 13.2 *Means, standard deviations and correlations*

| | Mean | SD | Grade | Age | Length of service | Trust in employer |
|---|---|---|---|---|---|---|
| Grade[i] | 2.85 | 1.1 | | | | |
| Age[ii] | 3.67 | 1.1 | 0.262*** | | | |
| Length of service[iii] | 2.03 | 1.1 | 0.354*** | 0.674*** | | |
| Trust in employer | 2.98 | 0.9 | 0.123*** | −0.261*** | −0.282*** | |
| Trust in line manager | 3.66 | 0.8 | 0.091** | −0.041 | −0.039 | 0.419*** |

* p<0.05.
** p<.01.
*** p<.001.
[i] 5 categories: 1 = manual, 2 = administrative, 3 = professional/technical, 4 = management, 5 = senior management.
[ii] 5 categories: 1 = less than 20 years, 2 = 20–29 years, 3 = 30–39 years, 4 = 40–49 years, 5 = 50 years or over.
[iii] 4 categories: 1 = 5 years or less, 2 = 6–15 years, 3 = 16–25 years, 4 = 26 years or more.

five years) showed a significantly *higher* level of trust in the employer (M = 3.24, p < 0.001). As length of service increased up to twenty-five years, the level of trust *decreased* (6–15 years service: M= 2.93; 16–25 years: M= 2.67) and then stabilized with the longest lengths of service (>25 years: M = 2.70). This therefore provides evidence of both associative (in this case job grade) and demographic (here, length of service) cultures impacting on employee trust in the employer.

Two of the case studies illustrate the impact of demographic cultures in more detail. At AdviceCo, a leading professional services organization, which had recently undergone restructuring and was implementing an incremental cultural change programme, levels of trust in the employer were high (see also Table 13.4). Here employees were largely young with relatively short length of service. Just under half of the survey respondents (46.9 per cent) were aged under twenty-nine and a large number (83.1 per cent) expected to stay with the organization for less than five years. At the time of the research, 78 per cent of the labour force at AdviceCo had less than five years' service. In addition to high levels of trust these staff recorded high levels of commitment to the organization and job satisfaction and had a strong sense of fairness concerning the performance management system. This situation was explained by respondents that whilst many felt that AdviceCo was not going to be their employer for life, they were satisfied with the transactional aspects of their employment relationship (AdviceCo was reported to be honest and straightforward about the nature of the employment relationship at the time of recruitment); moreover, they believed the training and development offered to them contributed to their employability outside of the firm.

By contrast at ProcessCo, part of a government agency where lean processing had been introduced into the organization of white-collar work, levels of trust in the employer were lower (see also Table 13.4). The respondents here typically had long service. Half of the respondents had worked for the Civil Service for between sixteen and thirty years and another 13 per cent had more than thirty years' service. Around half expected to stay with the organization for at least ten years, and one-third who were expecting to leave said that this would be due to retirement. The changes challenged their existing notion of the employment deal, representing work intensification and a threat to their security of employment in an environment where few alternative job opportunities existed.

Moving on to explore the variation between the culture groups in *trust in line manager* using ANOVA, there was much less variation by job grade and length of service. Job grade still showed a significant difference $(F(4,1378) = 4.232, p < 0.01)$, however, length of service did not have a significant effect $(F(3,1393) = 1.373, p = 0.249)$. The post-hoc tests (Tukey HSD) showed no significant differences between length of service levels. However, job grade did explain some variation: manual staff $(M = 3.45)$ showed significantly *lower* levels of trust in line manager $(p < 0.05)$ than professional/technical $(M = 3.73)$ and managerial staff $(M = 3.75)$. Unlike with *trust in employer*, only the job grade dimension of the cultural mosaic can explain some slight variation in the levels of trust employees have in their line management.

## *The relationship between trust at two cultural levels*

Considering the second question posed above, regarding how the levels of trust in employer compare with levels of trust in line manager across the different organizations, what is emerging here is that there is indeed a clear difference between these two organizational levels. Looking at the mean scores in Table 13.2, the mean trust in line management was 3.66, compared to 2.98 for trust in employer: employees were in general more positive about their line manager relationship. This then raises our third question of whether trust in line management can be seen as a reflection of the higher level organization and hence as an antecedent of trust in the employer as a whole.

The data were explored to uncover this direct relationship between trust in line manager and trust in the employer. The cultural groupings by job grade and length of service were also explored to see the extent to which they might play a moderating role in this relationship. The correlation between the two main variables (trust in line manager and trust in employer – see Table 13.2) is 0.419 (p<0.001). This correlation falls well within acceptable limits to assume multicollinearity will not be a problem.[1]

The results show, as seen above, that as length of service increases, trust in employer *decreases*, and as seniority increases, trust in employer *increases* (see Table 13.3, model 1). These associative and demographic variables alone account for 12.6 per cent of variance in trust in employer. By adding trust in line manager to the equation (see Table 13.3, model 2) a total of 31.2 per cent of variance in trust in employer is then accounted for. This shows that trust in line manager is a particularly important explanatory variable for trust in the employer $(\beta = 0.434, p = < 0.001)$. To test for moderation, the interaction effects of job grade and length of service are added. The results (see Table 13.3,

---

[1] In addition, a PCA factor analysis including all variables together produced a clear two-actor solution: one with items relating to trust in line manager, and the other to trust in employer. The tolerance (0.984) test also indicates a lack of multicollinearity.

Table 13.3 *Multiple regression results: trust in employer*

|  | Standardized $\beta$ | | |
| --- | --- | --- | --- |
|  | *Model 1* | *Model 2* | *Model 3* |
| Job grade | 0.245*** | 0.187*** | 0.060 |
| Length of service | −0.352*** | −0.327*** | −0.303** |
| Trust in line manager |  | 0.434*** | 0.373*** |
| Grade × Trust in line manager |  |  | 0.156 |
| Length of service × Trust in line manager |  |  | −0.024 |
| $R^2$ | 0.126 | 0.312 | 0.313 |
| Adjusted $R^2$ | 0.125 | 0.310 | 0.310 |
| $\Delta R^2$ |  | 0.186*** | 0.001 |
| Total F | 99.572*** | 208.076*** | 125.397*** |
| N | 1380 | 1379 | 1377 |

\* p<0.05.
\*\* p<0.01.
\*\*\* p<.001.

model 3) show that neither effect is significant, thus no moderating relation-ship was found. Hence the relationship between the trust employees have in their line manager and their trust in the employer is robust, and does not vary significantly based on an individual's job grade or how long they have been with the organization. The mean scale scores are used here in this analysis for a high-level comparison; individual scale items are reported further in the case descriptions below.

This analysis across the data set has shown that there is little variation in *trust in line management* according to the cultural groupings explored here. However, there is variation in *trust in employer*. Here, we find that the longer-serving employees and those who have not moved into manage-ment positions were most likely to be reporting *low* levels of trust in their employer (see Albrecht, 2002; Andersson, 1996; Dean *et al.*, 1998; Reichers *et al.*, 1997; Watt and Piotrowski, 2008). Those employees who were relatively new to the organization, or those who were already in management positions, were most likely to report *high* levels of trust in the employer. Subcultures aside, trust in line manager was found to be the strongest predictor of trust in employer, highlighting the important role that managers play in trust relationships. These findings have implications for how organizations manage trust during times of change, as will be discussed below.

## Comparative perspective: differences between organizations

Having explored the overall picture of the relationships between different subgroups and their levels of trust, we turn now to exploring how the different organizations compare with each other. Using ANOVA tests, we found *trust in employer* to vary significantly between organizations $(F(8,1393) = 59.910$, $p < 0.001)$, with the highest levels being reported in AdviceCo $(M = 3.66)$ and the lowest in ProcessCo $(M = 2.49)$ and RiskCo $(M = 2.28)$. *Trust in line management* was also found to differ significantly $(F(8,1391) = 2.315$, $p < 0.05)$, being highest in AdviceCo $(M = 3.89)$ but lowest in HealthCo $(M = 3.55)$. In order to explore these comparisons in more depth, we calculated the difference between trust in employer and trust in line managers in each organization (by subtracting the mean trust in line manager factor score from the mean trust in employer factor score per organization), which we term the 'employer–manager trust gap' (see Table 13.4).

AdviceCo records one of the lowest employer–manager trust gaps (0.23), as well as recording the highest levels of trust in both levels of the organization. For this reason, we present this company first as a case study. FoodCo has one of the highest differentials between trust in employer and trust in line manager of all the private sector organizations (0.35), and we explore the reasons for that also as a separate case. Table 13.4 also shows that the largest employer–manager trust gaps are recorded by all four of the public-sector organizations: CommsCo, AdminCo, ProcessCo and RiskCo. We explore one of these, ProcessCo, further as a case study to see why this might be occurring.

**Table 13.4** *Cross-company comparison of employer–manager trust gap*

| Sector | Organization | Trust in employer mean | Trust in line manager mean | Difference between means |
|---|---|---|---|---|
| **Private** | EngineerCo | 3.55 | 3.75 | −0.20 |
| | AdviceCo | 3.66 | 3.89 | −0.23 |
| | HealthCo | 3.21 | 3.55 | −0.34 |
| | FoodCo | 3.43 | 3.78 | −0.35 |
| | FinanceCo | 3.15 | 3.57 | −0.42 |
| **Public** | CommsCo | 3.15 | 3.79 | −0.64 |
| | AdminCo | 2.97 | 3.77 | −0.80 |
| | ProcessCo | 2.49 | 3.67 | −1.18 |
| | RiskCo | 2.28 | 3.67 | −1.39 |
| **Overall** | | 2.98 | 3.70 | −0.63 |

Looking firstly at AdviceCo where we found a low employer–manager trust gap (see Table 13.4), from the interviews we identified a number of factors which help explain the similarity between the trust scores for the employer and the manager. First, there was a relatively low degree of hierarchy in this organization. AdviceCo is a partnership with approximately one partner for every seventeen employees. Consequently, employees reported frequent contact with the partner they worked for resulting in more of a shared culture. Furthermore, given the ownership structure of the business, partners tended to be seen as 'the employer'. Second, in practice many employees spent much of the time out of the office and this may have prevented subcultures emerging. Whilst there were some differences between the various offices we researched across the UK, they were insufficiently strong to counter the overall culture of the organization. Third, this was not an organization in decline. Given past and present performance, employees had reasons to trust the managers of the organization. The cultural change programme was also generally seen as a positive initiative which was intended to help the organization grow, hence employees in this organization did not feel threatened by the change.

Across the private sector organizations in the study, FoodCo had the second greatest difference in mean scores between trust in the employer and trust in line management (see Table 13.4). This indicates a mismatch between the higher levels of trust employees have in line management, and the lower levels of trust in the employer as a whole. Here we found evidence of the gap having been created by the changes brought about by restructuring. The move to a global structure and the centralization of strategy had in some senses distanced the employer, although not the line manager.

Prior to the global reorganization, managers reported that they had autonomy in decisions about the operation of the company in the UK. However, they indicated that a consequence of the global reorganization was a change to where decisions were made in the organization. Managers reported that these changes had impacted on their roles and that they were now expected just to implement decisions in which they had had little input. They felt de-skilled, de-valued and disempowered as mere implementers of strategy and policy rather than formulators. Overall, there appeared to some resentment about how local managers were being treated, in part because it was seen as a waste of talented resource that had been developed over the years: 'we're just going to become a cog of the American machine'. One of the questions that illustrated such resentment was on the subject of senior management integrity. One interesting aspect to this is that of the 19 per cent who either agreed or strongly agreed that senior management would be prepared to gain advantage by deceiving the workers (see also Table 13.5), a high number of these

Table 13.5 *Attitudes towards senior management (per cent of respondents)*

| | | Advice Co | Engineer Co | Finance Co | Food Co | Health Co | Comms Co | Admin Co | Process Co | Risk Co |
|---|---|---|---|---|---|---|---|---|---|---|
| Our senior management would be prepared to gain advantage by deceiving the workers | Agree | 12.5 | 9.4 | 16.8 | 18.1 | 23.4 | 14.9 | 22.5 | 29.9 | 33.8 |
| | Strongly agree | 2.1 | 1.2 | 5.3 | 1.2 | 8.8 | 4.3 | 7.5 | 17.6 | 20.8 |
| I have a great deal of trust in management | Agree | 45.8 | 39.5 | 25.7 | 36.1 | 29.4 | 19.8 | 6 | 2.5 | 5.3 |
| | Strongly agree | 9.4 | 4.7 | 1.6 | 2.4 | 8.2 | 1.9 | 1.5 | 1 | 1 |
| My employer is open and upfront with me | Agree | 55.2 | 50 | 40.8 | 37.3 | 33.3 | 35.2 | 43.8 | 27.6 | 9.7 |
| | Strongly agree | 8.3 | 8.1 | 2.1 | 6 | 10.1 | 3.1 | 4.5 | 4.4 | 0.5 |
| Senior management are well informed about what people at lower levels think | Agree | 11.5 | 4.7 | 14.2 | 9.6 | 21.2 | 10.7 | 12.4 | 7.4 | 6.3 |
| | Strongly agree | 1 | 1.2 | 0.5 | 0 | 2.6 | 1.9 | 1 | 1.5 | 2.4 |
| Senior management can be trusted to make sensible decisions for this organization's future | Agree | 58.3 | 53.5 | 39.3 | 53 | 39.4 | 22.4 | 12.5 | 4.4 | 3.9 |
| | Strongly agree | 16.7 | 4.7 | 2.1 | 2.4 | 5.9 | 2.5 | 1 | 1 | 0.5 |
| I feel confident that senior management will always try to treat me fairly | Agree | 49 | 51.2 | 29.3 | 43.4 | 31.2 | 34 | 23.5 | 11.3 | 10.1 |
| | Strongly agree | 9.4 | 1.2 | 2.6 | 3.6 | 5.3 | 4.3 | 0.5 | 0.5 | 1.4 |

were senior managers themselves. This could be because they had issues with their senior managers in the global corporation. This was supported by comments in the interviews such as:

I'm not sure that actually people in very senior management really care about those in lower management. (Director/Senior Manager)

Looking at the survey data, only 38 per cent of respondents either agreed or strongly agreed that they had a great deal of trust in management and only 43 per cent either agreed or strongly agreed that their employer was open and upfront with them (see Table 13.5). In addition, only 10 per cent of the respondents agreed that senior management were well informed about what lower levels think and feel. Perhaps some of the uncertainties and frustration can be summed up in one person's statement that 'we joined a different organization'. People fondly talked of the fun and vibrant atmosphere that had characterized FoodCo in the 1990s and another reflected that 'the rules of the game' appeared to have changed for individual employees.

In FoodCo we also saw the impact of 'geographic' cultures (see Chao and Moon, 2005). The UK head office was located in a pleasant English county town about 100 miles outside London. It was characterized by a good quality of life, but with limited alternative employment opportunities in the immediate area. There was a sense that the location of 'EnglishTown' was an attraction and also a constraint and several respondents indicated that once people came to FoodCo they did not often leave. The environment of EnglishTown meant there was reluctance on the part of senior managers to step out of their comfortable world and from their perception that FoodCo UK was a cohesive and positive culture. Whilst the UK unit was an autonomous national unit, there was trust in the employer because for them the employer was the UK operation. After the global restructuring the employer became the US corporate centre. Through the restructuring they experienced a loss of status and de-skilling in the process; they felt they had unwittingly become middle managers in a globalized corporation. This loss of status and lack of involvement in decisions had effectively eroded trust. On top of this there was a sense of a national unit in decline and facing an uncertain future as production units were shifted to emerging economies. In the face of uncertainty managers may hold on to where they can find certainty, which is in the local culture of the past not the corporate culture of the future. In the absence of anything culturally positive from the USA that might replace the cohesion of the former UK culture, managers were unwilling or unable to accept their vulnerability and therefore trust in the employer declined.

Finally, ProcessCo recorded one of the highest mismatches between trust in employer and trust in line management across the organizations in this study. In particular, levels of trust in the employer were low, but with average levels of trust in line managers, comparatively speaking. Respondents perceived that there was in general a positive, supportive local office environment created by colleagues and line management. As many as 85 per cent either agreed or strongly agreed with the statement 'I get along with my line manager'. However, the response was somewhat different when asked about senior management of the government department. Only 5 per cent either agreed or strongly agreed that senior management could be trusted, and 48 per cent either agreed or strongly agreed that they would be prepared to gain advantage by deceit (see Table 13.5). Furthermore, 77 per cent either disagreed or strongly disagreed that senior management were well informed about people at lower levels thoughts and feelings. Upward and downward communication was seen as poor and half of respondents also felt that relations with the trade unions were mediocre. Levels of job satisfaction and organizational commitment were also very low.

The units we researched in ProcessCo were situated a long way from the central government department in London and in each unit a strong local/ geographic culture had emerged. A history of little performance accountability almost inevitably meant that a change intervention designed to measure and improve performance would be resisted. One theme that emerged was that although the processes and techniques had changed, the culture appeared to have changed little. This meant that for some, the acceptance of lean processing consisted of a certain amount of lip service, or was seen as a pragmatic move for avoiding job cuts by redirecting work:

So you have got managers who have got along, they are operating the change process because it says so on a piece of paper, but not because they believe it. (Senior Manager)

In some respects frontline managers seemed to have 'jumped into the trenches' with those that they managed. Line managers who had failed to tackle performance in the past were faced with a choice of showing loyalty to the local culture, or embracing the new environment. Since the change intervention was led by a consulting firm, it was easier for local managers to resist it too and ally themselves with their workforce. In addition, the threat of job cuts, coupled with few alternative opportunities in the local labour market, made employees feel threatened. In the face of threat they responded negatively to the employer.

## Discussion

Taking the survey and case-study data together, we see a picture emerging of where demographic and associative cultures have an influence on the level of trust reported in both distal and proximal exchange relationships. Whilst the levels of trust in employer were generally low, differences were observed on the basis of length of service and grade seniority, suggesting the significance of demographic and associative cultures. Furthermore, we found much higher levels of trust reported in the relationship with the line manager than with the employer, but with less variation according to different culture groupings.

These findings also reveal that levels of trust may vary at the distal level (the relationship with the senior management/employer) and the proximal (relationship with line manager) level. We have termed this difference the 'employer–manager trust gap'. The existence of this trust gap highlights an important role for line managers in the change-management process, since they may be able to maintain trust levels with employees, even where the levels of trust in the organization have been eroded. However, this role may also have a corrosive effect, since trust may be maintained by 'siding' with employee rather than employer interests.

## *Implications for practice*

These findings have important implications for practice. First, our results illustrate the significance of the employee–organization relationship and its effect on levels of trust in the process of delivering change in organizations. It is important for employers to consider the implications of trust levels in the design and implementation of change-management programmes. Second, practitioners should consider the influence of demographic cultures upon trust levels. Employees with shorter lengths of service reported higher levels of trust in employers, yet these factors did not significantly impact upon trust in line management. The case studies offer some explanations for these results: at ProcessCo the perception of the employer reneging on the long-standing public sector psychological contract for civil servants affected levels of trust in the employer. In FoodCo it was the loss of status for managers in the older generation that was the problem. Those at AdviceCo who were young and had good employability appeared relatively unconcerned by the transactional nature of their psychological contract. They had not experienced anything else and so did not experience a perception of loss. This may indicate that this is a generational problem – only time will tell.

Third, designers of change programmes should also consider the various local subcultures within an organization. In units which are both isolated and disconnected from the centre, like ProcessCo, strong subcultures can emerge. In the case of FoodCo this had been a deliberate business strategy in the past: multinational units were expected to develop as national profit centres and a strong culture might be expected. In both cases local cultures seemed attractive to employees, but the centre as the employer was seen to be eroding that attraction, hence the reduced levels of trust. In addition, the employer was perceived to put little effort into rebuilding a cultural future. It is difficult to transfer trust from a stable existing culture into something that is undefined.

Finally, in both the cases of ProcessCo and FoodCo we can see the critical role that local managers play in mediating between the employer and their local employees. They may be able to persuade their employees to trust in the future and help rebuild a new culture for the employer within their local units. However, in both these cases managers chose not to transform the reservoir of trust shown to them as individuals for the corporate good. In the way that change was being implemented in both these companies, little was done to empower the local managers (in FoodCo's case, the senior managers who were being de-skilled into middle managers) within the change process.

Furthermore, we can see the corrosive impact of change in organizational units that are in decline. Whether it is global restructuring or public-sector rationalization, these are change processes that communicate organizational decline and loss. When it is the employer that is instigating the change, trust is hard to maintain.

## Concluding comments

In conclusion, cultural mosaics are fundamental to understanding intra-organizational trust. Future research might be directed at uncovering further evidence of the importance of cultural subgroups, particularly in employer-level trust. The distinction between trust in different levels of the organization (employer/line manager) is also a key factor to understanding organizational transformation. This crucial role that the manager plays between employee and employer should be explored in future research, to help us draw out further the implications for practice. It could be argued therefore that managers have a crucial role in two areas: 1) shaping the responses of those cultural groupings whose levels of trust in the employer are low; and 2) ensuring that the strength of local subcultures within organizations does not undermine employees' trust in the employer. Generally speaking, this chapter records low levels of trust in the 'distal' exchange relationship between employees and the senior management/employer, but comparatively higher levels of trust in all but one of the organizations in the 'proximal' exchange relationship between employees and their line managers (see Coyle-Shapiro and Shore, 2007).

## Appendix: factor analysis

### *Trust in employer*

| Item | Loading | Alpha |
|---|---|---|
| I believe my employer has high integrity. | 0.870 | 0.943 |
| I have a great deal of trust in management. | 0.870 | |
| Senior management is sincere in its attempts to take account of the employees' point of view. | 0.858 | |
| I feel confident that senior management will always try to treat me fairly. | 0.852 | |
| In general, I believe my employer's intentions are good. | 0.845 | |
| Senior management can be trusted to make sensible decisions for this organization's future. | 0.839 | |
| Management cares about the needs of employees. | 0.806 | |
| I think my employer treats me fairly. | 0.735 | |
| My employer is open and upfront with me. | 0.735 | |
| Our senior management would be prepared to gain advantage by deceiving the workers (reverse). | 0.610 | |
| My employer treats me in a consistent fashion. | 0.579 | |
| *Eigenvalue* | 8.615 | |
| *Percentage of variance (extraction)* | 50.674 | |

### *Trust in line manager*

| Item | Loading | Alpha |
|---|---|---|
| My line manager is sincere in his/her attempts to take account of the employees' point of view. | 0.856 | 0.899 |
| I get support from my line manager when I have a problem at work. | 0.832 | |
| I get along with my line manager. | 0.831 | |
| My line manager is good at his/her job. | 0.807 | |
| I feel confident that management will always try to treat me fairly. | 0.748 | |
| My line manager gives me feedback on how well I am performing in my work. | 0.697 | |
| *Eigenvalue* | 2.815 | |
| *Percentage of variance (extraction)* | 16.599 | |

# References

Albrecht, S. L. 2002. 'Perceptions of integrity, competence and trust in senior management as determinants of cynicism towards change'. *Public Administration and Management*, 7(4), 320–45.

Adams, J., Hayes, J. and Hopson, B. 1976. *Transition: Understanding and Managing Personal Change*. London: Martin Robertson and Company.

Andersson, L. M. 1996. 'Employee cynicism: an examination using a contract violation framework'. *Human Relations*, 49(11), 1395–418

Balogun, J. and Johnson, G. 2004. 'Organizational restructuring and middle manager sensemaking'. *Academy of Management Journal*, 47, 523–49.

Bhattacharya, R., Devinney, T. M. and Pillutla, M. M. 1998. 'A formal model of trust based on outcomes'. *Academy of Management Review*, 23(3), 459–73.

Beckhard, R. and Harris, R. 1987. *Organizational Transitions: Managing Complex Change*. Reading MA: Addison Wesley.

Beech, N. and Johnson, P. 2005. 'Discourses of disrupted identities in the practice of strategic change: the mayor, the street-fighter and the insider-out'. *Journal of Organizational Change Management*, 18(1), 31–47.

Bridges, W. 1991. *Managing Transitions: Making the Most of Change*. Wokingham: Addison-Wesley.

Butler Jr, J. K. 1991. 'Toward understanding and measuring conditions of trust: evolution of a trust inventory (OTI)'. *Journal of Management*, 17(3), 643–63.

Chao, G. T. and Moon, H. 2005. 'The cultural mosaic: a metatheory for understanding the complexity of culture'. *Journal of Applied Psychology*, 90, 1128–40.

Cook, J. and Wall, T. 1980. 'New work attitude measures of trust, organizational commitment and personal need non-fulfilment'. *Journal of Occupational Psychology*, 53, 39–52.

Corley, Kevin G. 2004. 'Defined by our strategy or our culture? Hierarchical differences in perceptions of organizational identity and change'. *Human Relations*, 57(9), 1145–77.

Coyle-Shapiro, J. and Shore, L. 2007. 'The employee–organization relationship: where do we go from here?' *Human Resource Management Review*, 17, 166–79.

Dean, J. W., Brandes, P. and Dharwadkar, R. 1998. 'Organisational cynicism'. *Academy of Management Review*, 23(2), 341–52.

Frost, P. and Robinson, S. 1999. 'The toxic handler – organisational hero – and casualty'. *Harvard Business Review*, July–August.

Gabarro, J. J. and Athos, J. 1976. *Interpersonal Relations and Communications*. New York: Prentice-Hall.

Granovetter, M. 1985. 'Economic action and social structure: the problem of embeddedness'. *American Journal of Sociology*, 91(3), 481–510.

Hallier, J. and James, P. 1997. 'Middle managers and the employee psychological contract: agency, protection and advancement'. *Journal of Management Studies*, 34, 703–28.

Jones, G. R. and George, J. M. 1998. 'The experience and evolution of trust: implications for co-operation and teamwork'. *Academy of Management Review*, 23(3), 531–46.

Kramer, R. M. 1999. 'Trust and distrust in organizations: emerging perspectives, enduring questions'. *Annual Review of Psychology*, 50, 569–98.

Martin, J. 1992. *Cultures in Organisations – Three Perspectives*. New York: Oxford University Press.

Mayer, R. C., Davis, J. H. and Schoorman, F. D. 1995. 'An integrative model of organisational trust'. *Academy of Management Review*, 20(3), 709–34.

Morgan, P. I. and Ogbonna, E. 2008. 'Subcultural dynamics in transformation: a multi-perspective study of healthcare professionals'. *Human Relations*, 61(1), 39–65.

Pfeffer, J. 1983. 'Organizational demography'. *Research in Organizational Behavior*, 5, 299–357.

Reichers, A. E., Wanous, J. P. and Austin, J. T. 1997. 'Understanding and managing cynicism about organisational change'. *Academy of Management Executive*, 11(1), 48–59.

Rousseau, D. M., Sitkin, S. B., Burt, R. S. and Camerer, C. 1998. 'Not so different after all: a cross-discipline view of trust'. *Academy of Management Review*, 23, 393–404.

Sackmann, S. 1992. 'Culture and subcultures: an analysis of organizational knowledge'. *Administrative Science Quarterly*, 37, 140–61.

Sims, D. 2004. 'Between the millstones: a narrative account of the vulnerability of middle managers' storytelling'. *Human Relations*, 56(10), 1195–2011.

Unden, A.-L. 1996. 'Social support at work and its relationship to absenteeism'. *Work & Stress*, 10(1), 46–61.

Uzzi, B. 1997. 'Social structure and competition in interfirm networks: the paradox of embeddedness. *Administrative Science Quarterly*, 42, 35–67.

Van Maanen, J. and Barley, S. R. 1985. 'Cultural organisation: fragments of a theory'. In P. J. Frost, L. F. Moore, M. R. Louis, C. C. Lundberg and J. Martin (eds.) *Organizational Culture*. Newbury Park: Sage, 31–53.

Watt, J. D. and Piotrowski, C. 2008. 'Organisational change cynicism: a review of the literature and intervention strategies'. *Organization Development Journal*, Fall.

# 14 | The implications of language boundaries on the development of trust in international management teams

JANE KASSIS HENDERSON

## Summary

This chapter explores the concept of language boundaries in international teams in multinational companies which use English as their shared working language. Drawing on research in the fields of intercultural communication theory and sociolinguistics, and on references in the management literature, the analysis demonstrates how language boundaries in teams both foster trust within parties and hinder trust between parties. Empirical data from interviews with international executives illustrate how English as a shared working language can create as well as break down language boundaries. The chapter identifies the implications these boundaries have on the formation and maintenance of trust through cooperation and relationship building. Findings show that it is an awareness of language practices and sociolinguistic competence rather than expert language knowledge that fosters the development of trust in multicultural, multilingual teams.

## Introduction

Many management teams in multinational companies are not only multicultural, but also multilingual as they are composed of speakers of different mother tongues. The language factor has become omnipresent in international organizations, and globalization implies that they conduct their operations in multiple language environments and through multilingual teams (Feely and Harzing, 2003; Welch *et al.*, 2001). Language differences are often considered to be an obstacle and the concept of the language barrier is therefore a familiar one in such organizations. Indeed, it is so well known that its implications are often overlooked. Language barriers are visible obstacles to communication and occur when individuals who do not speak and understand each other's languages have difficulties working together. This can be a major source of problems for international teams. Research findings show

358

that people will be motivated to work through cultural problems if they want to cooperate 'but language may be an even bigger potential problem than functional differences and culture per se' (Schweiger *et al.*, 2003: 134).

To facilitate communication in international teams, English is widely used as a working language. Together with English, instantaneous communications through electronic media between members of virtual or distributed teams heighten the perception of a globalized, borderless, monocultural world. However, this apparent removal of barriers through the use of a common, shared language can cause less perceptible and less obvious language boundaries to form. Even if an 'international business language' or 'corporate language' is used to facilitate exchanges, the language factor continues to cause interference, misunderstandings and tensions both in face-to-face and in distance communications. Hence, language boundaries, although not readily perceived, exist between individuals in interaction and constitute a key influence on trust.

The issue of language and ways in which it affects trust and relationship building is rarely addressed explicitly or considered as a critical issue in the literature on teams. This chapter addresses these two factors, trust and language, explicitly and contributes to an understanding of how language-related issues influence trust. The questions addressed are:

1. How does using English as a shared working language both break down and create language boundaries?
2. How do these language boundaries influence the development of trust in multicultural, multilingual teams?

The chapter begins with a review of the literature on trust in multicultural teams and the theoretical background of the language question is then presented. This is followed by an analysis, illustrated by empirical data, of different language boundaries which may form in teams and the categories or parties within them. The final section identifies ways in which team members can develop more awareness in communication practices by recognizing language behaviour that prevents the formation of trust and by adopting behaviour that develops trusting relations.

Drawing on research in intercultural communication theory and sociolinguistics, and the management literature, the analysis demonstrates how language boundaries in teams both foster trust within parties and hinder trust between parties. In order to illustrate the implications of language boundaries on the formation and maintenance of trust, empirical data are taken from interviews with leading executives in a multinational company in the manufacturing sector in Europe with operations mainly in France, Germany, the UK and Spain.

## The language factor and trust in international teams

*Trust*

Given the interdependence of the individual members of international management teams, the notion of 'relational trust' developed by Rousseau (1998:
399) is of particular relevance to this chapter. In constituting evidence as to
the trustworthiness of the other party, concerning their ability, benevolence
and integrity (Mayer *et al.*, 1995), the trustor will be influenced by his or her
interpretation of interactions. These interactions are language dependent.
When communicating across languages, mistaken interpretations of the motivations and behaviour of an individual commonly occur and false attributions may be made about character or personality. This can increase the risks
of wrongly assessing ability, benevolence and integrity cues. Working
through a common shared language in a multilingual team therefore involves
an element of risk in the establishing of trustworthiness which is not present
when interactions take place between individuals in the same language community who share social meanings and interpretations implicitly. The latter
are less vulnerable as for them there is less risk of being misunderstood or of
false attributions being made as a result of language use. There is therefore an
additional element of vulnerability for individuals in multilingual teams.

A team member needs to establish his or her competence and reliability
before gaining trust; doing this when both parties are working through a
shared language requires an ability to interpret and share the social meanings
embedded in the communicative act and to show benevolence and integrity.
Benevolence is demonstrated when there is no 'egocentric profit motive' or
'extrinsic reward'; it is 'the perception of a positive orientation of the trustee
toward the trustor' (Mayer *et al.*, 1995: 719).

This chapter shows the extent to which the trust-building process is ren-
dered more complex by the language factor which can contribute to building
or eroding trusting relations.

*Culture*

When it comes to crossing geographical or linguistic boundaries, the notions
of 'language' and 'culture' tend to be bundled together under the heading of
'cross-cultural communication'. In this area of research the term 'culture' is
mostly used in its classic sense as a 'grouping' mechanism for nation states
(Chao and Moon, 2005: 1129). The aim of many publications in the field is to
prevent 'culture shock' by facilitating the adaptation of individuals moving

from one national, cultural context to another. Hence much of the work is comparative and the concept of culture is static and refers to identity and difference. Most research on cross-cultural trust development is said to still emphasize the obstacles resulting from cross-cultural differences (Möllering and Stache, Chapter 8). But as international organizations of today are characterized by multicultural team working which involves 'cultural recreation' (Holden, 2002: 46) a conceptual shift is needed in cross-cultural management studies from 'a hierarchical perspective of cultural influence, compromise and adaptation, to one of collaborative cross-cultural learning' (Holden, 2002: 306). This process can be slowed down as individuals tend to build on pre-existing shared cultural identities in order to form groups and to facilitate interactions.

Yet the research presented in this chapter shows that real or illusory 'shared cultural identity', often due to English being a 'shared' language, can be a *source of problems*, and that the challenge for teams is to create a working culture that transcends these illusory 'shared' cultures. This form of 'cultural recreation' corresponds to the proposition that cross-cultural relationships 'are formed in-between the cultures where they are partly disembedded from cultural constraints' (Möllering and Stache, 2007: 12). The analysis in this chapter of in-group and out-group identities in multilingual teams adopts the cultural mosaic perspective proposed by Chao and Moon (2005: 1134) and demonstrates that our cultural identities may reorganize themselves when new identities are learned or old identities shed.

## International teams and trust

Research on teams in multinational companies has demonstrated the importance of developing personal relationships for effective working relationships between members (DiStefano and Maznevski, 2000; Iles and Hayers, 1997; Lagerstrom and Andersson, 2003; Schweiger *et al.*, 2003). Boundary crossing has a significant impact on relationship building; frequently observed boundaries are organizational, cultural, linguistic, temporal or spatial in nature (Pauleen and Yoong, 2001). Relationship building necessitates trust; trust building is therefore a particular challenge in the changing, unstable and novel contexts experienced daily by boundary-crossing multilingual teams. It has been argued that trust decreases the costs of coordination in collaborative relationships and is the most important component of team development and effectiveness (Henttonen and Blomqvist, 2005).

Feely and Harzing (2003) demonstrate that the impact of the language barrier can be serious to multinational companies and that language should be managed as a corporate asset. These authors claim that 'the true cost can't be measured in terms of interpreting and translating … but in damaged relationships' (2003: 41), thus emphasizing the negative consequences of working across languages and the distrust and conflicts that ensue if the language factor is not managed.

Research has shown that the establishing of trust and relationships is closely connected with language issues and that language is a particular challenge in connection with socialization processes and less so for the technical aspects of work (Kassis Henderson, 2005; Lagerstrom and Andersson, 2003; Maznevski and Chudoba, 2000; Schweiger *et al.*, 2003).

Technical language competence without affective and behavioural competencies is acknowledged to be insufficient for relationship development (Griffith, 2002: 262). Reference has been made to the role of 'caring talk' and 'personal conversations' in trust building across spatial and language boundaries (Henttonen and Blomqvist, 2005: 115). These authors argue that socially based trust could emerge from a concern for the wellbeing of others and through creating a common culture and procedures.

According to Lagerstrom and Andersson (2003), social competence and flexibility are dependent on competence in the shared working language, which involves being receptive to other ways of speaking. Reporting on problems encountered in setting up transnational teams, the authors stressed 'the necessity of proficiency in the corporate language, English, for efficient communication. The gap between knowing a language in theory and using it in practice turned out to be crucial for the appointment of members to the team, and for team cooperation' (Lagerstrom and Andersson, 2003: 94). The words of one global team member explain this:

[Y]ou must speak decent English; it might sound silly but if you do not you cannot communicate with other team members … But we all speak our own kind of English, which means that we need to socialize and spend time together to learn each other's way of speaking. (cited in Lagerstrom and Andersson, 2003: 91)

The above remark is an explicit acknowledgement of the importance of observing divergent speech habits and modifying language use in order to adapt to others in the course of interactions.

Research shows that crossing language boundaries in international multicultural teams can have a negative effect on interpersonal relations, trust and the working atmosphere (Chévrier, 2000; DiStefano and Maznevski, 2000; Iles and Hayers, 1997; Kassis Henderson, 2005; Lagerstrom and Andersson, 2003; Schweiger *et al.*, 2003). Unfamiliar communication patterns or metacommunicative routines used by team members from different language communities influence interpersonal perceptions and attitudes, giving rise to uncertainty and ambiguity and inhibiting the creation of trust. However, findings also show that if communication in multilingual teams is managed effectively, language differences can be a key factor contributing to team building and group cohesion and even a source of trust (DiStefano and Maznevski, 2000; Goodall and Roberts, 2003; Holden, 2002; Schneider and Barsoux, 2003).

## Language

The topic of language in international business organizations covers a vast area of enquiry and is investigated in many academic areas, most of which are engaged in multidisciplinary research. Under the umbrella term of intercultural or cross-cultural communication are specialized areas of research such as sociolinguistics, discourse analysis, semiotics and translation studies. Aspects of language in business contexts are also investigated by other disciplines such as social and cultural psychology and linguistic anthropology. Intercultural communication theory as a subject is said to be in its infancy and the existing theories are a disparate collection reflecting the particular interests or beliefs of the scholars developing them (Guirdham, 1999): together they cover a considerable area of the potential behavioural ground, ranging from the motivations, emotions and cognitions of the intercultural encounter to the processes involved in effective intercultural interactions (Guirdham, 1999).

The theoretical perspective used in this chapter is from the area of intercultural communication theory concerned with adaptations in interactions, or interactional sociolinguistics (Pan *et al.*, 2002; Scollon and Scollon, 1995), which, as the term suggests, is a method used to analyse interactions in concrete settings. Practitioners in this field demonstrate how interaction involves individuals both inferring what others intend to convey and monitoring how their own contributions are received (Gumperz, 2003: 218). Their main field of inquiry is the inherent linguistic and cultural diversity of today's communicative environments (Gumperz, 2003: 220). One of the main purposes of interactional sociolinguistics is to show how diversity affects interpretation and this contributes to an understanding of the causes of miscommunication in multilingual teams (Kassis Henderson, 2005).

### Interpreting social meaning – communicating across languages
Individuals often have good foreign language knowledge but fail to achieve their goals when communicating across languages. This is because in addition to 'language' competence, 'communication' or 'sociolinguistic' competence is

required when operating across language boundaries (Hymes, 1971). This is building on Chomsky's (1965: 3) distinction between competence and performance:

> To study actual linguistic performance, we must consider the interaction of a variety of factors, of which the underlying competence of the speaker-hearer is only one ... We thus make a fundamental distinction between *competence* (the speaker-hearer's knowledge of his language) and *performance* (the actual use of language in concrete situations).

In this chapter the concept of 'sociolinguistic competence' is used to refer to the capacity of individuals to interpret the social meaning of language and to respond appropriately in the context of interactions. Sociolinguists reporting on over twenty years of research into intercultural intra-organizational communication have observed that

> most miscommunication does not arise through mispronunciation or through poor uses of grammar ... The major sources of miscommunication in intercultural contexts lie in differences in patterns of discourse. (Scollon and Scollon, 1995: xiii, cited in Kassis Henderson, 2005: 70)

### Discourse patterns, speech routines, conversations

When communicating across languages, even if team members are using the same working language, until they gain experience in international settings they tend to use and expect the routines, rituals and discourse strategies which are prevalent in their own native language communities. Actors who share the same context and speak the same language initially assume they share the same interpretations. Consequently communication behaviour tends to be judged according to local norms of appropriateness. In monocultural, monolingual groups communication competence is easy to identify as it corresponds to predictable norms. However, notions of what constitutes a good conversationalist or a constructive participant in a meeting differ greatly between individuals of different national cultural groups and therefore language communities (Kassis Henderson, 2005).

In the unfamiliar and uncertain environments that characterize multicultural teamwork, individuals are confronted with deviations from the patterns of speech and language routines to which they are accustomed. As discourse strategies are often misinterpreted this can have negative social consequences and result in the speaker being considered uncooperative (Gumperz, 1982) and so inhibit the development of trust.

Verbal communication is characterized by routine and the recurrence of regular discourse patterns. Examples of routine speech behaviour are greeting, thanking, apologizing, taking leave, forms of address, distancing. Other, more subtle forms of routine exist in conversations and there are significant cultural differences in this genre; for instance the way French and North American communicators perceive competence in conversations often causes misunderstandings since for the former conversation tends to be confrontational and competitive in style whereas for the latter it is cooperative (Carroll, 1988). This can be a cause of misunderstandings as conversation partners may be considered unfriendly or lacking in intelligence. The conversation style in certain milieus in the UK has been described in an analysis of British management practices as 'typically imprecise and vague, full of hints and subtleties' and hence misleading for outsiders used to clarity, decisiveness and demonstrative professionalism (Mole, 1992: 109–10). As Tracy (2003: 728) observed: 'a person's conversational strategies will be consequential for promoting relational satisfaction, minimizing group conflict or obtaining compliance'. One example of this is the different conventions for placing the main point at the beginning or the end of a conversation (Scollon and Scollon, 1995: xiii). Other important differences exist concerning the role of 'small talk' in a professional encounter. According to sociolinguistic analysis, problems arise in interpreting 'small talk' in cross-language communication (Scollon and Scollon, 1995: 6) as what is considered an unimportant part of a discussion by some may be considered crucial for others (Kassis Henderson, 2005).

Verbal routines and rituals are also played out in professional contexts such as meetings where particular speech codes and rhetorical styles are observed. In such contexts, opposite values can be assigned to certain discourse styles – silence, for example, indicating agreement or disagreement; consequently some participants may not be listened to or their contributions made in an unexpected mode may not be heard or taken seriously by others. Apart from these routine discourse patterns, the use of humour and attitudes to grammar mistakes or other technical language errors may differ and cause interference in multilingual contexts.

Being able to recognize the causes of tensions and misunderstandings in the course of interaction supposes the ability to 'read' the language routines of others, not only verbal language but non-verbal or paralinguistic features, which include 'body language', proxemics (the distance between people when speaking), speaking loudly or softly and the role of silence in communication.

### Sharing interpretations – using English in international teams

The above references to sociolinguistics and discourse analysis point to the complexity involved in using English in international teams as a 'shared', 'common', 'compromise' or 'working' language. Sharing a language implies more than exchanging messages according to the rules and conventions of a certain lexical, syntactical and phonological system. It implies sharing social meanings and interpretations and it is this aspect that poses a particular challenge when a language is used outside a context in which there is a close identification between speakers. When individuals are from a similar background and share a familiar context the intention behind the words expressed can be taken for granted as the speech is played out against a backdrop of common assumptions, common history and common interests (Bernstein, 1973: 231–2). But when individuals are from diverse backgrounds, as in international teams, the intentions of the speaker cannot be taken for granted and there is a greater need to make meanings explicit and to use an elaborate rather than restricted code.

## Language boundaries

All natural languages abound with conventions and markers of in-group membership such as characteristic pronunciations, specialized vocabulary and idiomatic phraseology and references to shared experiences and cultural background (Seidelhofer, 2001). The case of the English language is particularly complex as the majority of English speakers in the world today are those who primarily learnt English as a lingua franca for communicating with other lingua franca (or non-native) speakers (Seidelhofer, 2001: 139). In such contexts the English language is 'far removed from its native speakers' linguacultural norms and identities' (Seidelhofer, 2001:134) and can therefore be a misleading source of cues for initial trust. Hearing a different language or one's own spoken inexpertly signifies that the speaker has a different 'cultural tile' to the hearer (see Chao and Moon, 2005). As language signals in-group membership it therefore explicitly denotes a cultural boundary. Consequently, language boundaries do not only refer to the traditional demarcation lines between national or regional language groups or communities and cannot be assimilated to geographical boundaries.

The boundaries discussed in this chapter form as interactions between individual team members develop, and cultural tiles are reorganized to form new identities. A key distinction is made between monolingual native speakers of English (people who speak no language other than English) and non-native speakers of English (people with a mother tongue other than English and possibly an ability to speak or understand further additional languages). Taking each in turn:

Category (1): Monolingual native English speakers. (a) boundaries between native speakers of different English-speaking cultures. Trust is associated with a shared culture, history or outlook. Individuals tend to initially trust others whom they perceive to be similar; when 'the other' is perceived to be different trust tends to be harder to realize. So people who speak the same language expect to share similar interpretations of discourse; they hold tacit assumptions of similarity. This has been explored in previous studies. An example of this are the English-speaking international managers described in Welch *et al.* (2002: 620):

a transnational English-speaking elite had existed in the industry under study, thus nurturing a similar set of behaviors and beliefs regardless of national background. Elite managers came to know each other at international conferences and negotiations, and learned to regard each other, in the words of one manager, 'as similar sorts of people'. The existence of such an elite transnational culture is perhaps nurtured not only by frequent contacts, but also by MBA education programs and internal management training courses which are fairly standardized world-wide and which cultivate a similar jargon and outlook.

Consequently, members of this 'transnational elite' do not attach the same importance to building up relationships with each other as they would with members of what appear to be very different cultures.

The phenomenon of trust between native English speakers has been mentioned in the management literature (Welch *et al.*, 2001: 197), and perceived familiarity and supposed affinity have been reported to be a cause of problems in global teams. This is because native speakers from different countries tend, in the initial phase of collaboration, to trust each other implicitly – to have positive expectations of each other – in cross-cultural contexts, but they may fail to realize they are *not* culturally close, and that they may not share the same values along with the same language. This is known as the 'psychic distance paradox' (O'Grady and Lane, 1996). A good illustration of this is given in an article on relationship building and the use of ICT in boundary-crossing virtual teams (Pauleen and Yoong, 2001: 215). A misunderstanding in communication between a New Zealand team facilitator and an English team member whom she assumed she understood because of his supposed cultural similarity is reported as follows:

A.R.s virtual team consisted of New Zealand and Australian members and Asians and an Englishman on location in Asia. She did not consider the New Zealanders (she is one herself) the Australians or the Englishman to be culturally very different from herself and she thought that as a group she understood their communication styles. So when her e-mails on critical matters to the Englishman went unanswered time after time . . . she consciously made an effort to keep the lines of communication open: 'I telephoned him. Please tell me if I have offended you in some way.' He said, 'well I am a Yorkshireman and we go quiet when we are thinking.' I was astounded by this . . . This

Englishman had been hired as the lead consultant on the project at the last minute and A.R. had not attempted to build a relationship with him. She had assumed, until she learned otherwise, that she understood him, not only because he was an Englishman but also because he was a professional consultant like herself. (Pauleen and Yoong, 2001: 215)

This example of a Yorkshireman whose communication style did not correspond to the identity attributed to him (an 'Englishman') shows that distinctions need to be made within pre-defined cultural spheres and that there are drawbacks in using the concept of culture as a grouping mechanism for people of the same nationality. This incident can be explained by the Yorkshireman's cultural 'tiles' (regional identity and professional identity) remaining independent and thereby producing unpredictable and disorienting patterns of behaviour (Chao and Moon, 2005). Consequently the two parties do not attach the same importance to building up relationships with each other as they would with members of what appear to be very different cultures.

The two further categories will be analysed in detail in the context of the empirical findings reported later in the chapter:

Category (1): Monolingual native English speakers. (b) boundaries between monolingual native English speakers and non-native English speakers. This category can often be characterized by the illusion of trust. A supposed shared language and supposed shared assumptions mean that initial trust is taken for granted.

Category (2): Non-native speakers of English, for whom English is a second or foreign language and who are using English as a working language (a lingua franca). Although non-native speakers are themselves divided into subgroups by national language boundaries (German or French speakers, for example), these are insignificant compared with the boundary separating them from native English speakers. This second category is characterized by conscious or aware trust, where trust is a risk, but a confident risk (Rousseau *et al.*, 1998: 395).

## Method

The interviews were conducted in the course of a research project on the management of language diversity in senior management teams (Kassis Henderson, 2003). The objective of the interviews was to identify best practices for managing linguistic diversity and underlying cultural diversity which is expressed in speech behaviour. The interview guide (see Appendix) listed the following points to be explored: the policies and practices adopted to facilitate interaction and cooperation; the consequences of using English as the working language of a multilingual, cross-border team; the factors that hinder productive communication and team building; the particular challenges faced by native English speakers and speakers from other specific language communities.

The data quoted in this paper are from a sample of fourteen interviews conducted in 2003 with senior executives in a major European company. They refer to experience both in face-to-face situations (formal and informal) and in distance communications (telephone and videoconferences). Eight of the respondents were German and six were French; in their respective teams there were executives from other European countries, among them British and Spanish. Ten of the interviews were conducted by telephone and four using videoconference technology. They lasted between thirty and fifty minutes and were all conducted in English. The interviews did not explicitly address the question of 'trust'. The term 'trust' is used retrospectively by the respondents to characterize the nature of specific relationships and situations.

The recorded data were analysed with reference to the concept of sociolinguistic competence or the appropriate use of language in the context of interactions. In all of the interviews references were made to socialization processes, trust and relationship building. Patterns were identified by the recurrence of these and other key words or phrases such as 'trust relationships', 'time to learn how to interact', 'cooperation', 'trusting attitude'. The repeated use of certain terms such as 'sharing understanding' or 'isolating themselves' helped to identify the in-group and/or out-group identity of the speaker. The language boundaries and related themes were also identified on the basis of the assumptions behind the questions, namely those suggesting that particular language communities face particular challenges.

The answers to the interview questions showed a considerable degree of overlap between the concepts of 'language' and 'culture'; the respondents found it hard to attribute certain types of interference or difficulties to 'language' or 'culture'. In the analysis of the findings an attempt is made to separate the two concepts.

## Language boundaries and trust in teams

In detecting barriers to trust and sources of trust, the analysis of the data shows that individuals with sociolinguistic competence recognize trustworthiness cues reflecting ability, benevolence or integrity (Mayer *et al.*, 1995) in the behaviour of other members. The type of behaviour of team members described as leading to 'good relationships', 'confidence' or 'cooperation' is reported to be a source of trust. Although risk is a parameter in our analysis of the data, the term is not used by the team members as it is suggestive of vulnerability; when commenting on their relations in teams it is therefore unlikely that individuals would refer to the risk that is inherent in trusting relations as they would be unwilling to acknowledge it.

### Category 1b: Monolingual native English speakers and non-native speakers
*Boundaries not perceived by monolingual native English speakers communicating with non-native speakers. In this category trust may be an illusion or a 'trap' because of assumed mutual understanding and the status and role of English.*

One problem that frequently occurs when English is used as the working language of a team is that participants are under the false impression that they are sharing the same interpretation; that the same words and expressions have the same connotations for speakers of English from, say, the USA, India, Germany and Sweden, and that they use the same practices and routines.

One executive interviewed talked of the 'illusion [that] people were talking the same language and were on the same wave length', adding that 'people think they understand one another but the words, a part of the message, the intonation and body language say different things'. Another spoke of the 'fundamental misassumption that we all speak English and therefore we all understand each other'. Others pointed out the reluctance of non-native speakers to admit to not understanding for fear of losing face in meetings. One executive commented humorously that 'English people speak English so well they are not understandable', and then explained how he tends to react:

I do not hesitate to say to English people 'I'm sorry but I do not understand' but a lot of colleagues of mine do not want to say that. And when I ask my colleagues, they agree, they look as if they understand but in fact they understand nothing. This is a problem; during meetings it can lead to difficult misunderstandings.

Interpreting this behaviour in trust terms, it can be inferred that the colleagues referred to are not willing to take risks and feel vulnerable as they might appear incompetent by asking for an explanation of what they have not understood thus giving a wrong trustworthiness cue.

*Isolation of monolingual native English speakers: not trusted by non-native speakers; native English speakers are paradoxically outsiders in an English-language-speaking context.*

Although there are obvious advantages for native English speakers in teams which use English as the working language, there can also be negative consequences for communication processes in teams and for the individuals themselves who can be isolated or marginalized in a bilingual or multilingual group. One German executive interviewed stated that:

It is difficult if there is a group of colleagues and just one is speaking his native language. The other ones are speaking English as the common one. In our position we're better off as we have the same starting position. It is more difficult for the native speaker as he is more or less isolated from us with our 'continental English'.

It was also pointed out that native speakers are distracted by the way others use the English language and they tend to adopt a patronizing tone which irks other team members:

It also seemed to be that the British colleague was annoyed by the way the French or German were talking. They have a lot of difficulty not to teach the others how to use the English language rather than concentrate on common work.

Other data underlined this tendency of native speakers to try to impose a certain style and level of language. With the internationalization of organizations and the increasing use of English, Western (or 'Anglo-Saxon') interactional patterns and preferences are assumed to be transferable to multilingual and intercultural communication (Pan *et al.*, 2002). Relating an incident that occurred over the writing of a draft for a policy paper for an international organization, one executive reported that a native English speaker in the team prepared a very good comprehensive draft but that the vocabulary used, 'high level Oxford English', and the style was difficult for most team members to understand. For the paper to be understood by a third, external, party it had to be rewritten in international English, a process which was described as follows:

The native English speaker tried to reformulate, sometimes I made some proposals concerning international English, we discussed it and then we had not a totally other paper but we had some sentences written in another way then it was understood and this paper was accepted by the team.

Other remarks point to the fact that some native English speakers adapt their use of language more than others:

Usually our English is not so bad and the English people are polite enough if we are in discussion and communication to be a little bit careful with their language, pronouncing quite well and not too fast.

However, it is said of other native English speakers that they 'speak very quickly using words normally you never heard; for them it's difficult to adapt and take into account the other guys are not native speakers'. Another informant explained that it is a problem if the speaker is unaware of the difficulties the partners may have in understanding him, because, for example, of the speed of speech, low voice or use of slang expressions.

Applying the trustworthiness criteria of Mayer *et al.* (1995) to this example, our interpretation is that native speakers are not trusted as they are lacking one of the characteristics of a trustee, namely 'ability' (Mayer *et al.*, 1995: 717). This means they have insufficient aptitude, training or experience in the area of interpersonal communication with foreign speakers of English. If the other two trustworthiness criteria are applied here, benevolence and integrity, our interpretation is that the monolingual native English speakers do not care about the other party as they are unable to share their predicament of listening to a foreign tongue spoken without due care. Consequently, non-native speakers feel vulnerable and do not trust native English speakers sufficiently to explain to them that they have difficulties in understanding.

In their study on managing international joint ventures, Glaister *et al.* (2003: 101) give an example of native English speakers failing to take language differences into account and consequently alienating their partners and inhibiting the building of trust:

> another aspect of culture is the *lingua franca* to be used. In all of the International Joint Ventures in the sample, the English language was used between the partners. However, some European respondents noted that even though English was the agreed medium, they were at times irritated by the UK partner's failure to appreciate that they were communicating with those for whom English was not the mother tongue. This, in turn, led to operational tensions.

Team members who speak only their native language are unable to experience and benefit from the 'interlanguage' dynamics that characterize interactions between individuals; they do not have to struggle with a foreign language and hence are not able to extend emotional solidarity to colleagues. There may be unexpected consequences as when native English speakers, far from benefiting from the fact that a training seminar is taking place in English, are in fact at a disadvantage and 'missing out', not on the information, but on the 'interanimation' and on 'the emotional side of personal interactions' (Holden, 2002: 196, 199) as they are not having to argue their point in a foreign tongue. This can be explained by the fact that monoglots lack the experience that would enable them to share the feeling of vulnerability inherent in speaking a foreign language with native speakers of that language. Sharing a working language means team members are also implicitly sharing the same risk and this is conducive to an atmosphere of mutual trust.

## Category 2: Non-native speakers of English
*Non-native speakers of English have shared competence of crossing language boundaries (trusting attitudes towards each other). A sense of shared risk in relation to the language is implicitly present among non-native speakers and contributes to the building of trust.*

Research (Holden, 2002; Lagerstrom and Andersson, 2003) has shown that the use of English in teams composed of speakers of different languages tends to bring non-native speakers together and give rise to emotional solidarity as they are involved in the same act of crossing boundaries and communicating in a foreign tongue. They share a sense of shared risk: a risk of being misinterpreted concerning the task at hand or of their professional competence being underestimated. This creates a bond of collusion and trust between them and at the same time creates a new boundary between speakers of English as a foreign language and native speakers of English. Foreign speakers share the same competence of crossing language boundaries which contributes to mutual recognition and appreciation and helps to build trust among them. This bonding of non-native speakers over an unexpected common identity – 'against' the English speakers in some cases – could be interpreted as a self-organizing new identity (Chao and Moon, 2005: 1131–5).

In this connection a key factor is the building of trusting, working relationships through an 'internationalized' English that transcends cultural and linguistic boundaries. When English is not the native language of either party, for example when French and Germans work on a project together, a sense of equality and fairness is reported to exist (Kassis Henderson, 2003); this can be linked to the trustworthiness cue of integrity. Speaking the same kind of English facilitates the interaction and the cooperation 'because your partners have the feeling they are accepted as they are'. One executive observed that they all had the same starting point with their continental English. Another spoke of the advantages 'if there is the same level of bad knowledge of language'. This remark means that, in spite of an imperfect mastery of grammatical structures, they have a compatible way of speaking and do not feel vulnerable in each other's eyes.

One informant emphasized the fact that a high standard or 'Oxford' English is not a requirement in his team; he puts the stress on a common understanding, explaining:

Probably you feel that my English is not perfectly Oxford ... I'm pushing that also in my team members saying you're not obliged to reach a high degree Oxford level of English; what you have to reach is a common understanding in whatever papers whatever discussion you have to do.

Another described how they found a common language:

We built a new English language in that people found some word in order to have a common language between German and French, English language, but I'm quite persuaded it was not a good English language but we didn't care; that means we found a new word ... and during years we have a common English language but which was not real English ... it's a good way to have a common agreement on different words or topics and we use something that was not really English ... it means that if we put two people together and if they have the willingness to work together they can find a new language ... A lot of technical words directly invented by French or German people ... Always English words.

The concept of 'internationalized English' (Firth, 1990) can be applied to the analysis of the above quoted data. The development of specific network communication behaviour between partners communicating across linguistic and cultural boundaries is described as follows:

Within such a network, norms, standards and interpretive procedures are likely to be developed, becoming collectively recognizable as a 'style' peculiar to, or at least characteristic of the specific network; so standards of appropriacy, norms of spoken interaction ... become established ... over the course of regular communications ... In this way the use of English among specific 'networks' of individuals may become 'internationalized', with emergent norms or 'styles' that transcend cultural and, indeed, linguistic boundaries. (Firth, 1990: 277)

This points to the creativity that can result when cooperation and confidence in a team enable risk taking which, in turn, leads to the development of trust.

Other research has also drawn attention to emotional solidarity observing that in an international environment creativity and innovation occur through a healthy interaction of perspectives (Schweiger *et al.*, 2003). Embracing and enjoying differences is reported to facilitate the interaction and camaraderie of the team (Schweiger *et al.*, 2003).

## Language for 'technical' or 'social' purposes
The importance of social contact and building up relationships over time was emphasized by one informant, as it can override the effects of language:

[Y]ou have to understand them you have to see the body language how they act and react. This in my point of view has the same importance than just the pure language and the technical part of it ... So in my point of view, the way how I work, to know the people which I have to work with on a daily basis that they understand me, that they see me in a person and they can trust in me, this is important for me. I think in my experience, the language is not a blocking point or an obstacle. Different languages are an obstacle at the beginning if you want to be acquainted then they become a plus as you can learn new behaviours and new ways to act from each other. Colleagues get to know personal behaviour and reactions, then they build some 'trust relationships'.

He concludes on the necessity of viewing language and cultural differences as being opportunities not obstacles, saying that 'if individuals are positive minded, it is completely different'.

### Time and building trust relations

On questions concerning factors that facilitate communication in teams the importance of time for learning how to interact with people and build up relationships was a recurrent theme. One executive reported that in a new team if there are ten people that you do not know from ten different countries you need more time to read the people and understand them and to adapt your behaviour; 'it takes more time to read behaviour in an international team'. Others stressed the importance of the time factor and of knowing people personally before communicating with them satisfactorily through electronic mail or videoconferencing technology:

A lot depends on how well you know the people you're working with and you need to have teams built up over some length of time. If you know them you can go on a video conference and talk to each other, no problem at all. But if you go to a video conference and you don't know the party on the other side, it is quite difficult.

Others talk about building up 'trust relationships', and the need for patience, saying that it is not only language that is a barrier but differences from the past:

so the process of building such a trust relationship takes up to two years, and I would like to give advice to upper managers and shareholders . . . if they want to be successful they have to give time to that process.

Research has shown that the appropriate rhythm of virtual and face-to-face interaction is critical for team dynamics and effectiveness (Maznevski and Chudoba, 2000) and that the development of trust in distributed teams takes longer between previously unacquainted members (Wilson *et al.*, 2006). The importance of the time factor is acknowledged in the analysis of the trust-building process of Mayer *et al.* (1995: 722): 'as the relationship develops interactions with the trustee allow the trustor to gain insights about the trustee's benevolence and the relative impact of benevolence on trust will grow'. Also, integrity is assessed through the consistency of actions over time: 'The extent to which the party's actions are congruent with his or her words all affect the degree to which the party is judged to have integrity' (Mayer *et al.*, 1995: 719). But if the words are used in an unfamiliar way and hence misinterpreted this will have a negative impact on the trustor's assessment of the benevolence and integrity of the trustee.

## Using other languages in addition to English

The use of other languages as well as English, the working language of the team, is also reported to contribute to the development of trust. Research findings reported by Goodall and Roberts (2003) and Kassis Henderson (2005) show that establishing trust can be achieved through making the effort to speak the language of other team members from time to time even if it is not the dominant shared working language. This can be illustrated by the example of British executives making the effort to learn French which greatly improved relations; although English was the working language of the team, there was a marked increase in trust:

> there was enormous appreciation in the French team that their British counterparts were making this effort and realization that they will never be able to speak as fluently as us ... not for a number of years. This made a huge difference in terms of the team dynamics and in terms of the mutual trust which was not good. It really helps on trust.

This reference to trust can be explained by the trustworthiness cue of benevolence.

The importance of speaking the other languages of team members in aside communications and in 'small talk' was also commented on as a factor in improving trusting relations. The empirical data show a German who spoke French informally with his French partners commenting on his ability to build closer, more trusting relations. Analysing his experience, he said that personal relationships with the French team members can be built up more quickly if you speak each other's language as well as English:

> I recognize due to my knowledge of French there are different ways of understanding; if I didn't speak French I would have had many more problems.

He explained that personal relationships are formed more quickly with their language, French, and that he could form 'working friendships':

> If a normal neutral relationship ... I would see the problem Monday morning but if there's a friendship he will phone me this evening already to prepare that there will be a problem next morning. We try to exchange a lot of people to create a network; for months, a year or few years. Exchange programs to send people to other sites, to create personal relationships.

He added that this was not an official practice supported by human resources, for example but 'it's organized because we think it's necessary'. This example shows that it is an advantage for team members if they speak the language of the people they are working with, even if English is the language of communication and the language of a 'normal neutral relationship'. The term 'neutral' was used in other interviews, when the English language was referred to as 'a neutral basis'; as one person put it, 'but it is always good to try and talk in the other language if there is the possibility . . . it is helpful to give the sign'. Another German regretted he did not speak French as well as English, saying that 'English is not enough in Europe, with our global companies it's more likely we'll work with foreign colleagues'.

In an analysis of transnational project teams using English as their common corporate language, Schweiger *et al.* (2003: 138) commented on the advantage of multilingual team leaders being able to follow the 'side conversations' taking place in other languages.

## Discussion

Our main finding is that language boundaries can be both barriers to trust building and sources of trust in international teams. The empirical data draw attention to the fact that if team members understand the conditions contributing to trust building or being detrimental to it then 'more aware' language practices can be adopted in teams. Such practices could include, on the part of the speaker, the use of an elaborate rather than restricted code in order to make the intended meaning explicit and reduce ambiguity; on the part of the hearer, reformulating what has been understood and asking for confirmation that this was indeed the intended message. Aware communicators also know how to adapt the channels and means of communication to the context and to each individual.

The ways in which the executives interviewed talk about their experiences in multilingual teams show they are aware of the potential consequences of their decisions and choices concerning language use. They know that their trustworthiness is at risk and they can recognize trustworthiness in the communication behaviour of others; they know that it takes time to read behaviour in multilingual teams; they know that it takes time to create emotional solidarity. It appears that executives with experience of using English in international contexts distinguish between the ability to use language as a tool for transmitting objective information in 'neutral' relationships and as a means of building trusting relationships. One executive indicated to the author that taking part in the research interview was a valuable exercise for him as it forced him to think about everyday, taken-for-granted, communication practices and to make sense of them retrospectively. This shows that it is awareness of language practices – developed in part through reflection based on personal experience – and receptive attitudes to diversity in communication behaviour rather than expert technical language knowledge that fosters the building of trust.

## Implications for practice

This chapter is an invitation to think differently about questions of 'language' and 'culture' in the changing contexts that characterize international work settings today. Boundaries and groupings in international teams do not correspond to the ways in which questions of language and culture are generally framed in the management literature. Situations experienced by individuals do not necessarily fall into the neat, pre-established typologies or tables of the kind that list national communication styles or cultural behavioural traits. The chapter showed how language boundaries may form when English is used as a shared lingua franca in international teams and how language barriers can both foster trust and hinder trust formation. The analysis of in-group and out-group identities illustrated the predicament of native speakers of English in international, multilingual teams which use English as a shared working language. One conclusion to be drawn is that monolingual English speakers without previous experience in multilingual environments tend to be unaware that their own communication behaviour can create language barriers and inhibit the building of trust. Another conclusion is that individuals experienced in working in a foreign language are able to identify and work through language difficulties and build trusting relations that facilitate interaction.

With increased diversity in the workplace and speakers of different languages interacting on a regular basis, the link between the language factor and trust needs to be recognized in organizations. This has implications for recruitment, team leadership and training as, in addition to 'language competence', 'sociolinguistic' or 'communication' competence is required in multilingual work environments. As our findings show, part of this wider competence is the ability to speak the language(s) of the other team members as this guards against tribal behaviour and helps to build up emotional solidarity. English may be the shared working language in international teams, but additional language and communication competencies beyond a technical mastery of English are required for a trusting atmosphere to be established.

## Directions for future research

More empirical research is necessary on the impact of language-related factors on trust building in multilingual teams and more specifically on socialization processes in virtual teams in which communication takes place through communication technology: telephone, e-mails and videoconferences. A related field to explore is the effect on trust of the implicit transfer to multilingual management teams who use English as their working language of the interactional patterns and preferences used in English-speaking cultures. This takes place through educational processes – for example, management or language training seminars – and is said to be detrimental to the working atmosphere in multicultural teams.

## Appendix: Presentation of research topic and interview guide

### *The management of linguistic diversity in international teams*

#### Research project

Existing management research suggests that issues related to language diversity are often neglected or minimized in cross-border organizations or pluricultural teams. There is a widespread belief that there are no communication problems as 'everyone speaks English'.

In my study I am investigating how linguistic diversity is actually managed by team members. For example: What policies and practices have been adopted to facilitate interaction and cooperation? What are the consequences of using English as the working language of a plurilingual, cross-border team? What are the factors that hinder productive communication and team building? What particular challenges do native English speakers, and speakers from other specific language communities, face?

My aim is to identify best practices for managing linguistic diversity and underlying cultural diversity which is expressed in speech behaviour.

#### Interview questions

a) *Team focus*

1) How diverse, in terms of languages spoken, is your team?
2) How is this diversity managed? What policies and practices have been adopted to facilitate interaction and cooperation?
3) Can you think of any particular 'critical incident' or difficult situation which arose in your team because of the language diversity of the group members?
4) Have you observed any factors connected with speech behaviour or language use that (a) hinder, (b) encourage, productive communication?
5) Does language diversity add value to your team or is it an obstacle?

b) *Personal focus*

6) What languages do you speak/write/understand?
   What language(s) do you use in professional contexts?

7) What are the consequences for you of using English as a working language?
8) As a native speaker of ............ (French/English/German/Spanish/ other), do you face any particular challenges working in a plurilingual team? Are there any contexts in which you change your habitual speech behaviour or style of communication?
9) Have you ever facilitated intercultural/interlingual communication between team members? How did you do this?
10) What advice about managing communication processes would you give other management teams operating across cultures and languages?

## References

Bernstein, B. B. 1973. 'Language and socialization'. In N. Minnis (ed.) *Linguistics at Large*. St Albans, Hertfordshire: Paladin, 225–42.

Carroll, R. 1988. *Cultural Misunderstandings: the French–American Experience*. University of Chicago Press.

Chao, G. T. and Moon, H. 2005. 'The cultural mosaic: a metatheory for understanding the complexity of culture'. *Journal of Applied Psychology*, 90(6), 1128–40.

Chévrier, S. 2000. *Le Management des équipes interculturelles*. Paris: Presses Universitaires de France.

Chomsky, N. 1965. *Aspects of the Theory of Syntax*. Cambridge MA: MIT Press.

DiStefano, J. J. and Maznevski, M. L. 2000. 'Creating value with diverse teams in global management'. *Organizational Dynamics*, 29(1), 45–61.

Feely, A. J. and Harzing, A.-W. 2003. 'Language management in multinational companies'. *Cross-cultural Management*, 10(2), 37–52.

Firth, A. 1990. '"Lingua Franca" negotiations: towards an interactional approach'. *World Englishes – Journal of English as an International and Intranational Language*, 9(3), 269–81.

Glaister, K. W., Husan, R. and Buckley, P. J. 2003. 'Learning to manage international joint ventures'. *International Business Review*, 12(1), 83–109.

Goodall, K. and Roberts, J. 2003. 'Only connect: teamwork in the multinational'. *Journal of World Business*, 38, 127–40.

Griffith, D. A. 2002. 'The role of communication competencies in international business relationship development'. *Journal of World Business*, 37, 256–65.

Guirdham, M. 1999. *Communicating Across Cultures*. London: Palgrave.

Gumperz, J. 1982. *Language and Social Identity*. Cambridge University Press.

    2003. 'Interactional sociolinguistics: a personal perspective'. In D. Schiffrin, D. Tannen and H. E. Hamilton (eds.) *The Handbook of Discourse Analysis*. Oxford: Blackwell, paperback edition, 215–28.

Henttonen, K. and Blomqvist, K. 2005. 'Managing distance in a global virtual team: the evolution of trust through technology-mediated relational communication'. *Strategic Change*, 14, 107–19.

Holden, N. J. 2002. *Cross-cultural Management: a Knowledge Management Perspective*. London: Financial Times/Prentice Hall.

Hymes, Dell H. 1971. 'Competence and performance in linguistic theory'. In R. Huxley and E. Ingram (eds.) *Language Acquisition: Models and Methods*. New York: Academic Press, 3–28.

Iles, P. and Hayers, P. K. 1997. 'Managing diversity in transnational project teams'. *Journal of Managerial Psychology*, 12(2), 95–117.

Kassis Henderson, J. 2003. 'Managing language diversity in top management teams'. *Unpublished Research Project*, Chair of Executive Governance, ESCP Europe, Paris campus.

2005. 'Language diversity in international management teams'. *International Studies of Management and Organization*, 35(1), 66–82.

Lagerstrom, K. and Andersson, M. 2003. 'Creating and sharing knowledge within a transnational team – the development of a global business system'. *Journal of World Business*, 38, 84–95.

Mayer, R. C., Davis, J. H. and Schoorman, F. D. 1995. 'An integrative model of organizational trust'. *Academy of Management Review*, 20(3), 709–34.

Maznevski, M. L. and Chudoba, K. M. 2000. 'Bridging space over time: global virtual dynamics and effectiveness'. *Organization Science*, 11(5), 473–92.

Mole, J. 1992. *Mind your Manners, Managing Culture Clash in the Single European Market*. London: Nicholas Brealey.

Möllering, G. and Stache, F. 2007. 'German-Ukrainian business relationships: trust development in the face of institutional uncertainty and cultural differences'. MPIfG Discussion Paper 07/11.

O'Grady, S. and Lane, H. W. 1996. 'The psychic distance paradox'. *Journal of International Business Studies*, 27(2), 309–33.

Pan, Y., Wong Scollon, S. and Scollon R. 2002. *Professional Communication in International Settings*. Oxford: Blackwell.

Pauleen, D. J. and Yoong, P. 2001. 'Relationship building and the use of ICT in boundary-crossing virtual teams: a facilitator's perspective'. *Journal of Information Technology*, 16(4), 205–20.

Rousseau, D. M., Sitkin, S. B., Burt, R. S. and Camerer, C. 1998. 'Not so different after all: a cross-discipline view of trust'. *Academy of Management Review*, 23(3), 393–404.

Schneider, S. C. and Barsoux, J.-L. 2003. *Managing Across Cultures*, 2nd edn. Harlow: FT/ Prentice Hall.

Schweiger, D. M., Atamer, T. and Calori, R. 2003. 'Transnational project teams and networks: making the multinational organization more effective'. *Journal of World Business*, 38, 127–40.

Scollon, R. and Scollon, S. W. 1995. *Intercultural Communication: a Discourse Approach*. Oxford: Blackwell.

Seidelhofer, B. 2001. 'Closing a conceptual gap: the case for a description of English as a lingua franca'. *International Journal of Applied Linguistics*, 11(2), 133–58.

Tracy, K. 2003. 'Discourse analysis in communication'. In D. Schiffrin, D. Tannen and H. E. Hamilton (eds.) *The Handbook of Discourse Analysis*. Oxford: Blackwell, (paperback edition) 725–49.

Welch, D., Welch, L. and Marschan-Piekkari, R. 2001. 'The persistent impact of language on global operations'. *Prometheus*, 19(3), 193–209.

Welch, C., Marschan-Piekkari, R., Penttinen, H. and Tahvanainen, M. 2002. 'Corporate elites as informants in qualitative international business research'. *International Business Review*, 11, 611–28.

Wilson, J. M., Straus, S. G. and McEvily, B. 2006. 'All in due time: the development of trust in computer-mediated and face-to-face teams'. *Organizational Behavior and Human Decision Processes*, 99(1), 16–33.

# 15 | *The dynamics of trust across cultures in family firms*

ISABELLE MARI

## Summary

The aim of this chapter is to provide new insight into how chief executive officers of family businesses (who are themselves family members) create trust with the firm's owners. I argue that, in the family firm, three interacting subcultures (family, business and ownership) influence chief executive officer (CEO) and owner behaviour in keeping with their governance roles. Because of distinct values and norms of behaviour, the interactions of these three subcultures are often a source of interpersonal conflict, and often undermine relationships of trust built up over generations. Through an exploratory case study and application of the Economies of Worth Model, this chapter examines and illustrates how CEOs of family firms enhance their legitimacy and thus build, maintain, and repair trust.

## Introduction

Around the world, family firms dominate the economic landscape (Chrisman *et al.*, 2005; Morck and Yeung, 2004). Family businesses are those where ownership and management are concentrated within a family unit, and where its members work to achieve or maintain intra-organizational family-based relatedness (Litz, 1995). Their corporate governance structure may be composed of the same people, or at least people from the same family (Gersick *et al.*. 1997; Wortman, 1994). This overlap of ownership and management influences the relationships between the CEO, the board of directors and the owners, as well as the strategy of the family firm (Melin, 2001; Nordqvist, 2005). Indeed, their relationships are founded on three interacting subcultures (family, business and ownership) that may conflict. It is for this reason that family

I thank Nicole Gillespie and Mark Saunders for their very helpful comments and recommendations.

firms are particularly vulnerable to conflict arising from discord among relatives (Levinson, 1971) or to a form of inertia that can paralyse decision making and threaten the firm's survival (Meyer and Zucker, 1989, quoted in Shulze *et al.*, 2000). Family firms are dynamic organizations. Over time, parents, children, siblings and marriage partners may be involved in the business to a greater or lesser extent. The form of ownership, changing as well, may make the relationships between those involved in governance more complex and open to conflict as the values and norms of behaviour upon which these relationships were founded change, leading to distrust.

Under these difficult conditions, a critical issue faced by family firm CEOs is to make sure owners trust them. CEOs need owners to trust and support their strategic decisions and to keep their shares in the family, in order to maintain control of the firm. Trust may help family firm CEOs deal with conflicts with owners, ward off opportunistic behaviour and reduce monitoring costs (Steier, 2001). Trust and personal ties allow family firms to build informal, self-reinforcing governance mechanisms that may improve the quality of the firm's strategic decision making (Mustakallio *et al.*, 2002).

Corporate governance researchers have examined some of the governance problems faced by family firms in which ownership is concentrated and shareholders are directly involved in executive management (Corbetta and Salvato, 2004; Davis and Herrera, 1998; Gómez-Mejía *et al.*, 2001; Schulze *et al.*, 2001; Vilaseca, 2002; Ward and Hendy, 1988). However, although trust is a major component of corporate governance relationships, surprisingly little has been said about trust between corporate governance actors in family firms.

This chapter focuses on trust dynamics in family firms. It stresses family businesses, initially characterized by relationships of trust and prone to a dilution of trust as the family gets bigger. It examines the relationships among strategic actors – those involved in the corporate governance of the family firm, as well as in strategy making (referred to as 'corporate governance actors'). These relationships play out in informal arenas (Nordqvist, 2005) and family-firm-specific arenas such as family councils (Jaffe and Lane, 2004), as well as in formal arenas (board meetings, owners' assemblies, etc.)

The aim of this chapter is to examine how the family member CEO of a family business may enhance his or her legitimacy and thus build, maintain, and/or repair trust with the owners. In the first part of the chapter, I describe how the family business culture may evolve over time into three conflicting subcultures that can undermine the trust that binds corporate governance actors. In the second part, the Economies of Worth Model is used to explain how the CEO can use formalities to enhance legitimacy and create trust. This model provides a framework for understanding and dealing with multiple conflicting interests and subcultures. Next, this framework is illustrated through an exploratory case study of a Belgian family firm. Finally, implications for practice and directions for future research are discussed and concluding comments offered.

## Trust and cultures in family firms

### High trust organizations, strong culture organizations

In family firms, the relationships between corporate governance actors are usually governed by underlying informal agreements based on affect rather than on utilitarian logic or contractual obligation (Gómez-Mejía *et al.*, 2001). Emotions are part of these relationships and can be the foundation of a great degree of trust (Jones, 1983). Trust, then, is the 'willingness of a party to be vulnerable to the actions of another party based on the expectation that the other will perform a particular action important to the trustor, irrespective of the ability to monitor or control that other party' (Mayer *et al.*, 1995: 712). In family firms, governance actors' trust of each other can also be based on the shared values and norms of behaviour that underlie the family business culture.

Culture can be defined as 'a shared and learned world of experiences, meanings, values and understandings which inform people and which are expressed, reproduced and communicated in partly symbolic form' (Alvesson, 1993: 2–3). The family business culture results from 'beliefs, values, and goals rooted in the family, its history, and present social relationships' that are transmitted over generations and shape relatively stable cultural patterns (Hall *et al.*, 2001: 195). In the family business literature, the role of the founder in shaping the family business culture is always emphasized (Schein, 1995). This, along with occupation of leadership positions by family members, may account for the relative strength of family business cultures (Melin, 2001). Culture emphasizes the importance of symbolism – of rituals, myths, stories and legends – and how groups influence the interpretation of events, ideas and experiences (Frost, 1985). The family business culture influences the corporate governance actors' relationships, as well as the strategic decision making in family firms. Implicit rules prevail over explicit rules; family members understand organizational behaviour from weak signals and do not need rigorous systems of control. Shared values, attitudes, beliefs and behaviour contribute to cohesion, a shared vision for the future (Mustakallio *et al.*, 2002), and attachment to the firm, which are bases for trust.

These trust-based relationships allow family firms to improve the quality of the firm's strategic decision making and to strengthen the commitment of owners (Mustakallio *et al.*, 2002), as family shareholders trust the CEO to manage the firm in their interest. Over future generations, however, it may be hard to maintain the ties forged by members of the founding generation (Steier, 2001). In fact, as the family grows, the family culture often evolves into three overlapping subcultures that may conflict, undermining the foundations of trust.

## Family expansion and the evolution of trust relationships

Over time, family firms go through several stages or forms of ownership (Ward, 1987). Gersick *et al.* (1997) identify three stages depending on the number of generations that make up the family: controlling owner, sibling partnership and cousins' consortium. The culture of the family firm changes and may weaken when the founder has left the firm and the family has grown. As the family enlarges and several generations become involved in the business, values and norms of behaviour may no longer be shared, interest in and attachment to the business, as well as visions for the future, may differ widely. So the bases for trust may erode. According to Beckard and Dyer (1983), conflicts among family members increase with the number of generations involved in the firm. In particular, they intensify from the second to the third generation (Davis and Harveston, 1999, 2001) and can plague the firm with conflict.

## Family firms: a network of cultural mosaics including three overlapping subcultures

Not all family members can be involved in the family firm or in governance structures. Family members may act as relatives, owners or managers. These roles help characterize the behaviour of the corporate governance actors. Family firms, then, are three independent but overlapping systems: the family, the business and the ownership. Each system has its own values, norms of behaviour, rules and organizational structures, and they may conflict with each other (Gersick *et al.*, 1997). Each is described in turn:

1. The family system: family members are primarily concerned with the welfare and unity of the family. Value is given to internal unity and rivalry

among members is repressed or denied. The family system is emotional (Ward, 1987). Family members often have a conservative vision of the firm.

2. The business system: managers have a strategy-oriented vision of the firm. They will work toward operational effectiveness (Tagiuri and Davis, 1996). The business system is objective (Ward, 1987). Internal competition is encouraged.

3. The ownership system: owners are interested in return on investment and in the survival of the firm. They have a profit-oriented vision of the firm. Moreover, owners must provide equity.

The family business culture is no longer unitary, unique and characterized by a stable set of meanings. The family, business and ownership systems are subcultures with 'different outlooks of the world' (Alvesson, 2002: 145). These subcultures interact in complex ways (Schneider and Barsoux, 2003), influencing the behaviour of those involved in governance. As a result, family business culture can be portrayed as a network of cultural mosaics (Chao and Moon, 2005). Depending on their social situation, corporate governance actors will draw on different aspects of their multicultural heritage, 'and the different expectations associated with these cultural paradigms will affect their behaviour' (Chao and Moon, 2005: 1129). The family business culture is therefore composed of shared norms of behaviour that result from one subculture's domination of the others or are built on shared subcultures. It also includes norms of behaviour inherent to the different subcultures.

Family firm CEOs must deal with this complex shareholder structure created by the overlap of these three subcultures and by their divergent objectives and characteristics. These subcultures influence the ways people conceive their roles in the family business. Consequently, family considerations can easily intrude on strategic decisions. Some people may play several roles simultaneously, while others may have a single role. Therefore, corporate governance actors may face multiple problems: interpersonal conflicts, role dilemmas, conflicting priorities and boundary disputes (Gersick *et al.*, 1997). These problems may reduce trust or lead to distrust and prevent the CEO from governing the firm effectively. Maintaining and rebuilding trust means resolving issues regarding conflicting values, norms of behaviour, meanings and understandings.

## How CEOs create trust vis-à-vis owners in family firms

When subcultures compete, interpersonal trust may erode and the family CEO may adopt control mechanisms as substitutes for trust. These mechanisms help restore trust based on the symbolic legitimacy that accompanies the use of institutionalized procedures (Sitkin and Roth, 1993). In this chapter, I propose that the family business CEO may create trust with owners by enhancing his or her legitimacy. Legitimacy is the right to govern. In the process of building legitimacy, consent (Coicaud, 2002), as well as norms and values (Mari *et al.*, 2008), plays a major role. Indeed, the CEO sometimes needs owners to renounce their values or norms of behaviour in favour of new ones of interest to the firm as a whole. So legitimacy also means that the CEO and owners agree to share values and norms of behaviour.

The Economies of Worth Model (Boltanski and Thévenot, 1991) helps us understand how these new norms of behaviour can be created or arise from the interaction of the cultural mosaics of those charged with firm governance.

## Building trust through legitimate formal and informal control mechanisms

To understand what family business CEOs can do to build trust, we need to find out how they can be seen as trustworthy by corporate governance actors. Our perspective dovetails with that of recent literature on trust, which argues that trust and control are closely related (Bijlsma-Frankema and Costa, 2005), not contradictions in terms. For instance, when interpersonal trust has broken down, formal control such as legalistic mechanisms may create trust by strengthening task reliability. However, these legal remedies are ineffective in restoring trust when there is value incongruence (Sitkin and Roth, 1993). Since value congruence is critical for strategic decision making in family firms, examining how to achieve it is of great importance. The Economies of Worth Model provides a suitable framework for examining the achievement of value congruence.

Recently, Sitkin and George (2005) drew on institutional theory (DiMaggio and Powell, 1983) to provide a clear understanding of how, through the use of legitimate formalities, managers can earn the trust of their subordinates. Distinguishing between formal (decision criteria, organizational structures or practices) and informal (traditions and norms) control mechanisms, they suggest that the configuration of formal and informal mechanisms may create legitimacy and trust. This perspective may be used in combination with the Economies of Worth Model to understand how the CEO and the owners can create mutual trust through formal and informal control. Like Sitkin and George (2005), I posit that owners will be more likely to trust the CEO when there are easy-to-recognize markers of the legitimacy of the CEO, the CEO's decisions and the firm. To build trust, the family CEO will take actions that strengthen his or her legitimacy in the eyes of the owners by using formal and informal indicators to sustain his or her actions. For example, when unfamiliar with the business culture, owners may be more likely to trust the CEO's strategic decisions if they are the result of legitimate strategic decision making, or if they are viewed as legitimate by external directors.

More specifically, drawing on the literature on family firms and organizations, I propose that family CEOs can build trust through the following formalities: fair processes (Van der Heyden *et al.*, 2005), formal organization structure and decision-making criteria (formal control) and shared norms of behaviour (informal control). The Economies of Worth Model helps us understand further how informal control may be strengthened through the process of creating new norms of behaviours.

## Building trust by enhancing the legitimacy of family firm CEOs: applying convention theory

The Economies of Worth Model (Boltanski and Thévenot, 1991) highlights how, despite conflicting values, people use legitimate agreements to cooperate. Applied to the family business culture mosaic, this model shows how norms of behaviour from the family, business and ownership subcultures are brought together as new bases for trust.

### The Economies of Worth Model

The Economies of Worth Model views social coordination as achieved through rules (which become habits, common knowledge and culture) as well as price and exchange; in other words, sociology and economics join forces to understand cooperation among people with often conflicting values. Conventions reflect the expectations people have of one another. They are understandings that organize and coordinate action in predictable ways. They are habits, customs, routines, and standard practices that serve as signposts for economic interpretation and interaction (Biggart and Beamish, 2003). However, conventions imply 'a notion of coordination which is much more open to uncertainty, critical tensions and creative arrangements than the ideas of stabilized and reproductive orders' that characterize many sociologists' work (Thévenot, 2001) and Institutional Theory (DiMaggio and Powell, 1983). Finally, convention theory considers complexity and conflict a result not of group conflict but of 'the "same" human being's need to engage in different modes of conduct which vary from one situation to another' (Thévenot, 2001). This model takes the perspective that people are plural, meaning that different situations typically lead to different reactions.

Boltanski and Thévenot (1991) identify forms of behaviour in society and highlight the six general principles (motives, or, as they call them, 'logics of action' and 'worlds') underlying them. These worlds are historical constructions, drawn from classics in the field of political philosophy, and they reflect representations of the common good:

- Inspired world: giving value to creation and inspiration;
- Domestic world: giving value to tradition and hierarchy;
- Opinion world: giving value to reputation, recognition and success;
- Civic world: giving value to collective beings and general will;
- Market world: giving value to rivalry and competitors;
- Industrial world: giving value to performance and the future.

In addition to these principles, other characteristics such as objects and persons are used to describe and identify the worlds in a situation. These criteria indicate how people from each world think, behave, and act according to its specific values. Thus, each world entails a distinctive 'institutional logic' embodying specific orientations toward actions and evaluation of these actions.

Even though these worlds are governed by conflicting logics, they can coexist. The Economies of Worth Model sheds light both on the process whereby legitimate agreements (i.e. conventions) are reached to achieve cooperation and, at the same time, on the ways the worlds evolve.

When logics of action conflict, coordination becomes difficult. People may enter into conflict. Reaching agreements and committing to them means that these agreements must be considered legitimate by those in conflict. This legitimacy is built through justification. To justify their actions, people identify the worlds in conflict. For instance, a family CEO could justify his decision to keep a strategic activity in his portfolio instead of selling it by referring to the domestic logic of action: by tradition, the family has always been involved in the particular business. Even if it is less profitable than before, the CEO prefers to remain in the business. Through this process of justification, behaviour is qualified and evaluated. It is not a person's intrinsic qualities that determine his or her worth, but the qualities he or she exhibits in a particular world.

People in conflict must then decide on a common principle of equivalence to justify their views, take stock of what they have in common with each other and support a judgment based on their relative worth. When people refer to common criteria to define the situation, an agreement can be reached by reference to a common higher principle. This agreement is viewed as legitimate.

There are, of course, different kinds of agreements. Some are sustainable while others are momentary. Some are compromises within one world, while others result from trade-offs between several worlds. Of particular relevance to family firms is conflict involving several worlds; people refer to different higher principles drawn from different worlds. Agreements can be reached in a variety of ways:

1. One world is favoured: Several worlds are present and an agreement is reached by referring to one of these worlds.
2. Arrangement: In this situation, each person stays in his or her world, but a local agreement is reached. As this agreement does not relate to a higher principle, it cannot be applied generally. Arrangements are momentary and can change when people or situations change.
3. Compromise: Compromise is a more sustainable agreement. Compromises emerge from the association of different characteristics of different worlds.

I now take this approach to examine how agreements foster the evolution of family business cultures and build new foundations of trust.

### Applying the Economies of Worth Model to how CEOs create trust across cultures

The Economies of Worth Model can be used to depict the family business culture as a network of cultural mosaics; each subculture can be described through the values and norms of behaviour that characterize the world.

When the corporate governance actors face conflicting values or norms of behaviour, CEOs justify their strategic decisions by referring to the subculture of their decision. To be perceived as trustworthy, they will use the formalities inherent to this subculture to justify their actions. Others involved in the situation will justify their actions similarly. Agreement between subcultures is reached by invoking a higher principle of one of these subcultures. As a consequence, one of these corporate governance actors will adopt new norms of behaviour that will be the basis for trust. This process highlights how trust can be maintained or repaired in situations of conflict: people from one subculture can learn norms of behaviour from another subculture, while those involved in firm governance can abide by new norms of behaviour created by the merging of characteristics from different worlds.

It is then possible to describe the three processes whereby new norms of behaviour emerge from the interaction of subcultures:

1. Some norms of behaviour dominate others. When subcultures are in conflict, an agreement is reached by favouring one subculture (world).

2. Some norms of behaviour prevail as they belong to the same subculture and they are shared by the corporate governance actors who interact. They may also spring from the interaction of subcultures and from compromise.

3. Some norms of behaviour belonging to different subcultures are maintained (arrangement process) and express subculture-independent influences.

The family business culture evolves through this process, as do the dynamics of trust. These new norms of behaviour will be the foundations for the mutual trust of those involved in firm governance.

Through the Economies of Worth Model, it is possible to identify three processes in the dynamics of trust: building, maintaining and repairing of trust. Trust is built or repaired when the foundations of relationships among those involved in governance shift from one subculture to another. Trust is maintained when the foundations of trust remain rooted in the same subculture. I will illustrate this dynamics of trust by referring to an exploratory study.

## The dynamics of trust across cultures in family firms: an illustration

### Method

For the exploratory case study, in-depth interviews were conducted to analyse relationships between those involved in firm governance in the context of two strategic decisions. For each decision, five family and five non-family members, who were key participants in the decision, were interviewed. The interviews lasted at least two hours. They were audio-recorded, transcribed verbatim and coded. As Miles and Huberman (1994) recommend, I developed a first list of codes from the conceptual framework and research questions which I amended during data collection. To improve reliability, another researcher and I used this list of codes to categorize several pages. When we disagreed, we discussed the definition, pertinence of the code and decided to maintain or to remove it. We reproduced this process for other pages until we reached a rate of reliability of 90 per cent. Data analysis then involved the search for patterns of trust building. First, a detailed narrative of the strategic decision process was developed and two themes were identified: the nature of trust built and the process of trust building. Subsequently, the data were examined in greater detail to derive detailed descriptions of themes and subthemes. Following a brief description of the family firm studied, an understanding of how the CEO earned the trust of the owners is presented.

## The Wheels Company: background

The Wheels Company,[1] founded by Andrew Bower and his brother, is a large European family business in the automobile industry. The company employs about 2,000 people and manages over 80 subsidiaries around the world; 2003 turnover was in excess of 877 million euros. When Andrew Bower died in 1979, his successors (six children, among whom four sons are involved in the business) decided to take over the business and the youngest son, François Bower, was named CEO by the family members. The company, principally an automobile retailer, was in fact involved in different businesses (two-wheeled vehicles, car sales, real estate and office furniture) and each brother ran one of these four businesses. The four brothers took strategic decisions during family councils, which took place periodically at their mother's home (she had never worked in the company). Monthly board meetings took place at her home and brought the four brothers together. The four brothers were dynamic entrepreneurs, making career progress and managing their own businesses. Running the whole family firm together at the same time as the individual businesses wasn't an easy task. Each had to sacrifice personal interest to the interest of the family business as a whole. The mother didn't really take part in strategy decisions but helped them reach agreements. After their mother's death, and in view of the third generation's desire to enter the business, François Bower realized that it would be harder to keep the family united behind the company and that more formal mechanisms were necessary.

Corporate governance had to be changed and to become more explicit as conflicts arose between family members. One family branch wanted to sell its share and leave the business. There was a lack of information, of clear rules, which led to distrust between some family owners ... For me, there is a coherence of kin. We were all from the same nest; therefore, we all had had the same life experiences, which are our roots. Today, they are from different nests and the common experience, or backbone, is much more limited. (Family member CEO).

Whereas the sibling co-owners were bound by their common history and their close personal ties, the third generation could not understand or replicate this type of relationship. From generation to generation, family dynamics evolve, making it difficult to replicate the trust that characterized earlier generations. Some family relationships even evolved into relationships characterized by distrust. This distrust also emerged from the lack of clear rules and skills requirements for family members who wished to enter the business. Consequently, family involvement sometimes had negative consequences.

---

[1] For confidentiality reasons, the names of the company and the parties involved have been changed.

Some family members are still involved in the business. Some are in charge of business units. However, we observed that some of these business units perform less well than the other business units of the family firm. An internal audit showed that these business units were underperforming because of a lack of managerial and control competence ... And it takes time to resolve the problem. (Non-family member chief financial officer).

This problem highlights the complexity of dealing with family members when the performance of the business falters. Family firms tend to take care of family members involved in the business, as ties are emotionally based. The ties may also lead to conflict. But it is also important for the firm, in the broader interest of the family, to pursue performance.

To prevent conflicts between family members, rebuild trust and treat the family fairly, the CEO decided to create a new corporate governance structure.

## *The processes of creating, maintaining and repairing trust in family firms*

In this section, I will describe the processes of creating, maintaining and repairing trust and present the formal underpinnings of trust established by the CEO. The Economies of Worth Model is used to facilitate an understanding of how these formalities contributed to trust. Whether trust is created or repaired depends, naturally, on whether those involved in firm governance trusted each other to begin with. As a rule, creation of trust is typical of intergenerational relationships, as the members of different generations rarely know each other in the context of the business. On the contrary, although sibling relationships may be characterized by trust, a lack of communication between the CEO and the owners may erode the trust of those not involved in the firm.

I will present two conflicts that undermined trust. The first had to do with strategic investment decisions, the second with requirements for entering the business. For each, I describe how the CEO went about solving these problems by developing formal and informal control mechanisms to underpin trust. I then illustrate how the trust built through the resolution of these conflicts was maintained over time.

### Challenges to trust: lack of communication

This first problem required the repair of trust following a conflict between the family CEO and some of his siblings. Consistent with domestic logic, the corporate governance structure was rather informal: it involved an executive committee and a family council (composed of the four brothers) that met at the mother's home each month and was chaired by the oldest brother. After the mother's death, trust was threatened by a lack of information on strategic decisions. Some family members questioned certain strategic investments and feared opportunism from other family members involved in the business. One branch of the family wanted to sell out. The family CEO did not want the family to break up or lose control of the firm.

As the trust that once characterized the second-generation siblings had been threatened, more control-based forms of trust were necessary. However, the new corporate governance structure and the new rules of behaviour recommended by the family CEO drew on the business subculture (industrial and civic logics) and challenged domestic logic. Therefore, the CEO had to reassure corporate governance actors that the change was in their best interest. To do so, he involved them in the process.

First, he organized a family meeting and invited CEOs from other successful family firms. Here, the opinion and industrial logics are expressed. These CEOs were very well known. They explained to the entire family how they managed their businesses, the challenges they faced and the need to reorganize their corporate governance structure to favour professional management and remain competitive. As a result of this presentation, the family members not involved in the business became more familiar with the business subculture, its characteristics, and constraints. Family members trusted them. Ultimately, they agreed that, to stay competitive, The Wheels Company's governance would have to be reorganized.

Second, the family CEO hired a consultant to help redesign governance processes. This consultant brought all the family members together to discuss the business with them, what it meant to them, and how to keep it in the family. He favoured new norms of behaviour from the business subculture and helped family members accept them. As a result of these meetings, family members could express their opinions and attempt to justify them. Finally, family members took part in the decisions.

Hence, they created trust through formal control mechanisms (new corporate governance structures and fair strategic decision-making processes) and informal control mechanisms (new norms of behaviour). These were:

1. Creation of a board of directors to oversee strategy and ensure that the firm is professionally managed. Independent directors now sit on this board. The chairman is an independent director.
2. Creation of an audit committee made up of two independent and two family directors and led by an independent director. It oversees internal checks and balances.

3. Creation of a remuneration committee of two independent directors and the CEO. This committee determines pay for the executive committee and executive family members.
4. Rules for involvement of family members in the business: family members who want to work in the business need to have the diploma that enables them to apply for this job and three years of experience in another firm.
5. Strategic decisions: decisions must be made in formal business settings such as the executive committee, board of directors or strategic committee meetings (Mum's kitchen table is out of the question now).
6. Establishment of a family charter: family members commit to rules that govern their ties to the firm (corporate governance, pay, ethics rules).

As a result of these formalities, family members were more willing to trust the CEO and believe in the structure and the fairness of the decision-making process. The multiple meetings, the involvement of outside professionals (business consultants, outside directors) and the legitimacy of the outsiders were the cornerstones of the family CEO's ability to strengthen the legitimacy of the decisions he made to restructure the corporate governance and to create trust. The decision process helped those involved in firm governance become more familiar with the subcultures they were not part of. As they were involved in the process, family members accepted these norms of behaviour and committed to them.

### Challenges to trust: conditions for entering the business unclear to the third generation

The creation of trust emerged from a conflict that affected the family CEO and the third-generation family members who wanted to enter the business. They were arguing over the requirements for going into the business. The rules for involvement of family members in the business presented above resulted from the resolution of this conflict. Before the establishment of the new corporate governance structure and the new norms of behaviour, decisions to hire family members were made by the four brothers of the second generation. The family business culture is expressed through the three following logics of action: the four brothers used to decide who could enter the business because, as members of the second generation, they had hierarchical authority over the third generation (domestic logic). They also had a long and successful experience of the business, which gave them an authoritative voice in the industrial world. Indeed, they took over the firm after the founder's death. They each ran their own business units, which they knew very well because 'they had started them from scratch and had been through all the firm's problems and types of decisions'. Finally, the legitimacy of the four brothers stemmed from their consideration of the collective interest (civic logic). Although each brother managed his business alone without consulting the others, they sought to run the whole firm in the family's interest. They knew how to work together to manage the whole firm together and the performance was quite good.

Unfortunately, the rules and requirements weren't clear to the third generation, which didn't want the four brothers to decide on their careers. 'Indeed, with the previous generation around the family table, it was a black box for outsiders. They [family members from the third generation] didn't know what was going on' (CEO). The family CEO believed that new norms of behaviour had to be established. Moreover, some talented people from the third generation considered leaving, while the family firm suffered from a lack of competence among other family member employees. Here, domestic logic is called into question.

Establishing requirements for family members who want to enter the business put two views (worlds) in conflict. Consistent with market logic, some family members invoked their right as shareholders to be involved in the business. Other family members, who wanted to be considered like anyone else applying for a job in the firm, argued that a business degree and experience in another firm should be required. The family CEO, in keeping with this industrial logic, helped reach an agreement by relying on civic logic as well. He reminded family members that they were dealing with performance problems because some family members involved in running the business lacked the necessary skills. So an agreement was reached in the business subculture expressed through industrial and civic logics. A new set of rules for involving family in the business was created, and independent, external directors were invited onto the board to guarantee professional hiring practices. Family members approved these new rules of behaviour and this structure, and understood that respecting them was in the interests of both the firm and the family.

### Evidence of the maintenance of trust

Nine years later, the Wheels Company was exploring whether to acquire a European firm in the same industry. This decision involved the external board of directors, the family CEO and family owners from the second and third generation, including François's nephew (business line manager) and two of François's brothers (who had previously worked in these businesses and were now directors in the board council).

The relationship between the CEO and his nephew played a significant role in the decision: 'The fact that my nephew managed this question was a great comfort to me. I was reassured because, as a shareholder, he is deeply committed to the consequences of this deal not only on a short-term basis but also for tomorrow and after tomorrow'. This argument is an ownership subculture argument that relies on a mix of domestic (shared values inculcated during upbringing) and civic (the family legacy is at stake) logics of action. Indeed, it was easier to trust a family member than a non-family member because family members have a shared interest in the business, a shared vision of strategy and a motivation to take this risk. A non-family member, by contrast, might have shied away from the risk, as failure could have made him fear for his job. Or, just as easily, he might have viewed the acquisition as nothing more than a career opportunity, underestimating the risk for the firm. Trust is expressed in a shared understanding of the management of the family firm, which itself lies in a shared attachment to the business, a shared vision for the future of the firm, and a shared risk orientation that spring from a mix of domestic and industrial logics.

Trust is also manifested in the relationships of François Bower's brothers. François Bower communicated essentially with the chairman and his two brothers, who had long experience in the business and whose legitimacy made them the most influential directors. 'They were the most influential ones in the progress of this case as they knew the car industry, they knew the partners'. So, the members of the board trusted them: 'when they say that we must go, this is a good acquisition, the others follow' (nephew). External directors add value to the business subculture, through industrial logic, which favours competency.

Family members trusted the decision as it was made in a formal setting (board meeting). The legitimacy of the decision was strengthened by the backing of the chairman and the other outside board members. As one of the directors commented, 'now cases are very well prepared, very well analysed; profitability ratios have been included. I observe that decision-making is professional'. Formalities thus contribute to trust. Strategic decisions are justified. At the same time, family ties are maintained and swift decision making is facilitated.

## Discussion

In this chapter, I have shown that the mutual trust among those involved in the governance of family firms is often grounded on norms of behaviour shared by people from a single family. As the family expands, this family culture is more aptly described as a network of cultural mosaics made up of three overlapping and potentially conflicting subcultures. There is then the risk of an erosion of trust. The Economies of Worth Model offers a better understanding of the potential conflicts between these subcultures and the emergence of new norms of behaviour as a basis for forming relationships characterized by trust. The model highlights the production of legitimacy through formal and informal controls, and their contributions to trust. Trust, in short, is founded on the legitimacy of the CEO, the corporate governance structure, and decision criteria which enable him or her to make appropriate strategic decisions, as well as the fair process whereby these decisions are made.

The Economies of Worth Model emphasizes the justification process to address the question of the legitimacy of the agreement. Justification enables people from one subculture to be more familiar with other subcultures. It helps people understand, commit to or adopt norms of behaviour from another subculture, even if at first they conflict with those of their previous subculture. With the Economies of Worth Model, it is possible to delve into the process of negotiation between subcultures and to understand why some norms of behaviour dominate others and why new norms are created. Furthermore, new arguments that take into account the needs of family firms are advanced to design a traditional corporate governance structure. Through the case study, I have shown how such a structure can be implemented and how it can build, maintain or repair trust between those involved in firm governance.

## Implications for practice

Although this chapter focuses on the relationships between the CEO and the family owners, the framework proposed here is relevant for relationships between all those involved in corporate governance, not just the CEOs and members of a single family.

A great benefit of this framework is that it provides guidelines for the design of a structure for family firms that are seeking to preserve or build trust among those involved in corporate governance. As family firms link three subcultures (the family, the business and the ownership) and are emotionally based, trust is difficult to maintain. By taking into account the diversity of perceptions, values and interests that characterize governance relationships, this framework offers new insights for conflict resolution. First, it emphasizes involving governance actors in decision making. As these actors will approach in their own ways the decisions affecting them, they must understand the rationale for them. Involving family members will also make them feel recognized and valued. They will be more willing to accept or make decisions that might be unfavourable to them as they will be assured that their interests will be protected in the long run. A second insight is the importance of legitimacy for underpinning trust in the context of competing subcultures. Finally, this research underscores the necessity of using a variety of cues to signal legitimacy, which embraces and addresses the cultural and psychological diversity of corporate governance actors.

## Directions for future research

This research favours a dual trust/control approach, an approach that focuses not so much on the building of trust alone as on the use of trust and/or control to ensure that positive expectations of others are met. Several papers examine this trust-control nexus (Bijlsma-Frankema and Costa, 2005) by broaching ways of meeting positive expectations of behaviour (Möllering 2005; Bijlsma-Frankema and Costa, 2005).

In this chapter, I draw on Sitkin and George's (2005) framework to show that CEOs use formalities that, by adding to their legitimacy, may help generate trust. With the Economies of Worth Model, I propose that creating formal and informal controls helps those in conflict attain value congruence. It would be interesting to examine in greater depth the contribution to trust of each formality. In this respect, Arregle *et al.* (2007) describe a new theoretical model of board creation and composition. This model underscores the role of the board of directors in resolving conflict among family shareholders. Other research could go beyond this work and investigate the role of the board in building trust.

This chapter focuses on one underpinning of trust: legitimacy. The concept of CEO legitimacy is used to understand how CEOs can be seen as trustworthy by other corporate governance actors. Exploration of dimensions of trustworthiness such as ability, integrity and benevolence (Mayer *et al.*, 1995) could shed light on this concept. One possibility could be to explore the formalities (rules for the appointment of CEOs, corporate governance structures and the composition of the board of directors, etc.) that contribute to the development of these dimensions of trustworthiness.

In addition, CEO legitimacy is earned through a consensus reached on values and norms of behaviour regarding professional management of the firm and preservation of shareholder interests. In this perspective, the requirements family members must meet to enter the business underscore the importance of their earning legitimacy. Future research could focus more closely on the formalities and informalities that signal attachment to the family firm and on the means of legitimizing this attachment and thus creating trust.

This research is not without limitations. The analysis presented in this chapter relies on a small number of interviews, done at one point in time and interviewees were asked to reflect on past events. More robust analysis involving multiple methods of longitudinal research (observations, focus group interviews, diaries) and real-time data collection, would enhance confidence in the findings.

## Concluding comments

The Economies of Worth Model (Boltanski and Thévenot, 1991) enables insights into how a legitimate agreement can be reached when at least two subcultures conflict. For family firms, this approach is clearly relevant. Indeed, those involved in the governance of family firms may simultaneously play multiple roles inherent to potentially conflicting subcultures. We need theories that help us deal with this complexity. Unlike classic sociology, the Economies of Worth Model views people as plural, meaning that the cultures they are representatives of may depend on what they are experiencing. This model deepens our understanding of the dynamics of trust in a family firm by emphasizing the subcultures within the firm, as well as the family itself, and how they evolve across generations.

## References

Arregle, J.-L., Mari, I., Melin, L., Nordqvist, M. and Very, P. 2007. 'Board creation and composition in family firms: a conflict-resolution perspective'. *CeFEO Working Papers.*

Alvesson, M. 1993. *Cultural Perspectives on Organizations.* Cambridge University Press.

2002. *Understanding Organizational Culture.* London: Sage.

Beckard, R. and Dyer, W. 1983. 'Managing continuity in family-owned business'. *Organizational Dynamics*, 12(1), 5–12.

Biggart, N. W. and Beamish, T. D. 2003. 'The economic sociology of conventions: habit, custom, practice, and routine'. *Annual Review of Sociology*, 29, 443–64.

Bijlsma-Frankema, K. and Costa, A. C. 2005. 'Understanding the trust-control nexus'. *International Sociology*, 20(3), 259–82.

Chao, G. T. and Moon, H. 2005. 'The cultural mosaic: a metatheory for understanding the complexity of culture'. *Journal of Applied Psychology*, 90(6), 1128–40.

Chrisman, J. J., Chua, J. H. and Sharma, P. 2005. 'Trends and directions in the development of a strategic management theory in the family firm'. *Entrepreneurship, Theory and Practice*, September, 555–75.

Coicaud, J. M. 2002. *Legitimacy and Politics: Contribution to the Study of Political Right and Political Responsibility*. Cambridge University Press.

Corbetta, G. and Salvato, C. A. 2004. 'The board of directors in family firms: one size fits all?' *Family Business Review*, 17(2), 119–34.

Davis, J. A. and Herrera, R. M. 1998. 'The social psychology of family shareholder dynamics'. *Family Business Review*, 11(3), 253–60.

Davis, P. and Harveston, P. 1999. 'In the founder's shadow: conflict in the family firm'. *Family Business Review*, 12(1), 311–23.

2001. 'The phenomenon of substantive conflict in the family firm: a cross-generational study'. *Journal of Small Business Management*, 39(1), 14–30.

DiMaggio, P. J. and Powell, W. W. 1983. 'The iron cage revisited: institutional isomorphism and collective rationality in organizational fields'. *American Sociological Review*, 48, 147–60.

Frost, P. J. 1985. *Organizational Culture*. Newbury Park: Sage.

Gersick, K. E., Davis, J. A., McCollom Hampton, M. E. and Lansberg, I. 1997. *Generation to Generation: Life Cycles of Family Businesses*. Boston: Harvard Business School Press.

Gómez-Mejía, L., Núñez-Nickel, L. and Gutiérrez, L. 2001. 'The role of family ties in agency contracts'. *Academy of Management Journal*, 44, 81–95.

Hall, A., Melin, L. and Nordqvist, M. 2001. 'Entrepreneurship as radical change in the family business: exploring the role of cultural patterns'. *Family Business Review*, 24(3), 193–208.

Jaffe, D. T. and Lane, S. H. 2004. 'Sustaining a family dynasty: key issues facing complex multigenerational business and investment-owning families'. *Family Business Review*, 27(1), 81–98.

Jones, G. R. 1983. 'Transaction costs, property rights, and organizational culture: an exchange perspective'. *Administrative Science Quarterly*, 28, 454–67.

Levinson, H. 1971. 'Conflicts that plague family business'. *Harvard Business Review*, 49(2), 90–8.

Litz, R. A. 1995. 'The family business: toward a definitional clarity'. *Academy of Management Journal Best Papers Proceedings*, 100–4.

Mari, I., Petit, V. and Arregle, J.-L. 2008. 'Managerial legitimacy of top executives: a way to reconsider executive power in corporate governance?' *24th EGOS Colloquium*, Amsterdam, 10–12 July, 1–28.

Mayer, R. C., Davis J. H. and Schoorman, F. D. 1995. 'An integrative model of organizational trust'. *Academy of Management Review*, 20, 709–34.

Melin, L. 2001. 'Understanding strategic dynamics in family businesses through an integrative approach'. Paper presented at Theories of the Family Enterprise:

Establishing Paradigms for the Field – 1st Academic Conference, University of Alberta, Edmonton, September, 1–31.

Meyer, M. and Zucker, L. G. 1989. *Permanently Failing Organizations*. Newbury Park, CA: Sage.

Miles, M. B. and Huberman, A. M. 1994. *Qualitative Data Analysis: an Expanded Sourcebook*. Thousand Oaks, CA: Sage.

Möllering, G. 2005. 'The trust/control duality: an integrative perspective on positive expectations of others'. *International Sociology*, 20(3), 283–305.

Morck R. and Yeung, B. 2004. 'Family control and the rent seeking society'. *Entrepreneurship Theory and Practice*, 28, 391–409.

Mustakallio, M., Autio, E. and Zahra, S. A. 2002. 'Relational and contractual governance in family firms: effects on strategic decision making'. *Family Business Review*, 15(3), 205–22.

Nordqvist, M. 2005. *Understanding the Role of Ownership in Strategizing. A Study of Family Firms*. Jönköping: JIBS Dissertation Series No. 29.

Schein, E. H. 1995. 'The role of the founder in creating organizational culture'. *Family Business Review*, 8(3), 221–38.

Schneider, S. C. and Barsoux, J.-L. 2003. *Managing Across Cultures*. London: Prentice Hall.

Schulze, W. S., Lubatkin, M. H. and Dino, R. N. 2000. 'Altruism and agency in family firms'. *Academy of Management Proceedings*, 11, 1–5.

Schulze, W. S., Lubatkin, M. H., Dino, R. N. and Buchholtz A. K. 2001. 'Agency relationships in family firms: theory and evidence'. *Organization Science*, 12(2), 99–116.

Sitkin, S. B. and George, E. 2005. 'Managerial trust building through the use of legitimating formal and informal control mechanisms'. *International Sociology*, 20(3), 307–38.

Sitkin, S. B. and Roth, N. 1993. 'Explaining the limited effectiveness of legalistic "remedies" for trust/distrust'. *Organization Science*, 4(3), 367–92.

Steier, L. 2001. 'Family firms, plural forms of governance, and the evolving role of trust'. *Family Business Review*, 14(4), 353–67.

Thévenot, L. 2001. 'Organized complexity, conventions of coordination and the composition of economic arrangements'. *European Journal of Social Theory*, 4(4), 405–25.

Van der Heyden, L., Blondel, C. and Carlock, R. S. 2005. 'Fair process: striving for justice in family business'. *Family Business Review*, 28(1), 1–21.

Vilaseca, A. 2002. 'The shareholder role in the family business: conflicts of interests and objectives between non-employed shareholders and top management team'. *Family Business Review*, 15(4), 299–320.

Ward, J. L. 1987. *Keeping the Family Business Healthy: How to Plan for Continuing Growth, Profitability, and Family Leadership*. San Francisco: Jossey-Bass.

Ward J. L. and Hendy, J. L. 1988. 'A survey of board practices'. *Family Business Review*, 1(3), 289–308.

Wortman Jr., M. S. 1994. 'Theoretical foundations for family-owned businesses: a conceptual and research-based paradigm'. *Family Business Review*, 7(1), 3–27.

# PART IV

# Conclusions and ways forward

# 16 Emerging themes, implications for practice, and directions for research

MARK N. K. SAUNDERS, DENISE SKINNER
AND ROY J. LEWICKI

## Introduction

The conclusion summarizes the key findings presented within each section of the book, identifying the emerging patterns and themes across the conceptual contributions and empirical studies. These are considered in relation to our two initial questions. First, is there a universally applicable model of trust and trust development [*etic*], or do people from varying cultures understand and enact trust differently [*emic*]? And second, how can Party A from Culture #1 develop a trust relationship with Party B from Culture #2? We then highlight the implications of these patterns and themes for practitioners, and point to directions for future research.

We began this book with three vignettes that we believe highlight both the complexity and ordinariness of cross-cultural trust building in today's globalized business world. In the first vignette, we considered an Iranian businesswoman who is negotiating on behalf of her firm with male representatives from a German alliance partner; we particularly focused on the cultural implications for trust both within her own firm and between her firm and the German alliance partner. In the second vignette, we charted the trust relationship between a Dutch and an Irish employee representative, both engineers, working in and representing employees in Holland and England respectively, for an Anglo-Dutch firm during a period of considerable change, which culminated in the firm being bought by an Indian company. In contrast, in the third vignette, we reported production problems and the lack of trust between a French workforce and German contract technicians rectifying errors made in the company's German factory. We used these three vignettes to illustrate the importance of trust in securing sustainable working relationships in situations that are ambiguous and uncertain, and in a world where people from different and unfamiliar cultures are increasingly being asked to work together and manage their strategic business relationships. In each vignette, the cultures that individuals belonged to influenced the formation of trust cues within a relationship, and served as filters for cues encountered from other cultures, sometimes resulting in confusion, misunderstanding and miscommunication.

The vignettes highlighted the multiplicity of ways that cultures may group together. Schneider and Barsoux (2003) refer to these as 'cultural spheres' to which individuals invariably belong, and which extend beyond their national cultural sphere. Using Chao and Moon's (2005) metaphor of a mosaic, these spheres were portrayed as a series of 'tiles' operating both within and across organizations, each one representing a specific unique cultural identity of a person, such as nationality, ethnicity, religion, sector/industry, organization or profession. The existence and interaction of such 'spheres' or 'tiles', we argued, highlighted two essential questions with regard to the nature of culture and trust. *Question 1* is whether there is a universally applicable model of trust and trust development [*etic*], or do people from varying cultures understand and enact trust differently [*emic*]? *Question 2* is how can Party A from Culture #1 develop a trust relationship with Party B from Culture #2, given strong differences in intercultural interaction? Adapting Lewicki and Bunker's (1996) staged model, we presented our analysis as a five-stage model of trust development across cultural boundaries (Figure 1.3, page 7). This model represents the ways that the parties from different cultural spheres, and with different cultural tiles, might proceed through five key elements or stages: context, opening stance, early encounters, breakthrough or breakdown and consequences. Adopting the theoretical proposition that trust is fundamentally interpersonal but is shaped by latent and overt influences at multiple group, organizational and national levels, some of which are also cultural, the subsequent chapters presented their various interpretations of the trust-building and trust-repair processes across very different 'cultural spheres'. In Part I of this book, we considered the conceptual challenges of researching trust across different cultural spheres. Drawing upon both empirical studies and conceptual projects, the chapters in Parts II and III provided an 'emic' or integrated 'emic'/'etic' view of trust, in either between-organization relationships (Part II) or within-organization relationships (Part III). In this concluding chapter, we return to these two questions and, in our final discussion, we draw implications for practice and potential future research agendas.

## The conceptual challenge of researching trust across cultures

Following the Introduction, the three chapters in Part I offered distinctive insights into the challenges of researching trust across cultures. We consider these in relation firstly to the universal applicability of trust and trust development across cultures, and second, to the development of trust within relationships.

## Universal applicability

Our first question is whether there is a universally applicable model of trust and trust development [*etic*] or do people from varying cultural identities understand and enact trust differently [*emic*]. Addressing this issue, Ferrin and Gillespie proposed that whilst there is strong, consistent evidence that trust differs between national–societal cultures, there is also evidence that trust is universal across cultures. In other words, there are both culturally specific and universally applicable determinants and consequences of trust. Through the lens of their review of the predominately quantitative empirical research evidence on the effects of national–societal culture on interpersonal trust, Ferrin and Gillespie noted that countries differ in their average level of generalized trust. This difference was consistently associated with 'macro' factors such as national wealth, income equality, education, 'good' government, strong formal institutions and ethnic homogeneity, all of which are largely demographic and geographic rather than associative cultural tiles. Arguing that it is unclear from the studies conducted to date whether the influence of in-group bias on trust is culturally specific or holds equally across national–societal cultures, they concluded that there is mixed support for the role of cultural distance and similarity of societal background as clear and unambiguous determinants of trust. While past research suggests that the trustworthiness characteristics of ability, benevolence and integrity are universally applicable, there are also culturally specific unique manifestations and interpretations of these characteristics in at least some countries. Furthermore, there are additional, emic aspects of trustworthiness (such as thriftiness, respect for authority, organizational commitment) that appear to be more important in some countries than in others.

In Chapter 3, Reinhard Bachmann's contribution stressed the importance of cultural context as it relates to Question 1: the cultural specificity–universalistic debate. Bachmann called for a conceptualization of trust that is less universalistic and more context sensitive, placing emphasis on the emic component. Using examples comparing Germany and the UK, he cited national differences in their systems and orientations (geographic tiles), arguing that the resultant strong forms of individual power in each are not conducive to trust building. In contrast to the predominantly quantitative studies (reviewed by Ferrin and Gillespie in Chapter 2), Bachmann advocated using a mixed-methods design to build upon broader generalizations, and suggested using repertory grids as an appropriate way of understanding such contexts more fully. Focusing on the potential of repertory grids to build country-collective mind maps, he illustrated how these maps could provide the depth of understanding needed to understand and compare trust between cultures. Bachmann argued that universalistic concepts are useful for initial trust orientation, but that they lose explanatory capability when applied to real-world situations. Consequently, there is a need for a more differentiated understanding of how and why trust differs across cultures, combining both quantitative and qualitative research designs, so as to remain academically rigorous without losing practical usefulness.

Context, and the relational nature of trust, provided the focus for Wright and Ehnert's chapter (4), which, like Bachmann's chapter, also considered the wider utility of trust research in the world of practice. In this theoretical contribution, Wright and Ehnert proposed that because trust is dynamic rather than fixed or stable, it should be framed as a social construction. Like Gillespie and Ferrin, Wright and Ehnert identified limitations in the current academic literature which, they believe, reflect the limitations of trust researchers, rather than the realities of trust itself. They argued that while most researchers recognize that trust is relational and contextual, many researchers conceptualize and approach it in a universalist way, thereby ignoring the need to include contextual and relational aspects in their models. Provocatively, they argued that most existing research on cultural differences or similarities has limited use for practitioners. In drawing a link between trust development and the sensemaking literature, they propose that trust should be treated as a verb, as this allows it to be represented as a dynamic process. Going further than either Ferrin and Gillespie or Bachmann in relation to Question 1, they argued that trust is always shaped by contexts, histories and other actants, which need to be studied (an aspect addressed, for example, by Yousfi in Chapter 9). Culture (and its component tiles) is but one of several considerations that influence human organizing. Actors are always in the process of trusting, and trust is created through narrative, a social process of interaction and conversation. As illustrated later in by Kassis Henderson (Chapter 14), language is not neutral; power is always present in an encounter involving more than one person.

## Developing trust relationships

Turning to Question 2 (how can Party A from Culture #1 develop a trust relationship with Party B from Culture #2), Ferrin and Gillespie's chapter offered a useful overview of existing research. They noted that the few studies which have examined the mediating role of trust across cultural contexts, do provide preliminary supporting evidence that trust universally mediates certain relationships, such as between leaders and followers (an aspect addressed by Hope-Hailey and colleagues in Chapter 13) and supervisors and subordinates (addressed by Wasti and Tan in Chapter 12). However, they also noted that trust's mediating role in other empirical relationships, such as between leadership and subordinate citizenship behaviour, appeared to be culturally and context specific, highlighting the need for further research. In reviewing the predominantly quantitative body of research on this topic, they stressed how the use of country as a proxy variable for national culture could create difficulties and highlighted the problems inherent in isolating the effect of cultural variables. They questioned the impact of structural factors within academia on research design, and suggested that it is probable that the research literature overstates the true effects of culture on trust. They argued that these structural factors encourage the design, conduct, and publication of research on cross-cultural differences, while discouraging the design, conduct and publication of research on cross-cultural universals. The predominance of quantitative studies identified in their review also supports, albeit to a certain extent obliquely, the calls for alternative methods and methodologies in researching trust across cultures by both Bachmann in Chapter 3 and Wright and Ehnert in Chapter 4.

## Trust across different 'cultural spheres': inter-organizational studies

Building on the exploration of the conceptual and theoretical issues relating to researching trust across different cultures, Part II presented six chapters – five empirical and one theoretical – each considering aspects of trust across differing inter-organizational cultural spheres. These explored the professional (associative) cultural tiles of consultants and auditors and their respective clients; national (demographic) cultural tiles in German–Ukraine and French–Lebanese business relationships; a range of demographic and associative cultural tiles in the contexts of cooperation between micro-entrepreneurs in Nigeria and Ghana; and conflict resolution in multiple cross-cultural contexts from a theoretical perspective.

### Universal applicability

In relation to Question 1, the chapters in Part II offered further insights regarding how certain aspects of trustworthiness can have different foci in different cultures, and how the competing demands of different cultural tiles can, in some cases, result in conflict. They also highlighted how the applicability of the trustworthiness characteristics of ability, benevolence and integrity (Mayer *et al.*, 1995) varies across cultures. Considering conflict resolution in a cross-cultural context from a theoretical perspective, Kramer (Chapter 7) focused on dyadic negotiations between representatives of different cultural groups, arguing that, overall, the effectiveness of the negotiation process was affected by the level of trust between negotiators and that trust was difficult to achieve when individuals represented different cultural groups. He identified two principal barriers to trust: psychological and social. Psychological barriers are rooted in in-group bias, are the result of out-group distrust, and are sustained even in the face of evidence to the contrary. Trust-destroying evidence is weighed more heavily than evidence to the contrary. Social barriers relate to the roles played by third parties, such that third-party disclosure amplifies distrust to a greater extent than it increases trust.

Differences between work cultures, and in particular the competing demands of different cultural spheres and their influence upon trust, were the subject matter of chapters by Avakian and colleagues (5) and by Dibben and Rose (6). Avakian and colleagues considered inter-organizational trust and interpersonal trust in the context of client and consultant relationships, suggesting that trust was embedded in the alignment of cultural spheres, and that this alignment helped to reduce uncertainty. In Chapter 5 they argued (as did Ferrin and Gillespie, in relation to national cultures in Chapter 2) that, whilst there might be universalist principles of trust, these were manifested and interpreted within culturally specific contexts. They offered as an example the case of consultants who had to reconcile the corporate cultural values of their own organization with their clients' expectations, driven by the overwhelming need to build a positive relationship with clients while upholding their own organization's culture. Similarly, in their chapter on the auditing profession, Dibben and Rose argued that the competing demands of the different cultural spheres (organizational, professional, client and public cultural tiles) inhabited by individual auditors created complex implications for individuals' trustworthiness, and resulted in different trust (and distrust) requirements and criteria for different contexts. Their research showed how different cultural tiles assume greater or lesser importance depending on the auditor's varying roles, but that within the auditing profession, the prominence of the organization tile strengthens relative to the profession tile as an individual's career develops in that profession.

Differences between national cultures and their implications for trust provided the focus of the remaining chapters in Part II. In Chapter 8, Möllering and Stache explored the challenge of dealing with cultural differences between Germany and Ukraine, within a context of institutional instability and uncertainty. They argued that overcoming barriers requires a genuine interest in understanding the other party, questioning one's own assumptions, and searching for common aims and rules for initial interactions that produce positive mutual experiences through which a trustful relationship can grow. Within business relationships often characterized by dependence and power differences, trust across cultures emerged during interaction when people started to look beyond cultural differences and to work on setting up common rules for their specific relationship. Those rules could then contribute to a reflexive trust-building process by making each other's behaviour more understandable and less uncertain.

National cultural differences and the importance of demographic cultural tiles were also highlighted by Yousfi in Chapter 9. Yousfi explored the nature of trust in French–Lebanese contractual relationships, where relative differences in the importance of the ability and benevolence dimensions between the two national cultures resulted in different manifestations and interpretations of 'good cooperation', and, in turn, of trustworthy behaviour. These differences hindered the resolution of difficulties, as both parties interpreted the contract and its enactment differently; thus, while the trustworthiness characteristics of ability, benevolence and integrity may be universally manifest, the way in which they are likely to be interpreted and acted upon is quite sensitive to differences in cultural context.

## Developing trust relationships

The chapters in Part II also provided insights into how different parties from different cultures with different expectations might develop trust relationships, taking into account the range, relative dominance and interactions across cultural tiles. Kramer (Chapter 7) highlighted how, in dyadic negotiations, trust is difficult to achieve when individuals represent different cultural groups. He argued that trust between different cultures can be built through signalling one's own trustworthiness and willingness to cooperate, and trying to encourage cooperative behaviour in the other party. Creating positive personal bonds can build trust, as can creating appropriate institutional structures which create mechanisms for resolving questions of interpretation and concerns about compliance that allow an initial agreement to be reached (often representing associative cultural tiles, compare with Lyon and Porter, Chapter 10).

Avakian and colleagues (Chapter 5) and Dibben and Rose (Chapter 6) both focused on trust development in situations where there is likely to be cultural conflict. For Avakian and colleagues, consultants have to both uphold the associative culture tile of their parent firm, whilst also meeting the different cultural needs and expectations of the client. This often results in an internal role conflict for the consultant, resulting in interpretive tension. Like Yousfi (Chapter 9) and Kassis Henderson (Chapter 14), these authors argued that risk and interdependence are partly embedded in cultural values and artifacts. Different cultural expectations regarding trust across professional and organizational cultural tiles can work against trust development, and result in conflict as different culturally derived criteria are applied. In Dibben and Rose's chapter, the conflict was between professional and organizational cultural tiles. They argued that an auditor's level of trust/distrust determined whether or not she or he could switch from a professional cultural tile of scepticism to an organizational cultural tile of client-friendly values. Consequently, such cultural tiles appear to form a powerful source from which those involved can craft their understanding and expectations of a given context. In the consultant–client context, cultural tiles become aligned through sharing areas of agreement as to how the service will be deployed. Formal decision making, reporting and informal discussions also appear important in supporting trust development.

Exploring inter-organizational trust across national cultures, Möllering and Stache (Chapter 8) and Lyon and Porter (Chapter 10) both considered trust building in contexts where there were few institutional safeguards. Möllering and Stache noted that while trusted reliable institutions could be a foundation for trust when actors have no prior history of interaction, in Ukraine, where there is a deep distrust of the state, the reverse was true. Associative tiles such as informal personal relationships and reciprocity were more trusted and replaced institutional safeguards. In contrast, German managers were more used to relying on established institutional mechanisms. Möllering and Stache argued that where there is the potential for differences in institutional trust to cause insurmountable obstacles, the success of cross-cultural business relationships depends significantly on active trust and personalized development activities which are undertaken from a position of openness to the other culture and a willingness to deal reflexively with cultural differences. The building of cooperation and trust among micro-entrepreneurs in Nigeria and Ghana also happened without formalized institutional safeguards. Here Lyon and Porter demonstrated that, since formal agreements could not be enforced by a legal system, more informal personalized trust relationships were important as a means of reducing uncertainty. Individuals drew on personalized trust based upon information about the other party's prior behaviour and character, gained through three systems:

their own interactions; associative tiles derived from parallel institutional forms such as trader associations, chieftaincy systems and community leadership; and their own ability to apply sanctions. In such contexts they argued that associative cultural tiles embodying norms of reciprocity were critical, overriding potentially divisive demographic cultural tiles such as ethnicity.

## Trust across different 'cultural spheres': intra-organizational studies

Part III of this volume contains the remaining five substantive chapters, each of which empirically explored issues relating to trust dynamics across intra-organizational spheres and focused, in particular, upon demographic cultural tiles. In the first contribution (Chapter 11), Smith and Schwegler provided a bridge between inter- and intra-organizational studies by comparing and contrasting American and German Non-Governmental Organizations' (NGOs) cultural preferences in trust-building criteria and processes in the context of building partnerships and alliances. Wasti and Tan provided another alternative 'bridge', contrasting dyadic trust between subordinates and supervisors in Turkey and in China (Chapter 12), and again, offering insights regarding the universal applicability of models of trust and trust development. The trust relationship between line managers and subordinates was also examined within the context of major changes in nine UK-based organizations by Hope-Hailey and colleagues (Chapter 13), providing insights regarding trust differences and demographic cultural tiles relating to employment grade, age and length of service. Subsequent chapters focused upon different aspects of intra-organizational trust, highlighting the implications of language in relation to trust building (Kassis Henderson, Chapter 14) and how chief executives enhance their legitimacy to build and maintain trust, drawing on data from a large European family firm (Mari, Chapter 15).

## *Universal applicability*

The chapters in Part III supported earlier assertions that, whilst there are universally applicable trust concepts, the ways in which these concepts are manifest and interpreted is often very culturally specific. For example, using Doney *et al.*'s (1998) five routes for trust development, Smith and Schwegler (Chapter 11) found that although these routes could be distinguished in both American and German NGOs, in practice they were often combined and sequenced differently. In the United States, level 1 assessments (intentionality) were based on core values of a prospective partner organization. Subsequently, these American NGOs moved to level 2 assessments of their capabilities and competence, followed by an assessment of their track record (transference). In contrast, in German NGOs, while routes for levels 1 and 2 were still distinguishable, intentionality and capability were intertwined. As suggested earlier by Möllering and Stache (Chapter 8), German organizations preferred to utilize formal mechanisms, such as a code of conduct, against which to assess potential partners. Subsequently, they progressed to the next level (predictability), where they focused more on common history and previous shared experience than the American NGOs. These findings again support the earlier assertion that a universal model of trust needs to be sensitive to different cultural contexts.

Further support of the need for sensitivity to different cultural contexts was provided by Wasti and Tan (Chapter 12), comparing Turkish and Chinese organizations. They showed that while the ability, benevolence and integrity dimensions of trustworthiness identified by Mayer *et al.* (1995) are readily identifiable in intra-organizational contexts, their relative importance may differ between national cultures, and particularly in comparison to Western cultures. Within each organization, they identified differences in the way these dimensions were communicated, and specifically highlighted how, unlike in Western organizations, boundaries between professional and non-work associative cultural tiles were often artificial. Consequently, while ability, benevolence and integrity could still be distinguished, the way in which they were manifest differed among cultural groups. They argued that dyadic trust (subordinates' trust in supervisor) in collectivist high-context cultures places a much greater emphasis on relational and affective components than is suggested in the predominantly North American trust literature. Benevolence, for example, was found to be manifested more broadly, deeply and at an earlier stage of trust development, and encompassed behaviours such as magnanimity and concern for both the professional and personal welfare of the subordinate. Consequently, as with inter-organizational studies (for example Yousfi, Chapter 9), while universal models of trust development and the characteristics of trust could be applied at a broad level, these appeared to be moderated by culturally specific manifestations and interpretations, again supporting calls for a more differentiated understanding.

## Developing trust relationships

The chapters in Part III also provided further insights regarding how parties from different cultures within organizations might develop trust relationships. Hope-Hailey and colleagues (Chapter 13) found that trust during organizational change was associated with demographic cultural tiles relating to job grading, age and length of service. In particular, levels of trust within organizations varied between the distal (more distant) senior managers and the proximal (closer) line managers. They termed this the 'employer–manager trust gap'. Trust in the employer also declined in relation to length of service; as a result, in the context of organizational change, employees could not be treated as one homogeneous group. Subcultures aside, trust in line managers was found to be the strongest predictor of trust in employers, highlighting the important role that line managers play in trust relationships.

Mari (Chapter 15) also found differences between organizational subcultures in the development of mutual trust amongst those working in family firms. Trust levels were often rooted in norms of behaviour shared by members of the family, and membership in one of three interacting associative cultural tiles: family, business and ownership. Within these subgroups, the legitimacy of family-firm chief executives rested on the use of formal control (corporate organization structures) and informal control (norms of behaviour). As the firm grew and changed, these norms of behaviour were found to no longer be shared, and visions for the future began to differ among the subgroups, resulting in increased conflict. Based on this finding, Mari argued that, for trust to be built in a family-firm context, formalities of fair processes, formal organization structure and disciplined and transparent decision-making criteria were needed. This formalization, she argued, would help the chief executive to gain or maintain legitimacy and continue to be seen as trustworthy.

Finally, with regard to our consideration of how different parties from different cultures can develop trust relationships, Kassis Henderson's (Chapter 14) argued that while research has shown that the development of trust and relationships is closely linked to language issues, the issue of language and its relation to trust has not really been explored. Moreover, she challenged the assumption that using a commonly shared working language (usually English) removes barriers to trust creation. Rather, she argued that the use of a shared working language can create an illusion of a shared cultural identity which may ultimately be a source of problems. People who speak the same language expect to share similar interpretations of discourse; yet International English differs from that spoken by native monolingual English speakers. Consequently, language as a cultural tile could provide misleading cues for initial trust, resulting in, for example, native-language speakers not being trusted by non-native-language speakers.

## Discussion

Overall, our chapters have shown that while there appear to be universally applicable characteristics of trustworthiness such as ability, benevolence and integrity, these characteristics differ in their manifestation, relative importance and interpretation between cultural spheres, and are at least partially dependent upon which cultural tiles are dominant within a trust relationship. Trust relationships develop within specific contexts, and the cultural tiles are an integral part of those contexts. As a consequence, the way in which trust relationships develop and are maintained has both similarities and differences across cultures. We now turn to discussing the implications of these similarities and differences for practice and for future research.

## Implications for practice

Reviewing the chapters, it is clear that in developing trust within and between organizations, cultural differences matter! Individuals belong to multiple cultural spheres which influence the development and maintenance of trust. These differences extend beyond the most obvious demographic 'tiles' such as ethnicity and nationality, to include both geographic and associative cultural tiles. Each tile represents a culture or subculture component to which an individual belongs, and which serves as a facet of the context in which trust develops. The relative importance of each tile varies across trust relationships, both within and between organizations. Whilst our staged model of trust development in Chapter 1 simply emphasized the importance of context in trust relationships, the chapters within this book have illuminated how richly all three categories of cultural tiles, and the cultural spheres they represent, can influence the opening stances of the parties involved, their early encounters and the subsequent trust breakthrough or breakdown. Awareness, recognition of and sensitivity to the range of cultural tiles, the trust cues they embody and an understanding of their relative importance within a specified situation, is therefore crucial for those who are involved in the development and subsequent maintenance of trust within and between organizations and cultures. These dynamics are equally important in situations where there has been a breakdown of trust and trust repair efforts are required.

The nature and relative importance of factors that support the development and maintenance of trust are likely to be related to the dominant cultural tiles within any intra- or inter-organizational relationship. Where these differ between parties, and the resultant competing demands are not recognized or understood, there is likely to be conflict; as a consequence, trust will be more difficult to develop and maintain. In effect, the broad characteristics of trust are likely to be modified by culturally specific manifestations and interpretations. Whilst some cultures will place a greater emphasis on the relational and affective components of a relationship, emphasizing the benevolence component of trust, others will emphasize ability and/or integrity components. Of equal importance, where formalized institutional safeguards are weak or do not exist, the success of cross-cultural business relationships is likely to depend significantly on active personalized trust. In such situations, individuals will need to draw on personalized trust, information and the availability of other relevant and dominant associative cultural tiles. When developing such relationships, it is important to remember that a common language does not necessarily equate to common cultural tiles or shared understanding.

The chapters in this volume highlight a need for research and findings on cross-cultural trust dynamics to be useful to practitioners, and to be made available to them in a form that is accessible and easy to digest. This assertion echoes comments made by others about how management research can be made more accessible to practitioners (see Bartunek, 2007), and the need for management research to satisfy the dual criteria of theoretical and methodological rigour and, at the same time, practical relevance (Hodgkinson *et al.*, 2001). Although we would argue that it might not be appropriate for all research to be of direct relevance to practitioners or have immediate utility, considerations about the cross-cultural nature of trust are immensely important for practitioners, and the chapters in this volume have shown how both the relational and contextual aspects are likely to be of immediate practical use. Consequently, it is also imperative to ensure that, where appropriate, future research incorporates a full discussion of practical implications. We now turn to explore those areas where future research should be a high priority.

## Directions for future research

By specifically considering a cultural perspective on trust within and between organizations, our chapters have highlighted five interrelated directions for future research. These five directions are:

- establishing which dimensions of trust are culturally specific [emic] and which are universal [etic];
- examining the role of cultural distance and similarity in societal background between parties who are developing or maintaining trust;
- explicitly considering the impact of contextual factors other than culture, to understand better how trust may be built and maintained;

- adopting a longitudinal, time-series perspective to exploring the relative importance of different cultural spheres in the development and maintenance of trust;

and:

- recognizing the relative advantages of both quantitative and qualitative methods for addressing trust dynamics, and, where appropriate, exploring the utility of mixed-methods research designs.

Our first future research direction highlights the need to explore further and establish which dimensions of trust are culturally specific [emic] and which are universal [etic], incorporating the manner in which individuals interpret and give prominence to the apparently universal trustworthiness characteristics of ability, benevolence and integrity. Whilst the book's chapters have provided clear evidence that such cultural differences do influence trust development and maintenance, there is a need for more systematic work to explore how these trustworthiness elements operate and interact. Findings from such research could provide critical building blocks toward a universal theory of trust within and between cultures, expanding upon our staged model. Within such research, it is necessary to establish whether the influence of in-group bias on trust is culturally specific, and to develop an understanding of the critical role of multi-level modes of cultural antecedents and their consequences. This work is likely to offer further insights on both institutional and structural solutions to barriers to trust. Research in spheres where national and organizational cultures intersect is likely to be another fruitful avenue. Similarly, the implications of interactions between professional and personal cultural spheres, such as in friendships and their associated boundary conditions, is likely to provide further insights into those aspects of culture that moderate such relationships. These need to be considered at both individual and group levels.

The increasing interdependence of organizations across national, organizational and professional boundaries provides the broad context for our second future research direction. Organizations are increasingly asking people from different cultures to manage new relationships with new parties across cultures with which they are unfamiliar. This raises questions regarding the relative importance of factors such as the cultural distance and similarity in societal background between parties in the trust development and maintenance processes. In particular, there is a need to understand more fully the influence of cultural differences and similarities in relation to demographic, geographic and associative cultural tiles, their relative importance for particular trust relationships and the conditions under which certain cultural tiles become more dominant relative to others. As part of this exploration, there will be a need to distinguish clearly between trust within and between different managerial levels within organizations, including the employer–manager trust gap, as well as a consideration of how cultural distance affects trust between organizations. Building upon our staged model of trust research, such research could usefully incorporate the influence of each party's cultural preconceptions within different cultural spheres, as represented within their cultural tiles.

Throughout the book, authors have highlighted the importance of contextual factors other than culture in relation to the operation of trust. Other aspects that would benefit from explicit inclusion include the historical underpinnings of trust relationships, the role of organizational structures and the impact of language. With regard to the first, an understanding of how the past has influenced the present trust situation is likely to enable better understanding of how trust may be built. The stability and integrity of national structures, and organizations' and individuals' trust in them, appears likely to influence trust across national cultures. Similarly, organizational structures such as management boards, and formalities such as corporate governance rules, are also likely to influence trust, particularly where these differ between organizations. The impact of language-related factors on trust building is also worthy of further research, for example, exploring its impact in multilingual and virtual teams.

The chapters have also highlighted the additional insights that may be realized by taking a longitudinal perspective. This perspective allows the exploration of the relative importance of different cultural spheres in the formation, development and maintenance of trust over time, while explicitly considering how dimensions of trustworthiness impact on the process of achieving cooperation over time. This approach would specifically require the adoption of research designs and alternative methods that focus on longitudinal, rather than time-snapshot, data.

In undertaking this research, the chapters offer clear calls for invoking a broader range of data collection methods, and specifically highlight the importance of undertaking in-depth qualitative studies. Where survey research is used, it would benefit from looking explicitly at both cultural similarities and differences on trust. More important is to expand the use of qualitative research tools, and to realize the potential benefits of combining quantitative with qualitative methods. Many of the studies reported in this book have made use of qualitative methods, and offer compelling evidence on how these can offer additional explanatory capability and alternative insights to those provided by quantitative methods alone. Such qualitative methods could be used to better understand culturally specific manifestations of trust antecedents, which could then be operationalized by subsequent development of scales and other more quantitative data-collection rubrics.

## Concluding comment

Writing over seventy years ago, Lewin argued 'There is nothing so practical as a good theory' (1945: 129). Within that article, he highlighted the high degree of complexity in the world, emphasizing the need for careful diagnosis to enable the application of theory. As the chapters in this book have clearly demonstrated, the relationship between trust and culture is indeed complex, and requires careful diagnosis and the development of theories that are applicable to organizations and the people within them. The chapters have also highlighted how both quantitative and qualitative research methods can support this development of good theory, each providing complementary insights. There is now a need to undertake further research which incorporates culturally specific dimensions, but which will allow for generalizable findings to further support moves towards the creation of a good universal, but culturally sensitive theory of trust development and maintenance.

## References

Bartunek, J. M. 2007. 'Academic-practitioner collaboration need not require joint or relevant research: toward a relational scholarship of integration'. *Academy of Management Journal*, 50(6) 1323–33.

Chao, G. T. and Moon, H. 2005. 'The cultural mosaic: a metatheory for understanding the complexity of culture'. *Journal of Applied Psychology*, 90(6), 1128–40.

Doney, P. M., Cannon, J. P. and Mullen, M. R. 1998. 'Understanding the influence of national culture on the development of trust'. *Academy of Management Review*, 23(3), 601–20

Hodgkinson, G. P., Herriot, P. and Anderson, N. 2001. 'Re-aligning the stakeholders in management research: lessons from industrial, work and organizational psychology'. *British Journal of Management*, 12, Special Issue S41–S48.

Lewicki, R. and Bunker, B. B. 1996. 'Developing and maintaining trust in work relationships'. In R. M. Kramer and T. R. Tyler (eds.) *Trust in Organizations: Frontiers of Theory and Research*. Thousand Oaks, CA: Sage, 114–39.

Lewin, K. 1945. 'The Research Centre for Group Dynamics at Massachusetts Institute of Technology'. *Sociometry*, 8(2), 126–36.

Mayer, R. C., Davis, J. H. and Schoorman, F. D. 1995. 'An integrative model of organizational trust'. *Academy of Management Review*, 20, 709–34.

Schneider, S. C. and Barsoux, J.-L. 2003. *Managing Across Cultures*. London: FT/ Prentice-Hall.

# Index